National Manhood

New Americanists

A series edited by Donald E. Pease

National Manhood

Capitalist Citizenship and the

Imagined Fraternity of White Men

Dana D. Nelson

DUKE UNIVERSITY PRESS   Durham and London, 1998

© 1998 Duke University Press
All rights reserved
Printed in the United States of America on acid-free paper ⊗
Typeset in Trump Mediaeval by Tseng Information Systems, Inc.
Library of Congress Cataloging-in-Publication Data appear
on the last printed page of this book.

For Elsa Sophia Ross (b. 1998)

and

in memory of Lora Romero (1960–1998)

Contents

Preface

This book describes the formulation and historicizes specific negotiations of something I'm calling "national manhood," an ideology that has worked powerfully since the Constitutional era to link a fraternal articulation of white manhood to civic identity. I study the historical moment when the abstracting identity of white manhood—abstracting in the sense that it works to relocate men's affiliations away from more locally conceived identities—comes into focus as a supraclass ideal for guaranteeing national unity. Then I analyze examples of national manhood's ideological generalization, the processes through which individual "white" men assume the privileges and burdens of national imperatives, and how middle-class professionalization takes over and is authorized by the management of those imperatives.

National Manhood unpacks some of the consequences of the apparent democratization achieved through the ideological extension of "white manhood." This is a democratic expansion evidenced, the story goes, in the quickly evolving "universalization" of white manhood suffrage, a preliminary expansion across class divides that served as the precondition for suffrage extension first across the white-black divide, and then across the male-female divide. My argument turns our attention instead toward the antidemocratic structure of national manhood, and particularly two of its key entailments: first, that the process of identifying with national manhood blocks white men from being able efficiently to identify socioeconomic inequality as structural rather than individual failure, thereby conditioning them for market and professional competition; second and more importantly, that it entails a series of affective foreclosures that block those men's more heterogeneous democratic identifications and energies.

In this process national manhood substitutes itself for nascently radical, local democratic practices, energies, and imaginings, not replacing local manhoods so much as enlisting them for and orienting them toward a unified, homogenous national ideal. I will be arguing in a variety of ways that this symbolic interarticulation of race, gender, and nation cripples and haunts the U.S. democratic imaginary. National manhood erects an abstracting, atomizing circuitry that charges white men for market competition in the name of national unity. White men are promised relief from the anxieties of economic competition in the warm emotional space of civic fraternal sameness, of "brother moderation." But over and over national manhood's competitive individualism and hollowing logic of representivity vitiates the anticipated pleasures of fraternal exchange. As I repeatedly discovered, white men seem able to achieve the equalitarian reassurance of unmediated brotherhood only with dead or imagined men. The inability of civic fraternity actually to deliver on its affective promises emphasizes how the benefits of national manhood come at significant human cost to its others—the white women, Indians, blacks, primitives, poor, foreigners, and savages through which white manhood defines and supplements itself—and to white men.

We are not much in the habit of thinking about the implications of the Articles of Confederation or the variety of citizen's committees and out-of-door political actions preceding the Constitutional Convention for what they might tell us about alternative democratic possibilities for the United States. My own approach to the subject of national manhood reframes this so-called "crisis" era in just that way, as proliferating with signs of radical democratic energies, imaginings, and practices. Doing so enables me to attend to the ways that the ideology of national manhood effectively trains, curtails, and/or shuts them down. This ideology takes its start, I argue in chapter 1, in an important moment in U.S. history, when the Constitutional plan for unifying the confederated states holds out a reformulation of manhood—purified, unified, "vigorous," brotherly, national manhood—as a corrective to a whole range of frictions and anxieties men were experiencing as a result of postwar political, economic, and social dislocation. I contend that many men of the lower and middling classes were not as threatened by postwar political frictions—for instance, in emerging face-to-face democratic negotiations and actions—as they were by the costs entailed in the United States' rapid transition into a market economy. Indeed, those democratic practices offered avenues for addressing socioeconomic inequalities. But these various anxieties became undifferentiated through the powerfully conglomerating rhetoric of "crisis" and "fragmentation" deployed by the Constitution's defenders, which successfully attached political struggle to other very real apprehensions and difficulties men were experiencing in an accelerating market economy, and (at least partly tied to that) in familial order. The Federalists' explicit call for a reinvigorated, unified manhood exemplified in the body of a national executive—the president—promised relief for the "crisis" of household *and* civic order in a newly conceptualized, nationally unified fraternity. In the transition from Confederation to Constitution, U.S. democratic possibility became conditioned by presidentialism's powerfully homogenizing masculine ideal, one loaded up with unnecessarily rigid longings for self-sameness and self-subordination in the name of "unity."

While I'm not arguing that the passage of the Constitution documents men's wholesale subscription to the ideal of national manhood, I am arguing that its passage evidences at least in part the appeal of that ideal, and that in subsequent years we can trace the gradual cultural articulation of its symbolic arguments and inchoate logic. It is important to draw out the difference between the appeal of national manhood and its actual functional cultural installation, to emphasize the way that "white" men's learning to identify with national manhood also entailed an uneven, lengthy, continuing process of social—and even democratic—disidentification. For instance, we might hold up the first act of naturalization (1790) which identified free white men as potential citizens against the fact that free black men were not fully disenfranchised in the various states (North and South) until the mid-1830s—the era of "universal" white manhood suffrage. To emphasize the historical development of this process, I elaborate my arguments chronologically, concentrating on the period from the 1780s to the 1850s.

After charting the ideological coordination of nation, manhood, and whiteness during the early Federal period in chapter 1, I trace the transition from national manhood's articulation as a political ideal to its alignment of geographic and psychic territories. Here, through readings of the Lewis and Clark Expedition and a novel by John Neal, I concentrate on the way that one of national manhood's supplementary logics—the Indian—helped not only to authorize national expansion through territorial incorporation, but even more importantly to reterritorialize national stresses and economic inequality as individual responsibility. Chapter 2 also marks a transition in my argument's focus, where I move from outlining exceptional models pointing the way toward national manhood to examining its psychic recodification in individual men and then its inculcation as cultural logic. Chapters 3 and 4 study the polygenesis debate and early gynecology as examples of the way middle-class professionalization takes up the imperatives of national manhood, offering scientific documentation, institutional force, and career status for its proliferating investments in civic management. Chapter 5 then examines a variety of fraternal expressions (in essays, fraternal order ritual, professional friendships, and fiction) to detail another important dynamic: national manhood's functional melancholy. In the afterword, I return to the question of presidentialism, asking through a reading of a Poe story and two 1997 summer blockbuster movies what this ideal embodiment of national manhood means for the practice of democracy in the United States both then and now.

The structure of national manhood provides us an important key for understanding the referential power of white manhood. It also helps us understand how democratic energy is blocked and rerouted in the early nation as well as today. The political psychology of capitalist citizenship that I outline in *National Manhood* has powerfully conditioned individual lives, class logic, professional development, and civic practice in the United States. This ideology trained and continues to train citizens—and not just white male ones—to conceptualize U.S. democracy through antidemocratic modes. Imagining and building alternative possibilities for personal identity, socioeconomic structure, and political practice in the United States will mean confronting more than the individual expressions, local practices, and corporate structures of white male privilege. As *National Manhood* emphasizes, it will mean countering the affective foreclosures of heterogeneous democracy entailed by the fraternally homogenizing logic of national manhood.

I have had practical support from a variety of sources in the years I have worked on this project. I thank the Library Company of Philadelphia for a Mellon Foundation fellowship; Louisiana State University's Office for Sponsored Research for a summer grant; and the University of Kentucky, especially the College of Arts and Sciences (and former Dean Rick Edwards) and the English Department, for the research and leave support that allowed me to finish this book on schedule. In particular, my chair at UK, David Durant, has been actively supportive of my work on this project. For all his help, his ongoing interest in seeing me finish, and his constant good cheer I cannot thank him enough.

Thank you also to my research assistants at UK: Leigh Baldwin, Sydney Darby, Jessica Hollis, and most especially, Katherine Ledford, whose patience, resourcefulness, and good cheer I could not have done without. I appreciate the resources and help I received from staff at the Academy of Natural Sciences, the Pennsylvania Historical Society, the Library Company of Philadelphia, and the special collections libraries at LSU and UK. I thank Duke University Press and Cornell University Press for granting permission to use previously published articles on which some chapters are based: chapter 1 draws from an essay appearing in *Possible Pasts*; chapter 5 and the afterword draw from an essay appearing in the fall 1997 issue of *American Literature*.

I came to love the work of research and writing more than ever in this book for the places it felt more like community than solitary enterprise. My arguments have benefited enormously from conversations and writing exchanges with many people. I thank valuable interlocutors: Phil Lapsansky, Denise Larrabee, Mary Ann Hines, and Jim Green of the Library Company of Philadelphia, and Karen D. Stevens at the Academy of Natural Sciences, for source leads, informative conversations, and back-up eyes; Paula Garrett, David Mazel, Mary Katherine Politz, and Leonard Vraniak, former students who helped me think through some of these ideas in a graduate seminar at LSU; my colleagues in the Social Theory collective at UK, especially Jack Forbes, Fon Gordon, JoEllen Green Kaiser, David Kaiser, Wolfgang Natter, Ted Schatzki, Rich Schein, Paul Taylor, and Ron Witte; and especially Jerry Martin, who has been listening patiently and encouraging my work on this book in important ways from beginning to end.

A variety of conferences and panel invitations gave me a chance to develop my ideas for this book: special thanks to Robert Blair St. George, who organized "Possible Pasts," and to Carroll Smith-Rosenberg and Emory Elliott, who organized "Race in the Americas." Thanks also to Ed Dryden and the Arizona Quarterly Symposium, and Cathy Davidson's fall 1996 seminar students at Duke.

I owe a great deal to dear friends and colleagues who read and commented, early and late, on sections of the manuscript for me: Cathy Davidson, Tom Dillehay, Kevin Railey, Ivy Schweitzer, and Steve Weisenberger. Chris Newfield was an ideal reader—demanding, incisive, generous. Lora Romero read parts of this at every stage and was pivotal both to my thinking about and my confidence in this project from beginning to end; I could not have finished it without her. My book is better for her intellectual generosity as my life is immeasurably so for her friendship.

My writing groups have made intellectual work much richer: for vision, hard work, fun, and solidarity I thank Rick Moreland, Reggie Young, Virginia Blum, Susan Bordo, Suzanne Pucci, and most of all, Elsie Michie, who helped me figure out a lot more about the work I was doing writing this book than is evident in its main arguments, and whose watchful eye and demanding sensibility I could not have written this book without. My book's readers, T. Walter Herbert and Priscilla Wald, offered extraordinarily helpful local and overarching suggestions for the final revisions of the manuscript.

For crucial intellectual and/or personal warmth, I want to thank: Rick Blackwood, Al Blanton, Russ Castronovo, Eric Cheyfitz, Joan Dayan, Bill Demastes, Amy Kaplan, Carolyn L. Karcher, Susan Kohler, John Lowe, Pat McGee, Vivian Pollak, David L. Smith, and, in particular, my sister and gal-pal Julie Nelson Ross. I can't sing loud enough praise for my editorial team at Duke: abundant thanks to Richard Morrison and to Ken Wissoker for their enthusiasm for *National Manhood* and for the wonderful variety and steadiness of their expressions of support as I worked to complete it. A world of gratitude to my colleague Anna Bosch who dragged me to my first yoga class, and to my teacher Terry Landers who talks me through unbelievable postures and into unexpected relaxation—no mean feat. I dedicate this book to Elsa, whose heartbeat kept me going, and to Lora, whose passing came suddenly too soon.

Introduction: Naked Nature

Although we cannot control what happens to a perception before we become aware of it, we can retroactively revise the value which it assumes for us at a conscious level. We can look at an object a second time, through different representational parameters, and painstakingly reverse the processes through which we have arrogated to ourselves what does not belong to us, or displaced onto another what we do not want to recognize in ourselves. Although such a reviewing can have only a very limited efficacy, and must be repeated with each new visual perception, it is a necessary step in the coming of a subject to an ethical or a non-violent relation to the other. —KAJA SILVERMAN, *Threshold* 3

In 1855, Herman Melville published "Benito Cereno," a story about a Massachusetts captain at sea off the coast of Chile who encounters a slave ship. Melville's story was based on historical events: a slave uprising on the Spanish ship *Tryal*, intercepted and finally foiled by the U.S. captain Amasa Delano in 1805, and the 1839 slave revolt on board the Spanish schooner *Amistad*. Backdating the setting of his story to 1799, and naming the Spanish ship *San Dominick*, Melville links slave rebellion to questions of democratic order and revolutions for national independence at the outset.[1]

In Melville's handling, the story is centrally a mystery, in which Delano (and the reader along with him) is the detective. The action begins on a shadowy and gray day. Delano spots and boards an unmarked ship to offer assistance, speculating that they are in some kind of trouble. Evidently he is right, but the Spanish captain Benito Cereno evades Captain Delano's requests for specific information about that trouble, and his behavior is otherwise strangely elusive. He seems uneager to receive Delano's help, and keeps retreating from Delano to his cabin, accompanied by his ever-faithful personal slave, Babo. Delano remains on board to await supplies from his own ship and to negotiate an agreeable financial settlement for those supplies. Puzzled and a little unnerved by the odd, reclusive behavior of the captain of the *San Dominick*, Delano mentally questions the efficacy of Cereno's command and decides to have him relieved of it at the first possible opportunity. But this idea is only temporarily reassuring. Cereno's continuing evasiveness and unfriendliness thoroughly rattle Delano's own customary "genial" ease, a discomfort that increases as Cereno repeatedly denies Delano the fraternal exchange he seeks, in what Delano terms a "privileged spot"—that is, sequestered away from any of their social inferiors. Unable to find the authority he expects in a "brother captain" and unable to imagine it lodged elsewhere, Delano remains uncertain and uncomfortable throughout the duration of his stay on the ship.

In an earlier study of this text, I became fascinated by a particular, seemingly minor moment in the plot. Just at the point in Melville's "Benito Cereno" when Delano is both completely baffled and almost totally frustrated by his experiences on board the *San Dominick* and particularly by his inability to gain Cereno's confidence, he spots "a pleasant sort of sunny sight; quite sociable too." This sight, unlike others before it, calms the nervous Massachusetts captain as it reconfirms his sense of universal right-order:

> His attention had been drawn to a slumbering negress, partly disclosed through the lace-work of some rigging. . . . Sprawling at her lapped breasts was her wide-awake fawn, stark naked, its black little body half lifted from the deck, crosswise on its dam's . . .
>
>   There's naked nature, now; pure tenderness and love, thought Captain Delano, well pleased. (73)

He is provoked by this sight "to remark the other negresses more particularly than before," finding himself similarly "gratified by their manners." His musings over the women's ability to evidence both domestic gentleness and savage animalism culminate in an inward exclamation: "Ah! . . . these perhaps are some of the very women whom Mungo Park saw in Africa, and gave such a noble account of." As the narrator observes, "these natural sights somehow insensibly deepened [Delano's] confidence and ease."

In the midst of his worries that he's about to be ambushed, how does looking at a partially unclothed, enslaved African woman and her naked baby make Delano feel "well pleased"? Pleased about what? (Their *manners?*) How does thinking about sharing the sight of these well-mannered women with Mungo Park compensate for his discomfort with Benito Cereno? How does this odd concatenation of gazing at otherness ("naked nature") and imagining fraternal sameness (with an internationally acclaimed colonial explorer) stabilize Delano's sense of self, his "confidence and ease"? Though it goes by quickly, it's a moment worth pausing over. This moment indexes Delano's experience of himself as a man who commands: a "brother captain," a scientifically rational man, a philanthropic man, a white man. Delano enjoys the anthropological dissymmetry of looking on the African woman with her child because it fills out and confirms his whiteness and his manhood. The securing of this identity comes for Delano not just through the slave's unclothed "blackness" but also through her femaleness, her (apparent) mannerly passivity, her "natural" maternal performance, her seeming availability not just to him but also to another commanding man. In the powerful fraternal sensation Delano gets from viewing the slave woman "as if not at all" observed by her—where his subjectivity is occluded and hers is on display—he is able to regain a sense of rational command over a situation where he increasingly fears he has none.

"Benito Cereno" delineates a crisis in masculine subjectivity through the contrast between Delano's ongoing discomfort and this brief reprieve, and more particularly, a crisis in the intersubjective fraternity of white manhood. Delano finds this "sociable" moment with Mungo Park because he is near-desperately seeking one with Cereno and not getting it. That the Massachusetts shipper does not seek the company of the other people on board the ship (sailors and slaves) tells us something important about Delano's (American, democratic) notion of brotherhood. That he finds fraternal recourse in the "objective" exercise of a fantasy of shared ethnological ruminations on African women with the British explorer Mungo Park tells us something important too.[2] From this, we can see how Delano's "republican" subjectivity is consolidated through a triangular structure, in imagined affiliation with other men who have power over groups of people—the power to objectify, to identify, to manage.[3] Those powers collate discourses of science, legality, and property (personalty and realty) to certify a select, commanding, and specifically raced, masculine identity.

"Benito Cereno" highlights the practical efficiency of that identity structure at the same time as it underscores its affective failure. The story forces us to see the brutal (in)adequacy of white men's command. When Babo's lunge for Cereno reveals the slave rebellion to Delano and his men, the force first of avarice (or capital) and then law intervenes to restore "right order."[4] For Delano, these events serve to restore and confirm his "genial" optimism—like the "blue sea and the blue sky," Delano is prepared to turn over a new leaf. But Benito Cereno continues to bewail how the two men misunderstood each other so crucially that day on the ship: "You were with me all day; stood with me, sat with me, talked with me, looked at me, ate with me, drank with me; and yet, your last act was to clutch for a monster, not only an innocent man, but the most pitiable of all men" (115). The interruption of power is not as traumatic, Benito Cereno implies, as the interruption of fraternity, of that "privileged spot" where commanding men can be rightfully recognized and known by like-minded/bodied/propertied men. In "Benito Cereno," we see that brotherly space emerge only in the moment of Delano's happy musings over the African woman and her child in the imagined company of Mungo Park.

That scene offers a suggestive commentary on the promises and failures of white manhood—both as an "individual" identity position and a fraternal contract—in the early United States. The critique it sketches is thin but tantalizing, and so in this volume I have worked to unpack the broader cultural logic it suggests, a logic I describe as "national manhood." I have taken my cue loosely from Melville, studying the early national and antebellum period (1780s to 1850s)— from the era in which Melville set the story to that when he published it. I follow his story's lead in considering how white manhood came to be articulated in the early nation through multiple categories of national and civic identity, scientific standpoint, management, and fraternity. These are categories I will discuss below, treating these component aspects in some detail before summarizing the aims of my study.

National Identity

In *The Word in Black and White*, I characterized the Anglo-colonial recourse to "race," a strategy for hierarchically organizing diverse human beings, as being rooted in "an uncommon need"—which, I argued, sprang diversely from the epistemological and theological displacements of the Copernican revolution, colonial exploration, and the growth of a capitalist/mercantile economy. Responding specifically to Winthrop Jordan's and Edmund Morgan's contentions that the institution of lifelong slavery for African and African-descended peoples was either an "unthinking decision," or a "paradox" arising from various political and economic needs of the British colonial ruling elite, I asserted then that "it may be quite true that economic possibilities and social demands gave impetus to racial persecution and enslavement. But it was a cultivated and deep-seated sense of European (*cum* 'white') superiority that suggested African slavery as a 'natural' solution to Anglo-European economic woes" (12). As Theodore Allen's recent work compellingly establishes, though, the question I glossed over in that moment is the one that most demands our analysis if we are to understand the forces driving the racial categorization and racist institutions that emerged in that period and that we live in versions of today. Europeans did *not* at that point, as my formulation there implied, identify themselves *collectively* as a superior racial group (nor do they now, as a variety of recent events evidence). Rather, Europeans then identified themselves in a variety of aristocratic, trade, religious, ethnic, military, and protonationalist ways, not as "European," and not necessarily or primarily as "white," if white at all.[5] Nor did their various experiences of colonial life in America, or their experience of the Revolution, work to draw them into a seamless, common sense of identity. So the question we must ask, as Allen insists, is how and why these various—and often mutually antagonistic—groups of people came to identify themselves together, under the rubric of a new, abstract, overarching, and even counterperceptual, category of "whiteness"?[6] And to extend Allen's formulation of the question for the purposes of my study, under what conditions was "whiteness" attached to national identity and then middle-class professional formation?

Allen's work is part of a recent and growing body of critical studies that examine the historical construction of whiteness in politically, culturally, and economically specific contexts. For instance, David Roediger has recently analyzed the emergence of the white working class, beginning in the post-Revolutionary period, arguing that "working class formation and the systematic development of a sense of whiteness went hand in hand for the U.S. white working class" (*Wages* 8). This coordination of class identity with "whiteness" grew out of revolutionary ideals that created powerful fears about states of dependence: "the white working class, disciplined and made anxious by the fear of dependency, began during its formation to construct an image of the Black population as 'other'—as embodying the pre-industrial, erotic, careless style of life the white worker hated and longed for" (14).

Indeed, historians, sociologists, and philosophers concerned with historical manifestations of race/racism have similarly isolated the Revolution and its aftermath as the period when racial consciousness, and specifically whiteness, became more generally important as an identity category. Some, like Michael Goldfield, and Benjamin Ringer and Elinor Lawless, have located the intensifying appeal of whiteness in the late 1780s, in the Constitutional era. Though the South Carolinian attempt to add the adjective "white" to the Constitution was defeated, that adjective was appended to the nation's first naturalization law with no protest from Congress.[7] As Ringer and Lawless summarize, the only change was to gender the clause specifying the identity of eligible citizens as "free white persons," specifying that "*he* shall have resided for the term of one year at least" (U.S. Public Statutes at Large 1:103; quoted in Ringer and Lawless, 110; emphasis added). White *manhood* was thereby specified as the legal criteria of civic entitlement, attaching the "manly confidence" idealized by defenders of the Constitution to the abstractly unifying category of "whiteness."[8]

In this study, my aim is to analyze white manhood not so much in the range of its local formulations (such as white urban working-class manhood, or white patrician manhood), but in its broader symbolic attachment to national identity and civic organization. Adapting "white manhood" as the marker for civic unity worked as an apparently democratizing extension of civic entitlement. It worked symbolically and legally to bring men together in an abstract but increasingly functional community that diverted their attention from differences between them—differences which had come alarmingly into focus in the post-Revolutionary era. Men whose interests had been temporarily unified in wartime were increasingly encountering fellowmen not as citizen but competitor in an unstable, rapidly changing, postwar market economy. The national need to cultivate "sameness" was threatened by the differences structured not only through the variety of ethnic, religious, and political backgrounds of the colonial population, and the regional, colonial, and state affiliations that they had come to enjoy, but by the very market economy that supposedly ensured the nation's health. Thus we might think of the Constitutional "crisis" (as I argue in chapter 1) as an ideological transition that reworked the identification of the citizen: a move to consolidate a "sameness" abstract but compelling enough to take operative priority over differences that threatened the construction of national unity without jeopardizing the economic system it prioritized.

"White manhood" was a useful category for inventing national unity because it abstracted men's interests out of local issues and identities in an appeal to a nationally shared "nature." Its efficacy may also have followed from the way whiteness addressed capitalism's internal ambivalence: it simultaneously confirmed market logic (as a property that advantaged some) and seemingly defied it (in allocating "common" property). Former colonials of European descent, increasingly competitors in the market and political economies, could share collectively the exclusive property of "whiteness"[9] — a category that subordinated European national and colonial/state identifications as it "democratically" wedded men to the new United States. "Whiteness" became an "American" property, certified, as Crèvecoeur so richly and suggestively summarized, "in the broad lap of our great Alma Mater" (70). This grant or transition in identity (from local to abstract) was both "natural and common" (91). White men "recognized" this "natural and common" whiteness together as Americans, an identity they economically (and genocidally) wrested from, and imagined they held "in common" with, Native American men (a dynamic I explore in chapter 2).

Scientific Standpoint

Crèvecoeur also provides us with a clear diagram of the scientific standpoint increasingly adopted for the articulation of white manhood, the (occluded) Enlightenment vantage. When the happy and industrious Farmer James recounts his visit to Charlestown, he contrasts the decadent prosperity of the planter class to the oppression of the black slaves who supply white wealth: "the chosen race eat, drink and live happy, while the unfortunate one grubs up the ground, raises indigo, or husks the rice, exposed to a sun full as scorching as their native one, without the support of good food, without the cordials of any cheering liquor. This great contrast has often afforded me subjects of the most afflicting meditation" (169). His ensuing meditation provides an instance of what Forrest Robinson characterizes as "bad faith": the wiggly ethical standpoint of whiteness. Farmer James appeals to "Nature" as the ultimate arbiter of slavery's depraved foundations: "Oh Nature, where art thou? Are not these blacks thy children as well as we?" (169). Continuing in this argument, that slavery creates *unnatural* human relations, James ruminates on the doubled "burden of Nature," that afflicts enslaved black men when they father children, "a fatal present": "they are not permitted to partake of those ineffable sensations with which Nature inspires the hearts of fathers and mothers; they must repel them all. . . . Their paternal fondness is embittered by considering that if their children live, they must be slaves like themselves" (169). Having raised the emotional relationship dearest to his own heart—of fatherhood—James excoriates Southern planters for violating this sacred bond of Nature: "so inexperienced am I in this mode of life that were I to be possessed of a plantation, and my slaves treated in general as they are here, never could I rest in peace" (179).

Of course, he has already revealed to his readers that he does own slaves, and here he suddenly, apologetically seems to realize the sticky logical spot he is in. Identifying himself regionally now rather than individually, he assures readers that though "we have slaves likewise in the north . . . how different their lot, how different their situation, in every possible respect. They enjoy as much liberty as their masters [a remarkable assertion if ever there was one]; they are as well clad and well fed; in health and sickness they are tenderly taken care of; they live under the same roof and are, truly speaking, a part of our families" (171). He continues in a long (and ironically familiar, to those who have read Southern slave-apologist literature) catalogue of the advantages enjoyed by northern slaves: they "are not obliged to work more than white people"; they are "allowed to visit their wives"; they are "fat, healthy and hearty"; they "think themselves happier than many of the lower class of whites."

Obviously uncomfortable with ending his argument there, James turns from this difficult practical defense toward a more abstractly philosophical consideration of slavery: "Whence this astonishing right, or rather this barbarous custom . . . ?" he queries. "Is there, then, no superintending power who conducts the moral operations of the world as well as the physical? The same sublime hand which guides the planets round the sun with so much exactness . . . doth it abandon mankind to all the errors, the follies, and the miseries, which their most frantic rage and their most dangerous vices and passions produce?" (173). In categories ever more abstracted away from the specific question of his own personal culpability in a "violation of nature," James now orates on "the history of the earth" and in a fascinating twist of logic enabled by a universalistic, scientific perspective, is able actually to conclude that it is the very *cruelty of Nature* that creates slavery, allowing white Americans—barbarously or benignly—to enslave black Africans:

> In the moments of our philanthropy, we often talk of an indulgent nature, a kind parent, who for the benefit of mankind has taken singular pains to vary the genera of plants, fruits, grains, and the different productions of the earth and has spread peculiar blessings in each climate. This is undoubtedly an object of contemplation which calls forth our warmest gratitude; for so singularly benevolent have those paternal intentions been, that where barrenness of soil or severity of climate prevail, there she has implanted in the heart of man sentiments which overbalance every misery. . . . Yet if we attentively view this globe, will it not appear rather a place of punishment than delight? . . . Famine, diseases, elementary convulsions, human feuds, dissensions, etc., are the produce of every climate. (175)

From the objective and disembodied space of the universalist standpoint, here defined in Hobbesian terms, we are able to see, as James outlines it, "the frigid sterility of the north . . . the parched lands of the torrid zone . . . the poisonous soil of the equator." We see the ubiquitous depravity of humankind, how "[a]lmost everywhere, liberty so natural to mankind is refused, or rather enjoyed but by their tyrants; the word slave is the appellation of every rank who adore as a divinity a being worse than themselves" (176). His "general review of human nature" thus confirms indeed that all men are slaves, that slavery is but relative; that human tyranny and the practice of slavery are ordained *by* Nature. And Nature here is something that can be objectively recorded by impartial observers but not challenged. From the vantage of this general, scientific review it is impossible to find a willful agent, let alone hold him responsible for anything. Ethical recognition (there is a slave) is neatly shorn from social imperative (all men are created equal).

And just so, when he next relates his encounter with the caged and mangled slave, we see James walk away without rendering assistance, to dine with the planter who punished the slave with this brutal death sentence. It is *James's* "oppression" that is put on display at the close of the chapter, his enlightened philosophical anguish over the scientifically illustrated principles of "nature" offered for the reader's sympathy. Similarly "oppressed with the reflections that this shocking spectacle afforded," the reader is encouraged to share James's scientifically conditioned ethical standpoint, a standpoint from which the object observed is radically distant and divided from the observing subject, at once symbol for a "universal" condition shared by all, and radically "other." This is the vantage Abdul JanMohamed has described as "privileged stasis," where slavery can be decried and its privileges accepted in the same moment (or, in Farmer James's case, at the same meal).

The disembodied, objective, and universalized standpoint offered by Enlightenment science became useful for consolidating a perspective for "white" manhood. In the abstract space from which he conducts the global and historical survey of climate and human behavior, James himself is not present as an embodied agent: he remains personally (and ultimately, morally) outside the scope of his survey. Farmer James as a specific actor purchasing and managing slaves disappears in his universal and historical review. It is precisely this disappearance of his personal agency that authorizes his scientific authority. Standing above and apart from history, James accesses the godlike, dissymmetrical vantage of the objective recorder, whose face cannot be looked upon. The vantage of the Enlightenment scientific philosopher correlates neatly with the attitude of modern racism, which Collette Guillaumin describes as an occulted standpoint. Distinguishing between the autoreferential racism of aristocracy, and the altero-referential racism of modern democracies, Guillaumin summarizes the latter as follows:

> A fundamental trait of such a system is the occultation of the Self, of which people have no spontaneous awareness; there is no sense of belonging to a specific group, so the group itself always remains outside the frame of reference, is never referred to as a group. This can be seen clearly in the everyday ways in which groups are designated. . . . What conclusion can we draw from the fact that 'Christian' and 'white' are still used mainly adjectivally, whereas Black, Jew . . . and Asiatic have become nouns, if not that the dominant groups have escaped the process of substantivization which has befallen those whom they dominate? (50–51)

The occulted space of subject/authority formed the precise grounds for civic definition in the Constitution, as Eva Cherniavsky notes:

"[t]he particularized, or embodied, subject remains as such unrepresentable; the subject's specificity is precisely what is voided in his accession to the status of citizen" (9).

The famous defender of the proposed Constitution, Publius, claimed the occulted agency and rational vantage of the Enlightenment scientist/philosopher as a compensatory standpoint for American men. This was a space where men overlooked their own differences as they trained their focus on *other* "bodies," as, for instance, when Madison tacitly invites citizen-men to stand in the rationally authoritative space of the scientific diagnostician in approving the Constitution:

> A patient who finds his disorder daily growing worse; and that an efficacious remedy can no longer be delayed without extreme danger; after coolly revolving his situation, and the characters of different physicians, selects and calls in such of them as he judges most capable of administering relief, and best entitled to his confidence. The physicians attend . . . They are unanimously agreed that the symptoms are critical, but that the case, with proper and timely relief, so far from being desperate, that it may be made to issue in an improvement of his constitution. . . .
>
>   Such a patient, and in such a situation is America at this moment. (Hamilton, Madison, and Jay 184–85)

The recognizing, diagnosing, and managing of "difference" (the differences of democracy's Others) promised white men a unifying standpoint for national identity. This rationalist model promised men an experience of citizenship as fraternity in the abstracted space of universalizing authority over others.

Managing Sameness and Difference

The federal plan offered men a reassuring unity in the brotherly exercise of rational, managerial authority. But the precondition for the white man's authorization as a civic manager would be his ability to model the ideal of national unity in his own person: to train his own self-difference into a rationally ordered singularity. In this way, the new fraternal modeling of white manhood would accumulate imperatives for self-management and -regimentation. Perhaps nowhere are these imperatives more starkly outlined than in Benjamin Rush's 1798 essay "Of the Mode of Education Proper in a Republic." His tensely balanced model for educating American boys suggests the impossibility of the national demands being loaded into its manly civic ideal.

In his seemingly inexhaustible and contradictory list of what republican boys must learn to exemplify and perform, we can see this emerging civic mandate for "self" control; we can see how national political and economic concerns are handed off onto individual men, with the demand that they "learn" how to internalize and balance incompatible and even antagonistic claims as an expression of their "own" personal civic responsibility. The sheer length of this (excerpted) passage suggests the obsessive energies and expanding scope of national manhood's project for territorializing individual men:

> Let our pupil be taught that he does not belong to himself, but that he is public property. Let him be taught to love his family, but let him be taught, at the same time, that he must forsake, and even forget them, when the welfare of his country requires it. He must watch for the state, as if its liberties depended upon his vigilance alone, but he must do this in such a manner as not to defraud his creditors, or neglect his family. He must love private life, but he must decline no station, however public or responsible it may be. . . . He must love popularity, but he must despise it when set in competition with the dictates of his judgment or the real interest of his country. He must love character, and have a due sense of injuries, but he must be taught to appeal only to the laws of the state, to defend the one, and punish the other. . . . He must avoid neutrality in all questions that divide the state, but he must shun the rage and acrimony of party spirit. He must be taught to love his fellow creatures in every part of the world, but he must cherish with a more intense and peculiar affection, the citizens of Pennsylvania and of the United States.[10] . . . He must be taught to amass wealth, but it must be only to encrease [sic] his power of contributing to the wants and demands of state. He must be indulged occasionally in amusements, but he must be taught that study and business should be his principal pursuits in life. Above all he must love life, and endeavor to acquire as many of its conveniences as possible by industry and economy, but he must be taught that this life "is not his own," when the safety of his country requires it. ("Of the Mode" 90)

Rush's plan works structurally to reroute anxieties about national unity and sameness into the psychological interior of the American boy/man, who must equalize the contradictory demands of self, family, market, and national interests *in his own person.* National concerns for the reassuring experiences of unity and sameness are educationally recodified as the territory of national manhood, the white man's self-management of the "differences" loaded into him.

One might suppose that the appeal of this strenuous education for national manhood would lie in its fraternal bonds. Yet Rush reveals the inability of the fraternal contract to deliver on its affective promise. Indeed, he depicts emotional relations between boys-in-training as an actual *threat* to the purity of national manhood: "I cannot help bearing a testimony . . . against the custom, which prevails in some parts of America . . . of crowding boys together under one roof for the purposes of education. . . . The vices of young people are generally learned from each other. The vices of adults seldom infect them. By separating them from each other, therefore, in their hours of relaxation from study, we secure their morals from a principal source of corruption, while we improve their manners, by subjecting them to those restraints which the differences of age and sex, naturally produce in private families" ("Of the Mode" 92). Rush's goal, he shortly reveals, is to "convert men into republican machines," something that "must be done if we expect them to perform their parts properly, in the great machine of the government of the state" (92). But the sameness schooled by this mechanical/national manhood must be experienced only in the state of abstraction: these boys learn to "relax" not in the arena of fraternity but of the heterosexualizing family (more on this in chapter 4). Rush's "republican machines" are primed for competition, where the "individual" is called to the fore on behalf of national interest—an individual specimen of American manhood unfettered by the arguably contradictory (democratic?) impulses of fraternal bonds. National unity would not find its guarantee in fraternal bodies, then, except in the most ritualized, abstracted forms.[11] Instead, it will emerge as a condition of the citizen's mass-produced, radically individualized self, his tribute to national "sameness" rendered through his successful self-discipline.

After the passage of the Constitution, the nation began forming and reforming institutional devices for policing men who failed in their national self-discipline. Such individuals were exteriorized from the civic body as alien—figured in terms of effeminacy, sedition, insanity, and criminality (and these are precisely the categories to which Delano turns to manage his anxieties over the uncertain welcome of Don Benito). In his study of the centrality of penal reform to the articulation of U.S. democracy in the early Republic, Thomas Dumm notes that new standards for "uniform legal punishment underscored and supported a uniform model of behavior, so that there was less and less psychic space . . . for the development and nurturance of variety. U.S. citizens would have one dimension in which they could develop" (137).[12] But following in the narrow track of self-discipline promised a certain compensation in authority, an authority generated in the regimen and from within the standpoint of Enlightenment science. What Robyn Wiegman has termed the "universal disembodiment attending white masculinity" (67) became carte blanche for American men's title to civic management. The imperatives of national manhood thus created a two-order domain for management: American men were to internalize rational principles of (phobia-inducing) self-management as a precondition of authority for their (counterphobic) management of others. The occulted space of the managing "expert" became a democratic as well as a career ideal: a professional manhood.

The abstracting whiteness that expanded suffrage rights to "all" white men thus worked hand in hand (and however counterintuitively) *with* class stratification. Increasingly for the emerging middle classes, competitive mastery was defined in terms of professional expertise in civic, market, or social management. In his important study of "the culture of professionalism," Burton Bledstein characterizes the emergence of middle-class professional culture in the nineteenth century as an attempt "to eliminate wasteful competition and to establish universal standards for moral and civil behavior": middle-class professionals aimed to be "the world's organizer" (27). Professionalism would soon—and still does—function as a class/corporate enterprise of occluded authority (I develop this argument in chapters 3 and 4). National manhood's mandate to manage difference—in the name of social and political "unity" and for the sake of a national economy— underwrites middle-class professionalism and white-collar management, which generate scientific rationales for the organization and supervision of the national economy, and the civic, public, and private arenas.[13]

Through the emerging professional practices promising ever more precise aims for management (populations, bodies, business, workers, economy), civic actors consolidated more narrowly functional partnerships and imagined community that drove the formation of the middle classes. This was, in other words, a cultural shift that drew on the political psychology of national manhood to consolidate a more exclusive practice of it. Important work on middle-class women's history, literature, and culture has emphasized the extent to which women were active in the public sphere.[14] It seems equally important to keep in mind the competing ways that social sciences and medicine granted certain men access to and authority over the "woman's sphere." Jacques Donzelot has characterized the management of the "private" as a bourgeois technology; it is worth considering how this "technology" emerges in the United States in a complex series of cultural moves that work—at least in part—to consolidate the domain of middle-class manhood. In an era where women were testing new theories of public action, voice, and power, one way to reconsider the professional management of the "private" sphere by professional men is to understand it—at least in part—as a countermove to women's power on behalf of white manhood. Emerging sciences like gynecology, along with other sciences like the "American school" of ethnology (polygenesis and racial categorization), and, more generally, anthropological and social sciences, exemplified and exercised white manhood as an intellectual, professional, and social discipline. This exercise came over and against an ever-expanding arena of Otherness: women, nonwhites, the primitive/poor, the insane, criminals, laborers. Professional manhood diversified and formally articulated national manhood's investment in management logic on behalf of its own gender, racial, and class advantage.

My arguments in *National Manhood* suggest that we rethink the emergence of professional disciplines as one important aspect of an ongoing, national reorganization (and reenlistment) of manhood. The materials I study here suggest that, in the early national period, masculine aggression is symbolically reorganized under the banner of whiteness. This reorganization routes class, regional, ethnic, religious, and political rivalries away from dissensions manifested in such events as Shays's, Fries's, and the Whiskey rebellions, and toward market competition. National manhood provides a new ideological framing for interactions between men and for expressions of more locally organized ideologies of manhood,[15] seemingly guaranteeing that aggressive behavior will lead to the health (and wealth), rather than the fragmentation of nation. It trains men, as part of their civic, fraternal grant, to internalize national imperatives for "unity" and "sameness," recodifying national politics as individual psychology and/or responsibility. And its logic finds particular expression in the professional middle classes. Thus white manhood would come to work corporately on behalf of nation. But the question arises: how well does the democratic fraternity of national manhood work for *men*?

Privileged Spot

In this project, I examine national manhood not only for its ideological structure and material effects, but also as an affective space, for men individually and in groups. On board the *San Dominick*, Delano is almost perpetually in a state of "fidgety panic" (252); it is as if Cereno's reception of the Massachusetts captain, enigmatically alternating between iciness and warmth, throws Delano's own sense of self-command into crisis. Though he wants to regard Cereno as a "brother captain," he cannot rest until Cereno evidences a similar regard for him. When that recognition is not apparently forthcoming, Delano muses on the possibility that Cereno is an impostor seeking to take over his ship. Alternately, he justifies his desire to take over Cereno's. The brotherhood of command is in tense balance throughout this tale, always at risk of being lost between the clashing imperatives of fraternity and competition, brotherhood and self-interest.

As we see when Delano reveals the practical nature of his desire to speak alone with Cereno, his interest in finding an exclusive space of "fraternal reserve" is both material and emotional. He wants not just a financial but also an affectionate return on his offer to provision the ship. This privileged spot of white male mutuality is a stable and reassuring space only in Delano's imagining; its actual space is wracked by anxiety, by the tensions of white manhood's countervailing investments in equality and inequality (I detail this subject more generally in chapter 5). Indeed, a reading of white manhood guided by "Benito Cereno," would indicate that this abstracted identity is structurally unbalanced, anxiety-making at its foundation.[16]

We can better understand where this anxiety comes from if we make a list of the binaries governing Rush's plan for programming the republican machine. Rush's explicit terms look something like this:

Nation/Individual
Sameness/Difference
Fraternity/Competition

The national manhood that Rush maps depends structurally on particular "white" men to integrate all these categories, behaviorally and/or psychologically. The national investment in emergent capitalism made the yoking of the categories in this first list necessary. Indeed, the nation's economy depended, as Rush recognizes, on the practical prioritization of the secondary categories. The nation would be made strong by citizens who are well-conditioned for the market: industrious, competitive, individualistic.

It is also helpful to factor in the unconscious imperatives guiding Rush's plan, which might look something like this:

Unity/Fragmentation
Patriotism/Sedition
Equality/Inequality
Health/Disease

However commonplace both these sets of terms now seem, I have listed them here to emphasize how uncomfortably the secondary terms line up across the two lists; structurally, they create real instability. It is not just that the secondary terms (on the right side) of both sets come into practical and symbolic conflict with the primary terms (on the left), but also that the secondary terms from the first list—Individual, Difference, Competition—are tied structurally and symbolically to the secondary terms in the second list—Fragmentation, Sedition, Inequality, Disease—and for that reason are bound to produce anxieties in their routine enactment, both culturally and within "white" men. Ideally, the unstable secondary category would be conditioned through its attachment to symbolic structures of brotherhood—politically through suffrage, and more concretely in emerging party politics, in volunteer associations and fraternalism, and in emerging private corporate structures. All of these structures, though, are susceptible to producing more anxiety than they offset, in their invocation of intergroup competition and intragroup hierarchy.

More certainly and practically, the abstract identity of white/national manhood gains its structural stability in altero-referentiality. The "naked nature" moment in "Benito Cereno" outlines how Delano in fact achieves "brotherhood" only through altero-referentiality: denied the ritual forms of brotherly acceptance ("hospitality") by Cereno, Delano structures that emotionally reassuring space imaginatively by looking on and categorizing that African woman and her baby, finding his "brother" only by emptying another person and mythologizing her as his (their) "Other." This moment in "Benito Cereno" encourages readers to think about how, for national manhood as well as for professional, middle-class, managerial manhood, the commanding Self seeks stability (finds its supplement) through imagined and actual excavations of multiple others.

The altero-referential articulation of white/national manhood in the early United States depended on many others, their very multiplicity hard to keep simultaneously in focus: the "black" body (as a material/symbolic supplement for whiteness); the "Indian" body (as a material/symbolic supplement for Nation—and capitalism); the "woman" body (as a material/symbolic supplement for individualistic manhood); the "primitive" body—a category that can intersect with all three above as well as poor white male immigrants, criminals, etcetera—(as a material/symbolic supplement for progress). Though gynecology, the sciences of racial categorization, and Egyptology, territorial expansion, and fraternalism now all seem to be mostly unrelated cultural projects, my analysis in *National Manhood* encourages us to see them as genealogically linked to the articulation of capitalist citizenship. If national manhood "hailed" white men into an impossible discipline of self-division, the altero-referentiality of that standpoint provided a safety valve: they could reach for a sense of self-sameness through fraternal and managerial projections of self-division/fragmentation onto democracy's Others.

It is in just this way that Delano projects both his desire for loving recognition from Cereno and his confused, helpless anger at its denial onto the African women ("unsophisticated as leopardesses; loving as doves," 268). It is the fact that he must circuit the recognition he craves in this way that clues us into what does and doesn't work about white manhood in "Benito Cereno." It would be impossible to say at the end of the tale, with Babo's head on a pike in the piazza and the proceeds of the sale of the remaining slaves in Delano's trust, that white manhood had failed in its material, legal, and political aims. But the fraternity of white manhood reveals its human inadequacy, not only in its profound dismissal of the personhood and life of the man Delano had sworn he could never call a slave (57), but in the absolute failure of the "brother captain[s]" to connect in any meaningful way. Despite their attempts, they are unable to achieve the fraternal space each of them believes they are promised by the privilege of their person, their command. Their conversation, at the end of the story, ends in death-gathering silence. Their brotherhood is shadowed over by "[t]he negro," their Other; their attempt to satisfy their own desire for human connectedness is haunted by the very human, affective foreclosures that structure their privileged spot. The abstracting appeal of "white" manhood seems to work—it does certainly for Delano—on the promise of material privilege combined with privileged association. But in practice, it seems hardly to satisfy the latter condition even when it pays on the former. The communal space of national manhood seems unable to deliver on its fraternal promise—though it may be the very dynamic set up between its partial payments on those promises and its ultimate emotional inadequacy that keeps "white" men reaching for it.

Brothers, Husbands, Fathers, Sons

In his massive study of "the idea of fraternity in America," Wilson Carey McWilliams notes that the concept is one that has received little scholarly attention. *National Manhood* suggests, though, that fraternity is *difficult* to study, and is so because the idea works in the United States as an always-remote abstraction rather than as an embodied practice. Certainly that seems to be true in Rush's plan for national education, where embodied fraternity—boys associating—is presented as an actual danger to the national good. Neither my claim nor Rush's is commonsense within a culture that structures fraternal space in every arena from national government to national pastimes. But it is important to my study to read beyond the promises to patterns that emerge in the actual details. Doing so means realizing that what men are symbolically promised by national/white manhood is almost never what they get: a space where men can step out of competitive, hierarchically ordered relations and experience rich emotional mutuality of fraternal sameness.

It is worth paying careful attention to the symbols for difference that emerge within the logic of national manhood's "sameness." For instance, we can look at the way calls to fraternity in the early nation frequently rely on images that invoke relations not of male-male sameness, but male-female differences and relations between men and women that function in turn to *differentiate* men. A key image invoked in the *Federalist Papers* is the relation not of men to each other as brothers, but to their *wives*, as husbands. Before the Revolution, such images as Paul Revere's famous cartoon against the tea tax, "The Able Doctor, or America Swallowing the Bitter Draught," relied on an invocation of patriotism as chivalric protectiveness. In contrast to the British men, dressed in wigs and finery, who symbolically rape the vulnerable woman America, American men will stand in a protective, rather than exploitive relation, presumably too in plainer (more "manly," less foppish) clothes.

This implied contrast is drawn explicitly a year after the Constitution's ratification, by Royall Tyler. Though his play, *The Contrast*, advertises itself in its prologue as an American portrait of equality ("[w]here proud titles of 'My Lord! Your Grace!' / To humble *Mr.* and plain *Sir* give place"), the play itself, however, depicts not fraternal equality, but characterological rank ordering, sorting out "real" men from the dross. "The Contrast" between men (apparently after the Revolution as before) is drawn most emphatically in its comparison of how Billy Dimple, an elite "gentleman," and Colonel Manly, a Revolutionary War veteran, treat *women*. Billy Dimple is stringing numerous women along, variously for their looks or their money. Colonel Manly, as his name contrastively signals, is straightforward, aboveboard, honorable: a protector, not an exploiter of women. We know that because of his proud relation to "my late soldiers[,] my family" (1122). For Henry Manly (as for John Jay, whose sentiments in *Federalist* No. 2 he echoes), the "brother[hood of] soldiers" provides the model for national homosocial *and* romantic heterosexual relations, where citizens, like soldiers and spouses, are "united by a similarity of language, sentiment, manners, common interest, and common consent in one grand mutual league of protection" (1116).

Though this relation is posited as one of equality, it is figured as benign hierarchy, a model of "representation" founded on an ideal of sameness that is vertically ordered. Manly is in the city to petition Congress for funds for "*my* brave old soldiers" (emphasis added) who were wounded in battle. Because he acts in a heroically protective relation to the men who served beneath him in command, the audience is encouraged to see him as a good husband for Maria, who is unhappily engaged to the foppish Dimple. Indeed, Manly explicitly defines romance as a protective relation in a conversation with Dimple: "in our young country, where there is no such thing as gallantry, when a gentleman speaks of love to a lady, whether he mentions marriage or not, she ought to conclude either that he meant to insult her or that his intentions are the most serious and honorable" (1117–18). His ability to assume such responsibility marks him as the ideal type for American men, at the same time that it embodies him as America's representative, standing, honorably, for the Good of the Whole.

Curiously, though, this representative man has no equal in the play. None of the men the audience sees, besides Manly, served in the Revolution (Manly's patriotic waiter-who-will-not-be-taken-for-a-"servant"/"nagur," Jonathan, stayed home behind his father and brothers to take care of his mother; see 1105–6). Only one such encounter between Manly and an "equal" is implied: the day he enters

New York, he declines his sister's invitation to dinner becaues he is "engaged to dine with the Spanish ambassador," to whom he was introduced by "an old brother officer." (Though Manly expects only "freezing . . . compliment" from the ambassador, he was pleasantly surprised by his "true old Castillian frankness" and "friendly manner" and accepts his invitation for that reason [1104]). The *audience* sees neither the "brother officer" nor the ambassador; indeed, one of the laments of the play is for the loss of the spirit of patriotic brotherhood in the (effeminate) scramble for "luxury." Though the "brothers" remember each other (as Manly notes, "[f]riendships made in adversity are lasting" [1122]), brotherhood seems in danger of being forgotten, and forgotten by American men.

How could American men forget brotherhood? Though the play directs us to blame this on a growing fascination with European manners and consumer goods (an admiration figured as both unmanly and unpatriotic), the play's structure would seem to suggest something different. The play itself reveals that there are no practical grounds for experiencing brotherhood in the post-Revolutionary United States. In *The Contrast*, the training ground for brotherhood was the Revolutionary battlefield, now a fading memory. The field of civic engagement seems unlikely to provide Manly the equal he deserves—there are no men with whom Manly might forge civic brotherhood in the form of friendship, only men whose silly notions his role is to correct. Instead, his emotional relations will be channeled into his marriage with Maria as he learns to "mind the main chance"—that is, to engage in competitive economic relations in order to support his family.

This play then offers a blueprint for American manliness that would seemingly assuage Rush's worries: Manly's primary affective bond, after his nation and his geographically scattered "brother officer[s]" and "brother soldiers," will be defined in immediate exercise of his marital protectorate. Benignly ordered vertical relations, modeled on the relation of husband to wife, serve finally to justify the general relation of men to men in this play, of American "manliness" (I say more about this in chapter 1). Rather than representing this ideal American man in a field of equals, Tyler casts him as an isolated figure in a hierarchical field. Strikingly, the rigid hierarchy of the military, the social contract of marriage, and the new, sentimental family provide ideological glosses for the antifraternal function of the market—they are each "corporate" bodies founded not in equality but in hierarchy and submission.

If the "husband" was a figure invoked as a "Manly" positive category for equality-among-representatives, the father/son relation was ambivalently marked as a model for (in)equality in the early national period. Commentators like Burrows and Wallace, and Jay Fliegelman have carefully detailed how Revolutionary rhetoric mobilized powerful images of children rejecting bad parents, substituting more sentimental, equalitarian images and practices in the early nation. But as Michael Paul Rogin has observed, this revolutionary liberation from "parental domination" was not enough to ensure national unity after the war was over, "and, in the symbolism of the founders, the parents returned" (*Fathers* 34). I am less interested in the psychosocial implications of this "return"—which Rogin has impressively outlined—than in the meaning of that reinstallation to the symbolic construction of white manhood. Rather than conceptualizing (equalizing) friendships between men as a model for democracy, national manhood embodied democracy *in* the competitive, self-subordinating individual. As Rush's plan for national education helpfully outlines, American men learned economically to balance competing demands *inside* their person: they learned when to subordinate their "own" individual desire to the national power, when "to defend the one, and punish the other" (90).

In national manhood, civic identification *split* men, requiring them to manage "their" competing desires not through a paradigm of equality but rank-order: to "master" themselves.[17] Identification was directed not equilaterally, then, but *vertically*, toward the more powerful "interest" that overruled "individual" desire—nationally toward abstracted and idealized founding fathers, economically toward commanding men. Thus, though citizens "stood" symbolically in the same structural relation to nation as fathers did to their family and husbands did to their wives, citizen-men's experience of that relation was not from the vantage of the father but of the *son:* national manhood was symbolically and structurally oedipalized. Carroll Smith-Rosenberg has commented on the oddity of early national iconography, where key figures for America are powerful women and citizens are represented as infants, or miniaturized men (see "Dis-Covering," 870–73). National manhood promised its citizen/representatives the right to stand for (the authority of) the F/father, but it effectively left them in the space of the son, vulnerable and anxious (more on this in chapter 2).

National Manhood

National Manhood tries to keep both the affect and effect of national/ white manhood in steady focus, reading closely its system of delicately and brutally balanced demands. The civic "equality" proffered by the ideology of national manhood was conditioned by the structural inequality of emerging capitalism and the affective foreclosures necessitated in maintaining both capitalism and the "representative" construction of democracy. *National Manhood* analyzes the complicated desires—simultaneously democratic/communitarian *and* antidemocratic/anticommunitarian—of and for "whiteness" as they become imbricated with the production of national manhood, middle-class professionality, and individual men's identities. It studies the repeating thematics of white manhood—anxiety and disappointment, longing for and fear of equality and human connection—in political, scientific, and literary texts of the early national and antebellum periods.

I have drawn on a variety of texts across what we now regard as "disciplines" in order to pull into focus patterns that often remain submerged in individual texts. For instance, one tendency is for scientific texts—both published arguments and private correspondence— to be much more "in evidence" about the dynamics of racial and gender othering, whereas literary and political texts are often far clearer about affiliated desires for and anxieties about white male sameness. Reading them together, then, allows me to draw out a larger cultural logic that remains less accessible if our reading is restricted by the more historically recent logic of disciplinarity. The texts I examine were written and published in the nascent years of professionalism and modern academic discipline-formation. In some of the material I analyze in this study, the claiming of a "discipline" is exactly what is at stake. It seems important, then, to suspend "disciplinarity" as an automatic logic, instead historicizing and challenging it at the same time as I draw on a particular "discipline" for my approach to these materials.

I come to this study as a literary critic, and I consider *National Manhood* a contribution to literary as well as cultural studies, though many of the texts I analyze are now considered extraliterary as well as "popular," which is to say *non*literary literature. Here, I could invoke my training in early American literature, which, as those who share that training—and the task of representing it to undergraduate students—know, is culled from a body of writing (sermons, diaries, histories, news, tracts, etc.) hardly considered literature in the high sense now. Before the mid-nineteenth century, a far vaster array of written and printed materials were regarded as literature; *literature* as a specialized and professionally elite category of writing was only just being codified during the period of my study, in tandem with the emerging middle-class professions.[18]

Similarly in this period, science was only just beginning to establish itself as a (variety of) profession(s).[19] In order to differentiate between the political and social deployments of "scientific" expertise in the early nation, and its growth into a distinct employment category with discrete disciplinary conventions, I distinguish semantically between professionally oriented scientific writing and publication, and a more loosely defined scientific discourse, which can include works by a variety of people who may not have identified their primary avocation as "science" per se, but who deployed the positivistic energies of Enlightenment rationality toward the kinds of centralizing, unifying, and institutionalizing aims that Foucault has described (e.g., *Power/Knowledge* 81–85). For instance, disciplinary science today claims very little of the work of Thomas Jefferson and none of that by James Kirke Paulding or George Lippard as "scientific," but I will nonetheless consider in my analysis their appeals to scientific discourse or logic in Jefferson's *Notes on the State of Virginia*, Paulding's *Slavery in the United States*, and Lippard's *Quaker City*.

Though I make such semantic distinctions to clarify technical differences, I want to preserve for my study a focus that resists disciplinary categorizations. An important aspect of my argument is how the compartmentalization of knowledge in the early United States— disciplined in increasingly rigid professional arenas—contributed to the multiplex production of white manhoods under the umbrella of a national identity. For that reason, it has been essential to my project for intellectual and political reasons to cross disciplinary boundaries both in terms of primary material and theoretical apparatus. Bruno Latour has recently argued in his analysis of modernism and postmodernism that "our intellectual life is all out of kilter. Epistemology, the social sciences, the sciences of texts—all have their privileged vantage point, provided that they remain separate. If the creatures we are pursuing cross all three spaces, we are no longer understood" (*We Have Never* 5). In my insistence that we reconnect political, literary, geographic, scientific, and medical projects, which from our current vantage might seem discrete and unrelated, I am attempting to examine those aspects of the national/masculine self that have been split off or occluded from our study *by* disciplinarity, in hopes that studying them might help us better understand the raced and gendered mechanisms of national identity construction that continue to inform U.S. politics and culture.

I trust my readers to remember that I offer my arguments in the spirit of what philosophers Gayle Ormiston and Raphael Sassower have described as "narrative experiment"—a "re-collection" of stories that works to rethink these materials from a vantage that drops out of more "disciplined" studies. Postulating national manhood has helped me to understand with historical specificity how the interarticulation of race, gender, and nation produced a particular kind of civic and cultural logic in the early United States (and one that lingers with us today). It has helped me find productive and illuminating connections between events and texts I had been trained to see as unrelated. It has helped me to reconsider what I have thought about white men— about individual historical actors, and about the national/corporate structures that conditioned the kinds of dilemmas, responses, behaviors, choices that I have isolated for study here.

I have tried to achieve with this study what cultural theorist Kaja Silverman describes in the epigraph to this chapter as a "re-viewing": a kind of analysis that might allow us to achieve, however conditionally, an ethical and nonviolent relation to the subject of white manhood in the early nation. My readers might occasionally find me being startlingly sympathetic to some of the men, fictional and historical, that I describe here. After spending a good deal of my critical life sustained by feminist and postcolonial theory, being deeply angry at things white men have done, and at the vicious institutions and cultural practices white manhood has produced, it became important for me to experiment here with a more open stance. I wanted to figure out what would happen critically if I attempted to see the diverse humanity of actors within the institution of white manhood—to look around or "before" that category in just the same way that I am asking my audience to do as they read this book. This experiment emerged in the context of my own developing feminist, antiracist desire critically to cultivate democratic practice by working not just to appreciate "difference," but also functional disunity (more on which below). For me, one aspect of that latter project was to reject my own impulse to claim coherence for my critical position by othering the target(s) of my analysis.

At the same time, readers might also note that I am unrelentingly critical of the effects that the institutions and practices of white manhood produce for women and people of color—and critical of scholarship that works to excuse or distract us from thinking about those effects. These two positions do not seem incompatible to me: to describe the structure of white or national manhood as one that vigorously enlists certain people is not the same as saying that once caught within the momentum of that identification, they no longer have any ability to re-view individual or corporate behavior. It is entirely possible, and I would also say ethically important to the project of figuring out how to structure democratic community from out of "our" history in the United States, to register the trauma produced for individual "white" men by the political psychology of national manhood *and* to insist that its corporate results are always a matter of individual and group choice/consent and as such, available to interruption, struggle, and change.

National Manhood frames some early sites for the national production of white manhood. This is a project seldom attempted in disciplinary studies, not in the least because, as I have argued above, white manhood is (and is occulted in) the stance *of* the disciplined observer. Thus, the very altero-referentiality of white/national manhood—its rational, managerial directing of the gaze away from itself and toward its multiplying Other/supplements—makes it hard to pin down analytically. For that reason, I have structured my arguments in each chapter so as to foreground different sets of interlocking foci that generally inform my arguments throughout the book. In the first chapter, which draws on *The Federalist Papers*, Crèvecoeur's "What is an American?" passage from his *Letters of an American Farmer*, Jefferson's *Notes on the State of Virginia*, and Rush's essay on "Negro Leprosy," the focus is on the experimental reorganization of national unity through *white* manhood. In the second chapter, which studies the Lewis and Clark expedition, Nicholas Biddle's 1814 rendering of that expedition, and John Neal's 1821 novel *Logan*, I analyze how the idea of Indian-ness worked variously to train territorial expansion and to supplement and stabilize both corporate and individual articulations of national manhood. The third chapter, which rereads Samuel G. Morton's debate with John Bachman over polygenesis, foregrounds the construction of race in the terms of professional competition for cultural authority on behalf of white manhood. The fourth chapter studies how womanhood becomes symbolically useful not just to the articulation of racial/national purity but also for mediating anxieties emerging in the production of professional manhood, through cultural and medical articulations of gynecology. And the fifth chapter, which takes up another essay by Rush, the subject of male fraternalism and Morton's scientific correspondences, examines the intersecting desires of "representative" men with the practices of fraternity and male friendship before returning to "Benito Cereno" to read the tragically flawed emotional circuitry of national "white" manhood. Finally, in the afterword I address what emerged for me as an important aspect of my arguments in this study, the implications of a "unified" national ideal expressed by and in national manhood's icon, the president, for the U.S. democratic imaginary.

The Subject of National Manhood

In her recent study of how the bodily ego is constructed through the field of vision, Kaja Silverman insists that we reconsider our psychoanalytic and cultural assumptions about the ideal status of "wholeness" and "unity": "It seems important to note that the fantasy of the body in bits and pieces is only one way of apprehending the heterogeneity of the corporeal ego, and one which is inextricably tied to the aspiration toward 'wholeness' and 'unity.' Lacan suggested that it is 'organic disturbance and discord' which prompts the child to seek out the form of the 'whole body-image.' However, it seems to me that the reverse is actually true: it is the cultural premium placed on the notion of a coherent bodily ego which results in such a dystopic apprehension of corporeal multiplicity" (*Threshold* 20–21). Drawing on the work of psychoanalytic critics who have foregrounded the extent to which the subject is comfortable and even accustomed to heterogeneity and bodily fragmentation, Silverman underscores the *cost* to the subject of psychically internalizing rigid imperatives for "unity" or "self-sameness": "the aspiration to wholeness and unity not only has tragic personal consequences, but also calamitous social effects, since it represents one of the most important psychic manifestations of 'difference'" (27). It has cost all of us (U.S.). "White" manhood's identification with national unity has worked historically to restrict others from achieving full entitlement in the United States. At the same time, it has worked powerfully to naturalize "white" men as essentially unified subjects.

As I hope my discussion so far has made clear, national/"white" manhood, however effective for certain purposes, is *not* a "unified" identity. It is an impossible identity—impossible in the sense that it is an always-agonistic position, making it difficult for any human to fit into a full sense of compatibility with its ideal construction. That may be what makes it so difficult to critique, for when we, from the vantage of feminism or antiracism, critique "white" men, we are critiquing the ideal, the promise held out by national manhood. In response, "white" men often disidentify from that ideal-under-attack, claiming that its image does not apply to them personally; they never accrued such benefits from it. Indeed they well may say so. Ironically, their injured sense that they have been deprived of such benefits can still effect their identification with the privilege-bearing identity of "white" manhood. "White" manhood is not "guilty" these men insist, because they are not so (or so consistently) privileged. (Ironically, too, as they refute critics' negative definitions of that identity, such men do work on behalf of the national idealization of whiteness as a pure and "innocent" category—much like Crèvecoeur.) Recently, "white" manhood as an institution has conceded some space in the public and civic arenas, to those people formerly constituted as legal others—"minorities" and "white" women. But as the recent dismantling of affirmative action programs and their replacement with "new" civil rights laws designed to "protect" white men, and intensified national border phobias have demonstrated, such concessions have done nothing to dislodge or displace the referential power of "white" manhood, whether we agree that such men are privileged or "equally" victimized.

I have tried to reframe the question in this book. I am not concerned to uphold or vilify particular white men, but to begin asking how and under what conditions "white" manhood came to "stand" for nation, how it came to be idealized as a "representative" identity in the United States, and finally (in the afterword) how that representatively unifying routing of identity conditions the ways we are able to think about democracy. I want *National Manhood* to disturb the concrete referentiality of that term "white" man, bumping aside the abstraction in ways that let us begin considering the profound diversity of people who "fit" that label, and to begin asking what happens to those people and others when an abstracting group marker, such as white manhood, becomes socially attractive, legally desirable, aesthetically ideal, a national imperative.

I

Purity Control: Consolidating
National Manhood in the
Early Republic

I

Constitutional Crisis, or, (Dis)United States

When Jefferson formally asserted that "all men are created equal," he raised for the thirteen confederated states a question about political order and practice that could not sustain immediate attention in the exigencies of the Revolutionary War effort—more pressing then was determining the difference between Loyalist and Patriot. Jefferson's construction, endorsed by the Continental Congress, advanced a liberalizing reconceptualization of political entitlement. That loosely specified formulation arguably helped to produce a great deal of energy and dissent in the post-Revolutionary period. John Adams's response to Abigail Adams's 1776 request that in forming the new government he "remember the ladies"—his banteringly dismissive "I cannot but laugh"—is in itself hardly a clue to the disorderly potential that the Declaration's gesture toward universal political entitlement evoked for those accustomed to political leadership. Rather, those concerns surface in a letter to James Sullivan, which Adams would write a few weeks later. There, he evokes a specter of suffrage gone wild: "Depend on it, Sir, it is dangerous to open so fruitful a source of controversy and altercation as would be opened by attempting to alter the qualification of voters; there will be no end of it. New claims will arise; women will demand a vote; lads from twelve to twenty-one will think their rights not enough attended to; and every man who has not a farthing, will demand an equal voice with any other, in all acts of state" (*Works* 9:378). Adams seems precocious in these worries during the early years of revolution.[1] But after the war, people began to have manifestly different and patently disruptive ideas about what Gordon Wood has characterized as the "unintended" promises of the new nation (*Creation* 395).

There were multiple events and ideological developments during the 1780s that fed widespread fears about social, economic, or political fragmentation.[2] During the years preceding the Constitutional debates, residents of the United States found themselves facing a variety of social, political, and economic changes and upheavals. States debated furiously and split along sectional lines over Jay's negotiated treaty with Spain in 1786 surrendering U.S. claims to free navigation of the Mississippi in exchange for commerce privileges. The developing popularity of liberal abolitionist sentiment and its seizing on Revolutionary rhetoric and ideals had already begun exciting sectionalism. Western land speculation became rampant while postwar depression and inflation temporarily retracted wartime economic gains and undermined political idealism and interstate good will.[3] The need for higher tariffs to recuperate loans made during the Revolution excited group, class, and regional antagonisms. Dependence on foreign loans provided a source of symbolic anxiety, seemingly contradicting the Confederation's claim to "independence."

This ideal of independence began to motor disruptive socioeconomic claims. Indenture came increasingly under challenge, and the numbers of white indentured servants began a drastic decline, with former "servants" refusing their former "masters" and "mistresses" traditional forms of address. Ideological shifts interacted symbiotically with economic ones in the dramatic and rapid post-Revolutionary transition into a market economy. The prewar colonies had already been experiencing, as Paul Gilje emphasizes, the highest rate of economic growth in the eighteenth century; their break with England allowed them "to move in new directions that encouraged the development of capitalism even more" ("Rise" 10). This "development" was situated immediately in post-Revolutionary hyperinflation, and entailed for many a brutally rapid socioeconomic shift toward increased market dependence, nonlocal exchange, and profit "ethic." Class rivalry became threatening in interstate currency battles and violent in Shays's Rebellion (1786–87), as Massachusetts officials imprisoned many, tried over thirty, and condemned to death six of the Revolutionary veteran-farmers who blocked tax collection in an attempt to salvage their holds on property. Class revolt grew in more and less organized ways: the incidence of property crimes increased rapidly after the Revolution; robbers were subject to capital punishment, and were frequently portrayed as victims of state injustice in the proliferation of printed criminal narratives (see Cohen, 117–63 passim).[4] People began considering the necessity of equal distribution of property for the practice of democracy.[5]

Political leaders of the era and historians have offered such accounts to define the 1780s as a crisis zone that necessitated the formulation of a strong national government in the Constitution. They draw widely on the jeremiads of contemporaries, who warned against factionalism, complained against internal enemies, and worried about the collapse of the Revolutionary project. However widespread the register of "crisis" among Americans in the 1780s may have been, it is an assessment that historian Gordon Wood has described as "incongruous": "On the surface at least the American states appeared remarkably stable and prosperous. The political leaders at the uppermost levels remained essentially unchanged throughout the period. Both the Confederation government and the governments of the separate states had done much to stabilize the finances and the economy of the country. The states had already moved to assume payment of the public debt, and the Confederation deficit could not be considered serious. Despite a temporary depression in the middle eighties, the commercial outlook was not bleak. As historians have emphasized, the period was marked by extraordinary economic growth. In fact . . . it was a period of high expectations, clearly reflected in the rapid rate of population growth" (*Creation* 394–95). Wood argues that it was exactly the prosperity of the Revolutionary and postwar era that excited impossible expectations and exaggerated the sensation of crisis.[6] Some Anti-Federalists made very similar claims in answering Federalist arguments for ratification. For instance, the "Federal Farmer" (probably New Yorker Melancton Smith) points to the way wartime "confusion and the introduction of paper money, infused in the minds of people vague ideas respecting government and credit. We expected too much from the return of peace, and of course we have been disappointed" (qtd. in Ketcham 260). Pennsylvania's "Centinal" (Samuel Bryan) is even more scornful and direct: "our situation is represented to be so *critically* dreadful, that, however reprehensible and exceptionable the proposed plan of government may be, there is no alternative, between the adoption of it and absolute ruin.—My fellow citizens, things are not at that crisis, it is the argument of tyrants" (qtd. in Ketcham 236; original emphasis).[7]

However we measure and assess the actuality of "crisis," it is worth considering how Constitutional proponents rhetorically harnessed widespread concerns over emerging diversity, dissent, and evidences of disunity for a political counteroffensive against what John Adams had early labeled (again, precociously) "democratic despotism"—local and radical reconceptualizations of democratic practice increasingly present throughout the United States.[8] Contesting the British principle of virtual representation, citizens of the states began more and more to insist on *actual* representation. This movement was expressed in a range of practices, including new, strict residency requirements for representatives, expanded suffrage definitions framed to ensure structures for electoral consent, and a model of equal electoral districts that echoed the one-state, one-vote rule under the Articles of Confederation. Even more pointedly, citizens began showing up at legislative sessions to deliver instructions to their delegates. Certainly the laws enacted by these legislatures may have violated some peoples' sense of right order,[9] but these lawmaking bodies were, as Wood summarizes, "probably as equally and fairly representative of the people as any legislatures in history" (*Creation* 404). Intensifying emphasis was placed on the *local* as the best and most proper venue for democratic practice. New Englanders began insisting that the town was the real center for good government and fair representation, locus for the most meaningfully immediate social contract, and it wasn't long before Virginia counties began acting on similar claims.

This growing insistence on local democratic practice, on face-to-face democracy, was amplified in the increasing phenomenon of the extragovernmental organization of people, in county assemblies, watchdog committees, radical associations, and out-of-door actions.[10] A clear spillover from Revolutionary practice, these groups, commonly remembered in the dystopic rhetoric of vigilantism, riot, and mob, were present in every major city and across the countryside.[11] Commenting on Jefferson's own late-life advocacy of local, ward governance, Hannah Arendt observes that he "anticipated with almost weird precision those councils, *soviets* and *Räte*, which were to make their appearance in every genuine revolution. . . . Each time they appeared, they sprang up as the spontaneous organs of the people, not only outside all revolutionary parties but entirely unexpected by them and their leaders" (252). Political theorists and historians alike have failed to recognize, Arendt insists, the extent to which such councils represented a "new form of government, with a new public space for freedom which was constituted and organized during the course of revolution itself" (253). Though Arendt immediately moves to qualify her argument, C. Douglas Lummis grasps it as fundamental evidence for radical democracy's gravitation toward the local: "Again and again, in the phase where revolution was still revolutionary, the polity has broken down naturally into units small enough that the people can confront one another in genuine communities, talk to one another, and choose and act collectively" (113). Such radical practices threatened to make not only national governmental structures, but even state legislatures irrelevant to what Lummis calls the "state of democracy" in the early United States.[12]

Given the widespread outcroppings of emergently radical democratic practices,[13] my study of the 1780s always returns me to this question: why didn't the proposed structures of the Constitution—centralizing, abstracting, potentially monarchical—incur more organized opposition? Why didn't the revolutionary democratic spirit widely expressed in local, face-to-face practices lead people loudly to reject the virtualization of their democracy under the Constitution, given the way it rerouted energy for and relevance of local and direct self-governance?[14] History of Ideas offers no real help at this level for explaining not only cross-sectional support but also local acquiescence to ratification,[15] only because it is more concerned with the organized thinking of men at the center of state and national legislatures than it is with the more far-flung, disorganized, uneven practices of less socially and politically advantaged actors. And though arguments about the strategic fiat of the Constitutional framers and supporters offers somewhat more explanatory power on this point, arguments about rushed state conventions and bad roads don't explain broad cross-sectional popular support after the Constitution's passage.[16]

I'm going to propose that we look in a different direction from political philosophy's debates over liberalism and republicanism, or the Federalists' economic advantages and political machinations, and turn our attention instead to the way that proponents of Constitution, most famously "Publius," hold out a reformulated ideal of "manhood"—purified, vigorous, unified—as a counterphobic ideal for the kinds of social diversity and disruption foregrounded in emergently radical democratic practices. In other words, the conditional disunities and frictions of democratic negotiation entailed both by the more explicitly confraternal model of the Articles and by emergent local political practices is soothingly covered over by national self-sameness and unity, and embodied in the national executive.[17] This is a virtual (abstracted, imagined) fraternity, where the discomfiting actuality of fraternal disagreement disappears in the singular body of the President, who stands as a guarantee of manly constitution *qua* national accord. Importantly, his unifying energy is representatively routed through/supplied by male citizens in a way that can reassure individual men not only about political discord, but about other kinds of cultural and economic dislocations. In the end, what might have most effectively garnered support for—or at least blunted resistance to—the Constitution was the way it convincingly and insistently cir-cuited the ideal of political consensus through the similarly common ideal of a vigorous, strong, undivided manhood. The bribe of national manhood, a manhood that could be claimed through patriotic incor-poration (or subordination, as I'll be arguing), effectively undercut the radicalizing energy of local democratic practices and rerouted the con-ceptualization of democracy in the new nation, atomizing the idea of participation and fitting citizens out for market competition. To posi-tion my argument for considering a reformulated manhood as a key component in Constitutional ratification and postratification support, I want to back up and briefly consider another important dislocation affecting the confederated citizens of the early states.

Confraternity vs. National Manhood

In one of the most influential recent analyses of Revolutionary-era culture, *Prodigals and Pilgrims*, Jay Fliegelman has detailed how the Revolution was symbolically built, in large part, on the political energy generated by changing familial ideology: angry colonial chil-dren excoriated the bad parenting of Britain and declared their right to divorce those parents. What sometimes becomes obfuscated in Fliegel-man's analysis, though, is the highly ordered binary pattern of gender "logic" governing Revolutionary rhetoric.[18] In an earlier study, Edwin Burrows and Michael Wallace also examine Revolutionary-era con-tractualist ideology in England and America/the United States with regard to familial analogies. As they observe, the familial analogy to natural law was structured by appeals to the person of the King as "father," and the nation of Britain as "mother." Both "parents" were depicted generally in relation to "children," but specifically always in relation to *sons*.[19] From the vantage of those American sons, both King/Father and Britain/Mother were corrupt. Significantly, however, the form expressing that corruption was governed by highly loaded gender paradigms. The King/Father's corruption manifested itself as power ("tyranny"), whereas Britain/Mother's corruption was sexual ("prostitution").

In the newly United States, the analogical corollary for Mother (and therefore U.S. women) was Liberty, or Columbia, embodying prostitution's opposite, political and moral purity, though symbolically still expressed through the terms of sexuality. The U.S. corollary for Father was the Fraternity of Sons, given institutional structure in the Articles of Confederation.[20] But this replacement of Father with Brothers seemed symbolically to evoke anxiety and weakness, not confidence and strength. Carroll Smith-Rosenberg observes in her analysis of early Republican depictions of America, that iconography for conceptualizing "sons" was awkward at best. Men tend in these portrayals to be visually diminutive, backgrounded to the looming female figure of Columbia—and even feminized. As she summarizes, "what ambivalence surrounds the feminine iconographic representation of the virile and virtuous American Republic!" ("Dis-Covering" 870–71). If the analogical rhetoric of the Revolution made it possible to conceptualize and accomplish the overthrow of tyrannical patriarchy, it certainly did not resolve immediate questions about redistributions and coordination of male power and identity in U.S. culture. Breaking with the King/Father necessitated a reconfiguration not only of political power, but also—analogically and practically—of the ideals of manhood.

As Fliegelman stresses, the ideological and political modifications of manhood took practical expression within family structures. Within this (post-)Revolutionary family, there were economic and affective redistributions of power. Hierarchically ordered patriarchal models gave way to an affectionate model. Deference to biological fathers was no longer axiomatic but conditional: as Fliegelman puts it, "sentimental theory elevated the moral obligation to repay kindness above the natural obligation owed one's parent" (*Prodigals* 215). The new romantic pairing of husband and wife emphasized a nuclear, rather than extended, family organization and a more egalitarian sharing of emotional jurisdiction.

More recently, scholars have begun delineating how changes in

domestic manufacture and commerce—intensified by wartime boy-
cotts and exigencies—were also working to redistribute economic
power within middling and poorer families. Women's role in early
market culture has been virtually invisible to historians of various
schools. But as Jeanne Boydston argues, their economic role in the
early nation, contrary to the emergent logic of separate spheres and
the increasing ideological association of work with manliness, was
actually expanding: "the material conditions of transition [from market place to market economy] may have given rise, not to the exclusion of women from the market, but to an expanded dependence on
the market labor of women, performed both within and outside the
household. In both its material and ideological character, women's
labor tended to be more flexible than the labor men performed—more
easily adapted and redeployed to meet the changing needs of household economies. If anything, the transition moved many women into
a more critical relation to the market" (25). Such changes in economic
practices meant that more households became more dependent on
women's paid labor for "competency." And women became more evident as economic actors. Boydston observes that in cities of the early
nation, women could be found working as "sailors, morticians, day
laborers, iron mongers, and money lenders, as well as seamstresses,
mantuamakers and milliners" (29).

This potential rejection of patriarchy, however, was not celebrated
by men in the early nation (nor has it much been by historians since).[21]
Instead, women's labor seems rather quickly to have been conceptualized as a threat to men's post-Revolutionary project of reconstituting
their own "independence" in market culture. Ignoring actual women
workers, men struggled to reconstitute male power, training attention
toward their market interactions with other men as "manhood" became increasingly important as a category defined through economic
success. In a fascinating study of the correspondences of major Philadelphia merchants in the late eighteenth century, historian Toby Ditz
details how even those of the most economically privileged classes
were obsessed with "the precariousness of manly identity and reputation" (51). In their correspondence, "woman" operated not as an actor
but as a symbolic category that triangulated relations between men:
"as merchants negotiated the meaning of a rather elusive masculinity
with one another, they frequently triangulated their position with a
reference to a heavily symbolized femininity. Defining the male subject thus entailed the proliferation of images of femininity" (53–54).

Neither celebrated nor appreciated, female economic action was increasingly bracketed by men as "unnatural" and "disorderly," whilst they described male economic failure as evidence of effeminacy.

From privileged merchants to farmers,[22] shifts of authority, affiliation, and capital in the early nation seem to have reconfigured men's experience of and intensified their focus on manliness. Fears over masculine identity as experienced in the family, and about masculine rivalry foregrounded in the market transition became more urgent as these were attached to questions of national stability. The structure of the Constitution and the rhetoric of its supporters effectively harnessed these various anxieties to the lingua franca of manhood, a "common" manhood redefined in national terms, as national power. This nationally authorized manhood did not emerge sui generis but appealed generally to an assemblage of older cultural patterns, practices, and fears. It promised redress for men's various anxieties in a nostalgically configured fantasy of powerful manhood, revivified and certified through its attachment to national strength, unity, and economic expansion.[23] National manhood gained support precisely by mobilizing, generalizing, and guaranteeing manhood in a way that would shortly find ritual expression in "universal" white manhood suffrage.[24]

As I just indicated, it is most important to my argument to foreground that what is new in this reorganization of manhood is its appeal to and nationalization of *whiteness*.[25] The Constitutional period marks the beginning of an experimental reorganization and extension of whiteness to manhood through national incorporation (an incorporation that would alternately identify its fraternally "equal" subject through the terms of competitive individualism and market exchangeability). This incorporation promised to manage the potentially divisive effects of interpersonal, interclass, and interregional masculine competition by relocating them in a symbolically fraternal, reassuringly "common" manhood. One index to that new, more explicitly harnessed equation of national manhood with white manhood becomes manifest in the projection of cultural fears about dependence and rivalry onto groups of people who were excluded from that category. Anxieties about social and political disintegration were increasingly linked to women, racial others, and national "foreigners." Sentiment (one of the philosophical grounds of appeal for the nation's Declaration of Independence) was dissociated from an ever more self-interested masculine ideal, identified as a source of political "infection" and projected onto women. European immigrants (French and Irish democratic and anti-imperialist politicos in particular) were increasingly regarded with suspicion, as sources of contamination to the "democratic" spirit, a suspicion made lawful in the Alien and Sedition Acts. Race came, during this period, to be more intensively studied and negatively described in terms of bodily disease and political exteriority.

In the remainder of this chapter, I examine early manifestations of this national manhood, showing how that increasingly abstracted subject promised counterphobically to manage anxieties about masculine rivalry unleashed both by the nascent practices of radical democracy, and the cultural dislocations entailed by shifts in local and national economy. Specifically, I detail its symbolic (re)centralization as mapped in *The Federalist Papers*, its gender incorporation as modeled in Crèvecoeur's famous "What is the American?" passage, and its racial purification as suggested in two scientific texts about "race" by Thomas Jefferson and Benjamin Rush.

II

Sons of Liberty

One of the most useful strategies for assuaging postwar anxieties about male dependence and rivalry was to postulate a convincing, coherently bounded, and powerful fraternity of men, which is what Publius/Jay does in *The Federalist* No. 2: "It has often given me pleasure to observe, that Independent America was not composed of detached and distant territories, but that one connected, fertile, wide spreading country was the portion of our western *sons of liberty*. . . . A succession of navigable waters forms a kind of chain round its borders, as if to bind it together. . . . With equal pleasure I have as often taken notice, that Providence has been pleased to give this one connected country, to one united people, a people descended from the same ancestors, speaking the same language, professing the same religion, attached to the same principles of government, very similar in their manners and customs" (Hamilton, Madison, and Jay 7; emphasis added). There are several aspects of this passage worth noting: its abstracted, bird's-eye, geographical "reading" of the nation (recalling Jefferson's anthropological advice to Rutledge and Shippen to "go to the top of a steeple to have a view"); its evocation of boundary and identity that simultaneously appeals to secured property and corporate selfhood; its radical reduction of cultural, linguistic, ethnic, and religious diversity in the name of national "unity" (even as it tacitly acknowledges those differences in the necessity of "binding"); its apportionment of the geographical country to a masculine body-politic (sons of liberty)—what, in Lauren Berlant's terms, we can describe as the "double articulation of [white male] subjectivity and landscape" (*Anatomy* 35). The first powerful promise of the new nation is that it will provide the expansive security of empire for the united sons of liberty.

The self-containment in Publius/Jay's description grounds his subsequent appeal to the "nobly established . . . Liberty and Independence." Many recent historians have demonstrated how the idea of "independence" worked to consolidate exclusive models for civic identity in this period. David Roediger, for instance, has delineated the emergence of a "white" working class defining its own independence in increasingly sharp contrast to a "black" dependent class of slaves. And just as dependence became a new, essentialist category tagged to African and African-descended peoples, so too, as Joan Gunderson has detailed, was it attached to femaleness.[26] Civic identity was being defined in exclusive and increasingly excorporative terms. Drawing on powerful symbology, Publius argued for just such a carefully delimited and abstracted group identity (not the least in merging the three identities of the three authors into Publius, "the people" speaking in the Name of the One). It is precisely in this assertion of a national manhood, characterized by its unity (*qua* boundedness) and purity (*qua* sameness), that we find an angle from which to begin critically assessing the counterphobic structure of Publius's argument. Theirs/his is an argument that implicitly identifies local democratic practices *as* the fragmentation of male household management. In this rhetorical collapse, men are encouraged to view (healthy) democratic dissension through the phobic lens of a manhood imperiled by household disorder (women's more equal emotional and economic participation). Publius invites men to believe that hierarchizing remasculinization will simultaneously invest their personal experience of manhood with both familial and national order. This recharged manhood will provide a new arena for men to enjoy simultaneously their manhood and their "equality": the marketplace.

In positive terms, Publius describes Constitutional structure as one that manifests the masculine ideal of the scientific Enlightenment, and specifically a scientific system for managing government. National order indeed emerges from "cool" consideration, "[un]awed by power, or influenced by any passions" (Hamilton, Madison, and Jay 8). The reader is invited to adopt that very deliberate, dispassionate relationship to "the evidence of truth," that is, arguments for the Constitution (4). Publius/Jay posits those arguments to be, like Minerva, the pure offspring of a rational, godlike, male mind, that will be recognized as such by similar minds: "the more attentively I consider and investigate the reasons which appear to have given birth to this opinion, the more I become convinced that they are cogent and conclusive" (10).

So, the best vantage from which rationally to deliberate the merits of the proposed Constitution is from a distance, where one can take an "enlarged view of the subject" (Hamilton, Madison, and Jay 5). This ideal distance is, not coincidentally, the precise relation the constitutional government will assume toward its subject. For instance, in No. 9, Publius/Hamilton argues that what has been viewed as a fundamental weakness in the proposed Constitution is in fact the center of its strength: "the ENLARGEMENT of the ORBIT" that the Republic will assume with relation to the states and its constituents. It is precisely this distanced relationship that will enable the government to forestall the evils of local "factions," an argument which builds to a finer point in No. 10. Outlining the advantages of a republican system over local democracy, Publius/Madison details:

> The two great points of difference between a Democracy and a Republic are, first, the delegation of the government, in the latter, to a small number of citizens elected by the rest: secondly, the greater number of citizens and greater sphere of country over which the latter may be extended.
> The effect of the first difference is, on the one hand, to refine and enlarge the public views, by passing them through the medium of a chosen body of citizens, whose wisdom may best discern the true interest of their country. (46–47)

Thus rational distance works two ways. First, it "refine[s]" the vision by reducing the prominence of local difference, thereby suggesting that objective political rationality must function away from distractions of personality, away from local, democratic intersubjectivity (an argument Publius/Jay develops as well in No. 3).[27] Second, rational distance "enlarge[s]" the prospects of government, allowing for the kinds of ongoing territorial and civic incorporation that will provide adequate space for dispersing dangerous difference.

The integrity of national and civic expansion (a key point of debate with opponents of the Constitution who believed that only small nations could long remain viable) will be ensured by the firmness and potency of the government, a spirit summarized in the person of its executive. Publius/Madison notes in No. 37, "Energy in Government is essential to that security against external and internal danger." Publius/Hamilton correlates "energy" and "vigour"—both words that describe specifically masculine power—with the concept of "unity" in No. 70, where he advocates for a "vigorous executive" office. The "UNITY of the Executive" (Hamilton, Madison, and Jay 361) will both guarantee and represent the "uniform principles of policy," which will (in Publius/Jay's words) "harmonize, assimilate and protect the several parts and members, and extend the benefits of its foresight and precautions to each" (16). The executive will metonymically stand for the virility, the (manly) logic, and the coherence of the One: the United, over and against the (disorderly) States.

Publius posits masculine and, importantly, managerial "energy" in service of objective rationality as the particular contribution of the federal government. Various feminist historians and philosophers have observed that one of the Enlightenment's primary ideological achievements was that of correlating a disembodied, masculine reason with objective order.[28] Publius/Madison indeed suggests in No. 18 that insofar as the energy of government is trained toward "reason" it masters and removes itself from the corrupting tendencies of the disorderly, material body. Offering examples from ancient Grecian republics, the Amphyctionic confederacy and the Acheans, he summarizes the lesson thusly: "it emphatically illustrates the tendency of foederal bodies, rather to anarchy among the members, than to tyranny in the head" (Hamilton, Madison, and Jay 89).

Here it is then, the threat that Publius's model of civic management promises to put down. In responding to opponents' concerns about the curtailment of state power, *The Federalist Papers* manifest an ongoing emphasis on the management of diversity, "*United America*" as opposed to "*disunited* America" (Hamilton, Madison, and Jay 11; original emphasis). Publius is at pains to establish that a larger political threat is present in the fragmenting effects of unsubordinated diversity at any level, rather than from a centralized government. Over and over, Publius appeals to the harm brought by difference of interest. The judicious reader is reminded of the "danger of difference of opinion" (357), and asked to consider that a collective executive, like multiple sovereign bodies, suffer from a tendency to "be distracted and warped by that diversity of views, feelings and interests" (384–85).[29] Similarly, confederations tend to demonstrate an "excentric tendency in the subordinate or inferior orbs, by the operation of which there will be a perpetual effort of each to fly off from the common center" (73). Without the single, strong authority provided by the Constitution, there will be no way to control diversity; diversity will ineluctably lead to unmanaged competition, and thus to national disintegration.

Cannily, though, the key analogy for competition is not male-male rivalry, but male-*female* difference: Publius's key argumentative strategy is to compare the ideal, masculine political body provided by the Constitution to a feminine, disorderly body allegedly created by the Articles of Confederation. That latter "body" is governed by weakness and passion (see, e.g., No. 5, at Hamilton, Madison, and Jay 18–21). It is mobbish and disorderly (see, e.g., No. 58, at 294–99), even deviant. The Articles can only provide for "a system of government founded on an inversion of the fundamental principles of all government; it would have seen the authority of the whole society every where subordinate to the authority of the parts; it would have seen a monster in which the head was under the direction of the members" (231). It is a monster against which the judicious reader is encouraged to take a "firm stand": the "political monster of an *imperium in imperio*." Suggestively gendered, this monster is a "seduc[tive]" one, whose "fatal charm" it is necessary to "break" (70). Support for this political body can only lead the nation to a "national humiliation," and even death (see Nos. 15, 16, and 21).[30]

The Disorders of Women[31]

The above examples loosely connote the disorders caused by ungoverned womanhood. But "America" is repeatedly invoked specifically as a "woman" to portray a passive and even sickly body, one that can only be resuscitated by manly acumen and authority. "America," Publius/Madison argues, "finds that she is held in no respect by her friends; that she is the derision of her enemies; and that she is a prey to every nation which has an interest in speculating on her fluctuating councils and embarrassed affairs" (Hamilton, Madison, and Jay 317). Elsewhere, "she" is compared to a "patient," who has asked the medical advice of experts "most capable of administering relief": "She has been sensible of her malady. She has obtained a regular and unanimous advice from men of her own deliberate choice" (185). Suffering, in need of protection, in fact sensibly requesting masculine intervention, Miss America is no threat to masculine authority. It is when women demand not protection, but contractual equality that they turn "monstrous," like the women Publius/Hamilton invokes anecdotally in *The Federalist* No. 6, and much like contemporary women who were demanding the right to protect their property in prenuptial agreements. As a South Carolina lawyer argued on this topic in 1791: "Marriage settlements are . . . deviations from the fixed laws of the land and should not be carried to extremes. They will become dangerous instruments of domestic unhappiness. . . . The separation of interests between husband and wife, produced by marriage settlements, is calculated to produce many mischiefs, discords, loose morals and other ill effects. It relaxes the great bond of family union" (qtd. in Kerber 141). As Linda Kerber concludes, "the implication is that coverture, or more specifically, the power of the husband over his wife's property, is 'the great bond of family union' " (141).[32] If, as Rogin suggests, a key image of the Revolution was an image of patriots as loving husbands/suitors, protecting the virtue of a feminine and vulnerable "Liberty" (*Fathers* 24) after union, it would seem that their job is to be a *strong* husband, protecting and constraining disorderly women if necessary to assert the "bond" of union.[33]

An argument very similar to one on behalf of coverture guides the logic of Publius/Hamilton in No. 23:

> Who so likely to make suitable provisions for the public defence, as that body to which the guardianship of the public safety is confided—which, as the center of information, will best understand the extent and urgency of the dangers that threaten—as the representative of the WHOLE will feel itself most deeply interested in the preservation of every part . . . and which, by extension of its authority throughout the States, can alone establish uniformity and concert in the plans and measures, by which the common safety is to be secured? Is there not a manifest inconsistency in . . . leaving in the State governments the *effective* powers . . . [?] Is not a want of co-operation the infallible consequence of such a system? And will not weakness, disorder . . . be its natural and inevitable concomitants? (Hamilton, Madison, and Jay 114)

As Publius/Jay has earlier observed, "when a people or family so divide, it never fails to be against themselves" (18).

The logic of this repeating argument symbolically suggests that a subordinated (read: feminine) body has less to fear from centralized/representative (read: masculine) reason than vice versa, an argument figured most explicitly in Publius/Hamilton's invocation of "the influence which the bigotry of one female, the petulancies of another, and the cabals of a third, had in the co[n]temporary policy, ferments, and pacifications of a considerable part of Europe" (Hamilton, Madison, and Jay 23).[34] Because of the threat they pose, "women" who insist on equal power must inevitably be put in their place—if necessary, by force. Consider this symbolically resonant example from No. 5, where Publius/Jay is advocating against multiple state sovereignty (in, remember, an argument geared for citizens of New York): "The North is generally the region of strength, and many local circumstances render it probable, that the most Northern of the proposed Confederacies would, at a period not very distant, be unquestionably more formidable than any of the others. No sooner would this become evident, than the *Northern Hive* would excite the same Ideas and sensations in the more Southern parts of America . . . Nor does it appear to be a rash conjecture, that its young swarms might often be tempted to gather honey in the more blooming fields and milder air of their luxurious and more delicate neighbors" (20). "Opposite interests" result when the "members" are not subordinate to a strong "head," concludes Jay. Such disorder can lead only to "unfriendly passion"—and actions that suggest the forceful if illicit reestablishment of masculine authority through rape.

So we see there is a strong social logic attached to the gender symbology in *The Federalist Papers.* For however much the revolutionaries may have rejected a political patriarchy, for however much actual fathers may have been renouncing overt exercises of power in the newly configured, romantic/sentimental family, the appeal of this argument is predicated upon citizens and nation reemerging as strong husbands—as household managers, where national order is not so much built upon one strong and central patriarchal power, but upon the interpellation of husbandly, managerial power throughout every part of the national order, from top to bottom. Through this new interpellation of the old authority, the "authority of the union" can be "extend[ed] . . . to the persons of the citizens" (Hamilton, Madison, and Jay 71–72). This "common superior," the fraternally ordered figure of the president as *civic manager* (or, we could say, Miss America's proper husband), will supply the "necessary partition of power . . . by

so contriving the interior structure of the government, as that its several constituent parts may, by their mutual relations, be the means of
keeping each other in their proper places" (237; 261). All men will in
principle be civic representatives to the extent that they "stand for"
their family as its managerial authority.

Thus the patriarchal authority that was rejected as a political and
familial system is psychopolitically internalized to each "citizen" who
will be, like the male Oedipal subject, authorized in his subjection.
This is precisely the promise Publius/Hamilton makes in his argument about representation: "this dependence, and the necessity of
being bound himself and his posterity by the laws to which he gives
his assent are the true, and they are the strong chords of sympathy
between the representatives and the constituent" (Hamilton, Madison, and Jay 168). Their subjection to that order is precisely what will
allow "citizen" men to stand for that order. If the achievement of the
Constitution resides in its power to "hail" or interpellate its citizenry,
providing that "the people are always coming across themselves in
the act of consenting to their own coercion" (Warner 112),[35] we can
see more clearly from *The Federalist Papers* a fact of this interpellation that is perhaps somewhat more elusive, although not altogether
absent, from the Constitution itself: that is, the fact that the interpellation is strongly gendered. THE PEOPLE are "hailed" to nostalgically-
familiar gender order, "hailed" as male subjects. Patriarchal authority
seems, from this angle, not so much rejected as incorporated.

This incorporation produces what Cynthia Jordan has described as
a "new variant of patriarchy" (15)—and what I am calling national
manhood. This new variant depends upon two interpellative axes,
one vertical and one (that passes for) horizontal. The vertical axis
relies for its logic on the analogy of family. Husband is to wife as
reason is to passion as, finally, government is to nation.[36] The horizontal axis functions by means of analogy to fraternally ordered commerce. Man is to man as interest is to market as, at last, government
is to citizens.[37] Publius promises the Constitutional order will solve
the troubling questions facing men in the new Republic by relocating manhood, moving its emotional investment *beyond* the family.
A man's managerial role within the family will prepare him for civic
fraternity, where his best energies more properly will reside. There
he will become an equal actor; he will join other citizens in aiming
for what Publius/Hamilton describes in most evocative terms as "an
ascendent in the system of American affairs": "bound together in a

strict and indissoluble union," citizens will "concur in erecting one great American system, superior to the countroul of all trans-atlantic force or influence, and able to dictate the terms of the connection between the old and the new world!" (Hamilton, Madison, and Jay 54–55). If men lost power in Revolutionary reconfigurations of the family, it would seem that one possible response, implied by Publius and entailed in the nascent ideologies of Republican Motherhood and domesticity, was to "give" family as a province to women, in favor of a new (erotically charged) arena.[38]

In this domain, men's interests will be abstracted from particular ones of family, class, and region, and linked instead to those of other citizens "like" themselves; what they have in common will outweigh the threat of their differences. Independent, self-interested manhood will be the governing principle for capitalist citizenship, and here economy (or money) rather than familial sentiment, will be "considered as the vital principle . . . that which sustains its life and motion, and enables it to perform its most essential functions" (Hamilton, Madison, and Jay 143). This new, abstracted, and exchangeable "subjectivity" that functions like money will take relations not within and between families, but among men, as its provenance.[39] The new nation, in Publius's description, will operate by and through analogies to a masculine social body whose interactions will be governed by scientific, rationally managed market relations.[40]

III

The Broad Lap of Our Alma Mater

Publius's new mapping of the citizen-subject proffered an antidote against that "spirit of faction which is apt to mingle its poison in the deliberations of all bodies of men" (Hamilton, Madison, and Jay 72–73), and generally against the breakup of the fraternal/national order. Appeals to an already-extant fraternity work rhetorically to screen pervasive fears about masculine competition and rivalry—fears that were denied in their projection *onto* women. David Leverenz, in analyzing how "any intensified ideology of manhood is a compensatory response to fears of humiliation," emphasizes his disagreement with "the psychoanalytic view . . . that manhood compensates for various fears of women and mothering" (4). Instead, Leverenz insists that "male rivalry is the more basic source of anxiety, though the language of manhood makes ample use of maternal scapegoating" (4). As I suggested above, what fuels the rhetorical appeals to the corrective fraternal interpellation of patriarchal authority in *The Federalist Papers* is not, finally, the women who existed as the material correlative to the disorderly female symbolized in Publius's arguments. That symbolic female is an oppositional prop in *The Federalist Papers*. Her presence encourages readers not to think about the kinds of masculine rivalry—disorderly political, economic, local, intranational competition—that rest behind images of male-female relations.[41] For instance, when Publius/Hamilton details the history of international aggression in No. 6, he manages to suggest that women are the source of evil in four of his five examples, distracting readers' attention from the fact that *men* were the primary agents of aggression in four of the five instances.

This strategy, of transposing the blame for men's aggression to "woman," is also strikingly evident in two passages describing the national shame wrought under the Articles of Confederation. In No. 15, having asserted that the United States has "reached almost the last stage of national humiliation," Publius/Hamilton details at length his assertion that "[t]here is scarcely any thing that can wound the pride, or degrade the character of an independent nation, which we do not experience" (Hamilton, Madison, and Jay 68). This catalog of "national disorder, poverty and insignificance" focuses on the United States' international standing, in terms of both finance and military strength, as well as with interstate currency problems—all issues that concern men dealing with other men in the political/economic marketplace. But when Publius/Hamilton appeals for "a firm stand for our safety, our tranquility, our dignity, our reputation" (69), he suddenly figures his argument in terms strikingly reminiscent of No. 6: "Let us at last break the fatal charm which has too long seduced us from the paths of felicity and prosperity" (69–70)—invoking terms that suggest a female danger to men. In No. 62, Publius/Madison takes the more direct route, figuring national humiliation *as* a female: "But the best instruction on this subject is unhappily conveyed to America by the example of her own situation. She finds that she is held in no respect by her friends; that she is the derision of her enemies" (317). His description actually follows a political maxim that evokes homosocial or more properly, *homopolitical,* and not heterosexual, rivalry: "One nation is to another what one individual is to another" (316). Again and again we see fears about masculine rivalry experienced within the new, unstable sphere of political "equality" diverted to more re-assuring figures of man's putatively natural superiority over woman.

Such passages provide a useful illustration of how, as T. Walter Herbert formulates the point, "tormented relations of men with men that are intrinsic to male dominance get represented through re-lations of men with women" (*Dearest* 435).[42] The symbolic female therein grounds the structural conditions for male-male relations in the early nation. Called to their "common" manhood—in opposition to the "monster" woman, or as guaranteed by the "virgin" woman who will produce those "sons of liberty"—men who might otherwise be rivals can turn to each other as brothers in this sentimentalized region of pure masculine identity. In this affective collapse of purity and unity onto manhood we can begin to see how whiteness became central to the production of national manhood.[43]

If we examine Crèvecoeur's elaboration on the "regenerat[ive]" pro-cess of "this great American asylum" in what is surely our nation's favorite passage of *Letters from an American Farmer* (1782), we find precisely this homogenizing, subordinating vision in the picture of "pleasing uniformity":

> What, then, is the American, this new man? He is neither an European nor the descendant of an European; hence that strange mixture of blood, which you will find in no other country. I could point out to you a family whose grandfather was an Englishman, whose wife was Dutch, whose son married a French woman, and whose present four sons have now four wives of different nations. *He* is an American, who, leaving behind him all his ancient preju-dices and manners, receives new ones from the new mode of life he has embraced, the new government he obeys, and the new rank he holds. He becomes an American by being received in the broad lap of our great Alma Mater. Here, individuals of all nations are melted into a new race of men. . . . The Americans were once scat-tered all over Europe; here, they are incorporated into one of the finest systems of population which has ever appeared. (68, 69–70)

First, we might note that the exemplary American has a British patrilineage (and one vigorously male, judging from all those sons).[44] The family logic symbolizing Americanness here depends on the willed, legal subordination, under the British Common Law code of *feme covert*, of all "other" European immigrants, to the patrimony of the British original.[45] The passage prefigures the historically durable strategy of gynesis utilized by Revolutionary and Constitutional defenders to underwrite the early imagery of nationhood.[46] In symbolizing the land/nation as a fecund and nurturing woman, in fact, a *mother*, Crèvecoeur screens patrilineage and patriarchy behind the symbol of (immaculate) Maternity. The patriotic revolt was framed, as Fliegelman compellingly argues, as one against patriarchal authority. But registering the genuine significance of that psychopolitical and cultural shift should not lead us to ignore or to sentimentalize the gender hierarchy of national manhood's reconstruction. The men who participated in the creation of the United States reorganized male power through appeals similar to Crèvecoeur's, for a practice of a gentler, brotherly authority indebted to a symbolic originary Mother, a female symbolic figure. For instance, at a college commencement in 1780, one speaker, addressing the conditions of American political culture, declared that "I had rather be a woman—I had rather be Lucretia, that glorious woman, than all the Caesars that ever wore the imperial purple" (qtd. in Kerber 106). As Kerber summarizes, "it is true that the speaker considered Lucretia glorious—but only as an alternative to a tyrant" (106). Crèvecoeur, much like the commencement speaker, offers a formula for the new American that subtly protects British-descended male power while appearing to relinquish or even denounce its patriarchal manifestations. The site of incorporation—the powerful lap/womb of the white, female goddess America/Columbia/Liberty—simultaneously provides an alibi for the ongoing subjugation of actual women, and a repository for the "virtue" that secures the fraternity central to the early construction of U.S. civic identity.

Crèvecoeur's depiction of America as virtuous female participated in a genre of images that circulated widely in the early nation, simultaneous to debates over woman's place in the political order. During the Revolution, there is an imagistic progression from America as a bare-breasted (usually Indian) woman to more demurely garbed characters, embodying not just the continent, but the political ideals of liberty, peace, and wisdom. Linda Kerber has argued that these later representations of the nation as a symbolic female—Liberty or Columbia—presaged the Republican Mother, empowering women by making them the ideal of national virtue. Recently, though, Smith-Rosenberg has questioned this celebratory reading. In her reading of this symbology, she comments that "given men's problematic representation of women and the feminine, even Columbia evoked too many discursive conflicts and ideological anxieties" ("Dis-Covering" 870). In the narrative that these images provide about "naked nature," from women bare-breasted and innocent to women bare-breasted, virtuous, and pure; from women lying back in a forest bower to welcome Europeans, and then leading the way into a triumphant future, cultural attention is directed toward women's sexuality and its proper management. Colonial expansion derived from her welcoming accessibility; national manhood's strength will derive from her now limited, selective accessibility, her reproductive purity, her sexual virtue.[47] As Smith-Rosenberg concludes, in these images, the symbolic white woman works to confirm "the white man's superiority to the negative others who defined and contested his subjectivity" ("Dis-Covering" 873). In these colonial-*cum*-national appropriations of the feminine, we can trace the (arguably misogynistic) inception of an increasingly racialized obsession with "white" feminine virtue,[48] and even the interests at the symbolic root of gynecological medicine: the need to observe, repair, and guarantee the purity of "white" women's reproductive systems (I detail this argument at greater length in chapter 4). More immediately, we see throughout Crèvecoeur's *Letters* (as well as in, for instance, John and Abigail Adams's famous exchange over women's political entitlements), that the solicitous, even chivalric subordination of women is what, at least in part, mobilizes the identity of "this new [American] man."[49]

Crèvecoeur's delineation of the American man also hints at the regressive desires that will eventually figure more clearly in constructions of American manhood. Having rejected the sovereign law of the Father/King, the American man turns as a child toward the bountiful Mother. The intense move toward domestication in the post-Revolutionary period, following close behind the exaltation of the Republican Mother[50] may arguably correlate with this masculine desire to renounce a contaminated manhood in a return to the symbolic space of the womb, to an imagined, innocent past that would assuage the very real anxieties about political fracture, economic change, and social reconfiguration that followed the break with England. And alongside its certification of a blood fraternity (a "new race"), this image of America-the-Mother, evoking the innocence and purity of boyhood, prefigures a literal practice soon to be institutionalized by the U.S. middle classes, which Anthony Rotundo details as "boy culture."[51] In this way, the spectacular "desire" that is localized onto the figurative body of America-the-Mother mediates the brotherhood of the new American man, allowing us to begin considering with historical/political specificity the triangulated homosocial construction of American manhood *qua* civic identity.

Publius/Madison argues that the Constitutional order will certify "the vigilant and manly spirit which actuates the people of America, a spirit which nourishes freedom, and in return is nourished by it" (Hamilton, Madison, and Jay 291). In such laudatory images of the Republic-as-Mother we can trace the affiliated logical entailments of the rhetorical sleight-of-gender I have detailed above: reading closely here we must note that it is "manly spirit" that feeds "freedom," before the symbolically female "freedom" can in return nourish men. Through such imagery the authority of "independent manhood" appropriates the fertility of women's biologically reproductive role, and the nurturance of her socially mandated one.[52] If women hold "the secrets of life" (Margaret Mead, qtd. in Kittay 95), it is white men who—from the purity of their fraternity and from within managed masculine competition of the new market-nation—will hold the secret to political order. Their political order is homosocial; it is furthermore one that is imaginatively triangulated *through* national manhood's "common" and "rational" authority over (its) others.

IV

Purity Control

Scientific discourse plays a crucial role in U.S. identity formation; it offered intellectual strategies notably amenable to the psychosocial anxieties about political disunity, social disorder, and national fragmentation that Publius marshals for constructing strong national unity. With its scientific logic of identity and exclusion, the Aristotelian paradigm was well-suited for national manhood's territorializing ambitions. And the precise calculations, expansive boundaries, and sensation of mastery provided in the Newtonian universe and Baconian nature provided a positional authority for a unifying experience of national independence. Indeed, philosophers Gayle Ormiston and Raphael Sassower read the Declaration of Independence as an exemplary text of the scientific Enlightenment. They observe that "as is the case with many seventeenth-century narratives . . . the texts of Bacon, Hobbes, and Galileo are examples—nature is a book, a text to be deciphered and comprehended. Not only does the text legitimate the laws it claims are 'natural,' it legitimates the 'truths' it cites as 'self-evident.'" (56). The Declaration's scientific objectivism is refined by discourses of math and geometry in Publius's arguments for the Constitution, and indeed, in that document itself. Publius/Hamilton makes frequent appeals to ever more objective scientific rationality, as for instance in No. 38, where he urges readers to consider the "science of morals and politics" with the same dispassion that allows men to accept geometrical theorems such as "the INFINITE DIVISIBILITY of matter" (Hamilton, Madison, and Jay 148)—a principle the Constitution literally applies in its three-fifths designation for enslaved humans.

Enlightenment scientific discourse facilitated the constitution of a reassuringly bounded, yet symbolically expansive white manhood (a reassurance increasingly necessary in the turbulent years following the ratification of the Constitution).[53] Historians such as Allen, Saxton, and Roediger have recently begun analyzing how such an abstracted category, "white manhood," could take hold and become a lived and common sensation of selfhood that superseded the locality, class, and ethnicity of identity in the early nation. Rather than treating "race" as a corollary to culture—as ethnicity—they analyze race, and specifically, whiteness, as a system of social control through the development and maintenance of exclusionary classifications, institutions, and daily practices. It was in the name of systematization that Enlightenment science stepped forward for the project of racial categorization, a project that would quickly shift science's horizontal ordering of human "difference" to a vertical one. Racial science's hierarchizing description of "natural" order was complemented by a national organization of that "order" in law.

In this final section I consider, reading Jefferson's *Notes on the State of Virginia* and Rush's essay "Negro Leprosy," specifically how scientific discourse offered helpful equipment to U.S. national formation coextensive with its hierarchizing mobilization of the concept of "race." However different their political stances and their scientific interests, both Jefferson and Rush contribute to the consolidation of national manhood through the production of the racial Other. Jefferson and Rush produce, to borrow David Theo Goldberg's terms, a raced and gendered "social knowledge," establishing "a library or archive of information, a set of guiding ideas and principles about Otherness" (*Racist Culture* 150). They tabulate racial characteristics in the production of racial taxonomy as an epistemological exercise of power/identity. Both betray an anxiety over the potential stability of their racial logic, and both locate that anxiety onto the bodies of women.[54]

Such anxious moments emphasize their participation in a national project, that of installing "race" into the same paradigm of absolute oppositional and safely hierarchized difference that gender had come to occupy by the late eighteenth century.[55] Their desires for civic purity are routed into racial categorizations; their fears about racial (civic) instability are transferred into uneasy speculations about women's racial changeability. Jefferson and Rush insist that the "best" white women are absolutely distinct from white men — absolute gender binarity being their gauge of racial advance. But they worry that those same women are symbolically and actually liable to deteriorate into a barbarous, contaminatory strangeness, which reveals them to be, in Felicity Nussbaum's striking phrase, "joined by the genitals" to other races and other species (129).

Subjects of Natural History

In a recent article on Edmund Morgan's enduringly captioned "American Paradox," Alexander O. Boulton observes that Jefferson's *Notes on the State of Virginia* "to a large degree, was an explication of the Declaration of Independence; it grounded, as he thought, some of the grand philosophical principles of the Declaration in the empirical proofs of science" ("Slavery" 472). If science — "an investigation of Natural Laws" — would lead Jefferson to his assertion in 1776 that "all men are created equal," it would be the apparatus of science to which he would turn to stabilize his claims for the distinctiveness of a white civic body politic in the United States.[56]

The passage on "Laws" in Jefferson's *Notes on the State of Virginia* offers an intellectually and affectively tortured argument for the physical and cultural traits that separate black and white. He begins by asserting absolute and visible difference via a catalogue in which even the pluses he accords to "blackness" turn into minuses. "Whites" are more beautiful and symmetrical, "blacks" are less; "we" have more color, "they" are monotonously monochrome; "we" have more emotion, "they" have less; "whites" have flowing hair and more of it; "blacks" feel less pain. "Blacks" secrete more from their skin, but it gives them a less agreeable smell and makes them less tolerant of cold; "blacks" have as much bravery, but only because they have less forethought; "blacks" court more ardently, but only because they are less tender. In this racial calculus, Jefferson employs his beloved mathematics as a technique of dis-embodiment, in the service of splitting social bodies by anatomizing physical ones. This technique removes bodies from their localized physicality to categorical spaces produced by philosophical abstraction.[57]

Yet Jefferson's confidence wanes by the end of this section; he concedes "great diffidence" in offering *any* judgments about ascertaining racial difference through observation: "How much more [difficult to do so] then where it is a faculty, not a substance, we are examining; where it eludes the research of all the senses; where the conditions of its existence are various and variously combined; where the effects of those which are present or absent bid defiance to calculation." He concludes that "to our reproach it must be said that though for a century and a half we have had under our eyes the races of black and of red men, they have never yet been viewed by us as subjects of natural history." Jefferson's response to this failure is to appeal for further—and connotatively violent—scientific observation, "where the subject may be submitted to the Anatomical knife, to Optical glasses, to analysis by fire, or by solvents" (*Notes* 143). Here we can see the usefulness of "science" to the psychosocial construction of "race." It provides authority to categorize, restrain, and govern human reality based on abstractions of bodily particularity, and it offers a progressivist hope that today's failure may be overcome in the future, where the future is to be realized, as T. Walter Herbert observes, in "the use of force by white males upon dark bodies" (personal correspondence, 25 May 1994).

Jefferson's discussion of "blacks" in query 14 of the *Notes* elucidates the very process of splitting and excorporation, with its obsessive concern to locate and delineate bodily difference, that I have argued was central to the symbolic construction of national manhood. Here Jefferson seeks to enable a legal construction of a white body clearly separated from the "black" body, and simultaneously strives to construct the scientific individual/observer as distinctively separate from the subject of scientific scrutiny. But strategies of splitting and excorporation are psychologically corollary to desires that are about engulfment and *in*corporation, and the latter paradigm is more useful to understanding Jefferson's treatment of "Indians"—a treatment that, however different from his handling of "blacks," works in parallel ways to consolidate whiteness.

In the query on "Productions," Jefferson calculates Indianness differently. Here he focuses on the conditional racial equivalency of Native Americans: "Were we equal in barbarism, our females would be equal drudges. The man with them is less strong than with us, but their woman stronger than ours; and both for the same obvious reason; because our man and their woman is habituated to labour, and formed by it. . . . They raise fewer children than we do. The causes of this are to be found, not in a difference of nature, but of circumstance" (*Notes* 60). The paradigm of scientific debate—Jefferson's argument with Buffon—has perhaps disabled us from considering how this passage poses a scientific argument on behalf of (male) American identity not simply to legitimate its stability and progression for France and other "World" powers without, but also to justify its imaginative expansion in the form of territorial aggression within. In this case, equivalency functions to project racial *incorporation*, and gestures toward a construction of an assimilative, expansive "white" body (they are like, or could be like, us; we belong anywhere they are). Arguably, then, Jefferson's discussion of Native Americans in "Productions" has as much pragmatically to do with producing geopolitical identity (confirmation seemingly offered in Jefferson's subsequent and aggressive involvement with westward expansion, as I will discuss in chapter 2) as with defending intellectual legitimacy.

Clearly these two aims (incorporation/refutation) are not contradictory, but mutually confirmative in the exercise of defensive grandiosity that Jefferson terms a "proud theory": (white) American genius. Frank Shuffleton has recently argued that in the section on "Productions," Jefferson's "desire to refute Buffon's theory of New world degeneracy leads him to emphasize cultural production, a category in which he can include Logan as well as Franklin and David Rittenhouse" (272–73).[58] It is important to recognize, however, that Jefferson finally does not lump Logan *together* with Washington, Franklin, and Rittenhouse; rather his treatment of Native Americans is separated from his concluding remarks on the transplanted "white race" by a scientific/anthropologized assertion that he does "not mean to deny, that there are varieties in the race of man"—a pointed qualification of his earlier calculations of equality (*Notes* 62–63, 64–65). By asserting this hierarchized anthropology between Indian "productions" and "white" ones, Jefferson signals his regard for Native Americans as a resource for producing a white U.S. identity. Thus it seems less coincidental that this discussion appears not in the query on "Aborigines," but on "Productions." Despite the objective posture of science, we can see that Jefferson's argument about "Indians" does not function simply as a dispassionate response to Marbois's "cultural question-naire," or even as a defensive one. Rather it is more complexly an aggressive argument, one guided by territorializing ambitions.[59]

But in both passages, on "Productions" and "Laws," the calcula-tion of difference evokes doubt about the stability of racial definition. Strikingly, each chapter takes up "blackness" in the specific context of sexual reproduction. In his section on "Laws," Jefferson makes the (seemingly obligatory, for this period) observation about "the prefer-ence of the oran-ootan for the black women over those of his own species" (*Notes* 138), evidencing, as many commentators have ob-served, fears about both miscegenation and "racial" recrimination for the actualized desires of white men for female slaves. In the sec-tion on "Productions," he adds to his "catalogue of our indigenous animals . . . a short account of an anomaly of nature, taking place sometimes in the race of negroes brought from Africa." Herein he de-scribes four Albino "blacks" he has seen personally, and three more of which he has heard reliable accounts. Speculating that albinism is perhaps caused "by a disease in the skin, or in its colouring matter," he concludes that "it seems more incident to the female than male sex" (70–71).

Jefferson explicitly characterizes variability in skin color as "dis-ease," a disease projectively dissociated from both manhood and whiteness. It might seem that a man as preoccupied with quantifi-cation and calculation as Jefferson would not consider a sample of seven statistically valid. Yet even setting that quibble aside, we must, I think, carefully examine the symbolic and pedagogic intersections of "woman" with "race" in these passages on albinism and orang-utans.[60] Regardless of Jefferson's explicit intentions, the suggestion of female culpability for racial instability in this passage links it to what was by then an established eighteenth-century tradition of casting misogynistic anxieties about the reproductive powers of women in scientific discourse. Scientist-philosophers like Nicolas Malebranche, in his four-volume 1712 study, *De la recherche de la vérité*—a study that went through five editions between 1721 and 1772—argued that it was the mother, alone, who was to be held responsible for impos-ing, *in utero*, "pathological or teratological horrors" on the developing fetus (Stafford 313). More precisely, female emotional vulnerability— *her* penetrable and unstable psyche—were the direct cause of infant marking. Her secret passions literalized themselves on the skin of the offspring; as Barbara Stafford summarizes, "like a blank sheet of paper, the skin became marbled by pathos, mottled by an alien pattern of interiority" (313).

These "anomolies of nature," these "cadaverous[ly] white" black women serve further to refute Buffon's charge that white men are degenerating in America. If anything "degenerates" in the new world, Jefferson seems to suggest in response to Buffon, it is not white men but "black" women. Curiously, though, Jefferson tucks this account away in "Productions," sandwiching it between a list of the birds of Virginia, and an account of a nonindigenous honeybee, which the local Indians call "the white man's fly," since the bees "have generally extended themselves into the country, a little in advance of the white settlers." Suggestions of racial instability segue into a reminder of territorial expansion on "our continent" (*Notes* 71–72). Nature's potential ability to destabilize racial purity is left behind for a more comforting account of Nature leading whites across "their" continent, indeed, whitening everything in their wake.

Natural Whiteness

Rush had early staked a position quite different from the one Jefferson would take on Africans in *Notes on the State of Virginia*. In his earlier essay, "On Slave-Keeping" (1773), Rush extensively refutes the positions Jefferson would take on African character, sensibility, and "beauty" in "Laws" while anticipating the moral energy of Jefferson's section on "Manners." Both, of course, were slave owners, so we wouldn't want to overestimate the immediate relevance of their argumentative differences. Yet it would seem at first glance that Rush is even less invested in what we now think of as "racism" than Jefferson. Certainly his arguments about "negro leprosy," based on his observation of Henry Moss and careful study, demonstrate his willingness to see the possibility of likeness where Jefferson saw only irremediable—whatever its causes—difference. Precisely because of their intellectual and political differences, then, I want to draw attention to significant correlations in each man's scientific contributions to national manhood's racial archive.

Jefferson symbolizes destabilized difference as disease, where "cadaverous" whiteness corrupts "natural" blackness (*Notes* 70). For Rush, difference itself is apparently the disease. He characterizes the putative "blackness" of African skin as "morbid," and their physiology as "short, ugly and ill proportioned" ("Observations" 291–92), problems only remedied by salubrious nature effecting a recuperation of "healthy" or "natural" whiteness, and the attempts of a combined "science and humanity" to follow nature's lead in discovering an "artificial" method for "dislodg[ing] the color in negroes" (295). Rush envisions his search for a medical cure as a corrective to the tyranny of "whites" both ignorant and learned, the former supposing that "blackness" is the "mark" of "divine judgement," the latter arguing that it is correlative to their ability to work in "hot and unwholesome climates" (297).

Beneath Rush's optimism, however, lurk fears of civic/racial dissolution and collapse. As Sander Gilman has incisively argued, the figure of disease functions as a category of difference, and as such works to "determine the construction of the idea of the patient in a direct and powerful manner, drawing the boundaries between the 'healthy' observer, physician or layperson, and the 'patient.' The construction of the image of the patient is thus always a playing out of this desire for a demarcation between ourselves and the chaos represented in culture by disease" (*Disease* 4). That science now does not characterize "black" skin as a disease makes my point all the more emphatically: no matter how optimistic, humane, and incorporative Rush might seem, we must consider how, in figuring "blackness" as a disease potentially curable, he participates in the deployment of "race" as a "white" strategy for managing social anxieties about instability, chaos, and fragmentation. To put this somewhat differently: if, as Gilman argues, disease is a projective figure for personal disintegration, by ascribing it to black skin, Rush engages the black Other as a receptacle for social instability in the early Republic, and makes whiteness correlatively available as a recuperative (and supraclass) social order.

Linking "race" to an apparatus for social order and civic reproduction in Rush's thinking does not seem to be entirely unwarranted. In a passage from his earlier essay, "On Slave-Keeping," Rush raises a similar set of concerns, figured somewhat differently. There, in taking up the question of apparent biblical sanction for slavery, Rush observes that

we are told the Jews kept the heathens in perpetual bondage. The design of providence in permitting this evil, was probably to prevent the Jews from marrying among strangers, to which their intercourse with them upon any other footing than that of slaves, would naturally have inclined them. Had this taken place—their Natural Religion would have been corrupted—they

would have contracted all their vices, and the intention of providence in keeping them a distinct people, in order to accomplish
the promise made to Abraham, that "in his Seed all the Nations
of the earth should be blessed," would have been defeated; so that
the descent of the Messiah from Abraham, could not have been
traced, and the divine commission of the Son of God, would have
wanted one of its most powerful arguments to support it. (8)

Here Rush supports the *logic*, if not the practice, of slavery, in the
name of social stability and patriarchal order. Notably, he characterizes exogamous relations in terms of infection: "they would have
contracted all their vices." Rush evokes a most similar argument in
his embedded caveat about Negro "leprosy": "The facts and principles
which have been delivered should teach white people the necessity
of keeping up that prejudice against such connections with them [i.e.,
negroes], as would tend to infect posterity with any portion of the disorder" ("Observations" 295). Rush in effect appeals for a medico-racial
quarantine, placing his conclusions on the topic far closer to Jefferson's than their political differences might superficially indicate.

Strikingly, Rush locates his anxieties about infected populations
and racial "disease" in precisely the same way as Jefferson. Rush
hauls in the obligatory orangutan as he quotes Hawkins's observations about African albinos: "The difference of color cannot arise
from the intercourse of whites and blacks, for the whites are very
rarely among them, and the result of this union is well known to
be the yellow color, or mulatto. Many of the natives assert that they
are produced by women being debauched in the woods by the large
baboons, or ourang-outangs. . . . No satisfactory discovery has been
made to account for such singular, but not unfrequent phaenomena
in the species" (Hawkins, qtd. in Rush, "Observations" 291). And just
before his warning about maintaining the purity of the white population, Rush presents two anecdotes that underscore how women, via
sexual contamination, become culpable for racial impurity: "A white
woman in North Carolina not only acquired a dark color, but several
of the features of a negro, by marrying and living with a black husband. A similar instance of a change in the color and features of a
woman in Buck's county in Pennsylvania has been observed and from
a similar cause. In both these cases, the women bore children by their
black husbands" (294). Anxieties about "disease" are simultaneously
projected here onto two screens: sexually active females and blacks.
Rush here assigns responsibility for anxieties about loss of control

in the social body of the early Republic to two key groups against which unitary civic identity and its corresponding entitlements are increasingly being consolidated. The value of the scientific discourse on whiteness is that it provides a socially authoritative position for white men to manage such anxieties, one that "objectively" pointed toward the necessity of their managing raced bodies and white female bodies, to certify on the one hand white male coherence and on the other their virtue (through women's reproductive "purity").[61]

Gilman notes that a "fantasy of wholeness . . . lies at the root of all of the bipolar images of difference (health vs. disease; good vs. bad; white vs. black)" (*Disease* 5).[62] Whiteness increasingly became the symbolic correlative for the fantasized wholeness of nation and of manhood. Whiteness contained the centrifugal forces of an incipient, messier, more heterogeneously imagined democracy through the very process of ideologically extending whiteness to groups of men who otherwise might not have found that category a meaningful or primary social marker for identity. Thus the apparently democratizing grant of national (white) manhood worked to manage local democracy by virtualizing it, ensuring the establishment of a functionally centralized (and arguably counterdemocratic) political structure through the seeming decentralizing allocation of sovereignty to "the people." Insofar as "wholeness," "unity," and "purity" became not just a national ideal but the protectorate of national manhood, responsibility for and anxiety about civic fragmentation or social diversity were downloaded into citizens, nationally deputized civic managers.

Managing an always potentially fractured national identity through the "common" and more abstracted bodily bond of whiteness, men learned to train their own class, regional, and political rivalries toward the "managed" competition of the market economy. Men's unified embrace of this model for "equality"—an ideology of market exchangeability and competition—would, as Publius/Hamilton urges in *The Federalist* No. 11, insure the health of the nation. This model may have helped citizens explain to themselves the way that, in Wood's phrase, "Americans were thus both equal and unequal at the same time" (*Creation* 607). But as I will argue in the next chapter, it could also function powerfully to intensify men's personal experience of fragmentation, which, framed by the ideology of national manhood, increasingly became a "private" failure in quite the same way that "liberty" increasingly became a private good (see Wood, *Creation* 609).

"That's Not My Wife, That's an Indian Squaw": Inindianation and National Manhood

American Abraham

When confronted with the dismembered body of his wife, the nation's first parricide, John Yates, declared that she was not his wife: he insisted "that the woman was an Indian squaw."[1] Yates's mass murder of wife and family was first in an anomalous string of family mass-murders in the new United States. There were eleven such episodes between 1781 and 1836, with the highest rate—of six—occurring between 1800–1820; there were no more such events recorded in the nation until after 1900.[2] Yates's remark in this context, though exceptional to the pattern of early national parricides in its reassignment of the victim's identity from "family" to "alien," seems unexceptional read in light of a particular thematic running through early national narratives, a thematic I explore here in readings of the Lewis and Clark Expedition, Biddle's 1814 *History* of that expedition,[3] and John Neal's 1822 novel *Logan, a Family History*. Increasingly in the early nation, white male power was negotiated through imaginary and actual relations to "Indians." Yates's actions and his comment on his murdered wife provide a suggestive moment that might encourage us to recalibrate our understanding of identity politics in the early nation, to see the way anxieties about corporate and individual manhood get foisted off onto racially changeable women, to see Indianness not simply as a mythological oppositional/negative contrast to "white" identity, but as something more complex and flexible than that, less indicative of an achieved identity for white men than of their ongoing anxieties about it.

Yates's denial of the murders, and his identification of the maimed body of his wife as an "Indian squaw" dramatically captions one emerging strategy for securing white/national male identity. Rogin argues that Indians were a symbolic demon to emergent liberal society in the new nation: "Liberalism insisted upon work, instinctual repression, and acquisitive behavior; men had to conquer and separate themselves from nature. Indians were seen as playful, violent, improvident, wild and in harmony with nature. Private property underlay liberal society; Indians held land in common. Liberal relations were based, contractually, on keeping promises and on personal responsibility. Indians, in the liberal view, were anarchic and irresponsible. Americans believed that peaceful competitiveness kept them in touch with one another and provided social cement. They thought the Indians, lacking social order, were devoted to war" (*Fathers* 8). Rogin adverts to a psychoanalytic model of "regression"—a forbidden nostalgia for childhood—to explain the energy at the heart of the United States' westward expansion and its murderous consequences for Native Americans. Without disallowing Rogin's theory, I would argue that we might a bit more basically scrutinize that ideological fiction of the "peaceful competitiveness" of early U.S. capitalism (the providentially soothing logic of the "invisible hand") versus its experientially anxious, potentially vicious cultural and material results. Differently from earlier practices of manhood, which located men in a thick network of obligation and duty within family and community, newer formations of manhood, tied complexly to national ideals and emerging capitalist practices, affectively and ideologically isolated men in a newer form of individualist competitiveness.[4] It is important to my understanding of this episode and the complex interworkings of racial and gender management I understand it to emphasize, to pay attention to the economic anxiety that propelled Yates and other early parricides into desperate action (Yates bludgeoned to death not only his wife and four children, but also a dog, two horses, and two cows; see Fitzgerald 2).[5] This is a suggestive episode—however flimsy as evidence standing alone—that lets us begin considering how emerging models of competitive manhood, quite differently from the communal models they replaced, required individual men to internalize in terms of personal responsibility the political and economic vicissitudes of the early nation. These new "responsibilities" propelled a substantially intensified need for management and control and a particular pattern of emotional anxiety among white men.

Thus the Yates episode offers a starting point for my considerations in this chapter, as a dramatic instance of how racial projection could provide a means to convert the fragmenting evidences of one man's life into a coherent narrative of manly control *and* a specific disavowal of the violence entailed in its enactment. National manhood reached for stability through multiple, multiplying calculations of otherness; Yates's assessment of the wife he murdered defines her as three times his Other: woman, Indian, primitive. "Not mine," she is emphatically "not me," the (violent) performance of boundary maintenance rhetorically restoring Yates's unitary sense of self. In this respect, the Yates episode provides a suggestive preface to a complex thematic in the production of national manhood that I want to analyze in this chapter. The Lewis and Clark Expedition, Biddle's *History*, and Neal's *Logan* foreground the various ways anxieties newly located onto individual men were relocated—domesticated, managed—in exercises that defined, excavated, and occupied white men's Others in the early nation. Like Jefferson's appropriation of Chief Logan, these cultural instances and textual productions place in evidence a multivalent national narrative of manly inindianation.[6] This is a narrative that encapsulates men's tense, equivocal, simultaneous desires for equality and rank order, the longing to be part of a civic brotherhood and to gain exclusive recognition from the Father. Inindianation is the family romance of national manhood, a narrative that traces the anxious burdens of its structural oedipalization.

I

Mapping National Unity

In January 1803, President Jefferson made a preliminary move toward a coveted project: exploring a northwest water passage. In a confidential recommendation to Congress, he detailed his concern for securing access to the Mississippi and for gaining trading and territorial rights across the Northwest.[7] He warned that "Duty has required me to submit these views to the judgment of the legislature; but as their disclosure might embarrass and defeat their effect; they are committed to the special confidence of the two houses" (Jefferson, "Confidential Message" xxvi). One of his stated aims was to expand public commerce among Indian tribes. But, he underscored, this aim must necessarily be disguised from the various governments laying claim to the lands and trading rights with their inhabitants: the French, Spanish, and British.[8] Eager to circumvent the British stranglehold on fur trade in the Northwest, Congress approved Jefferson's proposal and appropriated necessary funds.

Jefferson noted the Congressional sign-off in a letter dated June 20, 1803, to Lewis, which began with the following nebulous charge: "Your situation as Secretary of the President of the United States has made you acquainted with the objects of my confidential message of January 18th, 1803, to the legislature; you have seen the act that they passed, which, though expressed in general terms, was meant to sanction those objects, and you are appointed to carry them into execution" ("Memoir" xxiv). The vagueness of Jefferson's specific injunctions about secrecy might seem curiously redundant (Lewis is obviously already familiar with "the act they passed"), and points ultimately toward the most important reason for that secrecy: the U.S. public. Prior to the acquisition of the Louisiana territory, the public (along with the soldiers Lewis enlisted for the first parts of the journey) was notified that the expedition was to explore the *Mississippi*, not the Missouri—this apparently to sidestep questions about the constitutionality of territorial annexation and expansion that might re-excite Federalist/anti-Jeffersonian opposition.[9] Clearly Jefferson felt that organized opposition to the expedition was a real threat: when Jefferson queried several medical and scientific experts about how best to prepare Lewis for undertaking the project, he enjoined them to strict secrecy, explaining to Robert Patterson: "I think it advisable that nothing should be said of this til [Lewis] shall have got beyond the reach of any obstacles which might be prepared for him by those who would not like the enterprise" (qtd. in Dillon 31).

Thus the expedition was, from its inception, structured by Jefferson's concerns about managing intranational political difference. President Jefferson camouflaged dissensus in the body politic through a twinned rhetorical strategy. First, he screened political opposition within the United States by highlighting international competition. Second—and for me even more interesting—he split off internal political dissent from the nation proper (or body politic), encouraging Congress to reconceptualize it as *individual* interest. Such competition from "interested individuals," Jefferson suggests, should obviously be managed by a united government: "The appropriation of two thousand five hundred dollars, 'for the purpose of extending the external commerce of the United States,' while understood and considered by the executive as giving the legislative sanction, would cover the undertaking [i.e., the exploratory expedition] from notice, and prevent the obstructions which interested individuals might otherwise previously prepare in its way" (Jefferson, "Confidential Message" xxvii).[10] Jefferson's argument defuses political difference through displacement. He appeals, in other words, to the national Selfhood expressed through presidential intent. His prerogative was claimed precisely to counteract the nationally disruptive quality of democratic intentions, forestalling recognition of those intentions as anything but individual (and unpatriotic) self-interest.[11] Here, then, Jefferson simply fulfills the vigorous and manly logic of the presidency promised by Hamilton and Jay in their arguments on behalf of the Constitution—that is, the executive will both guarantee and represent the "uniform principles of policy," which will "harmonize, assimilate, and protect the several parts and members, and extend the benefits of its foresight and precautions to each" (Hamilton, Madison, and Jay 16; cf. also *The Federalist* No. 70).

News of the United States' fait accompli acquisition of the Louisiana Territory on July 1, 1803, obviated Jefferson's need for further secrecy. But it did not eliminate, as I detail in my reading of the expedition, the specter of civic divisions. News of the Purchase allowed the exploratory mission—already underway—to become a public assertion of domestic possession, of the acquisition of scientific knowledge (biological, geographical, economical, ethnographical) about "our continent." The expedition now could be offered to the public as an enactment of expanding civic possibility: a fraternal mission to survey the new territory, its trade routes, natural resources, arable lands— and human occupants.

On Whom They Are to Operate: Science and Difference

Jefferson had previously marshaled the Mingo leader Logan's rhetorically elegant complaint against violent colonial expansion to prop up U.S. identity against scientific arguments coming out of France, that whites in the Americas were "degenerating." In this earlier appropriation of Indian "resources," Jefferson displayed a diplomatic and sympathetic regret over outrages against humanity, recording with admiration Logan's eloquent fury at the British troops who murdered his entire family. But for the expedition, President Jefferson's notice of Indian culture had shifted to a more clearly instrumental purpose.[12]

He charged the expedition with collecting information to add to the national racial archive.[13] The leaders of the expedition were to survey, anatomize, and catalogue Indian identity, as we see in one lengthy section of the detailed instructions Jefferson provides to Meriwether Lewis for the expedition:

> The commerce which may be carried on with the people inhabiting the line you will pursue renders a knowledge of those people important. You will therefore endeavor to make yourself acquainted, as far as a diligent pursuit of your journey shall admit, with the names of the nations and their numbers; The extent and limits of their possessions; Their relations with other tribes or nations; Their language, traditions, and monuments; Their ordinary occupations in agriculture, fishing, hunting, war, arts, and the implements for these; Their food, clothing, and domestic accommodations; The diseases prevalent among them, and the remedies they use; Moral and physical circumstances which distinguish them from the tribes we know; Peculiarities in their laws, customs and dispositions; And articles of commerce they may need or furnish, and to what extent. And, considering the interest which every nation has in extending and strengthening the authority of reason and justice among the people around them, it will be useful to acquire what knowledge you can of the state of morality, religion and information among them; *as it may better enable those who may endeavor to civilize and instruct them*, to adapt their measures to the existing notions and practices of those *on whom they are to operate*. ("Memoir" xxvii-xxviii; emphasis added)

Here, the emphasis is less on finding proof for a common humanity, as Jefferson's memorializing of Logan's speech and his according of "morality and religion" among the Indians here might initially suggest. Rather, the expedition's Indian ultimately offers a field for the science of human difference, a site for civilizing operations (a term chillingly evocative of his lament in *Notes on the State of Virginia* that science had not yet performed such invasive procedures as would yield definitive evidence for racial/bodily difference). For Jefferson "the Indian" offered flexible, imaginative access to the physical as well as psychological territorializing of U.S. identity. Defining "Indians" provided an opportunity for scientifically validating whiteness *qua* civilization, pedagogically mapping it for the body politic while extending it politically across the continent. Thus the usefulness of "Indians" may well have increased symbolically after the Louisiana Purchase, when remaining dissent within the civic body (those bitter Federalists) could be effaced in a national survey of Indian Others occupying "our continent" (this was certainly the focus that Nicholas Biddle chose in his magisterial rendering of the journey's *History* in 1814).

The "Indian" flexibly offered an admirable identity to share (as was true of the eloquent Logan), and an Other identity whose peculiarities needed "civilizing" (as would be true of the Indians on "our continent"); either way (and I would add that the boundaries of those strategies often remain highly fluid), the deep history of those moves was often competition—political, economic, professional—between "white men." The abstracting identity of white/national manhood found one means for stabilizing its internal divisions and individual anxieties *via* imagined projections into, onto, against Indian territories, Indian bodies, Indian identities. In this respect, Yates and Jefferson, read together, point up an important and complex thematic in the early formation and practices of national manhood. This thematic, which I trace in my readings of the Lewis and Clark Expedition, in Biddle's *History*, and in Neal's *Logan*, offers an important preface to the era of Indian Removal.[14]

II

Heroic Medicine

We find a pronounced—even startling—example of the defensive projecting of anxieties about manly/national dissipation onto the body of the Indian, at one of the tensest moments of the Lewis and Clark Expedition. It is an episode worth close analysis. During the second summer of their trip, on their way up the Missouri in June 1805, the party reached a fork in the river that neither their maps nor their informants had prepared them for. The party came to a standstill as the two leaders attempted to determine the correct route. It was an absolutely crucial decision. If they took the wrong branch and had to backtrack, it could delay the party long enough to prevent their crossing the Continental Divide before winter, necessitating their return to a safer encampment in the east. This would set the expedition behind an entire year. Frustrated at their informants and anxious to make the right decision with the least delay possible,[15] Lewis set off to explore the north branch, and Clark the south, each promising to return with their party to the fork within three days. Clark executed his mission and returned on June 6. Lewis did not return with his party until June 8, heightening the anxiety among the remainder of the Corps, who worried that he and his party had met with some misfortune. Finally, Lewis returned unharmed and also convinced that the southern branch was the correct route. His careful arguments convinced Clark.

But none of the captains' subordinates agreed with that decision. They were more persuaded by Cruzatte, an experienced waterman accompanying the party. Based on his superior knowledge of the Missouri, the men pressed their leaders to try the northern branch.[16] Finally, they agreed that they would "cheerfully" go where directed by the two captains even though they disagreed with the decision. To appease their doubt and verify that the south branch was indeed the Missouri River, Lewis went ahead by land as the party proceeded up the south branch, to locate the waterfalls promised by all his informants. In a gesture of self-confidence before departing, Lewis named the northern fork Maria's River, after his cousin Maria Wood, a woman whom he may have courted.[17] Lewis finally sighted the falls and sent a man back on June 14 to confirm it for the main party.

This crisis in direction and corps unity lasted nearly two weeks. The threat of disintegrating purpose and unanimity was seemingly symptomatized in the physical illnesses of Lewis and Sacagawea. Sacagawea, one of two wives of the French interpreter, Charbonneau, had joined the party as they wintered at Mandan. Lewis and Clark hired her husband for the remainder of the trip and unofficially commissioned her (leaving the other wife at Mandan), despite the fact that Sacagawea had just delivered a baby in February. They added this woman and her child to the expedition because Sacagawea offered the commanders a special advantage for this very perilous passage in their trip. As a Shoshonee who had been taken captive in her early teens by Hidatsas, she brought both geographical familiarity and the powerful bargaining tool of an emotional, surprise return to her kin. This was at least as valuable to the Corps as any directions she would offer, since they would need to court the favor of the Shoshonees in order to restock food and supplies, to purchase the horses, and to procure the directions and protection that would allow them to portage through potentially hostile tribal lands, from the Missouri to the Columbia River. Thus Sacagawea joined the party, the only woman traveling with over forty men.

As Lewis departed from the main party to forge ahead on the south branch, he notes both that he felt quite ill with dysentery, and that Sacagawea, too, was sick with similar symptoms. She was bled by Clark (this treatment prescribed for her by Lewis and apparently declined for himself),[18] who continued to treat "our poor Indian woman" in Lewis's absence with frequent bleeding, mineral salt solutions, and bark poultices applied to "her region" to redress her lower abdominal pain. Clark curiously and repeatedly correlates Sacagawea's condition and his treatments of her with the state of the river, as in this entry for June 11: "Indian woman verry [sic] sick, I blead [sic] her which appeared to be of great service to her, both rivers [apparently the Missouri and Marias] riseing fast" (Thwaites 2:143; cf. 2:161, 162). This is a correlation that Lewis echoes and amplifies, as we will see.

During this time, Lewis carried on overland with excruciating abdominal pain and a fever. He self-medicated with a chokecherry solution,[19] and forged ahead to discover the falls. Struggling conscientiously to be true to Jefferson's praise to Congress for his descriptive abilities, he paused to write a long passage worth quoting in full for the way it nervously appeals first to aesthetic and then to scientific discourses in order to record the sight that validated his risky decision:

> From the reflection of the sun on the sprey or mist which arises from these falls there is a beatifull rainbow produced which adds not a little to the beauty of this majestically grand senery. after wrighting this imprefect discription I again viewed the falls and was so much disgusted with the imperfect idea which it conveyed of the scene that I determined to draw my pen across it and begin agin, but then reflected that I could not perhaps succeed better than pening the first impressions of the mind; I wished for the pencil of Salvator Rosa [a Titian] or the pen of Thompson [a reference to James Thomson, author of "The Season"—ed.] that I might be enabled to give the enlightened world some just idea of this truly magnificent and sublimely grand object, which has from the commencement of time been concealed from the view of civilized man; but this was fruitless and vain. I most sincerely regreted that I had not brought a crimee [camera] obscura with me by the assistance of which even I could have hoped to have done better but alas this was also out of my reach; I therefore with the assistance of my pen only indeavoured to trace some of the stronger features of this seen by the assistance of which and

my recollection aided by some able pencil I hope still to give to
the world some faint idea of an object which at this moment fills
me with such pleasure and astonishment; and which of it's kind
I will venture to ascert is second to but one in the known world.
(Thwaites 2:149–50)

It's hard to read this as a moment of triumph. Confirmation of his decision to take the southern branch offers only limited relief from the
anxieties of his command. Worries about his leadership abilities convert immediately to apprehensions about his competence at circum-
scribing nature.[20] Lewis, dogged even in the moment of this victory
by fears of his inadequacy, returns to the camp and finds Sacagawea
still ill: "About 2 P.M. I reached the camp found the Indian woman ex-
treemly ill and much reduced by her indisposition. this gave me some
concern as well for the poor object herself, then with a young child in
her arms as from the consideration of her being our only dependence
for a friendly negociation with the Snake Indians on whom we depend
for horses to assist us in our portage from the Missouri to the Columbia river" (Thwaites 2:162).[21] Taking over the treatment from Clark,
Lewis observes that "she complains principally in the lower region
of the abdomen" and thus administers another bark poultice, mineral water, and opium. As the round of treatment begins to ease her
symptoms, Lewis concludes: "I believe her disorder originated principally from an obstruction in the mensis in consequence of taking
could [sic]" (Thwaites 2:163). As Elliott Coues knowledgeably summarizes: "Forgetting perhaps the tender age of her infant, they diagnosed
her case as 'suppression of the mensis' and undertook to regulate her
courses with the same precision with which they attended to those of
the Missouri River" (Coues 2:380 n. 35): Sacagawea was nursing her
four-month-old infant at this point in the journey and was probably
not menstruating for that reason.[22]

What seems significant here is not that Lewis misdiagnosed Sacagawea (it is not my intention to attempt estimating the particular
effects of this episode for Sacagawea), but the specific investment
of his diagnosis: its multiple symbolic and ideological implications.
This moment in the expedition provides a window on the ways in
which, as John and Jean Comaroff summarize in their work on Africa,
"'geographical mission' linked the advance of reason in the interior of
the dark continent with the biological thrust into the dim recesses of
the human person" (Ethnography 215)—here practiced with raced and

gendered specificity on "our squaw," "the Indian woman." Lewis was not professionally trained in medicine, and studied briefly in Philadelphia to prepare for the journey,[23] where lessons in the "disorders" of women were undoubtedly not high on the priority list given that there was no expectation that women would be part of the expedition. Moreover, gynecology had not yet emerged as a medical profession, and only hardly as a subject for male general practitioners to study.[24]

But Lewis's "heroic"[25] medical expertise was a prominent feature of the mission both for the party's leaders and for its national audience. The explorers frequently record their disgust at the spiritual, superstitous qualities of native medicine, as for instance in the following passage, from close to the end of the journey, where Clark makes fun of the Cheyenne leader's supposed ignorance:[26] "After Smokeing I gave a medal of the small size to the Chyenne Chief &c. Which appeared to alarm him, he had a robe and a fleece of fat Buffalow meat brought and gave me with the meadal back and informed me that he knew that the white people were all *medecine* and that he was afraid of the midal or any thing white people gave to them. I . . . again told him the use of the medal . . . informing him this was the medecine which his Great Father directed me to deliver to all the great chiefs who listened to his word and followed his councils" (Thwaites 5:352–53). Notably, Clark does not attempt to demystify medicine for the Cheyenne from his own scientific perspective. Instead, he displaces the power of the supposed superstition from whiteness to medal, suggestively relocating its mysterious power from the realm of culture to economy. The Cheyenne leader, placated, as Clark portrays him, by these reassurances, doubles his gift. This gesture certifies Clark's assessment that the Cheyenne is irrational: he has neither scientific understanding nor economic good sense. Native "medecine" thus stands as a foil for the rationality in which the corps prides itself. Failing to register the steady requests they receive from native peoples for their medicine either as gestures of spiritual reciprocity or diplomatic rapprochement, Lewis and Clark see instead only confirmation of their medicine's superiority, its rational and heroic ability to apply the force of reason directly to the body. I am not suggesting here that we discredit the successful application of such practices, for instance, in Lewis's decision to amputate the gangrenous toes of a Mitutankan boy during the winter in Mandan (see Jan. 27 1805; Ronda 105–6). Rather, I want to highlight the cultural construction of those values, the way their medical science interacts symbiotically with the expedition's domesticating agenda, as the taming of bodily excesses, of nature, through the managerial application of reason to Other bodies. The western reaches of the continent along with its current inhabitants, according to the mission of the expedition and its medicinal model, are all wanting the rational management embodied in and practiced by the head of the Corps of Discovery.

Despite the similarity of their symptoms (lower abdominal pain, fever, diarrhea), then, "heroic" intervention is prescribed only for Sacagawea.[27] Both Lewis and Sacagawea recovered, maybe because of and maybe in spite of the different regimes prescribed and applied to each. Without speculating on the quality of the science entailed in the different courses (chokecherry solution vs. bleeding and poultices), or even on their respective illnesses, I want here to continue focusing on the symbolic dimensions of this episode. Coues concisely highlights the archetypal associations between women's menstrual flow and the symbolic force of water—the connection between (in Klaus Theweleit's recent, pithy summary) "women, floods, bodies, history" in the ideological construction of modern masculinity. It is impossible to ignore the symbolic unruliness of the Missouri River in this episode, and the way Lewis manages it by imaginatively projecting its flow onto the Feminine, thus providing him the proper arena for dealing with it heroically.[28] In the moment of intensest anxiety, when he is lacking both a clear sense of direction and the support of his crew, he assigns the "wrong" branch to "Maria," letting chivalry prop his confidence. This naming, Maria, fortifies as it enacts Lewis's sense of command. In it, he becomes master of the flow; the unruly flow is named as his Other. He knows the way of the flow (south); he prescribes the flow for Sacagawea (bleeding).[29] In symbolic confirmation, he returns from the falls to name Sacagawea's ailment: (a blockage of) her feminine difference.[30] His diagnosis, then, confirms Lewis's qualification for the project of national, territorial domestication at the same moment as it confirms manhood (scientific, managerial, white, national) as the ultimate Law. Feminine excess, imagined here as the forking Missouri *and* as "Maria's" branch *and* as blocked menstrual fluid, must be managed by the rationalizing "view of civilized man" lest "it flow back and pollute [the] entire system."[31]

Analyzed symbolically, though, it's worth underscoring that the danger of pollution is less threatening for Sacagawea than for Lewis. In this episode at the rivers' fork—a word still being used to describe a body's crotch[32]—Lewis contemplates the symbolic crisis of national purpose. The situation jeopardized the unitary command of leadership in the same way that the original plans for the secret expedition threatened, if exposed to the U.S. public, to jeopardize the fiction of the president's unitary command over the emergence of political opposition. The fork in the river effects a crisis in the domestic/ating agenda for Lewis and Clark much as it symbolizes the threat of political opposition for Jefferson that guided plans for the expedition in its planning phases and early preparation. Lewis responds to this national crisis at the fork by projecting outward and taming his uncertainty. He overcomes his geographical confusion by naming it "Maria"; he minimizes his own bodily indisposition and recuperates his sense of scientific inadequacy and manly command by diagnosing Sacagawea's disorderly femaleness. The body and the landscape that troubles Lewis is converted, through discourses of science, into (at least temporarily) reassuring categories of raced and female difference; menstruation is invoked as a stabilizing sign of femininity, a difference that can be identified, controlled, and even prescribed by the civic manager.

What I want to caption for attention ultimately is Lewis's cooperatively oedipalized internalization of that national/fraternal division; he experiences personal and bodily disorder (his own mood swings and illnesses) that ultimately—perhaps—culminated in his suicide.[33] This is of course speculative, but it does seem fair to factor here his intensely close personal relationship with Jefferson—father-son is the term repeatedly applied by historians[34]—and a particular communication from Jefferson to Lewis while he was still in St. Louis preparing for the journey. Jefferson exhorts Lewis: "The acquisition of the country through which you are to pass has inspired the country generally with a great deal of interest in your enterprise. The inquiries are perpetual as to your progress. The Feds [i.e., Federalists] alone still treat it as a philosophism, and would rejoice at its failure. Their bitterness increases with the diminution of their numbers and despair of a resurrection. I hope you will take care of yourself, and *be the living witness of their malice and folly*" (qtd. in Coues xxiii n. 7; emphasis added). We don't need to validate the exact nature of the alleged father-son tie in order to realize the structural implications of Jefferson's affectionate charge for Lewis's particular, personal experience of responsibility for this journey.

Robert J. C. Young has recently highlighted the usefulness of Deleuze and Guattari's critique of the Oedipus complex for a postcolonial analysis: "[A]ccording to them the link between the family and the state is achieved through a form of interior, ideological territorialization of the psyche that turns questions and dilemmas from the social realm into the problem of the individual. Freud participates in this transaction by using the Oedipus myth to interpret the neuroses of family life—'not as effects of the society which the family represents, but as the psychic production of the children who suffer them.' The foreign is thus made domestic in a movement of psychic recodification" (171). Young's summary of how the "foreign" is made "domestic," highlights the applicability of this model for the subject of national manhood, here Lewis.[35] I want to foreground, somewhat differently from Young, the way in which the always-threatening, fragmentary qualities of the only fictionally unified body politic—the National Subject—are recodified as problems of the national subject, the individual, the male manager, on the colonial/imperial frontier. The threat of political disintegration is internalized as the threat of personal disintegration, and managed by its outward projection, the naming of racial and gender Otherness. For the "white man" this then is also a colonization, but a colonization that is able to depend on structural privilege (the fraternal/civic contract) for a temporarily comforting stabilization of identity through an assertion of hierarchizing order.

Fraternal Domestication

Despite Lewis's controversy-ridden stint as Governor of Louisiana Territory and his subsequent suicide, Jefferson recreated him after his death as an icon of national manhood, the characterization adopted by Biddle and consequently by the expedition's national audience. This was a man who could inspire national fraternity, precisely because he was so commanding. In his memoir of this "Lewis," Jefferson catalogued his qualifications for leading the expedition: "Of courage undaunted; possessing a firmness and perseverance of purpose which nothing but impossibilities could divert from its direction; careful as a father of those committed to his charge, yet steady in the maintenance of order and discipline; intimate with the Indian character, customs and principles; habituated to the hunting life; guarded, by exact observation of the vegetables and animals of his own country, against losing time in the description of objects already possessed; honest, disinterested, liberal, of sound understanding, and a fidelity to truth so scrupulous that whatever he should report would be as

certain as if seen by ourselves" ("Memoir" xxi–xxii). This "Lewis" exemplifies, indeed stands as the National Subject. He is, in short, "the
perfect man, a blend of older and new masculinities, both father and
frontiersman, scientist and civic ruler" (Susan Bordo, communication
to the author). "Lewis" is the Economic Subject, who knows what
h/we possess, and wastes no time in accounting for what h/we can
acquire; his manly vigor is wedded to the more disembodied, analytic,
mathematizing attributes of the Enlightenment observer. Through his
scientific instincts, his knowledge of Indian character combined with
his photographic reportage and his business sense about biology, this
idealized Lewis is, to borrow Lee Edelman's terms, "the *enactment* of
a masculinity whose distinguishing characteristic is its power . . . to
'look on' others 'with contempt and pity,' to occupy the place of the
non-'racialized' (because non-specularizable) master of the gaze" (50).
Unquestionably a leader, Lewis here represents the new nation's new
ideal Father, disciplining through nurture.[36]

The quality of Jefferson's characterization of Lewis's commanding nature abuts uncomfortably the historically common emphasis
on the expedition's fraternal enactment—what a Lewis biographer,
Richard Dillon, has described as "the two-headed exploratory freak
called Lewisandclark" (xiii). The fraternal performance, the integration of two men's authority into a single, purposeful command over
their party and the terrain it covered, was what fascinated the U.S.
public, the separate records of the two explorers crafted into a single,
continuous narrative for public scrutiny through the careful editing of
Nicholas Biddle at one end of the century (1814), and Elliott Coues at
the other (1893). But the narrative of that exhibition—the command of
white/U.S. brotherhood over a party of (not quite) fellowmen—though
embraced by an expanding republic, was always equivocal at heart.

The expedition is remembered as a joint exercise, but that memory
is crisscrossed with ambivalence about the value of fraternity, an ambivalence evidenced by historians' habit of treating Lewis as the "real"
center of authority. They are following, it seems, not only Jefferson's
description of Lewis, but also the War Department's unwillingness,
despite Jefferson's promise, to promote Clark to captain for the operation.[37] If the "equality" of national manhood was being imagined, as I
suggested in my reading of *The Federalist Papers* (chapter 1), through
a conception of fraternity increasingly based on white male equivalence, we see in this particular record strong traces of a simultaneous
desire to transcend the exchangeability that model liberally encodes.

Recognizing this ambivalence lets us start to conceptualize how fraternal manhood in the early nation—grounded in an economy of equivalence—could concomitantly produce an experiential anxiety among both participants and observers. Thus men would look for comfort and stability to a nonexchangeable version of manhood. National fraternity celebrates men through appeals to The (family) Man, the Father-of-his-men, here located in "Lewis." My reading here would foreground for more careful attention the profoundly conservative trends that flowered within what Jay Fliegelman has described as the "reconstituted family" in the early nation. This radical masculine leveling, the diminishment of the power of first-born men in the patriarchal structure and the renunciation of the absolutist quality of power attached to men *qua* fathers, argues Fliegelman, was actually celebrated and encouraged by new political ideals of fraternal democracy.[38] This new model of male identity, I would urge, was not lived in the pure space of its idealism, but rather in a tense ideological space where it interacted with changing political, social, and economic circumstances as well as enduring expectations about masculine authority and order, along with nostalgic longings for a stability gendered specifically as masculine. New ideals of manhood produced, in other words, intensified ideological dissonance about the place/s of manhood. The cultural strategies that emerged (from old ideologies and new) for managing these anxieties carried profound tolls for men as well as for the white women and racial Others who increasingly were made to share the burden of these anxieties.

I suggested in the previous chapter that one key strategy of a reconfigured, national manhood was to cede the family as an affective realm to the Republican Mother.[39] But attendant to that gesture was another, one that redefined the male citizen as a Family Man outside the family proper, redefined him as a man of, not in, the family: a civic manager. Not so much *domesticated* then, fraternal manhood assumed the practice—through models of increasingly professionalized manageriality—of *domestication*. In this sense (theoretically at least) all sons of liberty could stand for the nonbiological Father, as enforcers of discipline through "caring," civilizing familial order, to the world around them.

But only some within this imagined fraternity, the (virtual) democratic space of national manhood, could access the full benefits of such structural privilege (and probably none could experience it fully, as my reading of Lewis would suggest and my reading of *Logan* will corroborate). The expedition's national audience viewed Lewis and Clark as representatives of civic unity and national order, thereby participating both in the imaginary exchangeability of fraternal manhood and in the privileges of domesticating command. We would do well to remember: there were some forty other men on the expedition without the privileges of command. Fraternity in its actual practice was practically and ideologically most uneven while pretending otherwise. This, then—the maintenance of class hierarchy within a fictive space of equality—produced a structural tension that required constant rerouting, constant management.

To cast this point somewhat differently, we can recall the insistence of Homi Bhabha that "the concept of the 'people' emerges within a range of discourses as a double movement": "The people are not simply historical events or parts of a patriotic body politic. They are also a complex rhetorical strategy of social reference: their claim to be representative provokes a crisis within the process of signification and discursive address" (145). In the disjunction between national pedagogy and the performance of the national, Bhabha postulates a split national subject, a person who must always struggle to turn "the scraps, patches and rags of daily life . . . into the signs of a coherent national culture" (145). It is precisely such "splitting"—the ideological internalization of political and economic difference, papered over by the abstract identity of "whiteness"—in the construction of American manhood that I want to focus on in as much specificity as possible for what it can reveal about the "deep logic" of whiteness, civic identity, and compensatory articulations of manhood in the United States. Here, for instance, we can begin to theorize how "white men" in various economic and social spaces engaged the national pedagogy of competent, domesticating manhood in the form of their identification with the civic fraternity embodied in the Lewis and Clark Expedition, occupying an imagined equivalence that could in no way fully harmonize the dissonant lived effects of economic, political, and social competition among "white men." Here too we can begin to consider the way this particular ideological formation of white manhood worked to keep manliness, rather than nation, always at stake— as the United States made its rapid transition into industrial capitalism, urbanization, and westward expansion.

III

Pleasant Prospects

Bhabha calls our attention, then, to how "the narrative and psycho-logical force that nationness brings to bear on cultural production and political projection is the effect of the ambivalence of 'nation' as a narrative strategy" (140). In these next sections, I want to turn Bhabha's more generalizing theoretical point toward specific instances of the narrative and psychological force that nationness brings to bear on the cultural productions and political projections of *manhood*, examining Nicholas Biddle's 1814 rendering of the expedition, and then John Neal's 1822 novel, *Logan*. Biddle's project was to edit Lewis's and Clark's journals into a continuous account; he additionally drew on the journals of two of the expedition's sergeants, Patrick Gass and John Ordway, and personally consulted Clark, and another member of the expedition, George Shannon, for supplemental information. Training these diverse sources into a coherent narrative, Biddle effectively trims the dialogic qualities of Lewis and Clark's two, respective journals in favor of a unified account; his work in this respect allows us to analyze the thematic drive of his narrative agenda in comparison to the actual journals.[40] Somewhat differently, Neal's text, generically more receptive to the dialogic Biddle worked to suppress in his history, allows us to read through the thematic concerns Neal shares with Biddle, and analyze the structures of anxiety—less evident in Biddle—that *Logan* maps.

One recent historian has noted, in comparing Nicholas Biddle's 1814 edition of *The History of the Lewis and Clark Expedition* to the version of their journals brought into print in 1902 by Rueben Gold Thwaites, that "Biddle emphasized the search for unity which characterized nineteenth-century America; Thwaites exposed the diversity of its people which twentieth-century Americans recognized" (Barth 501). Gunther Barth observes that Biddle's narrative is relatively uninterested in the other men on the journey as anything other than the (virtually unnamed) supporting cast to Lewis and Clark, and that he systematically works the actual records to downplay significant temperamental differences between the two leaders in order to present them as being always of one mind. Biddle addressed his *History* to a national audience, argues Barth, by thematizing "unity" at the expense of "democracy."[41]

As Barth elaborates, Biddle (1786–1844) was motivated by concerns correlative (though politically not identical) to Jefferson's: "Biddle's prose [in the *History*] brought the reader close to the young patriot's image of a strong nation. His language strengthened the idea of national unity which he saw challenged again by the division of the country over the War of 1812. With that goal before him, in 1811, Biddle the politician delivered a Fourth of July oration before the Pennsylvania State Society of Cincinnati on the virtues of a divided country uniting against a common enemy" (513). His nationalist agenda extended into the literary realm;[42] he became a member in 1809 of the Tuesday Club, and was a regular contributor to the *Port Folio*, a periodical dedicated to building an American literature, and which he was actively managing while he was composing the *History*. Thus Biddle was interested in and well situated to turn the expedition's journals into a narrative that could address a national audience, to convert the continental expedition into a national narrative.[43] Though the initial printing did not sell well in its first edition (it was published eight years after the expedition's return), Biddle's was the only official record available to the U.S. public up to the end of the century, and it would eventually see more than twenty editions before new scholarly editions became available.

Biddle was without doubt scrupulous about his work, repeatedly consulting Clark to verify his literary rendering. But the stylistic and thematic divergence of Biddle's text from the journals is substantial, owing to Biddle's selection and rewriting of materials. Taken on its own, Biddle's *History* is a significant contribution to the national literary project, seldom treated as such by literary critics.[44] It certainly deserves a more systematic analysis than I can give it here. The editor of the *Port Folio* delivered a literary rendering of national mission that is simply stunning in its correlation of heroic achievement to national destiny. As Barth summarizes, "the nationalistic tone and the romantic sentiment of Biddle's language suited nineteenth-century Americans well. His prose gave their dreams of a continental empire reality" (509).

Biddle used the agreed-upon cocaptaincy of the expedition's two leaders as a metaphor for national purpose; he accordingly narrativized national identity in terms of a fraternally competent, rational, observant, economic, and occasionally heroic manhood. One particularly notable aspect of Biddle's strategy here was to frame the narration in the first-person plural, switching to proper third person (Captain Lewis, Captain Clark) to identify only the separate actions of the leaders. In relying narratively on the "we," Biddle not only fuses the two captains' observations into a single intent, he also invites readers imaginatively to join the expedition. "We" stands multiply for the fraternal endeavor of "Lewisandclark" (and the other men in the Corps of Discovery); for the United States they represented on their mission; and (a bit like the "we" of the Constitution) for the intersection of identity U.S./us.[45] Thus the "we" works powerfully for readers as a national-masculine pedagogy, drawing them into the (fictional) coherence of national purpose while offering a streamlined, rhetorically enhanced version of the expedition's accomplishments.

Biddle's streamlining additionally converts the real anxieties of the expedition's leaders into strategic silences or rhetorically glossy moments. We can compare as an example the passages from the actual journals that I already analyzed above. Sacagawea's illness and treatments are all but deleted; the Biddle text mentions on June 16 that "the wife of Charboneau [sic], our interpreter, has been dangerously ill, but she now found great relief from the mineral water of the sulphur spring," and again on June 19, "Our poor Indian woman, who had recovered so far as to walk out, imprudently ate a quantity of white-apple, which, with some dried fish, occasioned a return of her fever" (Biddle 1:271, 273; cf. Coues 2:377, 379–80)[46]—passages that suggest a digestive disorder and totally efface the two leaders' attention to, or Lewis's diagnosis of, Sacagawea's Other ailment. Historians have commented on Biddle's bowdlerizing sense of propriety, for instance, his conversion of Clark's account of the Mandan buffalo ceremony into Latin because of *its* circumlocutory mention of sexual intercourse. So we might speculate that Biddle deleted the numerous details of Sacagawea's illness and treatment *because of* Lewis's eventual diagnosis, which would make the whole scene indelicate. This hypothesis, though, doesn't stand up to the fact that Biddle includes sections of Lewis's numerous, endlessly fascinated commentaries on the experiences of Native women in childbirth—including Sacagawea's (see Biddle 1:160, 416, 432; cf. Coues 1:232, 2:551–52, 568). This in itself does not "prove" that the sections detailing Sacagawea's illness and diagnosis were deleted because Biddle read there, as I do, a certain anxiety that reflects back onto Lewis as well as the project of the expedition; but the fact that these numerous and significant passages become expendable to Biddle's narrative purpose says at least that they didn't—for whatever reason—further the image of the expedition he strove to represent.

What does further the image, of course, is Lewis's "discovery" of the falls. Biddle deletes all of Lewis's self-deprecating mentions of his inadequacy, honing the details Lewis did provide to the very certainty of tone Lewis despaired of being able to achieve. To enhance the effect, Biddle adds a stunning twist to Lewis's mention of an eagle's nest at the upper falls: "Here, on a cottonwood tree, an eagle had fixed its nest, and seemed the undisputed mistress of a spot, to contest whose dominion neither man nor beast would venture across the gulf that surround it. . . . This solitary bird could not escape the observation of the Indians, who made the eagle's nest a part of their description of the falls, which now proves to be correct in almost every particular, except that they did not do justice to their height" (Biddle 1:264; cf. Coues 2:369). Bruce Greenfield concisely summarizes: the eagle "suggests that it is not just a civilized man who has come to fulfill the destiny of the place, but a civilized American, whose totem, the eagle is also the presiding spirit of the place" (99).

Biddle's strategically enhanced excerpts, then, develop his motif of heroic national achievement, correlated specifically to images of civilization and rationality borne into the wild by the party's leadership. In particular, he thematizes national manhood through a repeating pattern of foregrounded ethnological contrasts between explorers and the Native peoples whom they encounter, pulling material out of its recorded order in the journals, and supplementing with information from Clark in order to provide ethnographic assessments of nearly every group the expedition encounters in the narrative moment of their encounter. The main effect in Biddle's casting, then, is constantly to keep "Indianness" *qua* difference on display, an emphasis not consistently prominent in the journals. In Biddle's *History*, the structure of the text keeps Indian peculiarity continually in evidence—Indian appearance ("diminutive stature," "ill-shaped," "thick ankles") Indian clothing ("the women are clad in a peculiar manner"), Indian behaviors (dancing, gambling, thieving), always surveyed and evaluated from the vantage of rational manhood. In this respect, the text depends on what Edelman details as the scopophilic exercise of racialized masculinity (46). Edelman characterizes this exercise in the terms of narcissistic fantasy: "If the fantasy of masculinity (and I would want that genitive to be read with the full force of its double meaning) is the fantasy of a non-self-conscious selfhood endowed with absolute control of a gaze whose directionality is irreversible, the enacted—or "self-conscious"—"manhood," . . . is itself a performance *for the gaze of the Other* . . . it is destined therefore to be always the paradoxical *display* of a masculinity that defines itself through its capacity to put *others* on display while resisting the bodily captation involved in being put on display itself" (50–51; original emphases). In fact, though Biddle does often include information about physical illnesses and sufferings of the men, he does not include visually descriptive summaries of the men of the expedition—we do not get to "see" them as objects of display in the way that we repeatedly do Indians. The *History's* achievement and its enduring effect is to provide a commanding display of national manhood as it—embodied in the gaze of the two captains and by the pedagogically trained, imagining gaze of the *History's* reader—puts continent and Indians on display.

Biddle highlights aspects of Lewis's and Clark's journals to flesh out this fantasy/display of national manhood, selecting from them and adding to them to give his *History* a thematic durability not nearly so present in the journals. Biddle has two particular foci for this display. First, Biddle forwards, even more frequently than the journals, Native "medicine" as a system of ignorance and superstition. Consider this inserted anecdotal elaboration on Mandan religious practices:[47]

> The whole religion of the Mandans consists in the belief of one great spirit presiding over their destinies. This being must be in the nature of a good genius, since it is associated with the healing art, and the great spirit is synonymous with great medicine, a name also applied to every thing which they do not comprehend. Each individual selects for himself the particular object of his devotion, which is termed his medicine, and is either some invisible being or more commonly some animal, which thenceforward becomes his protector or his intercessor with the great spirit, to propitiate whom every attention is lavished and every personal consideration is sacrificed. "I was lately owner of 17 horses," said a Mandan to us one day, "but I have offered them all up to my medicine and am now poor." He had in reality taken all his wealth, his horses, into the plain, and, turning them loose committed them to the care of his medicine and abandoned them forever. The horses less religious took care of themselves, and the pious votary traveled home on foot. (Biddle 1:138–39; cf. Coues 1:208)

Lacking even horse sense "in reality," the Mandans exemplify the irrationality of economy and medicine that Biddle, in this repeating theme, urges the reader to see in contrast to the expedition.

Native superstition provides not simply a contrast to the civilized perspective "we" bring to "our continent." More than that, it offers a material advantage to national claims, as Biddle repeatedly highlights the explorers' habit of scaling Indian burial mounds for the "delightful prospect" they present. Biddle frames the utility of these actions with particular clarity in the following passage, worth quoting at length:

[I]t was not till after four hours march that we reached the object of our visit. This was a large mound in the midst of the plain [scientific description of mound follows]. . . . But the Indians have made it a great article of their superstition: it is called the mountain of Little People, or Little Spirits, and they believe that it is the abode of little devils, in the human form, of about eighteen inches high and with remarkably large heads; they are armed with sharp arrows, with which they are very skillful. . . . The tradition is, that many have suffered from these little evil spirits. . . . This has inspired all the neighbouring nations, Sioux, Mahas, and Ottoes, with such terror, that no consideration could tempt them to visit the hill. We saw none of these wicked little spirits; nor any place for them, except some small holes scattered over the top: we were happy enough to escape their vengeance, though we remained some time on the mound to enjoy the delightful prospect of the plain. (Biddle 1:52–53; cf. Coues 1:86)

In this pedagogical contrast, between "our" understanding and Indian silliness, there is no place to consider that the story might well have been fabricated to keep the expedition away from a sacred site. Rather, the mound offers at once the vantage of geographical survey and the advantage of confirmed, heroic rationality to the Corps of Discovery and to the nation it stands for. The expedition literally and with symbolic import goes out of its way to stand on the bones of dead Indians in order to register its territorial sovereignty and rational superiority. Here, Biddle offers us yet another (artfully crafted) twist on the thematic use of Native bodies and Indian identity to elevate and consolidate the ad-vantage of national manhood.

Biddle also habitually composes ethnographic displays such that they sharpen the journals' focus on gender contrasts or introduce it to records that had a different focus. Two sets of passages provide a helpful sample. In the first, for instance, both leaders are thoroughly discomfited by the Chinook tribes they must deal with during their second winter on the expedition, at Clatsop, where the women had a great deal of political, economical, and sexual autonomy. Through the course of the winter they spent on the Pacific Coast, Lewis's and Clark's antipathy to their neighbors grew to the point even of paranoia (see Ronda, ch. 8). Lewis's ethnographical summary of the Chinook peoples attempts to explain his growing unease scientifically, in terms of alien and distorted gender relations, in a passage worth quoting at length:

> [T]hey do not hold the virtue of their women in high estimation, and will even prostitute their wives and daughters for a fishing hook or a stran of beads. in common with other savage nations they [Thwaites: Clatsop, Chinnooks, Kilamox &c] make their women perform every species of domestic drudgery. but in almost every species of this drudgery the men also participate, their woman are compelled to geather roots, and assist them in taking fish; which articles form much the greatest part of their subsistance; notwithstanding the survile manner in which they treat their womin they pay much more rispect to their judgement and oppinion in maney rispects than most indian nations; their women are permitted to speak freely before them, and sometimes appear to command with a tone of authority; they generally consult them in their traffic and act conformably to their opinions.
>
> I think it may be established as a general maxim that those nations treat their old people and women with most difference [Thwaites: deference] and rispect where they subsist principally on such articles that these can participate with the men in obtaining them; and that, that part of the community are treated with least attention, when the act of procuring subsistence devolves entirely on the men in the vigor of life. It appears to me that nature has been much more deficient in her filial tie than in any other of the strong affections of the human heart, and therefore think, our old men equally with our women indebted to civilization for their comfort and ease. (Thwaites 3:315–16; see also Clark entry of Jan. 9, in Thwaites 3:330–31)

Lewis seems to have difficulty processing the fact of Chinookan women's entitlement as anything but the confused or mistaken practices of Chinookan men. But his analysis in the second paragraph is perceptive in its recognition that social relations are often structured through or manifested by economic ones. He registers a thoughtful awareness of social relations between young men and old men, and young women and old women, a complex nexus of economic and affective exchanges that structure community.

In Biddle's handling, though, the complex apprehension of community and economy drops away, in favor of a schematic, binaristic emphasis on male-female roles, with manly virtue—or lack thereof—as its primary descriptive aim:

> The treatment of women is often considered as the standard by which the moral quality of savages are to be estimated. Our own observation, however, induces us to think that the importance of the female in savage life, has no necessary relation to the virtues of the men, but is regulated wholly by their capacity to be useful. The Indians whose treatment of the females is mildest, and who pay most deference to their opinions, are by no means the most distinguished for their virtues; nor is this deference attended by any increase in attachment, since they are equally willing with the most brutal husband, to prostitute their wives to strangers. On the other hand, the tribes among whom the women are very much debased, possess the loftiest sense of honor, the greatest liberality, and all the good qualities their situation demands the exercise. (Biddle 2:136–37; cf. Coues 2:781)

Lacking an investment in narrative continuity, Lewis does not push an agenda—which is not to overlook Lewis's closing emphasis on the salvific force of civilization, but to note the way his agendas are occasional, rather than narratively systemic. But Biddle does have a narrative agenda, and it is, as we see in this accumulating theme, about *disciplined* and *disciplinary manhood*. In numerous passages, he drives home a formulaic point: notions of virtue, proper order, and honor are attached to a model of manly strength, either manifested as hierarchical, brute male dominance (the only way Biddle recognizes "manliness" among Indians) or in combination with romantic devotion as the civilized patina on male dominance (this is a quality Biddle attaches exclusively to the two leaders, highlighting how Lewis and Clark name rivers for sweethearts and how Clark reprimands Charbonneau for his more severe mistreatment of Sacagawea). For Biddle, the fact that the Chinook proper and Clatsop women have autonomy within marriage is just one more evidence of their husbands' lack of discipline (their waste of time at their "attachment at games of hazard, which they pursue with a strange and ruinous avidity" being another important symptom [Biddle 2:140; cf. Coues 2:784–85]).[48] In Biddle's portrayal of the Chinook people proper, this lack of self-discipline corresponds to a profound deficiency in their behavior:[49] "No ill-treatment or indignity, on our part, seems to excite any feeling, except fear; nor, although better provided than their neighbors with arms, have they enterprise enough to use them advantageously against the animals of the forest, or offensively against their neighbors; who owe their safety more to the timidity rather than the forebearance of the Chinooks" (Biddle 2:116; cf. Coues 2:756). Biddle thus suggests that the Chinook, not lacking men, are lacking *manliness*. Though they are, in other words, properly equipped, the Chinook want the proper spirit, manifested both as masculine aggression and paternal restraint, that would make their possession of weaponry "advantageous" or "enterprising," beneficial in marriage, war, or commerce.

In strong contrast, my second example comes from an earlier moment in the journey, when the Corps is among the Shoshonee, Sacagawea's birth nation. Here, the leaders actually seem comfortable with the Shoshonee, despite what they consider to be some diplomatic difficulties with them. This is a comfort Biddle notices and emphasizes. He offers a far more extended depiction of Shoshonee character than is present in the journals; I am particularly interested in his characterization of their manhood:

> In their conduct toward ourselves they were kind and obliging . . . we recollected how few civilized chiefs would have hazarded the comforts or the subsistence of their people for the sake of a few strangers. This manliness of character may cause or it may be formed by the nature of their government, which is perfectly free from any restraint. Each individual is his own master, and the only control to which his conduct is subjected, is the advice of a chief supported by his influence over the opinions of the rest of the tribe. . . .
>
> In their domestic economy, the man is equally sovereign. The man is the sole proprietor of his wife and daughters, and can barter them away or dispose of them in any manner he may think proper. The children are seldom corrected; the boys, particularly, soon become their own masters. (Biddle 1:421; cf. Coues 2:556–57)

Here, then, is Biddle's example of an Indian manhood "we" can admire. If readers disapprove of men bartering away wives and daughters, Biddle still constructs the passage so that we are encouraged to appreciate the character of manliness that actuates itself (misguidedly?) in Shoshonee men's habit of disposing of wives as they please. Readers are tacitly asked to consider how the male privilege that results in this practice is also the foundation for their diplomatic hospitality, a trait Biddle's framing encourages his readers to rate highly. In other words, Biddle does not ask his readers to see Shoshonee men's brutality toward women as a compromise of their "manliness of character" but rather as another peculiar Indian expression of an admirable trait.

It is worth noticing that Lewis does not even use the phrase "manliness of character." In fact, his portrayal is somewhat less flattering of Shoshonee men, and less interested in offering a general commentary on manhood as a universal trait:

> like most other Indians they are great egotists and frequently boast of heroic acts which they never performed. they are also fond of games of wrisk [sic]. they are frank, communicative, fair in dealing, generous with the little they possess, extreemly honest, and by no means beggerly. each individual is his own sovereign master, and acts from the dictates of his own mind. . . . in fact, every man is a chief, but all have not an equal influence on the minds of the other members of the community, and he who happens to enjoy the greatest share of confidence is the principal Chief. . . . The man is sole propryetor of his wives and daughters, and can barter or dispose of either as he thinks proper. . . . They seldom correct their children particularly the boys who soon become masters of their own acts. (Thwaites 2:370–71)

We can see by comparing Biddle's version to Lewis's record that Biddle trims Lewis's description of Shoshonee men's self-sovereignty to "fit" better with U.S. notions of possessive individualism. Lewis seems to be casting for terms to describe what he sees as a cultural practice, whereas Biddle selects one specific set: rather than every man a "chief"—which would be the wording Biddle's anthropological emphasis on Indian peculiarity would predict—every "individual" is "his own master," a phrasing that strikingly orients Shoshonee manhood toward U.S. conceptions of manhood in this period. I would suggest, then, that this counterintuitive description of Shoshonee manhood is a pedagogical moment, framed obliquely. For Biddle, gentleman and scholar, it most certainly would be impolite to offer positive depictions suggesting that "white" men too could barter their wives. But "manliness of character," as imagined community between manly Indians and manly Americans, could nonetheless restructure U.S. manhood as a dominating enterprise, under the auspices of civilization. In this sense, readers were invited, much like Robert Bly and

Shepherd Bliss invite men today, to beat their drums and reject "feminization"—imaginatively, temporarily—for the pure spaces of manly
affiliation. This idealized, imagined, "interracial" male community,
then, offers us a helpful interpretive wedge into the mid- to late-
century exploding popularity of secret fraternal organizations, such
as the Fraternal Order of Red Men (a subject I treat in more detail
in chapter 5). For my specific analysis in this chapter, it offers an instance of the way imagined "occupation" of Indian identity could provide access to consolidating a national identity simultaneously white
and manly.

Biddle's *History* offered a space for U.S. men to imagine dominance
—over women—and to enact dominance—over Indians. But though
that exercise might palliate, it could not displace the economic, competitive, and professional tensions emerging between white men, a
dilemma that John Neal's 1822 novel *Logan* details. In his national
narrative, Neal locates the origins of the United States precisely in
Biddle's imagined manly community, claiming, after Jefferson and in
the fashion of Robert Beverly (1705), "I am an Indian," or, more precisely, "Logan is US."[50] Oddly (or perhaps predictably) this narrative
is less notable for its colonizing identification with Indian manliness
than for the anxieties in relations between white men that it foregrounds.

IV

Such a Noble Creature as Tecumseh

The disavowed fragmentation, self-division, and anxiety entailed by
the production and enactments of national manhood always threatened to return home. This threat is always looming in Neal's *Logan*,
where U.S. desire for (Indian) manhood is neurotically domesticated
through family/iarizing configurations of symbolic fathers and sons.
The novel neatly demonstrates, by extending and literalizing Jefferson's argumentational appropriation of Logan, the way Indian identity
became a resource for national/white manhood in the United States
through symbolic as well as literal expropriation and occupation.[51]

Behind Neal's plot for *Logan* was his theory that American literature could win recognition not by emulating the competition (the
British) but through a muscular style adapted from the heroic fearlessness and natural freedom of America's noble first inhabitants. He
would detail this theory late in 1825, in his *Blackwood's Magazine*
series on American literature:

Were Tecumseh himself, the great Indian warrior and prophet; were he alive now, we should say to him this, . . . if you go in your natural shape, in the true garb of your nation, you will never be laughed at. Grotesque, you *may* be; but, whether grotesque or not, you will be respectable. If you are wise, you will not undertake the part of a fine gentleman, at your age. You may spend half your life before a looking-glass, with a drill-sergeant or a dancing-master,—half your life; and yet, if you are made of real North American stuff, you will be no match, in the well-bred ease, for an English footman. . . .

[W]e now urge to the writers of America, who are coming out, one after another, in a vile masquerade—putting away their chief properties and aping the style of another people . . . It is American books that are wanted of America; not English books—nor books, made in America, by Englishmen, or by writers, who are a sort of bastard English. . . . Come forth naked, absolutely naked, *we* should say, to every real North American—savage, or not; wild, or tame; though your muscles be rather too large, and your toes turned the wrong way. (*American Writers* 198–201)

Neal forwarded his arguments on behalf of uncultivated, indigenous style against the cultured, derivative examples set by the likes of Irving and Cooper.[52] Neal's writing, characterized recently by David Reynolds as "subversive fiction"—a "deliberately outrageous, inflammatory, disquieting" style of writing (200)—followed the manic, aggressive character of his own career.

Born in Portland, Maine, in 1793, Neal was raised as a Quaker by his mother (his father died when he was young). According to his autobiography, he was literally beaten out of his pacifism by bullies in school, fighting back constituting his most important lesson during his years there (see Lease 7). After his schooling ended at the age of twelve, he worked as a clerk in a series of stores, moving on after the failure of each business.[53] In the early 1810s, he went into business with John Pierpont, first in Boston, then Baltimore. As Fred Lewis Pattee summarizes, "Neal with the impetuosity that soon earned for him the nickname 'Jehu O'Cataract' plunged into business like a gambler" (4). The two had a brief, spectacular success, but were quickly bankrupted in 1815, at the end of the War of 1812. Neal then decided to study law, and to fund those studies with a writing career. In short order, he published the novel *Keep Cool* (1817), *History of the American Revolution* (1818; co-authored with Paul Allen); *The Battle* of *Niagra* (1818); *Goldau: or, the Maniac Harper* (1818); *Otho* (1819; verse tragedy); and *Logan, a Family History* (1822)—all this while studying for the bar and editing *The Portico*, the magazine of the Delphian Club, which was a literary group that Neal helped found.[54]

It was from a developing and notably competitive professional investment in American letters that Neal posed his arguments for American literature, mined, it would seem, directly from his first publicly successful novel, *Logan*.[55] There, he extends and amplifies as a narrative of national origins Jefferson's adoption of the Mingo chief and orator, making his male descendants (and his namesake in the novel) white Americans not just analogically, as does Jefferson, but *genealogically*. Thus Neal effects, through family romance, the consolidation of national manhood—and a model for national literature—in (yet another) symbolic appropriation of Indian manhood. This arrogated identity, at once territorial and affective, legalizes its claims (yet again) through characterologically inconsequential, symbolically idealized Indian women.

The manhood envisioned in this national narrative, conceptualized as a natural and honorable counter to the overly refined, corrupted manhood of the British, is enacted through a heroically embattled model of fatherhood. This model works both to recategorize and assuage anxieties about relations among men in America through symbolic filiation. But this ideal and muscular fatherhood, despite its promises, fails to provide an affirmative masculine legacy or to guarantee a functioning civic fraternity for its anxious sons.

I Have a Legacy for My Land

Logan, as novel and as national narrative, works insistently through what Eric Lott has summarized in his study of blackface minstrelsy as "a destabilized structure of fascination, a continual confusion of subject and object" (127). That is to say, the story works through a systematic, productive confusion of biological and symbolic descent, between Indian-as-American and (white) American identity, between men who are enemies and those who are family. Identifying fatherhood as an exercise in agon and imperialism, the novel links the transmission of a symbolic paternal inheritance materially in the form of empire and spiritually in the form of patriotism, a legacy that must be heroically claimed by its properly manful citizen-sons.

The story proper is captioned by dying narrators (whether one or two remains unclear) who initiate the subject confusion that characterizes the story, between Logan-as-originary-Mingo and Logan-as-(British)-"incarnation"; between American as "Indian" and American as (British)-descended-sons-of-Logan. The first narrator introduces himself as a descendent of "Logan the MINGO CHIEF" before dying a dramatic, stage death in seven pages, bidding farewell alternately to "the blood of the red man" and "the sickly fluid of my white ancestors" (preface, unnumbered; 1:5). Following his demise, the narrative resumes with either a second or the same narrator, who indicates that with a recent witnessed death of either the first narrator or someone else altogether (possibly the character Harold), the "family of Logan, 'The Mingo Chief,' is now extinct" (1:6). This narrator elegiacally recounts the story of Logan, "friend of the white men":

> Who does not remember it? Suddenly, without provocation, or notice, this Indian patriarch, this Indian prince, in the very prime and vigour of his maturity, while about him sat his children and his children's children, and through ten thousand ruddy channels, the blood of the brave and good was rippling from the fountain of his being—in one moment, one little moment, he was smitten by barrenness and death. The shot rang, and many generations mingled their blood at his feet.
>
> All his hopes were prostrate. He was childless! He was no longer a father nor a husband. But a moment before, he had been the husband of many wives, and the father of a multitude. Now! he was alone, alone in the wide world. The channels of immortality were cut assunder—its sources and fountains locked up and hidden—and the rich fluid of many hearts was turned aside to the unfruitful sands of the desert.
>
> "There is not one drop of my blood," said Logan, "now running in the veins of a single human creature! What desolation!"
>
> "I would not turn on my heel," said he, "to save my life." Who does not believe him?
>
> "I took up the hatchet," said Logan. "I was glutted with vengeance." Verily, he was glutted, and his son, and his son's sons have been glutted after him. (1:7)[56]

The narrator almost immediately hereafter reveals that he too is of "the same blood" as Logan. In this disorienting reemergence of the "last of the Logans," we see condensed several layers of narrative and perspectival confusion strategically cultivated by Neal.[57] Despite the

British attack on Logan's progeny, Logan "sons" proliferate; despite the "extinction" of Logan's family with the death of the first narrator, another branch is seemingly revealed as if by magic. Significantly, the introduction brackets the "sons" as the *biological* offspring of the Mingo progenitor. But the narrative proper will shortly reveal that the Logan who looms in this narrative, a supposed descendant of the chief cited by Jefferson, is in fact a *British* aristocrat, George Clarence of Salisbury, third son of the last Cumberland, who renounced his seigneury because of his "ungovernable ambition" and journeyed to exercise it in America, disappearing there only to reemerge as the bloodiest "Logan" (1:12, 2:92). It is, in the logic of the novel, ungovernable ambition that identifies the "natives" of America; it is manly force of will that constitutes the route from identification to identity as we will see below.

This ungovernably ambitious man, the (British) "Logan," is father to the novel's American/Indian protagonist, Harold.[58] His (deceased) mother is a "true daughter of Logan," and it is through her, and others like her, that the (British) Logan stakes his claim.[59] For instance, though we know little about Harold's mother (except that "her heart was in perpetual travail for her people" [1:11]), we do know that while Harold is spending time with his adopted father, the British governor, "Logan," his biological father, claims as his betrothed Harold's Indian-maiden sweetheart, Loena. Loena later explains that "Logan" simply entered the village of Logan (Indian descendants of the Mingo original), demanding a wife; apparently his sheer strength of command leads the village council to decide upon Loena as their most attractive offering. We learn elsewhere that "Logan" desires to marry among the Logans to perpetuate Logan's lineage. The nominal confusion (Logan the Mingo? Logan the British George of Salisbury?) here is dazzling: thus behind the rhetoric of biological descent, the Name-of-the-Father exalted through "Logan" becomes a patrimony actually *detached* from biology, one that is instead staked through belligerent claims and acts of virility.[60]

We have—in "Logan's" claims to Indian/American manhood, in "Indian" acceptance of "Logan's" "wife bartering"—precisely the moment (and fictional triumph) of imagined fraternity between "white" and "Indian" manliness that Biddle suggested. Here the phantasmic "Indian" recognition of the British "Logan's" claims subtly works to authorize the superiority of (white) American manhood. As the narrator early summarizes: "Such was the father; a savage before he left the palaces of white men. But he was a great savage. He had a desperate but sublime ambition. He was full of the fiery element, that rises in the arteries like mercury in a thermometer, at the approach of greatness. His whole nature was heroick—but it was the nature of him who thundered against the battlements of heaven" (1:12). *Logan* here suggests that though the biological and affective unit of family was ceded to the Republican mother, civic fraternity would preserve the symbolic domain of filiation, where belonging is not descended biologically but manfully—racially, nationally—*claimed*, wrested away, and protected from the undeserving.

Logan repeatedly casts its fatherly ideal in the terms of uncompromising, purist manhood: "Let us talk of the father then; of him that never forgot or forgave. What a sublime constancy!" (1:11). Logan is the father par excellence, "gigantic" in his "self-possession" (1:116). Such self-possession, "individual and solitary," entails the renunciation of personal affective ties that are then replaced with divinely sanctioned drives, unencumbered by mutuality or obligation. In embarking for America, Logan, "snapp[ed] asunder every tie of sympathy and affectation—every filament of brotherhood or love—every chord of judgment, habit or feeling—bruising with an iron hand, and breaking, as in derision, with a profaning levity, the youngest and greenest tendrils of the heart, alike with the sinuous and gnarled roots of our toughest and most protracted habitudes—trampling on them all! scorning them all!—scattering them all without shame, or remorse, yea, without emotion!" (1:12). In that renunciation, Logan is divinely appointed to empire, as Harold later explains to the British parliament: "His dominion was an empire. It was given to him by Almighty God. He held it by no earthly tenure, no vassalage, no feud, no mediate nor intermediate sovereign, lord or man" (2:277). Owing nothing to anyone, this is a father, a citizen, of, not *in* the family.

In *Logan*, fathering is simply and magnificently an act of vengeance against the wrongs of a noble people; it is an act of domestic protection. Fatherhood guarantees familial/national sanctitude, and as such, fatherhood in its pure, pedagogical form is *patriotism*, as Harold argues to Parliament, appealing for Indian sovereignty on the (Jeffersonian) logic of human equivalence: "Look at yon warriour, stretching his glossy limbs in the shadow of yon rifted oak, teaching his naked boy how to feather his arrow and barb his javelin. He is a father. Is *he* not religious? lo! he is teaching his child to defend his inheritance. He is training him for he first lesson of patriotism, and is not patriotism religion?" (2:280). Patriotism—"acting as a father to one's country" (*OED*)—guarantees and purifies inheritance. The father *is*

Pater-of-nation, offering the national legacy in lessons of aggressive self-defense.

In this endless string of slippage—from father to Father, from local to national heritage, from acquisitive and dishonest colonizer to innocent and heroic colonized—we see the ends of the nominal confusion that structures the plot of novel *and* nation. This studied confusion enables colonial invasion and appropriation of Indian *lands* to be (re)conceptualized as genealogically sanctioned bequest, of "American" spirit, of "American" nation (this perhaps explaining "our" endless preference for the more flexible national substantive "America"). This calculated strategy, blurring colonizing agent with colonized object, encourages Neal's American ("white") reader to identify patriotically and manfully with the American, Logan, who is at once, flexibly, "white" *and* Indian.[61] This is an American who is—finally—an Indian solely by *act of will*, as we see in one scene where Logan realizes he is suspected by an Iroquois as being an impostor because he has forgotten to complete his disguise in the proper positioning of his feet: "Did his heart sink? No, no! His heart never sank. Did his eye quail? No, never! . . . He was Indian—Indian! body and soul! heart and spirit! blood and thought! There was no gesture: but his whole constitution was up in arms" (1:95). Logan is an Indian—even though he identifiably is not an Indian by the Iroquois' measure—because his "whole constitution" manfully *claims* Indianness. Thus for Neal's readers, Indian identity, or, to refine the point, identifying with the British "Logan," guarantees both national *and* manly identity.

This chain of abstraction from the local to the abstract works through means correlative to those I discussed earlier regarding "whiteness"; here again, a chain of abstraction serves as a guarantor of civic identity and national unity, relocating men's identities from the local, religious, class, and political into an overarching (fictive, imagined, abstracted) American Community. Though Neal invests Logan with an enduring hatred against "whites," the novel so thoroughly and effectively confuses British American with Native American/Indian identity that in the end, whiteness in *Logan* does not endure as a term of opprobrium. Rather it is abstracted out of view, is invisible to itself as such; *Logan*'s "white" reader is allowed to avoid confronting himself in the specific terms of his own "white" culpability as he glides manfully into the appropriated space of Americanness.[62]

Brothers Indeed They Were

In Neal's national narrative, the American Revolution completes the transfer of manhood from Britain to America as the narrator describes in closing: "Great God! What a revolution! My beloved country standing up, with her forehead in the sky, her bright hair streaming from ocean to ocean . . . and lo! her tyrant in the dust—where was *his* manhood now? where the presence, before which Europe trembled and was afraid? . . . and where the strong children of his youth?—the vast machinery of empire?—gone! gone! forever gone! in the retribution of the Eternal!" (2:340). This Revolution certifies the fraternal manhood of Americans in the testing ground of battle, like that of the mighty Iroquois, "not brothers by birth, but brothers more nearly and dearly allied—brother *by* blood and *in* blood" (1:94).[63] Completing the logic of Jefferson's argument with Buffon, Neal depicts America—interchangeably land and nation—as a place of masculine *regeneration:* Harold, after delivering his eloquent speech to the British Parliament, declares he and his party must return to America because "our minds are dwindling here" (2:327).

Oddly enough, however, in this land of regeneration, there seem to be no survivors. By the end of the narrative, Logan is dead, along with Harold, his brother Oscar, and Loena. The closing pages of the narrative stage the death of the second narrator: it would seem that Logans are dying off as fast as they can spring up. But more to the point, the narrative, despite its aggressive rhetoric and national vision, registers a deep ambivalence about the value of its own terms, most severely, the aim, scope, and legacy of the Father.

As I have suggested above, the affective value of symbolic fatherhood is the heart of the novel. The (second?) narrator begins the story proper as an ode to (the overwhelming idea of) the Father: "The father—I feel my heart growing warm again, as I recall the dear, dear spot to my remembrance and if I do not soon take my eyes from the picture that is, at this instant, assembling itself before me limb by limb; and feature by feature, I shall grow sick at heart, weary of my appointed trial, and throw aside my pen forever, fainting in the very wretchedness of spirit. But there is a cure for this—the father!—at his name I revive, my faculties arouse themselves. Let us talk of the father then . . . I will imitate him!" (2:11). As for the narrator, so too the protagonist. Over and again, in passages dizzying in rhetorical excess, Harold variously "claims" as fathers men of authority in his life—the British governor, the French governor of Quebec de Vaudreuil, God, and his "biological" father, Logan—and desires to claim "but dared not" numerous others (2:93; see also 1:244–45).

For instance, early in the novel, we see Harold denouncing Logan (whom he does not yet clearly remember as his father) to the British governor, an excoriation that ends in Harold's tentative expression of interest in the health of the governor, "my *father*" (1:64): "'Give me thy hand, Harold, my son!' cried the governour, pulling him down on his bosom—'yes, Harold, I *will* be thy father, and thou shalt be my son. God bless thee for the thought, Harold! God forever bless thee! my poor boy! There is none left, now, none! to dispute my title'" (1:65). The governor immediately asks Harold to renounce his vow to scalp Logan. This is a promise clearly difficult for the passionate Harold to make. But after an (erotic) agony, motored by his new spiritual union with the governor/father, Harold delivers up the promise: "The silence that followed [the governor's request] was uninterrupted for many minutes, by aught, but the supressed difficult breathing of Harold, who appeared occupied in some profound study. He sat with his hands strongly pressed upon his forehead, his eyes glittering, motionless. Their heads almost touched, as they leaned towards each other; the sweat was upon their lips . . . At length, with a deep hollow sigh, he lifted his head" (1:65–66). Within pages, Harold will enact a similar (and similarly eroticized) scene, from the son's claim of recognition to his promised submission to the desires of his "father":

> "Thy son!" [Harold] articulated, as their cheeks touched, "thy son! Oh God! my father! my father!"
> For minutes they were locked to each other, soul and body.
> (1:109)

Logan informs Harold he is dying, wounded by the Iroquois and two of his compatriots, who earlier identified him as a "white" man. He demands that Harold forgive them and forbear from revenging his death on them. Harold replies in the terms of a marriage vow:

> "Choose thou thy course. Avoid blood shed. Wilt thou forgive them? Speak, speak quickly my son."
> "I will, I do."
> "Well then. Now swear that thou wilt pursue the whites to extermination, day and night, forever and ever—" "Father!" (1:110)

Soon, Harold will be claiming yet another, de Vaudreuil, as "Father!" and submitting to his wishes—this time a less dramatic demand that he travel to Europe for an education.

A desire to be *repeatedly* recognized by the Father powers Harold, and indeed, this story. By contrast, the narrative places virtually no value on *fathering;* the recognition the Father can bestow in the form of "inheritance" and authority upon anxious sons bears literally no relation to the material and emotional duties of biological parentage, as we see when Harold's son Leopold (by Elvira, one-time wife of the British governor) dies virtually unnoticed by Harold.[64]

This odd disjunction between rejected fathering and the desire to be subordinate to a Father points up a key feature of the narrative: its perspective is insistently governed by that of the anxious son, demanding fatherly recognition from virtually every masculine source—and most especially, from men with power.[65] In fact, the narrative closes with the second narrator delivering his deathbed demand that Britain dignify (U.S.) America with exactly such recognition: "you will acknowledge us, as we are, the strongest (though boastful and arrogant) progeny of yourselves" (2:340). This excessive desire of "sons" for the fatherly recognition overfills the Father as a symbolic category, suggesting the value of Deleuze and Guattari's more politicized understanding of oedipalization in order to reconceptualize the anxieties that propel the specific narrativization of this desire.

It is not a stretch—as the passages I've been quoting amply advertise—to argue that *Logan* maps how the homoerotics of white male democratic culture, and of increasingly masculinized work and social culture in the early nation, was narratively rerouted through heterosexual domesticity ("a family romance")—through symbolic father-son relations and through incestuously heterosexual relations with women who circulate between father and son, brother and brother.[66] Or to cast this in terms of my prior suggestion that we read this novel as a national narrative, *Logan* forwards national manhood as a structure of identity that is aggressively homosocial, disciplinarily heterosexual, and structurally, if tacitly here, homophobic. Even more particular to my interests though is the way the novel attempts repeatedly to route the homoerotic energies generated within masculine competition into hierarchized relationships between men based on affection and devotion—on the symbolic son's desire for loving subordination to symbolic fathers. In other words, even in positions of authority, the national oedipalization suggested in *Logan* guarantees that men will experience the anxieties of the son. They are unable to conceptualize the enjoyment of the Father (let alone fathering), because they are always standing emotionally apart from His place, seeking His recognition in the experience of loving subordination.

In this sense, the novel points toward the ideological consolidation

of "friendly inequality," which, Christopher Newfield argues, came to
structure democratic liberalism and its subject, the "corporate individual," by mid-century.[67] In the specific terms of my arguments in
this chapter, the novel's obsession with loving subordination between
men emphasizes a dynamic similar to the one I highlighted in my
discussion of the Lewis and Clark narrative, in which commentators alternately cast the two men as equals (in authority over the
other men of the party), or stage Lewis as the expedition's "father." In
Harold's repetitive claiming of symbolic fathers, we can more clearly
locate the affective dimensions of the history of ambivalence between
fatherly leadership and fraternal equality. Here, we can see fraternal
anxiety in its doubled aspect, a complex worry over both *equality* (experienced as equivalence) and *inequality*.

Recognizing this tension in emerging ideals of U.S. fraternality,
an anxiety that suspends men between their fear of being excluded
from the cultural capital of civic (white) manhood and of being made
interchangeable by it, allows us to analyze how, though the novel
forwards a "blood brotherhood," it is able to imagine fraternity only
as it is able to conceptualize fatherhood: symbolically. There is no
actual fraternity in *Logan*. Oscar and Harold, like Harold and Leopold,
have no motivating interest in or affectional bonds with each other;
more clearly, in their alternating sexual relationships with Elvira and
Loena, they are competitors. Harold is an isolated man, which the
narrator goes to great lengths to caption as both choice and the consequence of his superiority: "His ambition was silent, meditative,
solemn. His deep voice, his gathered brow . . . the fearful steadiness
and lustre of his eye . . . the bright, eager, broad flash of mind that
broke out, when he was suddenly excited were altogether so significant of a peculiar and high intelligence, that the most familiar of his
daily associates, those with whom he went about the commonest affairs of earth, constantly beheld him with an instinctive and profound
veneration. This was not shown in words, for, indeed, they hardly
knew it, and would never have acknowledged it themselves" (1:144).
This, seemingly, is Jefferson's "natural aristocracy," an equalizing philosophy that promised to do away with artificially maintained social
hierarchies. But, the novel belatedly reveals, it is biological aristocracy too, an imaginary melding of George of Salisbury's line with
Jefferson's romanticized Mingo "chief"—an equivocating jointure of
aristocratic legacies with democratic practice. *Logan* seems to want it
both ways, and it seems unable to commit to either.

The narrator assures the reader of Harold's ultimate suitability for fraternal relations, emphasizing Harold's ability to cultivate "passion and admiration" among men. "Harold never attempted to make a friend, even of an enemy—but he succeeded. He never trifled, no unhallowed levity was about him. But if he smiled, indeed; brief but delightful" (1:144). (We might see this manly ideal still in healthy circulation a century later in Wister's *Virginian*.) Despite the narrator's efforts, though, these assurances provide less a vision of fraternal equality than of what Newfield summarizes as "anxiously hierarchical, democratic heterosexuality: love no one as you love the master" (*Emerson* 128)—a social arena where men should experience isolation as noble superiority, watching always for powerful men to call "Father!" Beyond the Iroquois who (attempt to) murder Logan, the novel is nowhere able to depict a functional "brotherhood." In fact, the narrative begins with a denunciation of the narrator's compatriots that we might read as a practical refutation of the American fraternal ideal: "I do not dedicate my book to any body; for I know nobody worth dedicating it to. I have no friends, no children, no wife, no home—no relations, no well-wishers;—nobody to love and nobody to care for. To whom shall I; to whom *can* I dedicate it? To my Maker! It is unworthy of him. To my countrymen? They are unworthy of me" (preface, unnumbered). The novel's narrator is presumably speaking from the period of the novel's publication; it is not entirely unwarranted to urge that we read the narrator's obvious hostility to his fraternal compatriots in the early nation through the lens of Neal's biography—losing his father in youth, having his pacifism beat out of him, strategizing his career frenetically, and with increasing anger watching one route after another close in financial failure. As a corrective, we might speculate that Neal offers a national genealogy, an imagined community structured by symbolic fatherhood to provide an imaginary haven from the agon of competition that was increasingly an ineluctable feature of U.S. capitalist citizenship.

But even in the shelter of this imagined community, there is no relief. The construction of these imagined families between men do *nothing* to ameliorate the terms of their competition: Logan, not recognizing his son, kills Harold at the end of the novel.

The trend of my reading suggests, then, that the centrality of symbolic fatherhood in *Logan*, and in the early nation, may have been less a sign, as Fliegelman argues, of patriarchy's *rejection* than of what Newfield terms its "transistorization": "The transistorization of nineteenth-century group circuitry only allowed libido switching to make a father out of anyone. . . . The beauty of such a democracy is that it makes democracy entirely compatible with hierarchical patriarchy" (*Emerson* 111–12). If transistorization made democracy among (white) men compatible with hierarchical patriarchy, it simultaneously functioned to disguise its own central effect through the palliative agency of "choice." Anxious Sons *chose* their "patriarch"— imaginatively domesticating (family/iarizing) their competition even as they subordinated themselves to it. They constructed a narrative of willing and loving submission, and explained the effects of that subordination in the symbolically resonant terms of fatherly love. Transistorized fatherhood thereby offered both a means to manage recognitions of, and to domesticate anxieties about, (in)equality among white men in the early nation.

If emergent ideologies of corporate liberalism allowed men to domesticate anxieties about democracy and individualism within capitalism in the terms of loving subjection, that reconceptualization entailed their more thoroughly internalizing unequal results of capitalism as their own failures. The advantage of whiteness for men, then, perhaps more immediately than the cultural capital it entailed in the marketplace of democracy, was the disavowal and projection of internal fragmentation that it allowed—even while flexibly identifying with imagined aspects of its Others, even while remaining relatively, or entirely invisible to itself as such, as I have shown in my readings of Jefferson, Lewis and Clark, Biddle, and Neal. What I am foregrounding here is perhaps best described as a chain of political, economic, social, and psychic displacement that runs through, fragments, and then racially (re)unites the white nation/male. My analysis insists—particularly in the context of Marxist, feminist, and postcolonial theories that have so profoundly influenced me—on the importance of reading, without reducing, the human costs for men who variously struggled with and in white manhood in the early nation, while refusing to qualify or sentimentalize its real effects on others. Inasmuch as white women, Native Americans, and Africans came to be explicitly—scientifically and popularly—Othered during this period, their national minoritization came as a counterphobic remedy to white men's experience of their own (in)equality. As the conjunction of materials in my study suggests, this counterphobic consolidation of white manhood came *multiply*, through the "claiming" of the cultural capital of whiteness by (emergently) working-class men, as historians like Roediger and Allen, and social critics like Lott have so carefully and insightfully detailed, and through the corollary claiming of professional status for civic management by (emergently) middle-class men.

Political access converged with scientific discourse to produce structures of containment for the abstract community of national manhood and for the somewhat less abstract interests of the middle classes as they began to consolidate their managerial aims in the terms of "career" status. When Lewis and Clark arrived in Washington, D.C., in 1807, Jefferson details how Congress "granted the two chiefs and their followers the donation of lands which they had been encouraged to expect in reward of their toils and dangers" ("Memoir" xxxviii). Like George of Salisbury, the force of the captains' will and the fact of their achievement entitled the explorers to occupy title ("chiefs") and lands. But even more to the point, as Jefferson continues, "Captain Lewis was soon after appointed Governor of Louisiana and Captain Clark a General of its militia and Agent of the United States for Indian affairs in that department" (xxxviii)—appointed as official managers of the lands and Indians they so ably surveyed.

The "Indian" has served ably as a multiuse repository for the burdens of national, as well as professional and class formation since Boston's "tea party." Jefferson's interest in Indian mounds and Lewis and Clark's repeated pleasure at the "prospect" of the country from atop them, would soon transform into Ephraim Squier's professional excavation of such mounds (what he and his scientific friends called "moundology") for the purposes of Samuel George Morton's project of racial categorization, the dynamics of which I take up in the next chapter. In the same historical moment, imagined occupations of Indian identity found organized expression in the Fraternal Order of Red Men, who claimed as their date of "founding" the year of 1492, and whose induction ceremony, "Inindianation," serves well to encapsulate the complex aims and effects of what I have described here.[68]

3

"Our Castle Still Remains Unshaken": Professional Manhood, Science, Whiteness

Early in the years that science began consolidating as a middle-class career domain in the United States, Samuel George Morton gained his first professional recognition by describing the fossils collected by the Lewis and Clark Expedition. This project made him, as Thomas Gossett notes, "the founder of invertebrate paleontology in this country" (58). He would win international recognition as the "father" of another scientific project—the "American school" of anthropology—by measuring and cataloging Indian skulls. Through a carefully built network of casual-scientist contributors all over the Americas, and through a few well-placed friends like mound excavator Ephraim Squier, Morton amassed hundreds of aboriginal crania for his measurements. We have seen how Lewis and Clark rationally discredited tribal superstitions, offering scientific documentation for Native inferiority by athletically scaling sacred mounds of Indian remains. The similarly intrepid Squier excavated such mounds so that Morton, measuring crania with bird shot, could scientifically "document" the source of native superstition: their "smaller" cranial capacity.

Morton's most decisive and enduring contribution to the professionalization of science came not so much from his "proof" that aboriginal crania were smaller than Caucasian,[1] but from the use he put them toward: developing his arguments on behalf of polygenesis. This was the scientific theory that argued for separate racial origins, insisting that different "races" were in fact diversely originating species. Morton began his work to establish the separate origin of the races in the 1830s, an era that was marked in the United States by rampant land-speculation and economic inflation followed by market panics and depression; by the "universalization" of white male suffrage and of professional/white collar employment; by Indian removal; by the emergence of domestic ideology; and by a marked intensification of abolitionist organization. In this chapter, I want first to examine an episode in abolitionist debate before turning to consider how that debate anchors another key episode, this one in the professionalization of science. In particular, I want to challenge the terms of traditional analyses of Morton's famous debate with Bachman over polygenesis in the late 1840s. My own reading suggests that it is worth paying more attention to the racialization not just of the "white" working class(es) but also of the "white" middle classes in their transition from merchants to managers. My interest in this particular episode lies in the way it lets us begin considering how, as middle-class manhood began to articulate itself through professional title, it took up the imperatives of national manhood, claiming for its own particular provenance the terms of rational objectivity and scientific, civic management. In so doing, (emerging) middle-class professionals secured a style of managerial expertise,[2] the fundamental trait of which Collette Guillaumin has summarized as the "occultation of the Self." This style of authority interwove the strategies of scientific discourse with the agendas of domesticating manhood, arrogating the prerogatives of that union for men of the middle classes.[3] It ensured the ability of this professional class of managers to stabilize and reproduce their own authority in captioned and ever-multiplying displays of the "other."

Science's disavowal of Morton's theories should not lead us to overlook science's revalidation of Morton's professional status, nor should it lead us to ignore his enormous cultural influence as a scientific architect of whiteness. The "factual" popularity of Morton's work did much to consolidate whiteness as a natural identity category and an exclusionary political and social logic, and it did so with a power that continues to manage our understanding of that episode to this day. Reconsidering this episode helps us attend not just to the ways Morton's science worked to articulate whiteness simultaneously as a powerfully exclusionary domain and a universalized standpoint, but also to the ways polygenesis helped culturally to undergird an emerging, specifically white, middle-class cultural hegemony.[4] And even more specifically, my reading of this episode will point toward the importance of heeding the social power of "white" middle-class women, claimed through rhetorics of civic virtue (Republican Motherhood), and of "sympathy." Polygenesis provides a cultural logic that locates and refutes the politically and emotionally miscegenational works of female domestic reformers. My framing arguments for this episode thus also outline the way emerging gynecology would provide a way to extend and actualize the purity campaign of polygenesis—its "natural repugnance" from all contaminatory mixing—into the space of sentiment, the domestic, female space.

I

Pardon the Americanism

Lydia Maria Child published her *An Appeal in Favor of that Class of Americans Called Africans* (1834) early in a career that spanned more than five decades. This unusual text followed two novels, a series of short stories, and a number of domestic advice books, including her popular *The Frugal Housewife* (1829). Child's attentiveness to race and gender issues in her early career carried into her abolitionist compendium history of slavery. Carolyn L. Karcher notes that, "Although the *Appeal* violates the prevailing norms of feminine discourse by its very engagement in political controversy, as well as by its authoritative display of erudition and its preoccupation with such matters as law, economics, and congressional apportionment, it simultaneously presents a woman's perspective on slavery. Repeatedly, Child focuses on the special ways in which slavery victimizes women and makes a mockery of the domestic ideology glorifying 'true womanhood'" (185). *An Appeal* was unprecedented in the scope of its historical sweep and the synthesizing quality of an argument grounded in political, economic, social, and theological history. Child's study was radical in two specific respects: for the originality of her willingness to analyze how the maintenance of slavery depended internationally on racial, gender, and class despotism, and for her defiance of gender norms in forwarding abolitionist arguments against laws prohibiting intermarriage.

From the outset, Child is at pains to detail how "the white man's avarice" has fueled the institutionalization of slavery (11). Very early on she directs readers' attention to "the influence of slavery on the *'white man's* character'": "The very first step in their business is a deliberate invasion of the rights of others; it combines every form of violence, bloodshed, tyranny and anguish" (16; original emphasis). But Child counterintuitively leaves documenting white men's cruelty toward slaves for later in the volume, and turns instead to examine their cruelty toward subordinate white men: "There is a great waste of life among white seamen employed in this traffic, in consequence of the severe punishment they receive and diseases originating in the unwholesome atmosphere on board" (16–17). Citing the British abolitionist, Thomas Clarkson (1760–1846), Child points out that sailor mortality is forty times higher per trip on a slaver ship than on other expeditions, and argues that the difference is directly attributable to a combination of "cruelty" and disease: "The instances are exceedingly numerous of sailors on board slave-ships, that have died under the lash or in consequence of it" (17). Not only could this class of men depend on being physically abused by their social superiors, they could bet on being financially cheated by them: "the wages of the sailors were half paid in the currency of the country where the vessel carried her slaves; and thus they were actually lower than in other trades, while they were nominally higher" (17). If the appeal of whiteness in the early United States was its promise to equalize male citizens, Child begins her arguments against race-based slavery by pointedly exposing the myth that stood for its logic. One notable contribution of her volume to the abolitionist debate is a focus on gender in terms of women's experiences as slaves and slaveholders; another important aspect is surely her surprising gender analysis of the white men's exploitation of "fellow" white men.

Child's analysis takes national unity formulated through human equality as its central aim; over and again she highlights the ways in which slavery works to divide humanity *and* nation along fault lines of race, gender, class, and region: "Instead of calmly examining this important subject on the plain grounds of justice and humanity, we allow it to degenerate into a mere question of *sectional* pride and vanity. [Pardon the Americanism, would we had less *use* for the word!] It is the *system*, not the *men*, on which we ought to bestow the full measure of abhorrence" (30; original emphasis and brackets).[5] As she would throughout her career, Child refuses to reduce slavery and racial prejudice to a question of personality, but rather analyzes them as national institutions, insisting that passive acquiescence functions as institutional maintenance. Her method for redressing this combines moral suasion with middle-class manners, actually attempting to marshal the mannered culture of passivity toward reform: "All are not able to do so much as Anthony Benezet and John Kendrick have done; but we can all do something. We can speak kindly and respectfully of colored people upon all occasions; we can repeat to our children such traits as are honorable in their character and history; we can avoid making odious caricatures of negroes; we can teach boys that it is unmanly and contemptible to insult an unfortunate class of people by the vulgar outcry of "Nigger!—Nigger!" . . . If we are not able to contribute to African schools, or do not choose to do so, at least we can refrain from opposing them. If it be disagreeable to allow colored people the same rights and privileges as other citizens, we can do with our prejudice, what most of us often do with better feeling— we can conceal it" (215). Though these admonitions seem both laughable and frustratingly white bourgeois now, I urge readers to consider how, in calling on the class whose penultimate boundary-defense was "manners," Child ends her *Appeal* insisting that "manners" be turned toward practices of inclusiveness. Child's argument in this instance is an extension (and perhaps a reduction) of her understanding of the way manners reflected the state boundary apparatus: laws against intermarriage. Child unveils the alchemy of laws and manners designed to protect class homogeneity, by refiguring class as a police-force for "race": "I know two or three instances where women of the laboring class have been united to reputable, industrious colored men. These husbands regularly bring home their wages, and are kind to their families. If . . . their wives should become heirs to their property, the children may be wronged out of it, because the law pronounces them illegitimate. And while this injustice exists with regard to *honest*, industrious individuals, who are merely guilty of differing from us in a matter of taste, neither the legislation nor customs of slaveholding States exert their influence against *immoral* connections" (196–97; original emphases). For Child, domestic morality could only be certified through civic inclusiveness and heterogeneity. But according to James Kirke Paulding, who weighed in with his counter-history, *Slavery in the United States* in 1836, the nation's domestic harmony could only be protected through the recognition of its racial exclusiveness, precisely by guarding its (supposed) racial homogeneity.

In the earliest of his many reversals of Child's arguments, Paulding insists that her so-called inclusive philanthropy is really a form of exclusion, the exclusion of whites: "In applying . . . the great precept of the Saviour to the blacks alone, and considering them as our neighbors to the entire exclusion of the whites, we place the latter in the relation of stranger and alien; we cast them out of the pale of human nature and make them victims of our one-sided philanthropy" (33). Paulding here makes clear the very different terms of his argument, that "races" are separated not primarily by law or custom, but by a complex interweaving of custom and manly exertion that both asserts and certifies nature. Both race and nation are patrimonial grants in Paulding's argument: "The government of the United States, its institutions, and its privileges, belong wholly and exclusively to the white men; for they were purchased not by the blood of negroes, but by that of our fathers" (42). In a curious twist on the notion of patrilineal "purchase," Paulding later grants that the United States exists on territory the largest portion of which was obtained by "conquest alone" from Indian tribes. Echoing Neal's logic in *Logan*, Paulding insists that "however defective such a title may be originally, it acquires force and authority by the lapse of time" (97). The force of law over a period of time constitutes natural races and legitimate possessions (in other words: sure we stole it, but we held onto it fair and square). His "logic" here provides a nice diagram of Guillaumin's argument that over the course of the eighteenth and nineteenth centuries, "biological continuity came to replace juridical continuity" in the enforcement of race (41).

Paulding is forced by the terms of Child's arguments about intrarace class exploitation to frame an argument that will salvage "white" unity without disrupting its (useful) class divisions. He appeals to a God who functions with the economic wisdom of Adam Smith's "invisible hand": "The Saviour of mankind, in propounding that pure, rational, practical and perfect system of morals and religions under which we live, refrained from all innovation on the civil institutions of the nations to which he addressed himself. . . . His principles are of universal application; and his precepts can never, without the most impudent perversion, be made to sanction violations of private property or public law" (291). Though he acknowledges discrepancies in wealth inside the national "family," Paulding reminds his readers of the universal benefits of civic inclusion: "It is here alone, of all the civilized regions of the earth, that he equally shares the opportunities of fortune and the rights of a citizen" (266), arguing elsewhere that there are no "natural" distinctions between the white men of Europe that an "equal distribution of civil and political rights" wouldn't redress (270). Such passages concisely evoke Alan Dawley and Paul Faler's argument that in the 1820s and 1830s, the trend toward universal white manhood suffrage worked to dampen the potential for class-based political movements in a period of increasing economic inequality: "Just as inequality waxed in economics, it seemed to wane in politics" (475).[6] Thus Paulding invokes the very national/racial mythology of manly equality that Child sought to unpack.

One of the more fascinating aspects of Paulding's response (one that seemingly confirms my assumption that he is in fact responding to Child's arguments) is the way he draws an argumentative line straight from fears of fragmenting national fraternity to men's remediative domestic management of white women. At the outset of his argument, Paulding argues: "in asserting the natural rights of one class of men, the constitutional rights of another have been denounced as violations of the law of god; and . . . a ferocious, unrelenting, unbrotherly warfare has been, still is, waging against a large portion of the good citizens of the United States, which, if continued, must inevitably separate this prosperous and happy Union into discordant and conflicting elements, that, instead of co-operating in the one great end of human happiness, will be productive only of contention and ruin" (6). He concludes by identifying the agency of abolition as female: "From the various notices we have seen of abolition meetings in Boston and elsewhere, it would appear that the abolition societies consist principally of females" (309). In the final paragraph of the volume, Paulding, "with respectful deference to the sex, which is the distinguishing characteristic of freemen" (309-10) remands women to the domestic sphere: "It is not at midnight meetings of conspirators against the repose and integrity of the United States; nor in listening to the brawling declamations of sublimated incendiaries, advocating violations of the laws of man as well as the decorums of woman, that she can qualify herself for the fulfilment of those sacred duties, the performance of which makes her the guardian angel for the happiness of man; his protector and mentor in childhood; his divinity in youth; his companion and solace in manhood; his benign and gentle nurse in old age. Thus she is twice his mother; once in the cradle and again on the verge of his grave; and thus while supporting the fabric of men's happiness she lays the surest basis for her own, in the bosom of HOME" (311-12; original emphasis; NB: "HOME" is the last word of the text). Paulding fights Child's arguments for racial integration (or incorporation) by characterizing them as a national prostitution (cf. 62–63; 310). As corrective discipline, he insists on more thoroughgoing feminization of white women—responding, it would seem, as much to Child's "unladylike" arguments on behalf of social and sexual intercourse as to her explicit and indemnifying analysis of the economic fractures within the community of white manhood.

Paulding shrewdly suggests a change of venue for the abolitionist debate at several points in his argument. Rather than engaging Child's moral/philanthropic argument on its own ground, or trying to counter it with political or economic arguments, Paulding insists that science will provide the most proper arena for the debate. Certainly, "science" did enthusiastically take up the debate during this period, and it is worth remembering in this context that early U.S. science was considered internationally distinctive in only two areas—racial science and gynecology. While I do not wish to argue here that early U.S. science was simply the handmaiden of national manhood, I do want to draw out the ways that their interests interwove in a particular historical moment, in the context of a particular set of cultural imperatives.

Paulding seconds with far less "diffidence" Jefferson's opinion that African and African-descended peoples "are inferior in the faculties of reason and imagination" (*Notes* 143; cf. Paulding, *Slavery* 65–66). In noting that "the difference seems more than skin-deep," Paulding echoes Jefferson's interest in relocating questions of what Paulding terms "the universal sentiment of our race" (antiblack prejudice) from the realm of the social to the domain of the biologized, anatomized body. Indeed, racial science would soon efficiently remap the social and political arguments of the abolitionist debate to the spaces of human interiority.

II

Remembering Polygenesis

Dr. Samuel George Morton (1799–1851) was at the historical center of the scientific debate over polygenesis in the United States. This was a debate that had far-reaching historical and geographical influence. As Robert J. C. Young observes, "it was the Americans who invented the terms, though not the ideas, of monogenesis and polygenesis" (*Colonial Desire* 123). Morton had studied at the great race theory medical schools in Europe (Edinburgh and Paris) after taking his degree in Philadelphia. As Professor of Anatomy at the University of Pennsylvania, he began collecting human crania for research in 1830, "in which year having occasion to deliver an introductory lecture on Anatomy, it occurred to me to illustrate the differences in the form of the skull as seen in the five great races of men" (Morton, *Catalogue* 1849). With the aid of medical colleagues, casual scientists, and foreign diplomats,

Morton gradually amassed over nine hundred skulls, building the largest crania collection in the world by the time of his death.[7] The great majority of the collection was devoted to skulls of Native Americans, out of which Morton published his first major work, *Crania Americana* (1839). Here, in a prefatory essay on the various "families of men," Morton began carefully to build his case for the separate origins of the "great races" by invoking distinctive differences in cranial shape, as well as in mean cranial capacity of the racial groupings.

A substantial section of the collection was supplied by George Gliddon, U.S. Consul in Cairo, who indulged an avid interest in Egyptian tomb excavation. Morton categorized these skulls as "Ancient Caucasian" and "Ancient Negroid" and based his second major work, *Crania AEgyptiaca* on them (1844).[8] In this work, he was able extensively to confirm a hunch that he noted in his first work, where he speculatively rejected the "supposed affinity between the Egyptians and the Negroes" (*Americana* 29). From his examination of ancient crania of Egyptians and "negroids," Morton argued that not only were there different cranial capacities in the ancient "white" and "black" races, but that these significantly corresponded with contemporary differences. Thus he was able scientifically to corroborate his suggestion that the "races" had been "separate" from the start, firmly seizing the achievements of ancient Egyptian culture for the category of "white," and discrediting abolitionists like Child, who argued against notions of African inferiority partially on the basis of the achievements of Egyptian civilization (Child 150–51).[9]

In 1849, Morton published a compendium catalogue, where he felt able, at last, to document conclusively what he seemingly set out to find in 1830: a hierarchical difference in the cranial capacities of the various "races." In thirty skulls culled from the most favored "Teutonic family," (Germans, English, and Anglo-Americans), Morton found an average nine-cubic-inch cranial superiority over the average of seventy-four "Native African" and "American-born Negro" skulls in his collection.[10] Morton's deployment of the term "race" was absolutely central to the construction of his cranial researches. Morton's contemporaries, working under the assumption that humans originated from the same stock (namely Adam and Eve) typically used the word interchangeably for the Linnean subcategory of "species": "variety." But Morton, with increasing emphasis, used the word "race" to designate the more exclusive category of species. In 1847, bolstered by the support for his work, as well as by his friendly working partnerships with George Gliddon, Josiah Nott, Ephraim Squier, and Louis Agassiz, Morton began to say in print what he had been arguing in anatomy lectures at least since 1844: that the five "great races" sprang from different "primitive centres" thus indicating that "race" indeed designated distinctive "species" of men.

For the purposes of scientific history, Morton's attempt to document a polygenesis of human races is a dead letter. Not only is the theory of separate origins now considered by (most) professionally accredited scientists to be incorrect, but also, the cranial measurements upon which the theory rested have been entirely discredited.[11] Yet William Stanton, in his still-definitive history of nineteenth-century polygenesis, finds both historical and scientific value in Morton's legacy. "Despite Morton's primary concern with raciology," Stanton argues that he was working on precisely the same puzzle as Darwin, the fixity of the species (116). Along with that inquiry, and as important in Stanton's estimate, Morton's work led the way toward modern science's decisive break with the superstitious biases of theological naturalism in the United States, paving the way toward its expanded and professionalized status.[12] Stanton insists that polygenesis should not be remembered as a disgrace to the record of scientific progress: not only was it not completely "wrong," its errors did not result from lack of scientific objectivism. He discounts the notion that political motives drove any of the pro-polygenesists excepting Josiah Nott: "the conscious extrascientific bond which linked many of these men together was not sympathy for Southern institutions but anticlericalism and anti-biblicism" (193). This "extrascientific bond"—an opposition to the interpretive stranglehold of Christianity—rather than tainting these men's scientific motives, actually served as the enabling condition for the emergence of modern science. Thus Stanton frames the scientific errors of the polygenesists as scientific growing pains.[13]

More recent historians of science, often disputing the quality of Stanton's enthusiasm for the polygenesist scientists, still tend to confirm two of his basic arguments: that the "best" of the polygenesists demonstrated a commitment to good (that is, objective) science, and that they ushered the way toward modern, professional science, out of the dark ages of its affiliations with and bondage to Christian biblical exegesis. Gould, who offers the strongest critique of polygenesist science and disagrees with Stanton on the value of Morton's work to scientific history, reluctantly confirms Stanton's assessment of Morton's scientific detachment, highlighting as "the most intriguing aspect of the case" that it is virtually impossible to portray Morton as anything but disinterested and objective, that is, a good scientist. Gould was able to find "no evidence of conscious fraud; indeed, had Morton been a conscious fudger, he would not have published his data so openly" (*Mismeasure* 54; see also 68–69). Robert Bruce views the episode as evidence of the "racism that polluted the mind of antebellum America from top to bottom." Yet his conclusion otherwise coincides with Stanton's, that "in the long run, the 'American school of ethnology' was significant . . . [to science] for investigating hybridization as a mechanism of variation and for weakening religious fundamentalism" (124–25). Unable to find evidence for an explicit agenda against "blacks," Gould puzzles over the "honest self-delusion" of Morton's work, noting that "Morton was widely hailed as the objectivist of his age, the man who would rescue American science from the mire of unsupported speculation" (*Mismeasure* 69).[14] Unable to conceptualize science as anything other than progression from superstition to factual knowledge, Bruce must maintain the "value" of this otherwise discredited scientific legacy for scientific modernity.

For social historians interested in charting the development and modifications of racist thinking in the United States, the impact of polygenesis both inside and outside the scientific community becomes important. Following Stanton's cue and long national habit, these historians often cast the question of support for polygenesis in terms of North-South sectionalism. For instance, though Wilson Carey McWilliams notes that "more than a few" in the North showed enthusiasm for Morton's theory, he documents at length only its Southern cheerleaders. Similarly, George M. Fredrickson glances at Morton's apparent political disinterestedness and focuses on Nott, an Alabama physician whose "preconceived racial attitudes probably drew him to ethnology in the first place" (78). Most historians signal surprise at Morton's involvement, because he was from the North, and because he didn't own slaves.[15] Such a focus works repeatedly to suggest that the South is where racism resides, thereby downplaying Northern racism and investments in racist institutions privileging whiteness.[16] The tendency of this regional focus is to make racism coterminous with an involvement in slavery, a formula that operates to keep good science separate from a political interest in slavery, and by extension, racism. John Bachman (one of Morton's opponents) and Josiah Nott (one of his supporters), both Southerners, owned slaves and were therefore agenda-driven, interested pseudoscientists; Morton, a Northerner, did not own slaves, and therefore, though his work in craniology now looks more like racism than science, we can safely conclude that he was in fact a well-intended and disinterested (objective), if finally mistaken, scientist.

I am concerned with what these binaristic oppositions—science vs. religion, science vs. racism, objectivity vs. slaveholding, North vs. South—allow us to miss in our reading of this historical record, which is precisely the way whiteness works as a sociopolitical/scientific construct and a gendered domain. For instance, Gould indicates that "prevalence of *unconscious* finagling [of scientific data] . . . suggests a general conclusion about the social context of science" demanding a reconsideration of the "myth that science itself is an objective enterprise" (*Mismeasure* 55–65, 21; original emphasis). Yet in his inability to explain Morton's "honest . . . self-delus[ion]," Gould still falls prey to the mystification these binaries enable. If racism is measured only insofar as and when it is violently enacted on the bodies of "dark" others, then "racism" cannot be read as such in the moments where it simply benefits—consolidates the affective, political, sociological domain of—whiteness. The inability of historians and critics to engage such analysis in this episode suggests that the ideological construction of whiteness is more difficult to focus on—more subtle in its permutations—than whiteness's construction of blackness. It would seem, then, that this is precisely the direction—the direction of whiteness—we must look if we are to really understand the national, institutional durability of white racism.

In other words, the insight these various puzzled historians seem to be missing is this: Morton's "prejudice" did not necessarily have to be against "black" people for it to work on behalf of racist practices and structures. Rather, Morton's prejudice seems to have been located in supporting whiteness. Seeing this allows us to begin assessing the ways scientific calculations of racial hierarchy consolidated the discursive, subjective, and professional spaces of white, scientific manhood. We know that Morton corresponded perhaps more extensively and regularly with Josiah Nott than with any other of his political and scientific friends excepting George Gliddon—and that both of these men regularly used the term "niggerology" when referring to Morton's "craniology" in their letters to Morton. And we also know that Morton rushed Secretary of State John C. Calhoun an advance copy of *Crania AEgyptiaca* for his use in preparing negotiations over

the annexation of Texas and the question of slavery with the international community (see Fredrickson 77; William Stanton 61–63). Thus,
though Morton did not have any pecuniary interest in supporting
racism on behalf of slavery, it is still possible to adduce from the
record of his scientific work, correspondence, and political affiliations that he did have, as Gould notes, a powerful (if for Gould finally
inexplicable) interest in racial hierarchy. We come closer, perhaps, to
understanding that interest by examining more closely the permutations of one argument fundamental to Morton's polygenesis theory.

Natural Repugnance

When Morton set out to accredit his argument that the human "races"
were separately originating species, he faced a powerfully "self-evident" refutation: the fact that the so-called black and white "species"
could, against all rules, successfully interbreed. Acknowledging the
fertility of cross-"racial" unions meant, by the Linnaean criterion,
identifying "race" as *variety*. So to have his "species," Morton had
to discredit the axiomatic test. He therefore makes a series of related claims. First, invoking examples from ancient and contemporary anecdotal sources, he argues at length that some species in
rare instances can successfully produce fertile offspring (e.g., Equines,
Bovines, Ovines [sheep], deer, camels, dogs, cats, birds; cf. "Hybridity
in Animals" 203–10). This capability, which Morton terms "latent
hybridity," exists particularly in animals that are most amenable to
domestication. By extension, since humans are the most highly developed of "domestic" animals, Morton argues that it stands to reason
that their "latent hybridity" would likewise be most fully developed,
therefore permitting more extensive hybridity (or miscegenation, as
it would later come to be called). For these reasons, argues Morton,
"hybridity ceases to be a test of specific affiliation" ("Hybridity in
Animals" 212).

Postulating this, Morton must still account for the otherwise fully
explanatory value of Linnaean categories. So he then argues, "If different species mixed their breed, and hybrid races were often propa-
gated, the animal world would present a scene of confusion. By what
method is the confusion prevented? The fact seems to be, that the
tribes of wild animals are preserved distinctly, not only by the sterility of mules, but that such animals are never, in the state of nature,
brought into existence. The separation of distinct species is suffi-

ciently provided for by the natural repugnance between individuals of different kinds" ("Hybridity in Animals" 210). It is in Morton's theory of "natural repugnance" that we could begin to trace some ideology manifesting itself as a desire to protect white purity. His theory needs interbreeding, but it seems likely that the same impulse that led him to rank "caucasian" at the top of his catalogue and "negro" at the bottom (separated by multiple intermediary "races") would similarly propel his thinking on hybridity. Thus he cannot resist developing an argument for "natural repugnance" between "races," particularly, as he terms it, between the "two extremes of the *genus Homo*" ("Appendix" 150). Morton argues that, "the repugnance of some human races to mix with others, has only been partially overcome by centuries of proximity, and, above all other means, by the moral degradation consequent to the state of slavery. Not only is this repugnance proverbial among all nations of the European stock among whom negroes have been introduced, but it appears to be almost equally natural to the Africans in their own country, towards such Europeans as have been thrown among them; for with the form a white skin is not more admired than a black one is with us" ("Hybridity in Animals" 210–11). Morton invokes scientific objectivity for his observations about "repugnance" by attributing it bilaterally, thereby universalizing "race" prejudice and proving a natural basis for its particular political manifestations in the United States. Here Morton mines the travel literature of fellow whites Hawkins, Browne, Burkhardt, Caillet, and others for evidence of the "fact" of African "natural repugnance" from non-blacks (see 210–11). He thus paved the way toward rehearsals of so-called "in-group" genetic coding that, as Martin Barker has incisively detailed, still underwrites the racist theorizing of some late-twentieth-century sociobiologists and ethnologists (most recently, Herrnstein and Murray). And, Morton's reliance on an international community of explorers and scientists provides a clear example of Balibar's arguments that whiteness was at the same time a national and an international project (Balibar and Wallerstein, *Race* 43).

In his exchanges with Bachman, Morton's own "natural repugnance" would lead him to contradict further the logical impulse of his own theory of hybridity by arguing, following his friend Josiah Nott, that in the case of "high races" interbreeding with "low" ones, although they might immediately produce fertile offspring, their progeny would, within a few generations, become infertile, thus eventually *confirming* the Linnaean test for species. He does this through a fairly tortured argument, proposing that "natural" evidence points toward the multiplicity of races (read: species) of man, since evolution from one couple (i.e., Adam and Eve) would have created an incestuously weakened population pool:

> There is . . . a physiological objection to the propagation of any animals from a single pair, because this incestuous intercourse tends eventually to the deterioration and extinction of the races that are subjected to it. I do not believe that the earth could ever have been furnished with animals on this plan, unless a miracle had been wrought at every stage of it. The process of breeding *in and in* is extremely difficult and often impossible. . . . [E]ven among our domestic animals, we have a degree of that same difficulty that is proverbial among admitted hybrids. As to man, let us suppose that mulatto offspring of a black man and a white woman (or the reverse) were compelled to marry among themselves, without any access of other individuals of either race, how long do you suppose this mixed breed would last? Not beyond the third or fourth generation. ("Letter to the Rev. John Bachman" 17; original emphasis)

Clearly this is an argument that logically works against Morton (he does not, for instance, seem to be bothered by the implications of "whites" "breeding *in and in*"). Nonetheless, this argument does amply demonstrate Morton's anxieties about demonstrating and maintaining the group purity of whiteness, anxieties that he locates and analyzes here specifically as questions of sexuality.[17] So he postulates a purity both of sexual immediacy (natural repugnance) and of biological eventuality (granting that if the races do "mix," they will eventually be disabled from continuing to do so). One way or the other, it would seem, the security of whiteness can be scientifically corroborated, and thus, as Morton's mailing of *Crania AEgyptiaca* to Calhoun would suggest, implemented as or augmented by social and political policy.

Dark Weirdness

For my interest, finally, the question of *whether* Morton himself was a racist is less interesting than one that would lead to a more careful consideration of the racist praxis that his science—and subsequent scholarly assessments of it—enable. This consideration is disabled if we acquiesce to the binaries that have guided much prior inquiry. Morton's work in craniology and racial categorization did more to credit U.S. science internationally than the work of any of his scientific colleagues before the Civil War. When he died, the *New York Tribune* declared that "probably no scientific man in America enjoyed a higher reputation among scholars throughout the world, than Dr. Morton" (qtd. in W. Stanton 144). Swiss naturalist Anders Retzius wrote to Morton that "you have done more for ethnography than any living physiologist," and he was similarly lauded by the British James Prichard: "it is in the United States of America that a remarkable advancement of this part of physical science has been at length achieved (qtd. in William Stanton 51–52). Scientists all over Europe were soon relying on Morton's figures, for all aspects of the debate over "racial" types.[18] Morton's international panache arguably contributed to the seriousness with which his work was treated in the United States among scientists aspiring toward professional status.[19] The "factual" popularity of Morton's work in the United States thus ended neither with the war nor Darwin: Morton's racial rank-ordering and arguments about "natural repugnance" transposed smoothly into late-century social Darwinism, lent themselves as readily to eugenics, and offered "scientific" evidence to popular theories that fostered racial and ethnic prejudice. Thus, as the historians of science and U.S. culture allocate racism to men like Nott and Bachman and scientific objectivity to Morton, they participate in the installation of "disinterest" as an authoritative discursive register both for professional science *and* for the occluded managerial agency of whiteness. In acquiescing to these constructions, by seeing science and racism only as opposed, rather than as mutually constructing discourses, we allow ourselves to be "scientifically" disabled from mounting analyses of the way "objectivity" certifies white privilege.

We can see such disabling in the *New Republic*'s editorial introduction to an article by Richard Herrnstein and Charles Murray, excerpted from their controversial study of IQ "differences" between "races," *The Bell Curve* (1994):

> The notion that there might be resilient ethnic differences in intelligence is not, we believe, an inherently racist belief. It's an empirical hypothesis, which can be examined. Since it's an idea that has fueled the most monstrous crimes in human history, it

is not a hypothesis that should be explored casually or unseriously. No attentive reader can believe that Charles Murray and Richard J. Herrnstein's essay . . . that follow[s] in these pages is casual or unserious. Our view, put simply, is that the burden of proof for suppression of a responsible debate about a vital public issue should lie with those who want to suppress it.

What other editorial impulse could there be? Many, it seems. First, a suspicion of the motives of the authors. But Herrnstein was, until his recent death, a distinguished professor at Harvard; Murray has written many superb books and articles, not least for TNR. Neither is a racist.

Clearly, professing and publishing vet one's objectivity. Once "attentive readers" have concluded that these scientists are professionally "serious," we are able to know that they are objective, and therefore not racist. The editors continue: "While one always suspects people with a fascination with race to be prone to *dark* weirdness, neither author is weirder or *darker* than many other writers to be found in our pages. They can be *tarred* (perhaps rightly) by remote association; but ultimately they must be judged on their data and their arguments. How can that happen if their data and their arguments are not brought to *light?*" (*New Republic*, October 31, 1994: 9; emphases added). The editors appeal for an objective review of their objective scientist-contributors. They appeal, in other words, to the scientific perspective for "fair" evaluation. But curiously, they appeal to a rhetoric mixing science with images of race, and specifically, racialized violence. "We" must bring Herrnstein and Murray's arguments "to light"—that is, into the light of the scientific Enlightenment, where a bravely rational, objective debate prevails in finding "truth"—aver these intrepid editors. They develop this racializing rhetoric in their assertion that "to say a debate simply cannot be had is to enforce a taboo utterly at odds with free inquiry" (9). Like Morton's debate with theological naturalism, then, this debate will help us readers overturn primitive ("taboo") superstitions in favor of modern, freely found truths. We can trust these men in this debate, the editors insist, because they are neither "weird" nor "dark"—presumably they do not deviate from standards of normalcy, and, one must assume given the rhetorical accumulation here, whiteness. Recognizing this, readers must be careful not to "tar" them, but instead rely on the objective and sanitizing process of scientific review, through which the two scientists may be found controversial but "ultimately" innocent of the racism that might arguably contaminate their study.[20]

It seems worth pointing out, then, that this editorial invokes the very same signifying chain that Morton appealed to in his debate with Bachman: science = objectivity = manly heroism = truth wrested from contaminating superstition = purity = whiteness.

Cui Bono?

Just prior to publishing his compendium catalogue, Morton went public with his arguments about the separate origins of the races. From 1847, when he published "Hybridity in Animals," until his death, Morton engaged in a debate carried out through a series of articles in the *Charleston Observer* with the spokesperson for monogenesis, John Bachman. Though Bachman was an established naturalist who had collaborated on a three-volume work on "viviparous quadrupeds" with John Audubon,[21] historical summary often tends to downplay Bachman's scientific qualifications for the debate and to emphasize his religiosity and his racism (he was a Lutheran clergyman; he explicitly supported slavery). This emphasis works to uphold the predominant reading of the debate, casting its significance in terms of how it contributed to preprofessional science's enabling break with theological interpretation.[22]

The apparent aim in historical accounts of this episode—keeping objective science categorically away from the subjective contaminations of both religiosity and racism—is complicated because Bachman was arguing for the unity of the human species, whereas Morton was arguing each "race" was, in fact, a separately created species. Let me clarify at once: I am most definitely not interested in rescuing Bachman from charges that he was racist in order to turn that charge against Morton. I do want to insist, though, that their different modes for investing in racist practice held out significantly different political possibilities to a culture negotiating the philosophical and social implications of "sympathy"—implications that Child drew on in her *Appeal.*

Without attempting to ignore Bachman's assumptions about racial hierarchy, I want briefly to consider the assumptions about human community that structure, at least partially, his refutation of Morton, because doing so helps us to reconsider this episode outside the framework Morton provides. Bachman quotes Humboldt midway in

Doctrine of the Unity of the Human Race: "By maintaining the unity of the human species, we at the same time repel the cheerless assumption of superior and inferior races of men. There are families of nations more readily susceptible of culture, more highly civilized, more ennobled by mental cultivation than others; but not in themselves more noble. . . . Deeply rooted in man's most inmost nature, as well as commanded by his highest tendencies, the full recognition of the bond of humanity, of the community of the whole human race, with the sentiments and sympathies which spring therefrom, becomes a leading principle in the history of man" (169). Using designations of "improved race" to describe Europeans and "degraded" to describe Africans, Bachman insists that it is not "color" or "race" that significantly differentiate the condition of humans, but rather, that "it appears more in unison with the laws of nature to believe, that civilization and Christianity have mutually contributed to the improvement of man, in form and feature, mental endowments and moral elevation" (*Doctrine* 157). Thus Bachman's insistence that "race" be housed under the category of "variety" contains explicit and implicit potential for political expression. Explicitly, Bachman's argument asserts as part of the flexibility of "racial" categories, a paternalistic/patronizing moral obligation on the part of the "improved races" toward those designated "degraded," to extend the benefits of "civilization and Christianity." As Gossett points out, Bachman completely backs away from the most radical implication of monogenesis by appealing to history, both biblical and secular, for the "naturalness" of African enslavement. Arguing instead for the explanatory value of "psychological races" (*Doctrine* 200), Bachman echoes the patronizing attitudes of liberal abolitionists, who perpetuated the notion of African "deficiency," but argued that it could be "corrected" by changing the habits of mind, through proper socialization and education—for Bachman, aims achieved through Western enslavement.

His vision of human community is without doubt hierarchically structured, but it is also clear that he took the acommunal implications of polygenesis very seriously, as we see in a passage of his "Second Letter": "If this loose unphilosophical and most unscientific mode of discussing this grave question be continued, needless excitements will be produced in minds that know nothing of the subject on either side. . . . I ask, *Cui bono?* Why bring these subjects before promiscuous assemblies, or discuss them in the newspapers?" (658). It is here, as Bachman questions "who benefits?" from the theory of polygenesis, that we can locate the implicit potential of his position. Monogenesis, however reluctantly and inconsistently Bachman himself was willing to realize, implied "racial" equality, an expanded human community rather than a constricted one (much as his debate with Morton relied on a larger, more cooperative definition of scientific community, as we will see below). Morton's response on behalf of polygenesis thus arguably parallels the mid-seventeenth-century attacks on alchemy in Europe that Evelyn Fox Keller analyzes in her account of "The Birth of Modern Science." She observes that alchemy was not so much targeted by the Baconians for its lack of scientificity so much as for its countervailing politics: "As Bacon's metaphoric ideal was the virile superman, the alchemist's ideal was hermaphrodite. Whereas Bacon sought domination, the alchemists asserted the necessity of the allegorical, if not actual, cooperation between male and female" (*Reflections* 48). Much like the alchemists in Keller's analysis, Bachman was not arguing for any *actual* equality. But his scientific definition of humanity was guided by a principle of communitarian inclusion, placing "blacks" in the same human pool with "whites"—a concept that, as we have seen, was tremendously unsettling for Morton, who, along with Louis Agassiz, insisted on "natural repugnance" as both the mechanism by which, and self-evidence for which, "blacks" were specially segregated from "whites."[23]

Bachman framed his arguments against Morton's theory of "natural repugnance" in terms both scientific and social: "We could heartily wish in behalf of good morals, that these views of our esteemed friend could be verified by our experience in regard to the two varieties to which he alludes. Charleston has from time to time received the majority of its male inhabitants from our Northern United States and Europe. Personal observation does not verify his assertions that it requires centuries of proximity to remove this natural repugnance; on the contrary the proofs are sufficiently evident, and to a melancholy extent, that if it existed on the day of their arrival here, it faded away not after the lapse of centuries but in a very few days" (*Doctrine* 104). Bachman sees "repugnance" as a *social* mechanism, not at all a "natural" one. He offers for consideration the fact that Europeans are far more permissive about interracial union than U.S. "whites." He recounts having seen an interracial couple in Stratford, concluding that "[h]owever revolting this sight was to our American feelings, yet it did not appear to be regarded with the same repugnance by the communities in Europe" (104).

Alongside his strategy of calling into question the sources Morton relies on for his anecdotal evidence of interspecies hybridity, Bachman's most insistent argument is that the racial categories Morton constructs do not have any consistently valid explanatory power:

> In a dissection of a negro by an anatomist, it was discovered that in the specimen examined there was one lumber vertebra more than was contained in the skeleton of the white man. The parties, who had been laboring to prove that the negro was of a different species, now triumphantly proclaimed this fact to the world as an evidence of the truth of their theory. For a time the believers in the unity were placed under the harrow. Presently, another negro was dissected, and it was ascertained, that he had no more vertebrae than those found in the white race, and finally the skeleton of a white man was found that had an additional lumber vertebra, such as had been previously detected in the negro. After this discovery they prudently said no more about it. (*Doctrine* 73)

Here, Bachman attacks Morton's arguments on hybridity, and further implies that his quantifying measurements of crania—those which made him the darling of the international scientific community—could be disproved as well. Whatever basis for scientific measurement the polygenesists choose, Bachman is confident he can find exceptions for, and in finding the exceptions, refute the category, as he summarizes with reference to the question of color: "If we have not said sufficient to convince our readers that colour is not an essential characteristic in deciding on the human species, and that 'identity of tint is not an essential character of race,' we would yet remind them that almost every variety of colour is found in each of the five varieties of Blumenbach. We have heard some of the believers in the plurality of species remark that the only difficulty in their minds in receiving the doctrine of the unity consisted in the existence of the black pigment under the skin of the negro, which was absent in the white man. We would remind them of the fact that there are very dark if not black men among all the races that are arranged under the Caucasian family" (*Doctrine* 232). Strikingly, Bachman's observation on this score would seem to fall in with the contemporary scientific consensus on the question of biological "races." As James Shreeve puts it in his recent article, "Terms of Estrangement," "despite the obvious physical differences between people from different areas, the vast majority of human genetic variation occurs *within* populations, not *between* them" (60; original emphasis).[24] Some pertinent questions could be raised here: why doesn't Bachman get more note for that in histories of this debate? How is it that, even in the most careful accounts, Bachman's arguments are still summarized such that they serve as an "unscientific" foil to Morton's professional, if finally mistaken, science? But more pertinent to my interests here: if we set aside traditional terms of analysis (conservative, interested racist theology versus progressive, disinterested science), what other aspects of this episode might emerge? How can a more careful and skeptical analysis of this episode and the patterns of its historical evaluations help us reassess ongoing national investments in the sociomanagerial aspects of professional science and occulted whiteness?

III

Occulted Authority

We might pose such an alternative analysis by comparing the two projects rather than opposing them to each other. As I have already indicated, Stanton is certainly correct in noting that Morton and Bachman were operating out of a substantially similar set of assumptions about the social (if not biological) relations between "whites" and "blacks." Bachman shares Morton's confidence that there is a hierarchical ordering for variously designated types of humans. They also share a set of scientific procedures, despite Morton's portrayal of the debate and historians' differentiating treatments. Bachman set out to repudiate Morton's particular arguments about special hybridity and natural repugnance with a methodology virtually identical to Morton's.[25] Both culled evidence from books published by other naturalists, zoologists, and ethnologists. Like Morton's comprehensive survey of "races" in his craniological catalogues and essays and his essay on "hybridity," Bachman's argument evidences a scientific gaze that moves confidently in global sweeps—sweeps enabled by the existence of a print archive already devoted to a delineation of racial difference.[26] Bachman, also like Morton, maps the authority for his argument through the exercise of what Michel Foucault has described as the gaze of medico-scientific authority in the nineteenth century, and Laqueur has characterized as the "scopic drive" (76). His arguments evoke the "suzerainty of the visible" commanded by an "absolute eye of knowledge" (see Foucault *Order* 128–32; *Birth* 164–

70). In this manner, *both* Bachman and Morton situate themselves as a disembodied and disinterested observing subject, surveying, evaluating, and categorizing local others.

It is worth paying attention to how the construction of a disembodied, universal authority is characteristic of both scientific procedure *and* much modern racist discourse (see Wetherell and Potter 127). Modern science, as feminist historians and philosophers of science have extensively argued, processed itself through notions *of* otherness. Its contributions in the eighteenth and nineteenth centuries were instrumental to consolidating powers that worked "through the identification of new categories of people and new methods of assessment and surveillance of population" (Wetherell and Potter 83). As "other" bodies were investigated, inventoried, and invested with particularized materiality, scientific authority located the Observing Subject in what Denise Albanese has described as "an artificial space of evacuated materiality" (180). This evacuated materiality of science, its disembodied reason serving as the condition for its claim to universal authority, is strikingly similar to the ideological condition of whiteness, according to Richard Dyer: "I was taught the scientific difference between black and white at primary school. It seemed a fascinating paradox. Black, which, because you had to add it to make a picture, was, it turned out, nothingness, the absence of all colour [*sic*]; whereas white, which looked just like empty space (or blank paper), was, apparently, all the colours there were put together" (45). Dyer notes that though this explanation of color is now "outmoded," its usefulness to ethnic categorization is not: "black is always marked as a colour (as the term 'coloured' egregiously acknowledges), and is always particularising; whereas white is not anything really, not an identity, not a particularising quality" (45).

In the United States, then, modern science, very much like the new, socially and politically operative categories of whiteness and middle classness, processed itself through paradigms of alterity and incommensurability. Recognizing these similarities as affiliated strategies might lead us to reexamine Morton's debate with Bachman, and Morton's career trajectory, particularly as a cultural exercise in the consolidation of white scientific manhood. We should be able to understand Morton's investiture in "whiteness" as a very specific one (however abstracted), one that was indeed linked to his sense of authority—and authorization—as scientist.[27] Scientific authority merged with and stood for the occulted white manly Self. As Guillaumin elaborates: "[S]ocial discourse is no longer directed out from a dominant sense of Self, but towards a dominated Other. Race is no longer associated with power, but with lack of power. Whereas in auto-referential societies difference is the declared property of the dominant group, and used to its advantage, in altero-referential societies it is the Other (in the form of various dominated groups) who is always different. And underlying this difference is the fact that the Other has now become a regulator, rather than a producer, of social discourse; a regulator deprived of power and so reduced to the status of object" (51). To say this somewhat differently, the vantages of science and "whiteness" collude to produce the occulted space of the "normal." From this vantage, as Deleuze and Guattari summarize, "there are only people who should be like us and whose crime it is not to be" (*Thousand Plateaus* 178). The perceived need to identify, categorize, and regulate "abnormality" that accompanied this occulted scientific authority served as one base for the expansion of professions and disciplinary knowledge in the mid-nineteenth century. Formally occupied, these professional civic managers would work as certified guardians of the normalcy of nation.

The Arena of Battle

In staking his argument for polygenesis, Morton was carving out a position for what was coming to be known as "the American school" of ethnology. We should be able to acknowledge the importance of his stake here in territorial terms. By castigating monogenesis and natural theology along with it as being insufficiently scientific, Morton was arrogating to his "American ethnology" the status of science and the territory of profession. His strategy was by no means unusual; as George Daniels observes, "in the process of defining a position for a new profession, a measure of encroachment upon already established professions is almost inevitable; that is to say, the new profession generally claims special competence in some area that has previously been the exclusive domain of another." Daniels points out that science's competitor had long been theology, "for both groups considered themselves to be dealing with natural laws, and both considered themselves competent interpreters of those laws" (*American Science* 51).[28] As Morton sought to increase acceptance for his school of science, he excited a debate that would establish its authority in a competition.

Morton, his supporters, and his earliest biographers, Charles Meigs and Henry S. Patterson, all cast his debate with Bachman in terms that evoke a scientific martyrdom like that of Galileo. But Bachman vowed from the beginning to keep theology out of his dispute with Morton. In a personal letter dated October 15, 1849, he assures Morton that, "we are both in the search of truth. I do not think that these scientific investigations affect the scripture question either way. The author of revelation is also the author of nature and I have no fear that where we are able to read intelligibly we will discover that both harmonize. We can investigate these matters without the fear of an *auto de fe* from men of science. In the mean time all must go with respect and good feeling toward each other" (Morton ms. collection, Library Company of Philadelphia). Likewise, Bachman openly avows his intentions to engage the question of polygenesis on its own grounds in the title he carefully chooses for his printed response, *The Doctrine of the Unity of the Human Race Examined on the Principles of Science*. A careful reading of his book, as well as his article-responses to Morton, confirms that although he forwards his theory of monogenesis as a biblically confirmed "truth," he criticizes and engages Morton's arguments about polygenesis in specifically scientific terms, attacking him for using bad sources and bad logic, with the result being bad science. He seldom adverts to a specific discussion of religion; these usually come directly in response to Morton's goading (e.g., see Morton, "Letter to the Rev. John Bachman, D. D." 17; Bachman, "Reply" 506–7).

Given, then, that it is Morton who insists that Bachman take up theology in the debate, it would seem that we might at least bracket the interpretive choice Morton and his supporters provide for this episode, between innocent science and persecutorial theology.[29] Looking from a different direction, we can see that it is less an attack against Morton's religiosity that is being mounted, and more an attack against theological authority that Morton himself is mounting. In the context of Daniels's observations about the process of professionalization, what we can discern in Morton's debate with Bachman is a developing model of authority for a new professional arena, tested against and emerging precisely in its contest—by Morton's account— with a well-established authority on the order of things: theology. In other words, one way to refocus how we consider this debate is to see it not as a contest over how bodies get categorized (their hierarchical organization was hardly in question), but over *who* gets to categorize and manage them. It would seem that accrediting polygenesis provided a wedge by which Morton could discredit theology's right to interpret "natural order," and claim that authority as the spoils of the "battle" for "science."

Despite Bachman's gentlemanly protests in his letter to Morton, it is clear from his subsequent publications that he relishes a combative engagement with Morton. Refusing to frame their opposition in extra-scientific terms, Bachman evidently takes a sporting adversariality as being intrinsic to the business (and language) of science: "Thus far we have acted on the defensive. We have met and grappled with our opponent in all the points in which they conjectured our citadel was weak or unguarded, and where they imagined their success was attainable. We have traced their stratagems and maneuvers, and listened to their shouts of fancied victory, but our castle still remains unshaken, and they have not succeeded in removing even one picket that guards the outposts of our strong fortress. We may now be permitted to assail them in turn and carry the war into their own camp, by pointing out the very great difficulties that present themselves against their theory" ("Reply" 120). It is impossible to overlook the aggressively—and erotically—masculinist quality of Bachman's rhetoric here, which figures science as a "field of gender" (Jeffords xi). Here, in the heat of the contest between men of science, all women and men of other "races" and classes recede from vision, appearing only in subsidiary ways, as sites for engagement, as the "field" for battle between these professional men.

Morton does not deploy an overt rhetoric of military engagement (he saves his real ammunition for measuring cranial volume), using instead what is a now-familiar academic rhetorical style, grounded in objective, rational refutation and negation.[30] His purpose, however, escalates Bachman's playful rhetoric to professional strategy: his arguments, if successful, aim to eliminate his opposition entirely from the field of scientific debate. In his argumentative maneuver to make Bachman's interpretations exogenous to science, Morton engaged in a remapping of the cultural authority of the scientific profession. Bachman's arguments take for granted that a *shared* authority will emerge in an eventual scientific consensus resulting from the debate. Quite differently, Morton situates Bachman *entirely outside* scientific consensus, and figures the newly consolidated power resulting from the debate not as shared, but exclusive. In his recasting, scientific authority will disprove the misplaced authority of theological naturalism. As Morton argues roughly at the midpoint of their exchanges,

"what is mis-called *Theology* is a Protean compound, that has probably made as little progress, in ten centuries, as any branch of human
knowledge" ("Additional Observations" 7; original emphasis). Thus
the scientific point of view will demonstrate science's authority over
inferior "branch[es] of knowledge" precisely as it verifies white men
as the climax of the "natural" order.

Morton engages in a competition for dominance in science that
repeats and normalizes an imperative becoming characteristic of
middle-class manhood in the second quarter of the nineteenth century. This is the (still prevalent) equation of manly autonomy with
competitive opposition.[31] Here then we can begin to see with historical specificity how science comes to participate in consolidating
(indeed, professionalizing) a particularly "masculine point of view"
(Jeffords xiii) in the nineteenth-century United States, legitimizing by
providing an altero-referential (or "objective") discourse for establishing individual as well as class/group autonomy, realized in the social
structure as dominance.[32] Despite his refusal to engage Bachman's
colorful military rhetoric, it is possible to argue that Morton's is actually the more aggressive project. Morton's scientific/masculine point
of view multiply authorizes a radically denatured meaning for professional as well as political, legal, and social communities. We might
therefore reconsider this episode as a turning point in the emergent
culture of professional disciplinarity, grounded in tropes of purifying
competition and exclusion, rather than interdisciplinary inclusion.
Through this professional episode, and in precisely this way, disciplinary authority for science increasingly becomes modeled upon the
exclusionary and hierarchizing prerogatives of "whiteness" within
the framework of "natural" (market) competitions of expertise.

And so I return to the questions I raised earlier: Why doesn't Bachman get more note for the quality of his arguments in contemporary
histories of this debate? Why are Bachman's arguments finally remembered, even in their most careful and favorable portrayals, as
being "unscientific" and "seriously compromised both by his religious
ideas and commitment to slavery" (Gossett 63, 62)? How is it that
Morton, not discarded as "seriously compromised by his pro-white
racism," continues to rank as a scientist, as Bachman is abandoned to
the realm of theological irrelevance? Our best answer now sounds a
little like something from Oz: what Morton had that Bachman didn't
was a closet full of skulls.

Let me be precise in attempting to explain what I see as a pervasive blind-spot in our historical understanding of this episode. If, as I have argued, the immediate stakes of the argument were not so much *how* the "races" of men were categorized as *who* was assigned the right to categorize, then we should pay close attention to how contemporary evaluations still portray the debate in the terms of its victor. Morton seems to be able to maintain his respectability as "scientist" in a way that Bachman cannot, precisely because of his massive project of cataloging human skulls that proceeded with all the careful trappings of scientific objectivity. Unlike Bachman, who split his time between his passionate interest in science and his duties as a minister,[33] Morton spent most of his career, as Daniels summarizes, "actively engaged in research" (*American Science* 218). His career commitment as well as his methods thus advertised the kind of disinterested and occluded subjectivity increasingly linked to practices of population quantification and human mathematicization—that is, to the civic-economic, domesticating priorities of professionalized management. Though his arguments on hybridity proceed precisely as do Bachman's—out of anecdotal evidence culled from scientific writings—they issue from the authority (objective, scientific) that Morton accrued in his crania collection and measurements, a scientific-cultural capital that Bachman lacked. So, though the debate on hybridity takes place on both sides as a debate between "armchair naturalists," Morton can appeal to his craniological work in the new, professionalizing areas of laboratory/field science in a way that Bachman cannot, no matter what other validity might adhere to his arguments. Historians of science and culture still rate Morton's scientific credibility over Bachman's, it would seem, on this basis—usually refusing even to factor Bachman's arguments in the category *of* the scientific. That is precisely the result Morton looked for.

As Daniels notes, "scholars have failed to understand that natural theology, in terms of the science of its day, was a perfectly respectable scientific discipline, and furthermore, all its chief proponents were scientists" (*American Science* 53). Morton's strategies for discrediting Bachman's scientific qualifications should thus be scrutinized with more care.[34] As Morgan Sherwood concluded from the Dana-Lewis controversy, it would also seem that for Morton and Bachman, "the main source of friction was nothing more than a matter of intellectual jurisdiction" (314).[35] Though Morton did not here achieve for "science" a conclusive fracture from theology, he participated in strategizing for modern, professional science a project that would not conclusively culminate until after the Civil War. Morton's move toward racial cataloguing simultaneously culminates the larger cultural transition carefully detailed by David Theo Goldberg, from religious to racial modes of identity that characterize modern epistemology and social organization. It is therefore in no way irrelevant to U.S. professional science that one of its most successful early bids for disciplinary separation from religion occurred over the subject of "race."

Maximizing Whiteness

In the skull-capacity measurements that "disproved" Bachman's theoretically postulated human community, craniology's objective, descriptive demeanor performed a practice/theory split that reduplicated and borrowed energy from the public/private (and rational/ emotional; rational/intuitive; masculine/feminine) binary increasingly undergirding the practices of middle-class "democracy" in the United States. William Stanton observes that growing support from the international scientific community for the theory of polygenesis worked effectively to remove questions of morality from the project of racial categorization (111–12). I also want to use this episode as a wedge that could help us think more generally about how science became professionalized in the U.S. middle-class arena precisely through a move toward acommunal, amoralistic positivism, however commonsensically "scientific," "objective," and "correct" that movement appears to us now. Ludmilla Jordanova elaborates on the centrality of positivism to the scientific practice of the early nineteenth century: "Positivism was a movement which, although firmly rooted in experimental science, had far-reaching social and political implications. Its reformist rationalism valued science as a major tool for social progress. Positivism, as it was generally received, was thus antitheoretical, while it generated optimism about the progressive growth of reliable, objective knowledge. . . . For this reason, what started in the eighteenth century as the science of man, and developed in the nineteenth century as the moral and social sciences, was an important test case for the universal applicability of scientific method" (Languages 30–31). Appealing to the pragmatic value of its universal applicability, this professional science, the "American school" of ethnology, participated in and provided a strong logic for a disciplinary narrowing of human community and of democratic possibility. In these examples from Morton's career and his debate with Bachman, we can see more clearly what Michel Serres means, when he concludes an essay by asserting that "Western man is a wolf of science" (28). Describing science since Bacon and Descartes as a rationalist strategy in a militaristic sense, Serres insists that the hunt for "natural" laws in science is the hunt for a strategically "winning" move: "as soon as laws are written, they allow man [sic] *always* to have access to the inaccessible. The stability and constancy of certitudes or precisions are conceived in the beginning as the end of a prior game" (23). Enlightenment science provided the positivistic rationalism that begat the authority of Jefferson's Declaration.[36] Morton's craniology carries forward the Founding Fathers' positivism to resolve the internal dissonance of "self-evident" relations between men. Adverting to the efficacious purity of scientific rationalism, Morton effectively purges the question of "equality" in the Declaration of its ethical, democratizing impetus. Thus Serres would describe Morton's craniological cataloging as a "maximal move," a scientific strategy in service of a political order that would "freeze . . . the game space in a single pattern of order and hierarchy" (22).

IV

Competing Manhoods

This new positivist articulation of professional human science bolstered the practical logic of managerial authority in two mutually constitutive directions—it collated whiteness and manhood on behalf of an emerging middle-class by articulating professionalized identity as one that would, from its rationally disembodied position of occluded authority, manage democracy's Others. Yet while Morton's scientific theory operated ideologically as a guarantor for the corporate identity of "white" men, his professional method participated in a logic of competitive manhood that experientially destructured the imagined fraternity of national manhood.

In the context of this battle between a preacher and a doctor, we might usefully recall Anthony Rotundo's observations about the effeminate status of both ministry *and* medicine in the antebellum United States. He observes that "these two professions were overwhelmingly male, and they demanded both 'manly reason' and book learning. However, they conducted their activities away from concentrations of men and power, and they directed their activities as much at nurture as competition . . . [for this reason] they conferred a lower status on a man than other nineteenth-century professions" (205; see 205–9 passim). Thus, Morton's insistence on disciplinary competition—a debate not between (armchair) naturalists, but between science and theology—becomes a way of testing and validating professional science for emerging, competitive, acommunal standards of manhood. The production of scientific racialism is not simply a manifestation of uneven power relations between whites and blacks in the early nation: its articulation becomes the means for negotiating and indeed legitimating uneven power relations between white men.

In their personal correspondence, Morton, Nott, Gliddon, and Squier spend a good deal of space speculating on forthcoming "attacks" by their opponents; their rhetoric casts such professional disagreement in the terms of personal—even physical—assault, and they rehearse for each other plans to answer in kind.[37] Clearly, the aggression entailed in staking of disciplinary authority invoked anxieties that were not experientially counterbalanced by the abstractly unifying effects of whiteness. Here it's worth paying attention to the way the staking of disciplinary authority reduplicates the logic of market and class competition; indeed, as sociologist Magali Sarfatti Larson argues in her study of the rise of professionalism, "the development of specialized roles and functions is broadly determined by the structure of inequality from which it is inseparable: dependent upon the unequal distribution of wealth, power and knowledge, the institutionalization of specialized functions itself contributes to the unequal distribution of competence and rewards" (2).

White manhood worked as a transistor for a chain of political, economic, class, and professional displacements between "white" men. It circuited political and economic inequality as individual failure, and routed frustrations into projects of disavowal, into "healthy" market and professional aggression toward other (white) men, into endlessly multiplying practices of (civic, labor, market, population) management. This is exactly the routing Paulding chooses in his debate with Child. He rearticulates the intraclass threats to the fraternal/national brotherhood that Child highlights as the national danger of degraded, prostituted white womanhood. Adapting a gesture from Jefferson and Rush, Paulding's response to Child's pointed analysis of discrepant economies of various white manhoods recouped the alibi of a unified national manhood by claiming its domesticating prerogative, the fused role of husband-as-civic-manager.

Domestic Reform vs. Domestic Management

In the maximizing posture of competitive, dominative white manhood that occurs in and through the debate over polygenesis, we can locate a specific instance of how, in Balibar's formulation, "racism always presupposes sexism" (Balibar and Wallerstein 49). Science in the United States early provided a disembodied "masculine point of view" that moved over and against not just other races, and not just other (white male) cultural/managerial authorities (i.e., theology).[38] Perhaps as significantly, Morton's debate with Bachman signals an aggressive strike against the emotionally and politically miscegenational culture of (sentimental) domestic reform—and morally independent womanhood—being variously consolidated in middle-class women's culture of the period.[39] This was a reform movement that shared with Bachman's monogenesis at least an impulse toward (without necessarily committing to the various or full implications of) social and political equalitarianism.

It's worth thinking about how the contemporary emergence of scientific professionalism works in part as a cultural countermove against women's growing claims to a civic agency formulated through the moral logic of domesticity, on behalf of a dominative construction of managerial manhood.[40] In other words, *contra* Ann Douglas's thesis that a "feminization" of American culture occurred during this period, I would argue that we have equally compelling evidence for seeing the antebellum period as one when national manhood braced itself in the mantle of professional authority, its sanction fueling the formation of a new, managerial middle class. In an ideological shift that paralleled the ceding of the family to "white" women as "white" men took up the pose of civic manager, certain realms of culture were bracketed for middle-class women as white middle-class men assumed the stance of professional manager. This era, in my reading, can only be regarded as being "feminized" insofar as we neglect to analyze (or as we stand in the space of) the occulted identity and growing authority of the "professional."

This argument finds suggestive confirmation in Mary Ryan's observations about an important shift in domestic advice literature for women during the period of my concern here, from the early 1830s to the 1850s. She notes that early advice manuals, like Child's *Frugal Housewife*, counseled women as household managers, advising them how to function competently in architectural design, financial planning, and home medical remedies, along with cooking and cleaning. But by the 1850s, advice literature more and more instructed women to rely on male professionals—doctors, architects, accountants—and depicted women not as competent managers but "as a separate species of humanity whose distinctive identity was the subject of metaphysical and scientific inquiry" (*Empire* 36; see also 25, and ch. 1 passim). The cultural authority that professional men claimed over crucial aspects of the "female domestic sphere" during this period—over "their" homes, families, hygiene, habits, and bodies—should point us toward considering how racial science authorized the very project Paulding outlined, protecting national manhood through a project that disavowed concerns about inequalities between white men, projecting them to the interiors of always potentially impure white women, a project I will analyze in the next chapter.

4

Gynecological Manhood: The Worries
of Whiteness and the Disorders
of Women

Late one night in August 1848, future gynecologist[1] Josiah Nott (1803–73), a general practitioner with a locally noted surgical reputation and a scientific commentator increasingly infamous for his aggressive arguments on behalf of polygenesis, sat writing a letter to his friend Ephraim Squier (1821–88), whom he had met through their mutual friend, Samuel G. Morton. The letter ranged through topics of common professional interest. He discussed their different work in documenting separate racial origins, rehearsed professional frictions each were encountering in making those arguments publicly, and conveyed news of other friends engaged in promoting their scientific cause. Here's how the letter ends: "Well, I must close this hasty scrawl—here I am 5 miles from home, at 2 o'clock at night, sitting up with a woman in labor! It is all science however—exploring a woman and a mound are pretty much the same" (Aug. 19, 1948, Squier Papers, Library of Congress). This is a "naked nature" moment: a triangulated, compensatory articulation of professional male sameness. It evokes concisely the masked anxieties and the desires that structure the imagined community of professionalized manhood at the same time as it points toward its very real effects on its others. Professionalizing the desire(s) of national manhood meant institutionalizing as "sameness" the abstracted qualities of "white" manhood through physicalizing, abjecting scientific/medical investigations of otherness, now mobilized as "careers." Specific projects such as Nott's and Squier's symbolically supported a broader cultural logic. More generally, professionalization formalized, institutionalized, concretized the displacement strategies of national manhood; professionalization extended (by diversifying) national manhood's "corporate" project as it bolstered its individuating rationale in the form of "career success."[2] In such careers, anxieties generated in competitive economic relations between white men are structurally and professionally displaced: through the discourse of and managerial rationale provided by science, both positively and negatively charged emotions generated between white men could be triangulated through and transferred onto "others."[3]

This chapter unpacks Nott's suggestive correlation, exploring how the cultural interests of racial science converged with the professional emergence of gynecology in their mutually reassuring stabilization of white manhood and professional masculinity. Gender difference and specifically diseased female sexuality was, like the "Indianness" I examined in chapter 2, being fitted to carry the symbolic burdens of national manhood and the particular anxieties of professional competition and economic climbing. Professional gynecology in its early days promised to stabilize a whole range of social, economic, and political samenesses and differences between white men, by rerouting those anxious negotiations to a mapping of female difference, a rerouting that a quick reading of Charles Meigs's introductory lecture to *Females and their Diseases* will help us see. This rerouting is by no means specific to the professional discourse and practices of gynecology; we can trace it in the cultural arena. George Lippard's 1845 novel *Quaker City* suggestively thematizes cultural phobias emerging out of questions about individual men's power within the contradictory domains of (equalizing) friendship and (hierarchizing) competition. But these anxieties are repeatedly diverted into plots about endangered/endangering white women, their threatened sexual purity, their threatening sexual *impurity*. Indeed, the novel's literal and symbolic structure depends on this rerouting: Lippard's key symbol for the corrupt city, "the *Whited Sepulcher*" finds its concrete reference in the corpses of sexually contaminated white women.

In a recent article, "Sexual Desire and the Market Economy During the Industrial Revolution," Thomas Laqueur takes up how the free-market economy created its own logic of appeal to sexuality: "passion and desire were integral to the new order, and there was no clear conceptual boundary between its sexual and economic manifestations" (186). His analysis focuses on how the promise of unbounded upward mobility in the competitive marketplace threatened to pollute the social body: "Society seemed to be in unprecedented danger from the marketplace. And the sexual body bore the widespread anxieties about this danger" (213). Beyond Lippard's fictionalized Philadelphia, gynecologist J. Marion Sims's autobiographical account of his early career provides a concise instance of the counterphobic repair of such anxieties: worries about being a man—having manfully to pit himself against professional competition in the name of career building— can be projected onto the sexual bodies of women, from whence he can reroute them into cleaner and more properly productive channels. Reading his career in gynecology culturally, through the lens of *Quaker City*, lets us begin to consider more generally how the very anxieties generated with the middle classes' move toward professionalization—the promises of upward mobility, in other words, combined with men's desires for the (differentiating) *status* and the (equalizing) *guarantees* of whiteness—could be managed by and through their gynecological projection onto women's bodies.

I *Excelsior!*

In 1847, the eminent Professor Charles Meigs, MD (1792–1869), offered a "Lecture on Some of the Distinctive Characteristics of the Female," an introductory address to a series of essays on *Females and their Diseases* (published the following year). Meigs would need nearly seven hundred pages to rehearse women's various reproductive and sexual disorders there; here, he introduces the topic literally as a rhapsody on the female uterus and specifically "the germiniferous tissue of the female"—her ovaries. Meigs emphasizes the powerful purity of the female reproductive system for his male audience: "It is from her stroma that issues the generic as well as the genetic force! What a wondrous law! What a wondrous power tis that which maintains each genus and species so pure and unalloyed as when it issued from the creator's hand!" (8). In this twenty-page lecture, Meigs poses the object of study—woman—as one not simply of scientific classification and investigation, but an exploration of "the history of those wonderful functions and destinies which her sexual nature enables her to fulfill, and the strange and secret influences which her organs, by their nervous constitution, and their functions, by their relation to her whole Life-force, whether in sickness or health, are capable of exerting, not on the body alone, but on the heart, the mind, and the very soul of the woman" (6). Laqueur notes that "the theory of the menstrual cycle dominant from the 1840s to the early twentieth century rather neatly integrated a particular set of real discoveries into an imagined biology of incommensurability" (*Making Sex* 217). It is the imagined absolute difference of "woman" that ties gynecological study to an investigation of her "very soul," where her spiritual essence serves as a mirror for her reproductive being. The pervasiveness and significance of female incommensurability makes the gynecological study a comprehensive and even heroic inquiry for the medical student:

> The Medical Student has, then, much to study, as to the female, that is not purely medical—but physiological and moral rather: such researches will be a future obligation lying heavily upon you, upon all of you.
>
> Every well educated medical man ought to know something more of women than is contained in the volumes of a medical library. Her history and literature, in all ages and countries, ought to be gathered as the garlands with which to adorn his triumphant career as a physician; but these insignia of his power he can only gather by the careful and tasteful study of his subject among the rich stores of learning that are gained in the belles-lettres collections, whether archaiological, medieval or modern. (Meigs, *Lecture 6*)

This passage suggests one key aspect of Meigs's project, to outline a theoretical system and a practice grounded in discrete oppositions: woman's body to men's intellect, woman's passivity to men's activity; woman's mutability to men's permanency; woman's domesticity to men's professionality; woman's "low" germiniferous matter to men's "high" work at civilization. Meigs's categories and their historical sweep heterosexualize both medical inquiry and world history, defined as they are in this account through a stabilizing range of essential differences between "woman" and men.

But the contrasts defining sexual difference are presented so emphatically, so repetitively, that they begin to feel somewhat strained. Meigs captions his subject from the outset as one of stark contrast, indeed, of manly erection, noting how all the "high concerns" of civilization and history emerge from the "lowness" of women's "germiniferous tissue." Pronouncing women's ovaries and wombs the "ark that contains the law" of species reproduction, Meigs emphasizes for his male audience that "the male tissues are nowhere endowed with the power of this yelk [*sic*] production, and the sole elaboration of the stroma of ovaries is germ-elaboration" (*Lecture* 8). "How can you study this subject sufficiently?" Meigs rhetorically queries, and continues: "[b]ut let us pass to other views. Let us go to look upon woman in the phases of her intellectual nature" (8). Having just named women the origin of life, the guarantor of species *and* the spirit of civilization ("Versailles and Marli, and the Trianons, had never been built for *men*. . . . Even literature and the sciences are in good measure due to her patronage and approbation, which is the motive power to all endeavor" [7]), Meigs then spends literally pages counting out what women *cannot* do: they can't think well, or organize, or administrate, or orate, or navigate. They can't write epics, let alone poetry, they're not artistic, *and* they would be too afraid of Satan to write about him, as did Milton. While there have been strong women, those were unnatural, even monsters: most women can't watch battles stoically; they do not "glory" in the "commingling of the spears" (11). Having named "her" as the most important object for human study, Meigs now spends pages miniaturizing "woman," reducing her human and scientific interest solely to her womb, and describing that amazing organ as "no bigger than my thumb" (18; see also 5).[4]

We might conclude, then, that Meigs is insecure in his relation *qua* male to the female object for his study. If indeed she is all that he says she is, then men are, by logical extension, second best. It would be that realization that he is anxiously skirting in his lists of all the big things men do, even if they're only doing them for women who, constitutionally, haven't the least clue how to appreciate them. But I think there might be another index to the anxiety that seemingly underwrites Meigs's performance, an anxiety not about men and "woman" but one about his standing as a professional man among men. Having offered to his audience the "key that unlocks" the secrets of woman's distinctiveness ("that she is peculiar because of, and in order that she might have this great, this dominant organ concealed within the recesses of her body" [*Lecture* 18]), Meigs concludes his lecture highlighting his own inadequacy to the topic: "But why should I attempt, or why should I have attempted a theme too great for a volume, and far beyond my abilities? You see how I have failed. It requires the eloquence of a Roussel, and the learning of a Virey, to present even a sketch of a topic so vast, so interesting, so closely related to what ever may be called happiness, whether domestic or social or political" (19). Measuring his abilities here, at the end of a talk sprinkled with classical allusions and rhetorical elegance, against that of other learned, professional men, Meigs captions his own medical and rhetorical impotence as an inspiration to his audience to aspire for better: "does not the most highly cultivated intelligence to be found among men, leave them at last, even the most gifted among them, blind, groping, feeble worms of the dust? What should be our motto and our cry, from the lowness of the human nature in which we lie groveling?—*Excelsior! Excelsior!*" (20). Though it's tempting to read this image of men groveling as worms (no bigger than a thumb?—smaller than that? sperm?) as a disingenuous rhetorical trick that actually signifies its opposite, grandiosity (particularly in light of the way Meigs has already framed woman's "sex" as the "lowness" from which all civilization arises), I want to pressure this moment interpretively, reading it more carefully through Meigs's own remarkably insistent but notably equivocal sexual geography. What seems to me noteworthy about this address is precisely Meigs's multiple ambivalences about the durability of the supposedly essential differences that ground human progress in sexual distinction—for instance, those strong (erect) women he both names and discounts as unnatural.[5] Meigs begins his address by situating the Sex—"woman"—as the moral force behind the social contract: "The medical man, surely, of all men, ought to be best able to appreciate the influence of the sex in the social compact. But for the power of that influence, which one of you would doubt the rapid relapse of society into the violence and chaos of the earliest barbarism?" (6). According to this argument, then, medical men of all professionals are best situated to understand the deleterious effects of male-male competition—what men would do to each other, to male humankind, without the moral influence of woman. Framed negatively there, male-male antagonism is later elevated as Meigs turns to detail woman's essential unsuitedness for battle. He quotes at length a poem by the (aptly chosen) popular poet, Mrs. Felicia Hemans, that actually romanticizes warfare as men's "crusading chivalry" (11). Halfway into the lecture, then, Meigs seems to be praising that in men which he had earlier explicitly denigrated. Here their proclivity to beat up on other men is now framed as producing not chaos but heroism. Interestingly, when Meigs studies male combat on its own terms—homosocially, we might say, or without women in the picture—it looks barbarous. Viewed heterosexually—with women as audience, object, and influence—male combat can be read positively, not only as a productive good for Christianity and civilization, but as another benign proof of male-female difference. As Meigs summarizes of Hemans's verses: "for my part, I cannot but see in these verses of that most sweet poetess, proofs of her liveliest sensibility to both the nature and the intenseness of those male passions, which, however they may be fitted to enkindle her admiration, and enslave her heart, as forming a perfect antithesis to her own gentle nature, would, as existing in her own breast, demoralize and deform it" (12). Meigs is comfortable, in other words, with male combat only when he represses male competition (male-male differences) by focusing on romanticized and singularized male-female difference.

Or—and this reading is somewhat more speculative, but allied to the first—Meigs valorizes male combat by focusing on romanticized and abstracted suggestions of male-male *sameness* that simultaneously exclude women while depending structurally on "her" symbolic presence. At the beginning of the paragraph from which I have quoted the last sentences, Meigs exhorts his students: "I would have you fill your souls with knowledge; I would have you bathe in it as in an ocean." Michael Moon has extensively analyzed how the "fantasy of male selves flowing in and out of each other and dissolving into each other" powers Whitman's poetic and fictional uses of "fluidity." As important to my reading here is Moon's analysis of the ways in which the "heaven of sentimental relationship between males" emerges as a "counterdiscourse" to new cultural emphases on male individualism and competition in the 1830s and 1840s (*Disseminating Whitman* 245–46). Beginning his lecture with a negative invocation of male rivalry, Meigs concludes with an explicit figuration of anxiety about his own status among fellows, which he generalizes outward, abjecting *all* cultivated, intelligent, aspiring professionals as "worms in the dust" striving to raise themselves from "the lowness of human nature in which we lie groveling"—together. The rhetoric is excessive, explicitly figuring a degraded image of impotent men but suggesting in its invitational appeal an abjection from which *intellectual men* can rise heroically (*Excelsior!*), leaving the contaminating "dirt" (which his rhetoric encourages us to see both as "woman" and as male impotence) behind for a transcendental male-only realm of disembodied knowledge. Meigs focuses on male-female difference, culturally, professionally, medically, as a way of stabilizing cultural, professional, and medical anxieties about male-male competition in the new middle-class professional realm. These are anxieties equipoised by sameness (civic entitlement depending on the sameness of whiteness) and differences (professionalization depending on differentiation experienced individually as success or failure in competition and manifested corporately in class/occupational stratification). These differentiations, individual and categorical, symbolically threatened the sameness that guaranteed the fraternal contract of national manhood. It is important to my reading then to clarify how the "counterdiscourse" that Moon highlights for our attention emerges plurally, as counterdiscourses—both abjecting and utopian—that can be deployed by the very men who adhere to practices of "self-reliant male rectitude" (Moon, *Disseminating Whitman* 246).[6]

Despite Meigs's obsessively binaristic scheme, there emerges finally no single, clear logic, but an unstable mixture of logics, suggesting uncertainties not only about the character of relations between men and "woman," but between men. This more complicated example suggests with a bit more detail than Nott's letter to Squier the way that Meigs's conceptual system of gender binarity is finally not adequate to sustaining a sense of stable achievement within the homosocial professional realm. But I want to foreground the *dynamic:* that very inadequacy powers his compensatory gesture toward stabilization in the ongoing practice of medically investigating "woman's" reproductive body. Laura Brown has analyzed for eighteenth-century British culture how the female body comes to represent "the 'enigmatic character' of the commodity" and how in literature of that era, the obsessive "dressing and undressing of [women] can be seen as an attempt to strip away the mystifying 'clothing' of the commodity and to discover the lost human essence that lies beneath" (120). Using Brown's insight, we might consider the burgeoning medical interest in gynecology in the nineteenth century as an index to the transclass quality of white men's ambivalence—like Meigs's—over the human costs of being in the marketplace. Displacing that ambivalence onto women's bodies, their obsessive struggle to "know" that body and (to borrow Brown's phrasing) "to understand and control female sexuality is in this sense corollary to the struggle with the process of alienation" imposed by the abstracting discipline of white/national manhood in a competitive, insecure, and rapidly changing economy (133).

George Lippard's infamous 1848 novel *Quaker City* maps these dynamics, allowing us to read in greater detail a cultural thematic of middle-class (or professional) male identity in early gynecology, the way anxieties about impurities within the (male) civic body can be transferred to the sexuality of women; the way men can gain a purchase on positive differentiation within the civic realm by repurifying "fallen" women; the way these displacements ultimately map a melancholic loss of democratically imagined human connectedness.

II *Quaker City: Purity and Danger*

Set in the cradle of liberty, the City of Brotherly Love, Lippard's scandalous and best-selling novel[7] advertised itself as a broad exposé of that urban icon of religious, social, economic, and patriotic ideals. In its opening pages, a dying, kindly, and honest lawyer offers the narrator/"author" a packet of papers that will disclose not simply that "Philadelphia is not so pure as it looks"—as the naive narrator puts it—but will reveal the city to be a "Whited Sepulcher." The dying lawyer offers the narrator an alternative geography to the "regular streets and formal look" of the city, one instead which, though pure on the outside, is "within, all rottenness and dead men's bones . . . rankl[ed]" with "festering corruption" (3–4). To the extent that the novel has been read in this century, it has been viewed as a denunciation of the secret vices of the wealthy elite, calling attention to the overwhelming urban squalor and poverty that they fostered, or at best turned a blind eye toward, and from which they profited. Based, according to editor David Reynolds, on an 1843 case in which a Philadelphian was acquitted of the murder of a man who had allegedly seduced his sister, *Quaker City* caused a great deal of public speculation over which other "local celebrities Lippard was trying to expose in his various subplots" (Lippard xii–xiii).

Within pages of the novel's opening, readers are introduced to an astrologer who "disclose[s] the remarkable fact, that the great, the good and the wise of the Quaker City" are engaged in all kinds of schemes, lies, and adulteries. Lippard renders Philadelphia as a dark and brutal urban landscape of stark class discrepancy, "row[s] of massive buildings, dwellings and warehouses, with a small frame house, arising near the centre of the square, like an image of starvation in the midst of plenty" (403). In one of the most painfully human (as opposed to surreally painful) scenes in the novel, the wealthy and well-fed banker Job Joneson ridicules an unemployed mechanic who is pleading that Joneson return his six-hundred-dollar deposit. The bank has declared bankruptcy, defaulting on its depositors, and though the mechanic Davis explains that his daughter is ill, Joneson callously urges him to find a job or take out a loan, refusing even to give him a single dollar: "The fact is, were I to listen to all such appeals to my feelings, I would be a beggar tomorrow" (408). Banker Joneson is a suitable representative of the type of men who frequent Monk Hall, the multistoried and mostly subterranean site of the most sensational actions in the novel, and a secret nightly gathering place for Philadelphia's social and political elite. Reynolds observes that: "Lippard's notion of a huge Monk Hall where the wealthy gathered to revel was by no means a complete fabrication. Very exclusive social clubs for the wealthy formed during this period. The Philadelphia Club, founded in 1834, had 160 members by the mid 1840s . . . [such] clubs represented a highly visible, arrogant display of status on the part of the urban elite. The main pastimes at the clubs were card playing, smoking, chatting and wine drinking. From Lippard's working-class perspective, the clubs seemed nothing less than demonic" (Lippard xxxiii).[8] In Lippard's handling, the club of Monk Hall becomes the sinister heart of the city, breeding evil and subsuming goodness.

If Lippard offered *Quaker City* as an exposé of the wealthy elite, he just as arguably offered it as advice literature for the laboring classes. From the opening chapters of the novel, it would seem he is as concerned to correct or prevent dissipation among men of the middle and working classes as he is to excoriate the villainous debaucheries of the wealthy.[9] Well before we see or even hear of Monk Hall, readers are introduced to the Oyster Cellar, which the narrator details for unknowledgeable readers. He traces the physical layout, summarizes the clientele ("not the very select, you may be sure"), and then moralizes:

A strange tale might be told, could the stairway leading into the Oyster Cellar be gifted with the power of speech. Here Youth has gone down laughing merrily, and here Youth has come up, his ruddy cheek wrinkled and his voice quavering with premature age. Here Wealth has gone down, and kept going down until at last he came up with his empty pocket, turned inside out, the gripe of grim starvation on his shoulder. Here Hope, so young, so gay, so lighthearted has gone down, and came up transformed into a very devil with sunken cheeks, bleared eyes and a cankered heart. O merry cavern of the Oyster Cellar, nestling under the ground so close to Independence Hall, how great the wonders, how mighty the doings, how surprising the changes accomplished in your pleasant den, by your jolly old Giant of a Decanter! (10)

Lippard here deploys what was by the mid-1840s an increasingly familiar temperance rhetoric. Numerous critics and historians have recently insisted on the central importance of temperance to the social culture and class formations of the new nation. Paul Faler has argued that "[t]emperance reform must be viewed as an integral part in the larger process of social disciplining, the tightening of the moral code and the creation of a system of values compatible with the needs of an emerging industrial society" (130). He insists that it would be "erroneous to view industrial morality solely as a bourgeois or middle class way of life that was imposed on the rest of society" (137), detailing how the economic changes of the early nineteenth century reinforced the appeal of what he terms "industrial morality" *across* economic groups. The artisan and working classes as well as the emergent middle classes could and increasingly did demonstrate, in Faler's words, an "extreme orientation toward work, maximum productivity and material accumulation" (137).

The male-purity movement emerging in the second quarter of the century held this orientation over and against all of the social ills associated with intemperate drinking: poverty, vice, loose sexuality and illegitimacy, idleness and self-indulgence. To the extent that no atrocity in the novel fails to include the willing and/or forced intake of alcohol and/or drugs, Lippard's novel could arguably be read as a temperance or male-purity jeremiad,[10] warning not just against the antidemocratic implications of elite corruptions in the early nation, but as insistently against the self-corruption of working boys and men in the cities. Indeed, the narrator emphatically locates the beginning and (near) end of the novel's disastrous course of events *in* the Oyster Cellar. In this sense, the novel aggressively advocates, mostly by negative contrast, the regime of the male-purity movement, which recommended dietary, sexual, and economic self-restraint. And it is important to recognize here that anti-onanism and temperance arguments aimed not simply at masturbation and drinking. As Carroll Smith-Rosenberg has observed, the stringent control of self advocated by those movements promised to hold the line not just against "unproductive" sexual pleasures and drunken mobs, but more especially against emergent forms of urbanized male autonomy and democratizing association (see "Sex as Symbol").

Indeed, cultural anxieties that underwrite the male-purity movement pervade *Quaker City*—anxieties recently and helpfully summarized by Michael Moon—are "about the loss of boundaries between mind and body, of erotic boundaries between males, of boundaries of gender between men and women, and of boundaries between races and social classes" (*Disseminating Whitman* 59). The novel, to encapsulate my point, is a complicated and even contradictory mixture of arguments: (1) against the antidemocratic ramifications of class stratification, (2) for working- and middle-class males' advantageous self-suiting for democracy *and* industrial capitalism through temperance and self-restraint, and (3) for the maintenance of careful social boundaries, the crossing of which threatens, it would seem, to turn the Quaker City into a "Whited Sepulcher" of Sodom. In other words, in a cursory look the novel does seem indeed straightforwardly to be a radical critique of the way class stratification threatens the City of Brotherly Love. But a closer reading suggests that in the Quaker City the radical social ramifications *of* democratic "brotherly love" threaten at least equally to undermine the city's "purity" in a riot of sexual excess, violent pleasures, disorderly mixing, and uncontrolled hybridity.[11]

Repeatedly, the novel reveals that the disorder and deceptions of the unregulated social mixing unleashed by class climbing menaces civic order at least as much as the heartlessness of the wealthy. Algernon Fitz-Cowles, for instance, is a class-climbing con-man, for which practice he employs a variety of costumes and identities. In an interesting exchange with his servant, "Dim," Fitz-Cowles demands: "Now Dim, answer me, one question. *Who are we?* " Responds Dim: "Massa take de chile for a philly sofer? Dat berry cute question! Sometime we are a plantaw from the Souf—sometimes we are a son of a Mexican Prince; oder time we come from Englan' and our fader is a Lord. De High-Golly! We are so many tings, dat de debbil hisself could'nt [*sic*] count 'em—" (Lippard 155). If the novel's villain, Lorrimer, is infamous for his sexual seductions, Fitz-Cowles, as well as "the Jew" with whom he temporarily associates,[12] is infamous for his economic swindles. As the characters of Fitz-Cowles and Lorrimer suggest, then, it is virtually impossible, thanks to the elasticity of "whiteness" within democratic urban culture, to know any man's class origins or motives with any surety.

But, as we might expect, it is a woman—Dora Livingstone—who serves as the novel's central example of this threat. From a laboring-class background, she leaves her first love, Luke, for the wealthier merchant Livingstone, whom she proceeds to plot to kill with her new aristocratically titled paramour, Fitz-Cowles. Dora's "very soul," as Fitz-Cowles exclaims in some amazement, "seems absorbed in this ambition to rise," her desire to be, in her own words, "the Cobbler's grand-daughter with a *title*" (Lippard 188). Dora uses her beauty to practice deceit, impersonating innocence: "she, so beautiful, so queenly, and so like the impersonation of a pure Thought in every outline of her form! . . . this, was once a confiding, loving and boasting girl; but the Canker of Ambition has warmed itself into her Soul, the atmosphere of Sensuality has changed her inner nature while her outward beauties remain the same!" (251–52). Dora's primary threat is not to the poor of Philadelphia (though with financial power she becomes, presumably, complicit with the exploitation of the "poor mechanics") so much as to the tender and faithful heart of Livingstone, who turns out, as luck would have it, to be possessed of a *real* aristocratic lineage (as opposed to the sham one that con-man Fitz-Cowles assumes to gain Dora's affection and her widow's inheritance).

It seems to be less for the debaucheries *of* the wealthy, than for the unguarded, profligate nature of social/sexual mixing and class-climbing from out of the laboring classes that Devil-Bug's dream suggests the city, like Sodom, will be destroyed. With the sole exception of Mabel Pyne/Izole Livingstone (who is revealed as the illegitimate daughter of Devil-Bug), all the other harmed "innocents" in the novel court their own seduction. Mary, for instance, violates the social purity of her class by consenting to talk with both female and male strangers on the street, which behavior leads to her entrapment and rape. Her brother, Byrnewood, meets the "Libertine," Lorrimer, on the streets as well, and sets the action of the plot into motion when he baits Lorrimer into a bet, questioning Lorrimer's projected schedule for finishing his next (as yet unnamed) target for seduction. *Quaker City* seems to suggest that everyone is accountable for the defilement of the "Whited Sepulcher" and that even those who aren't directly culpable are contaminated by it. The song Devil-Bug hears in his apocalyptic dream is: "a lament for the dead who were to die on the morrow. It was a lament for the young maidens, for grey haired and helpless men, for smiling and sinless babes. All were to be mingled in the destruction of the morrow, all were to share the doom and the death of the Last Day of the guilty and idolatrous city" (383). "WO UNTO SODOM" is the refrain of Devil-Bug's dream. Drawing on the work of historians Vern Bullough and Martha Voght, Newfield observes in his reading of this passage that "sodomy before 1890 did not so much convey an idea of a specific deed as a form of compulsive male depravity . . . a social as well as a sexual crime" (*Emerson* 96), evoking a wide sense of inappropriate social and sexual mixture, quite differently from today, where it denotes a particular sexual act.[13] G. J. Barker-Benfield's analysis of male-purity crusader John Todd's use of the word reveals that in 1867, even heterosexual, maritally sanctioned sex could be condemned as sodomitical if it wasn't used for the proper ends of reproduction and race purity (211).

Devil-Bug, with his "tawny cheeks" and "swarthy visage" (Lippard 221, 242) only epitomizes, then, what emerges as the most threatening criminal element in the novel, the creolization of his patent phrase— "I wonders how that 'ud vork?" (554)—literally spelling out the irregular and hybrid results of a forfeited pure group ideal. The reckless affiliation of Mary and Byrnewood with Lorrimer is physically manifested in characters who either are suggestively racialized or literally confirmed as Creoles. From the fallen Bess's "very faint brown . . . complexion" (77) to the Creole servant Dim/Endymion, to the "sallow paint which marred the eternal manhood" of Ravoni's face (461), the novel both hints at and literalizes the threat of unguarded social mixing as *racialized* hybridization. The threat left looming at the end of the novel after the death of Devil-Bug and Lorrimer reaches well beyond the boundaries of Philadelphia: this threat is precisely one aimed at the purity and boundedness of the white nation. A mysterious "Personage" appears, who is hinted (at the verge of the Mexican War, 1846–48), to be a *Mexican Prince!* He does identify himself as the father of Fitz-Cowles, pronouncing his son "the bastard of a creole slave" (553, 551). He reveals the mission of his appearance in Philadelphia as nothing less than the takeover of the United States: "By the God, that rules the fate of nations, when I look over their crumbling fragment of a republic, I see rising above its ruins, the Giant Image of a [*sic*] Empire and a King!" (550). Already infiltrating the "pure" nation with illegitimate, creolized spawn, the mysterious Personage threatens political and sexual defilement of the U.S./us, a corruption threatening from outside the border that will take advantage of boundary weaknesses within.

On Homoerotic Heterosexuality and Its Discontents

This looming threat points us not so much toward international politics as toward what I take to be an important remapping of difference and sameness increasingly useful for negotiating male working-culture anxieties in this period. While the novel's driving plot has to do with the seduction of two innocent women, Mary and Mabel, its shadow plot—competition and attraction between Byrnewood and Lorrimer—is articulated through the impending doom of territorial competition and hostile national takeover. Or we could say, the novel carries through with a two-layered diversionary plot only in a hollowly formal sense, leaving off the "brown peril" plot without resolving it, and unconvincingly giving Mary the novel's last (heterosexual) word ("Lorraine!"). Between those story lines, the novel insistently returns to a different emotional center: the strong attraction between Lorrimer and Byrnewood, whose fates, the astrologer tells them when they visit, "are linked together till death" (Lippard 29). The astrologer elaborates that he has coincidentally cast horoscopes for both these young men, only to discover that the future of each is "as like . . . as night is to-night" (30). He warns them that only by staying away from each other can they avoid their disastrous fate. Presented with a choice, these two men, equally handsome, equally privileged, equally leisured, and equally guilty of cruel seductions, refuse to heed the astrologer's warning. Byrnewood urges Lorrimer along toward their bet, the success of which they will confirm together that evening at Monk Hall: "Lorrimer you are not frightened by the preachings of this fortune-teller? . . . You will not give up the girl? Ha—ha—scared by an owl! Ha—ha" (32). Lorrimer responds: "Give up the girl? Never! She shall repose in my arms before daylight! . . . Come on Byrnewood—let us away."

The intensity of the men's desire to carry through this bet evokes what Patricia Cline Cohen has characterized as a "homoerotic dimension" in the construction of nineteenth-century urban middle-class heterosexuality. In her analysis of the 1834 murder of Helen Jewett, a "fancy brothel" prostitute in New York City, Cohen uncovered a striking pattern of behavior among the men—mostly clerks—who engaged her services. From the ninety letters recovered from Jewett's room, Cohen has argued, "[s]everal common themes emerge." The men who utilized Jewett's services corresponded with her "as if they were gentlemen suitors," with one striking exception: "[n]ot only did they acknowledge that she had other clients and lovers; they seemed to welcome, promote even, sharing with her friends" ("Unregulated Youth" 35–36). Evidence from the letters suggests that men took pleasure in the exchange of information about the evenings they shared with Jewett. Cohen summarizes, "[t]he elaborate rituals of yielding

place and the concern to be knowledgeable about each other's performance suggest that for these young men, heterosexuality had a homosocial dimension to it: it was comprehended and validated through
the eyes of male friends, instead of being an entirely private matter
between a heterosexual couple" (36). Similarly, Lorrimer and Byrnewood construct a homoerotic ritual of heterosexual exchange, which
turns bad (which is to say, the homoerotic exchange is foreclosed
by the retributive obligations of compulsory heterosexuality) when
Byrnewood discovers the victim to be his sister.

The novel leaves us with a vision of Byrnewood, acquitted of Lorrimer's murder, but hopelessly obsessed with his memory and image.
Byrnewood has retreated, with the servant woman he himself had
seduced, now his wife, and his defiled sister Mary, to the very locale
Lorrimer promised Mary they would live after their marriage, Wyoming (Pennsylvania). And we find that Byrnewood's study has become the secret temple of Lorrimer. "Oh Byrnewood, do not enter
that chamber today," pleads his wife Annie: "I have never sought to
know the Secret of that dreary place, I have never crossed its threshold. But this I know, that you are always dark and gloomy, after you
have spent but a moment, within its walls" (Lippard 573). Byrnewood spends his time in the room compulsively rehearsing Lorrimer's
seduction of Mary, and his own trial for Lorrimer's murder. But that
heterosexual ritual of affective displacement does not finally succeed:
"The Avenger knew that he was right in the sight of God, in the execution of the fearful deed which had been death to the Libertine, but
still there was one thought, never absent from his soul. At his board,
on his pillow, in the walk through the wild wood or the crowded city,
the face of Lorrimer was ever with him. He found an awful pleasure
in contemplating the portrait of the Libertine" (574). Deliberately self-
secluded from the company of men, Byrnewood is only able to think
of Lorrimer. When the women, uninvited, enter his study, Byrnewood
reacts with alarm: " 'Ha!' he cried, with a sudden start as he perceived
the intruders. 'Mary have I not told you, never to cross that threshold—' " (575). Though the women's exclusion is ostensibly for their
"protection," Byrnewood's irritation at their sudden intrusion documents something different than their protection and points instead
toward his attempt to preserve in death the sanctity of a bond and the
enjoyment of a connection that could not be sustained in life. The
violent termination of competition, then—the necessity of one man
having to kill his "equal"—is the traumatic center of the story, the

heterosexual and national crisis plots serving ultimately as dramatic repositories for anxieties of attraction and competition, for the fore-closed desires, generated between men.[14]

Mapping Difference

Lippard, like his hero Byrnewood, relies on the thematic rerouting of these anxieties into questions of women's fallen purity as a first-order strategy. The novel's resolute focus on female sexuality is a multilay-ered structure—not only does Lippard use Mary's seduction and rape as his framing device, but he also claims in the 1849 author's preface that the specter of imperiled female innocence is what drove him to write the book:

> I was the only Protector of an Orphan Sister. I was fearful that I might be taken away by death, leaving her alone in the world. I knew too well that law of society which makes a virtue of the dis-honor of a poor girl, while it justly holds the seduction of a rich man's child as an infamous crime. These thoughts impressed me deeply. I determined to write a book, founded upon the follow-ing idea:
>
> *That the seduction of a poor and innocent girl, is a deed al-together as criminal as deliberate murder. It is worse than the murder of the body, for it is the assassination of the soul. If the murderer deserves death by the gallows, then the assassin of chastity and maidenhood is worthy of death by the hands of any man, and in any place.* (1–2; original emphasis)

Analogizing the vices of a city and an economic system to the seduc-tion of an "innocent" woman and seating female sexual "purity" in her soul, Lippard locates questions of civic order in women's mys-terious interiors. Men's criminal dramas are mapped across female bodies. Using a sexual geography that echoes Meigs's, Lippard re-peatedly depicts women's seductions in elaborate tableaux of arousal, where their "high" innocence struggles with their "low" animal na-ture, where swelling sexual excitement overflows and colors their "pure" whiteness. Reader attention is trained virtually not at all to-ward actual sex acts between men and women; rather the excitement of these scenes depends on watching women battle it out with them-selves.

Mabel is paradigmatic in this respect. Drugged and transported to

Monk Hall for the perverted pleasures of the man who passes himself off as her father, Reverend F. A. T. Pyne,[15] readers are treated to pages of Mabel's drug-induced arousal.[16] In her usual state of innocent lucidity, Mabel increasingly recognizes her "father" as a sexualized threat, though she is hardly able to articulate that threat from the vantage of sanity. When we first meet her, she has fled from her father's house, and is raving, "—Stand back from the bedside! Back! Back, I say, or you will drive me mad!" (Lippard 209). "Brother Pyne" has her removed from her refuge to his house, where when we see her again, she lies sleeping, "dressed in spotless white." Her temptation for Pyne is her beauty, "of that peculiar cast which mingles high intellect and purity of soul with all the enticing loveliness of a fair young form, soft limbs, a delicate bosom, throbbing with the impulses of youthful blood and a lustrous black eye beaming with the undeveloped love of a stainless soul" (292). Her sexual purity manifests itself in physical whiteness, her "countenance white as marble . . . without the warm hues, which tint the lips with love, and fire the cheek with passion" (293).

Lippard presents Mabel's purity as physicalized whiteness; Mabel herself identifies sexuality as death. When she revives, already under the influences of drugs, she sees her "father" and his uncanny double: "Father, look, look! There, at your very shoulder, stands a skeleton, winding a grave-shroud round your limbs!" (320). As the drug begins to take its full effect, Mabel's countenance colors voluptuously as her "animal nature" takes over: "the girl stood erect, her form raised to its full height, her eyes gathering new fire every instant, her cheek blooming with unnatural freshness. . . . Oh how beautiful the picture—a vivid impersonation of beauty, mere animal loveliness, yet still bewitching loveliness, utterly deprived of intellect! The long dark hair falling over the shoulders, the erect attitude, the extended arms, and the flowing robes of snowy white, the large dark eyes, dilating every instant and swimming in a strange light, the pale face with the burning freshness in the centre of each cheek, the red lips and the young bosom rising faintly into view. Oh beautiful as a dream, and yet more terrible than death!" (322–23). Perhaps more generously than Meigs, who insists that women's intellects are fully tied to and limited by their reproductive mission, Lippard grants women "high" intelligence, of which they become deprived by sexual arousal. Like Meigs, though, he locates women's sexuality in the lowness of "animal nature." Strikingly, Mabel's sexual arousal is characterized in phallic terms—she is "erect" and "raised" and fiery. In this powerful state of sexual arousal, she, like her libidinous "father," is a specter of death.

Sexual Mabel is described in terms surprisingly evocative of the narrator's description of the aroused Lorrimer just before he rapes Mary. Readers there witness an elaborate seduction, with Lorrimer describing in sensuous detail the "fair valley of Wyoming" (Lippard 126), where he proposes they should live. As Lorrimer offers Mary an imaginative tour, readers watch his hand traveling to reveal Mary's (soon heaving) breasts. Just at the point that she is fully revealed to the readers and her lover, Mary begins to resist her rising sexual passion, and Lippard redirects the reader's gaze from the girl to Lorrimer: "Playing with the animal nature of the stainless girl, Lorrimer had aroused the sensual volcano in his own base heart. . . . He stood before the crouching girl, a fearful picture of incarnate LUST. . . . His form rose towering and erect, his chest throbbing with sensual excitement, his hands hung, madly clinched by his side, while his curling hair fell wild and disordered over his brows. . . . His blood-shot eyes, flashed with the unholy light of passion, as he stood sternly surveying the form of his victim. There was something wild and brutal in their savage glare" (133). (Lorrimer, who has bragged that he never forces women into sex, but rather makes a woman "the instrument of her own ruin" by arousing her animal nature through conversation, now perpetrates the "crime that has no name," raping Mary.) Descriptively, Lippard doesn't differentiate between the sexual "nature" of men and women: both can be overtaken by the deathly specter of illicit sexual arousal. But he differentiates by locating "innocence" in women, as their purview. *All* the key male characters in the story are revealed to be seducers, from Lorrimer and Pyne to Byrnewood and Livingstone. It is women who are "naturally" innocent, and it is toward women that Lippard insists we must look if we are to comprehend with outrage the corruptions of the Quaker City.

Though sexuality is figured as death for both male and female characters, death itself is sexualized in the female body—the "Whited Sepulcher." The narrator lavishes extravagant detail on the dismembered corpses in Ravoni's Dissecting Room; for instance, the following passage: "Here lay an arm, whose soft and beautiful outlines, were terminated by a small and graceful hand, and over the alabaster arm and the snow hand, the blue taint of decay spread like a foul curse, turning loveliness into loathing. . . . the head had been severed and below the purple neck two white globes, the bosom of what had once

been woman, were perceptible in the light. And the Rainbow of corruption crept like a foul serpent around that bosom. . . . And on this
fair bosom hands of affection had been pressed, or sweet young children had nestled; or maybe the white skin had crimsoned to a lover's
kiss!" (Lippard 437). Given the novel's strong associations of sexuality with animality and death, the visual logic here seems hard to
miss, particularly considering the evocation of the "foul serpent." The
careful reader already "knows" what the narrator suggests, that the
woman died of carnal knowledge. Though her sexuality is repurified
by the blanch of death, her body cannot but recall the recombinant
corruption of sexuality and death that placed it there. This abjection
of women's sexuality is a repeating motif in the text. For instance,
after Byrnewood reels away from the deathbed of the servant girl he
seduced, Ravoni appears to claim the corpse, apparently for his own
scientific uses. As the sheet covering Annie is removed, "Ravoni gazed
at the lifeless girl. Death was there in beauty. . . . The neck was snow-
white, and as the sheet was lifted slowly up, a gleam of light shone
upon a fair young bosom—dainty food for grave worms!" (411-12).

In her analysis of how women's bodies are mapped by "libidinal
pathways," Elizabeth Grosz argues that in the West, women's bodies
have been constructed with more complexity than poststructuralist
terms like "lack" or "absence" allow us to see. Rather, she considers
the ways in which "women's corporeality is inscribed as a mode of
seepage," a "disorder that threatens all order" (203). Lippard's evocation of the worms that will feed on this dead woman's torso presages
an observation that the Philadelphian Meigs would make two years
later in his study of *Females and their Disorders:* "When a woman becomes pregnant, the breast very speedily begins to grow larger; the fat
deposited upon it is sensibly increased in quantity, and if the gland be
taken between the thumb and four fingers, it is found that the fascia
which encloses the materials of the gland is fuller and more tense,
and has a granular feel; in many it feels as if it were full of strings or
ridges, *giving in some women, a sensation as if it were filled with hard
earthworms*" (650; emphasis added). In *Quaker City,* as in Meigs's
lectures on women's "distinctive characteristics," women's sexuality
and sexual reproductivity threatens symbolic and actual death, decay
and disorder.

This theme is even clearer in the next passage, where Meigs muses
on the way the physical changes brought on by pregnancy actually
threaten to overcome the whiteness of the "Caucasian" female sub-

ject: "At the same time this process of augmentation within begins, the aureole increases its area, and, what is very singular, and worthy of your observation, the corpus mucosum of the skin beneath the areole, *acquires the power of excreting pigmentum nigrum;* just as if the corpus mucosum had now become endowed with a pigmentary membrane, like that that lies beneath the skin of a Negro, a Malay, or an American Indian; but does not exist beneath the skin in the Caucasian race" (*Females* 650–51; emphasis added).[17] As for Lippard, a woman's own sexual arousal replaces her "innocent nature" with an animal presence, so for Doctor Meigs, the bodily changes associated with pregnancy seem capable of overflowing a woman's whiteness with a marked raciality: for both men, sexuality "colors" the "innocence" of white women. Or, we could say, sexual women are always already contaminated/contaminatory hybrids. Grosz provides a nice summary here for what Meigs and Lippard (much as we have seen in Jefferson, Rush, and Lewis) are arguably circumnavigating in their mapping of women's unstable boundaries and flows: "The metaphorics of uncontrollability, the ambivalence between desperate fatal attraction and strong revulsion, the deep-seated fear of absorption, the association of femininity with contagion and disorder, the undecidability of the limits of the female body (particularly, but not only with the onset of puberty and in the case of pregnancy), its powers of cynical seduction and allure are all common themes in literary and cultural representations of women. But these themes may well be a function of the projection outward of their corporealities, the liquidities that men seem to want to cast out of their own self-representation" (203).

Worrying Sameness

Lippard runs into the same difficulties with his plot that Meigs runs into with his medical argument: this transfer of dis-ease from male corporeality and masculine socio-professional relations to female bodies and heterosexual plots provides a durable but finally insufficient ordering system for those anxieties. The very excessiveness of the novel, with its surreal imagery, its obsessive returns to underground pits, subterranean dungeons, rotting bodies, and body-rending violence signals the energy that drives concerns about fixing sameness and difference. The aggressive presentation of dissolving corpses and dismembered bodies betrays a fear of dissolution, a compulsive concern for the installation of difference, of a bounded nation, city, and manhood. The recurring rape/seduction plot then provides both structural and symbolic recourse to the ordering of gender oppositionality, which promises to structure a whole series of relations, not simply between male and female, but also sameness and difference, external and internal, high and low, active and passive, life and death, subject and object.

The concern to secure a "hard," bounded male body/self is nowhere more evident than in Ravoni's medical theater. This scene foreshadows Byrnewood's ascension to the status of the Avenger. Ravoni, the mysterious scientist, recently arrived in the city from "God knows whence," has utterly captivated local medical and scientific students. As Dr. McTorniquet explains to Byrnewood, "He walked into our Medical Halls unbidden, and proved himself a great Anatomist, a splendid Surgeon. No one has had the bravery or impudence to question him concerning his former life, because there's a cold impenetrable gleam in his eye, that few men would like to brave—" (Lippard 435). Ravoni has widely advertised his promise to reveal "some new Theory of the origin of life, which he will illustrate by the dissection of a subject" (436). The event draws a national audience of medical men but is thwarted when the medical subject turns out to be a pauper's corpse livid with smallpox.[18] The audience mobs out of the room in panic; only Ravoni and Byrnewood remain. As the narrator describes it, Byrnewood "had seen the crowd, he too had looked upon the corse, he too had felt some throbbings of panic, palpitated in the air of the room, but he still stood, silent and firm, tho' ashy pale." The scientist praises his fearlessness in the face of infection and certifies him in the highest (and most intimate) of terms: "Thou hast a firm soul . . . And by my soul, yes . . . By the Soul of Ravoni thou shall be one of the Chosen; thou shalt be a Priest of the Faith!" (442).

The firm souled, courage-bounded manhood of Byrnewood and Ravoni provides a strong contrast to the "sweet maiden-man . . . sweet virgin-man" earlier lambasted by the narrator (Lippard 305). *This* man is an urban subject unsuited to stare death in the face, as Byrnewood and Ravoni do. An unnatural mix of male and female sentiment, the "be-pantalooned girl . . . Mister-Miss . . . maiden-man" (305–6) is no help to the project of redeeming the city: "Your perfumes agree but sorrily with the thick atmosphere of this darkening vault, your white-kid gloves would be soiled by a contact with the rough hands of Devil-Bug, your innocent and girlish soul would be shocked by the very idea of such a hideous cavern, hidden far below the red brick surface of broad-brimmed Quakertown. . . . Our taste is different from yours. We like to look at nature and at the world, not only as they appear, but as they are!" (305). This passage differentiates the effeminate, other-man from the male collective, the "we" who assume a flinty, objective, scientific vantage, who can look at, see into, and know the truth of a subject. Hard men armed with science can redeem the corruptions of the "fallen" woman, as we see when Ravoni dramatically and by the simple force of his own magnetic will brings Annie back to life.

Science provides a dramatic arena for the heroic man's recuperation of the racially/sodomitically degraded female. This fantasy of masculine recuperation is played out simultaneously as a decontaminating heterosexualization and a hierarchizing professionalization. Ravoni's handpicked followers, culled "from the various medical schools, and from the haunts and nooks of the wide city" (Lippard 444) are initiated into the "New Faith" by the miracle of Annie's revivification; their faith is summoned in a theater of male performativity, over the dead body of a fallen woman. In the range of scientific application, this "miracle" is presented as its ultimate performance. Ravoni's apprentice men of science will learn to enact a sanitizing mastery over all the otherness loaded onto "woman"—sexuality, corruption, disease, death. They will "look into the bosom of the Universe, and make the secrets of nature your own, train the lightnings to your will, and sweep the souls of men in adoration at your feet! . . ." (448).

That Ravoni's promise slips easily from revealing the "bosom" of nature to subjugating other men demonstrates the usefulness of heterosexuality, as Cohen suggests, for forging disciplined relationships between men. These twenty-four apprentices, who share "haggard faces, high pale foreheads, well developed in the ideal organs and white hands tremblingly grasping rolls of manuscript" (Lippard 444) come together in a context that (temporarily) converts the male aggression that always threatens men with competition, into a reassuring sameness. These men, embracing a heroic and active manhood that defies death, are as different from women as they are from the "sweet virgin-man" for the very fact of their aggressive pursuit of "naked nature." Ravoni's gospel negotiates the demands of fraternal sameness and differentiation, promising them simultaneously that their share of God—the ultimate manhood—exceeds that of other men not in the room, and that each man in the room has equal access to that manhood. He reassures, in other words, their need to experience fraternal sameness as individualizing differentiation:

All men from the slave to the prince, from the dull boor to the man of genius, are connected with each other by an universal sympathy, an invisible influence. . . . This influence or sympathy, call it what you will, is the atmosphere of souls the life of intellects!

Some men absorbing a larger portion of this invisible life than others, become men of genius, warriors or statesmen.

. . . These men demonstrated the great truth, that the AWFUL SOUL having created us, hath left us all to our own salvation or our ruin, as we shall by our deeds determine; thus we shape our own destinies; that we are the masters of our own lives; that we, by developing the mysteries implanted in our bosoms, may walk the earth superior to the clay around us, each man a GOD *in soul!* (447; original emphasis)

In her discussion of "Race and Gender: The Role of Analogy in Science," Nancy Leys Stepan outlines the powerful influence of metaphor in organizing scientific categories. "Without the metaphor linking women and race," she argues, "many of the data on women's bodies (length of limbs, width of pelvis, shape of skull, weight or structure of brain) would have lost their significance as signs of inferiority and would not have been gathered, recorded and interpreted as they were. In fact, without the analogies concerning the 'difference' and similarities among human groups, much of the vast enterprise of anthropology, criminology and gender science would not have existed" (48). In short, the metaphor linking white women to "other races," analogizing women's and men's biological relation of difference to that between Caucasians and "other races," provided, in Stepan's words, "a program of research" (49). Lippard's depiction of Ravoni and his apostles suggests that gender and racial *difference* was not, however, the primary metaphor: rather, the troubled and troubling metaphor of *sameness* that guided civic/market identity propelled the metaphor-driven search for locating "difference" in ever-multiplying "others."

On Mobs, Manhood, and Men

In the intimate and reassuring spaces of the scientific priesthood, the urban mob and its threatening degradations drop away. Men, bathed in their intellectually heroic sameness, are individualized through their relation to pure male/scientific authority. In the classroom, the men sit, "their eyes enchained to [Ravoni's] . . . with a singular intensity," an intensity that recalls the particularity of their selection by Ravoni. Byrnewood's gaze upon the scientist in the amphitheater returns the look that Ravoni gave him when he invited him to the "New Faith": "the eyes of Ravoni were fixed upon him; he felt his veins fire and his heart kindle as that glare shot into his soul, like a ray of light from the eternal world" (Lippard 444).

But in this exchange, "[t]hey were no longer the same men" (Lippard 448). The mobs of the street are banned only to recur in that very assemblage of students, whose enthusiasm converts them into frightening sameness:

> Every face was stamped with an excitement that corded the veins on the forehead, and fired the eyes with a blaze like that which streamed from the dark orbs of Ravoni. It was a terrible picture of Fanaticism.
>
> "We are thine!" they shouted in one voice raising their hands in the light. . . .
>
> Byrnewood Arlington was no more himself. . . . he joined in the chorus of fanatics. "I am thine!" (448)

Lippard seems not so much to question the differentiating scientific project of "look[ing] into the bosom of the Universe" so much as he seems to fear the bathetic sameness that converts groups of like-minded men into mobs. After all, Ravoni does revive the dead Annie, and in the same spirit, Byrnewood marries her, socially resurrecting the woman whose "fall" he earlier engineered. Take away the sex and rotting bodies, and we have a plot structure that would satisfy Rush's instructions for building "Republican Machines." Men verify their manhood not amongst each other, but in their sexual rescue of (corrupted/diseased) women: they claim their manhood not just heterosexually but *gynecologically*.

For Lippard, there seems to be no middle ground, in the City of Brotherly Love, between the debauched male friendship of the Oyster Cellar and Monk Hall, and the threatening professional "priesthood" of Ravoni's science. Dangers for men lurk everywhere; there is no safety in male affiliation.[19] Both social and professional association result in the murder of the key figure: Byrnewood kills Lorrimer, Devil-Bug kills Ravoni. Devil-Bug kills himself, and Byrnewood, lesson learned, retreats to an all-female enclave. The only safe relations for men seem to be with women. But the only ones that matter, as Byrnewood's lingering obsession with Lorrimer reveals, are with men.

III

J. Marion Sims

Lippard's presentation of Ravoni's science pulls in multiple directions: he leaves readers hung between its promises and its threats (much as working men undoubtedly felt stretched by the unstable, rapidly changing economy of the 1830s and 1840s). Lippard's strategy for tidying the story is finally the "straight" sexual rescue: a heterosexual marriage. J. Marion Sims (1813–83), operating medically and not fictionally, strove for the scientific rescue, surgically rerouting women's flows into proper channels. In Sims's work from the mid-1840s forward, we see the thematic transfer of cultural anxieties into programmatic and surgical imperatives.

Sims is known to medical history as the "father" (or, the "fountainhead") of gynecology.[20] Sims's biographer, Seale Harris, MD, describes Sims as "one of a few outstanding nineteenth-century pioneers who added more to the basic knowledge of medicine and surgery in three or four decades than had been accumulated in all the thousands of years preceding" (xix, xvi). Less enthusiastically, G. J. Barker-Benfield chronicles Sims's medical achievements: "His first and most indisputable claim was his surgical cure of the vesico-vaginal fistula—a tear or tears in the walls of the vagina during parturition—causing continual and hitherto irremediable leakage from the bladder. . . . His greatest general influence was to encourage an extremely active, adventurous policy of surgical interference with woman's sexual organs. He was a pioneer in several operative techniques, including pre-Lister cleanliness; the speeding up of healing of the vagina by covering the cut surface with mucous membrane; and the surgical treatment of cancer in women. He was a prolific inventor of surgical instruments, [and] the moving spirit behind the founding of the Woman's Hospital (in 1855)" (91).[21] Sims experimented in artificial insemination as part of his interest in fertility treatment. Serving as the president of the American Medical Association (1876), he worked to enact the licensing and regulation of prostitutes in cities.[22] He was one of the first doctors in the United States to earn real wealth from his practice; as he wrote to Samuel D. Gross, "No man in our country 'solitary and alone' ever made as much as I have by my profession" elaborating that

he could make as much as fifty thousand dollars a year from his practice in Europe (qtd. in McGregor 265).[23] He worked later in his career
to overturn AMA codes forbidding physicians from advertising and
taking out patents on surgical tools.[24] Despite his enormous professional clout, he was widely regarded as a contentious, difficult man;
Sims repeatedly felt betrayed by and fell out with close associates.

I am reading Sims's own account of his early career in gynecology thematically, as an alternative to medically driven histories of his
work. I want to use my reading of *Quaker City* to draw out the cultural concerns that run through and orient Sims's early investments
in gynecological surgery. I do so in order to highlight how Sims's
work in gynecology had a national as well as a class interest—in stabilizing samenesses and differences such that they helped to consolidate the purview of national manhood and professional masculinity.
I want to be clear about my argumentative aims in this section especially, because of the way the larger issues I am studying can easily
be lost in focusing on an individual actor. It is not entirely evident
to me, for instance, that Sims was personally a rampant misogynist—
in fact, his relationships with women seem better throughout his life
than those with men. That said, I would never be willing to exoner-
ate him from accusations of profound medical cruelty toward women,
particularly black women and poor white women.[25] But I am far less
interested with questions of his individual "culpability"—however
that might be assessed—than with those about the cultural logic of
his contributions toward navigating, consolidating, and professionalizing the interests of white/national male desire(s) in the practice of
gynecology.

G. J. Barker-Benfield has analyzed Sims's anxieties about career and
"horror" of women, finding in Sims's career support for his argument
that "[h]ostility toward women and competition among men were the
conditions for the rise of modern gynecology" (96). Though he does
not overlook race as a dimension in Sims's career, his analysis does
not position it as a fundamental term in a history of early U.S. gynecology. I want both to acknowledge the debt I owe to Barker-Benfield's
germinal work on Sims while I supplement and redirect his emphasis on male gynecologists' fear and hatred of women's genitals (see,
for instance, 107) toward one that takes the synergistic imperatives of
whiteness and national manhood more fully into account.[26] I begin
my assessment of what we can learn from Sims in an analysis of
three sets of episodes taken from his 1885 autobiography, *The Story of
My Life*.

1. Of Lice and Men

Sims's autobiography begins conventionally, tracing not just a familial but a national lineage. In chapter 1, he offers a brief history of his father and mother, his rural childhood, his modest beginnings. In chapter 2, he tells a story about his maternal grandmother, Lydia Mackey, who pregnantly and bravely faced the British Colonel Tarleton during the Revolution to gain pardon for her husband Charles, who had been sentenced to die for (patriotic) treason. In chapter 3, as if anticipating fellow gynecologist T. Gaillard Thomas's eulogy, which ranked him with George Washington and William Jenner as one of "three men who in the history of all times had done the most for their fellow men," Sims recounts—explicitly comparing himself to Washington—a humorous and pedagogically instructive lie (qtd. in Barker-Benfield 91).

Pedagogical instruction is in fact the theme of that chapter, titled "My Early School Days." It is organized chronologically, a "humorous" string of anecdotes, mostly vignettes of cantankerous teachers beating, humiliating, and threatening students. We are introduced, for instance, to "old Quigley," who makes it "a rule to whip, when once he began, till the remedy worked either up or down" (i.e., either students vomit or wet their pants; Sims, *Story* 58; see 56). There is Mr. Sanderson, "an Irishman" who "thrashed" his students even when "nearly grown, though he was a small man" (61). There is Mr. Patterson, his father's business partner, who, when Sims was eight, happened to ask him for the "proper name" of a weed growing in the corner of a fence. Records Sims: "I certainly must not appear to be ignorant, so I drew myself up, feeling my importance," and answered decisively, "Jimson weed, sir," whereupon Mr. Patterson chides him for answering out of ignorance. Sims summarizes the episode: "I was never so humiliated in all the days of my life" (65). Then, there is William Williams, "the first native American teacher that we had among us" who douses Sims's novice passion for the Jew's harp by humiliating him with his inability to spell the word. Sims offers "juice-harp," listens with "complete discomfiture" as the boy next to him spells it correctly, and reports, "I never played it afterward" (66–67).[27]

In the midst of these scenes of "the mysteries of pedagogism" (*Story* 57), Sims offers a series of reflections on two less formal sources of instruction, girls and "the black race." Remembering that "when I was a boy I always had a sweetheart," Sims tells the story of a love gone bad. The little sister of a girl he had previously admired, Sallie Caston, was, Sims offers in retrospect, "unsympathetic, and . . . altogether a very stupid girl"—this because she tattles on him for throwing water on her. The schoolteacher, Mr. Williams, questions him, and Marion does not lie: "As long as I had acknowledged it, there was nothing more to say, and Mr. Williams knocked the love for Sallie out of me in about three minutes, and I never was in love with her again after that. She was a poor little forlorn creature" (69). Not so very remarkable, really, until, reading on, the reader confronts a fascinating, and I would say telling, series of associations. The next paragraph begins: "Mr. Williams and I were great friends after that. He was my father's deputy sheriff. He was an admirable teacher, and did the best possible for the advancement of his pupils, and succeeded with all of them who were willing to work. In 1824 [some two years later], my father removed from Hanging-Rock Creek to Lancaster village. I think he went on account of Mr. Williams's school" (69). The pattern of association and displacement in this passage is arresting. Sims, humiliated at the age of nine by a little girl and spanked by his teacher, becomes "great friends" from that moment forward with the agent of his punishment, regarding the girl only as a "poor . . . creature." Deputy sheriff to the father Sims rarely sees,[28] Mr. Williams becomes, it would seem, a deputy father to Marion in the moment of the beating: in the three minutes of pain, Marion learns the asymmetry of heterosexual manhood, and chooses to align himself with male authority.

Sims's father soon decides to move nearer to Lancaster to be closer to duties and the deputy/schoolteacher. In arranging for that move, the father leaves Marion and his brother (temporarily) behind on the farm. Sims explains: "My brother and myself were left at the old place, in charge of a manager and the negroes. Here we were very much neglected; and white children living among negroes, if they were not looked after carefully by the mother, were sure to become lousy. The servants who had charge of us had neglected us entirely, and I shall never forget the mortification that my mother experienced when my brother and myself went to Lancaster to see her, when she found our heads and clothing infested with these little creatures. They belong always to the black race" (*Story* 69). Choosing racial authority this time, Sims displaces his sense of excessive "neglect"—now onto lice-infested "negroes"—the only company he and his brother have in the absence of his parents. In a chapter where humiliation is always instructive, Sims learns not to subject "the mother" to the "mortification" resulting from his (neglect-driven) association with black slaves. He portrays this lesson—the color ban on affection—as his mother's desire for cleanliness. Though he and his brother became "lousy," Sims is careful to allocate ownership: the lice "belong always" elsewhere.

The string of affective dislocation continues into the next paragraph, in another extraordinary story of "infection." The lice that "belong always to the black race" apparently remind him of another affectionate relationship, with a "negro by the name of Cudjo," whom he remembers from the age of "seven or eight." I quote from a lengthy passage: "He was about four feet high, remarkably well built, and his face was beautiful, but horribly tattooed, just as it appears to us, symmetrically done. He said he was captured and brought to this country when he was a boy. He was a prince in his own country, and would have risen to become a king or ruler of the nation or tribe, if he had remained at home there. . . . This man told wonderful stories—ghost stories—and would eat fire, and knock himself with a stick on the head, when he was telling them. I remember how anxiously I looked for him every Saturday night to tell stories that were really poisoning my mind, and infusing into it and my nature a sense of fear which should not have been cultivated in children" (Sims, *Story* 70). A beautiful man with the air of immense authority who wins young Marion's admiration, is later, from the vantage of Marion's identification with his sheriff father and the father's deputy, abjected: the beauty and wonder and kindness that attract Marion to Cudjo must be renounced as "poison." Free-associating here, and violating a chronology that seemingly rules elsewhere in the chapter, Sims offers a chain of memories and signification that begins in humiliation and punishment by white men with authority, and moves to young girls, to lice, to the "black race," and finally to a particular and particularly kind black man who "infected" his childhood. Mediating these associations are figures of authority, the absent one of his father, and the father's two deputies, Marion's teacher and "the" mother.

This chapter would seem to detail and complicate David Leverenz's central argument in his study of "manhood and the American Renaissance"—that male rivalry is the more basic concern in negotiating American "manhood" than fears of women—all the more so as it proceeds into its concluding anecdote. Seemingly redressing the anxiety his tale of "infection" has raised, that he has been feminized, "infus[ed]" in "mind" and "nature" by Cudjo's influence, Sims's next anecdote is about becoming himself an agent of penetration and humiliation. It is also the story of his lie: "It was said Washington never told a lie. I am very sure I am not Washington, for I told one lie in my life and it was a 'whopper'; but I told it very mildly" (*Story* 73). In this episode, Sims plots with a boy in the class to injure another boy, "the best of remarkably good boys" who studies in the schoolmaster's seat while the other boys play. Sims agrees to fix a two-inch pin in the center of the schoolmaster's chair while his cohort distracts the good boy. The distraction, however, works too well: the good boy stays out to play, and the next person to sit in the seat is the schoolmaster himself. When the notoriously bad boys in the class deny placing the pin with a convincing show of innocence, Mr. Connelly is unable to find the perpetrator. He questions Sims; Sims denies it, and Connelly, already believing Sims to be innocent, accepts the lie.

That is not, however, the end of the story. In its conclusion the story returns structurally all the humiliation that teachers have dealt out to Sims. Years later, Sims runs into Connelly on a New York street. He invites him over to dinner where, the story having clearly become a favorite among his children, Connelly is recognized as Sims's victim. As the children giggle over their vicarious participation in the joke, Sims finally offers his former teacher the truth: "Mr. Connelly, I have something to say to you which has been on my conscience for more than a quarter of a century." Mr. Connelly does not take this revelation in the spirit of fun: "He took it in great earnestness and bad humor and could not enjoy it. He was mortified to death" to discover that Sims was the agent of that humiliating pinprick, and refuses to meet with Sims afterward (*Story* 77). Sims, knowing the end of the story as he begins it for his readers, does not seem distressed so much as amused with the outcome: "I always felt sorry that I had to lie, but I can not say I have regretted so much that I did" (73).

Leverenz maps Emerson's attitude toward domesticity and female nurturing as a "depressive strategy of displacing resentment," a maneuver necessitated if he is to maintain his identification with male power (63). For Sims as for Emerson, "[f]eeling" clearly came to mean "pain, powerlessness, resentment and the perils of the body" (Leverenz 62), and thus Sims, well-schooled by numerous beatings and humiliations by his teachers, does not identify with the humiliation he caused Connelly but rather the power he experiences in inflicting it. "We are what we are by education," Sims later asserts (*Story* 99). This chapter records the education of young Marion's desire for human intimacy and democratically imagined connection. His recounting of childhood instruction reveals how such "depressive strateg[ies] of displacing resentment" locate not only an affiliation with male power but also with *whiteness*. Choosing male authority over the nurturing presences of his childhood, Sims adopts the sanitizing, categorizing imperatives of white purity. Blacks, he learns, like girls, humiliation, and lice, "belong always" elsewhere: no mixing allowed.

2. Theaters of Difference

Sims's identification with whiteness may have been more completely achieved in his early education than his affiliation with manhood. In *Vested Interests*, Marjorie Garber explains the "logics, and the effects, of cross-dressing as an index . . . for the notion of category crisis" (16). Garber positions cross-dressing as an index to the permeability of cultural binaries that we might otherwise believe to be "naturally" uncrossable. And despite the severe lessons of his youthful training, Sims presents an episode of cross-dressing in his college years—arising in seeming consequence of a crisis of anxieties about manhood.

Sims emphasizes his aversion to finishing college. At the end of his training at Columbia College, he recalls, "I felt real sorry that the time was drawing near that I would have to assume the stern duties and responsibilities of real life and manhood" (*Story* 113). Returning home, he soon informs his father that he wants to study medicine, knowing his father will disapprove ("There is," declares his father, "no science in it" [116]). Sims departs for Charleston to continue his studies at the new Charleston Medical School. Here he applies himself more diligently to his studies:

> I felt that, as I had failed in my duty as a student in my college course at Columbia, the responsibility of life was now doubly on me, and weighed heavily upon my shoulders. I felt that I had to prepare for a period that I looked forward to not with pleasurable anticipations but with dread. Most of the young men that I had associated with all my life, from ten years old upward had looked forward to manhood with joy and satisfaction; but with me, it was exactly the reverse. I was afraid to be a man; I was afraid to assume its responsibilities, and thought I did not have sense enough to go out into the rough world, making a living as other men do. I was small in stature, and I did not feel that I

had intellect enough to grapple with or to pit myself against such opposition as I should encounter in life. (118)

Like Meigs, Sims is concerned with his stature among men. He follows this confession with details of a couple of episodes just prior to his graduation from Charleston, of enjoyable times spent in the company of his good friend Dick Baker.

Dick, it would seem, did not suffer Sims's anxieties. Sims describes him as "a jolly companionable fellow, and one of the best of men" (*Story* 119). Sims recounts how he allowed Dick to talk him into dressing up as a girl to attend a masquerade ball. Dick's plan is that he will dress as a "country wagoner," with Sims as a "daughter." Sims at first protests: "Dick, that I won't do, for I am afraid it will be discovered. I don't want to put on girl's clothes and do that" (121). But shortly, as though seeing an opportunity to experiment with an alternative to the manhood he dreads entering, Sims agrees. They borrow the costume from Dick's cousins. Discovering at the door that the ball has been canceled, Dick proposes they go to the theater and Sims assents. Thinking that they can sit in the back without drawing much attention, he is dismayed to realize that Southern chivalry will allow no such thing: all the men around him insist on "the lady" moving to the front of the balcony. In the "brightly illuminated" gallery, Marion Sims becomes the object of general scrutiny: "In an instant every opera-glass in that theater was leveled at me and not on the play, until I was nearly crazed" (123).[29] Manhood may be something to dread, but the place of a woman, object of chivalry and subjected to the relentless gaze, is seemingly far more agonizing for Sims. Kept for the entire play "in durance vile" by his friend Dick, Sims is miserable with the scrutiny of the crowd and his fear that "I should be taken up by the police and carried before the court the next day for appearing in public in women's clothes" (125). He never sees Dick again after that evening. The next chapter recounts his medical training, his decisive progress toward the assumption of his manly duties.

This episode seemingly provides one example of how, as Judith Butler has framed it, "sexuality is regulated through the policing and shaming of gender" (*Bodies* 238)—from the intense shame and fear he feels as a man-dressing-as-a-woman, Sims puts down his anxieties about manhood, and mentions them no more. He moves into career and marriage; within ten years, building an ever-more successful local practice, Sims publishes his first surgical article, and begins his career in gynecology. This is a career that allows him to convert the shame and policing that constructed his manhood into agency: his regulation and management of *women's* (damaged, excessive) sexuality.

Thomas Laqueur has argued that "the instability of sameness and difference lies at the very heart of the biological enterprise" (*Making* 17); this is especially true for Sims's gynecology. It is as if his aggressive interventions into women's "difference" is the ground on which he can subsequently build his professional manhood.[30] Or to put this somewhat differently, it is as if Sims is able to define his manhood by becoming one of the most active agents of the eighteenth- and nineteenth-century project outlined by Laqueur, of "translating facts about reproduction into 'facts' about sexual difference" (*Making* 175). These are, of course, assertions that are difficult to "prove." What is certain is that a theatrics of gender became central to Sims's career from the very beginning of his experiments in gynecology, where he scientifically performs Ravoni's promise. In these surgeries Sims presided in the spotlight over a woman, whose subterranean female "disorders" he exposed and manfully repaired under the admiring gaze of fellow doctors.[31] In 1873 the Board of Supervisors of the Woman's Hospital asked for a cap of fifteen spectators for surgeries, complaining that the crowd (sometimes as high as seventy) had become excessive and detrimental to the comfort and modesty of the patients who, often conscious, were perhaps similarly "crazed" by the spectacle they became during the operation. Sims was incensed to the point of resigning.[32]

3. As Different as Our Faces

Before he could rise to prominence as a gynecological surgeon, however, Sims had to overcome his habitual disgust for women's genitals. Sims spent the first ten years of his practice referring out all cases having to do with "any functional derangement of the uterine system" (*Story* 226). But his increasing surgical expertise, particularly his successful surgical technique for harelip, combined with an accidental encounter with a gynecological case, led him to his professional destiny. A certain Mrs. Merrill, a "respectable" if "stout" wife of a "dissipated old man" fell and injured herself one morning, and sent for Sims. When he arrived, he remembers, she was in bed, suffering from back pain and pressure on her bladder and rectum. Sims felt unable to avoid the situation, and reluctantly proceeded. As he recalls:

"if there was anything I hated, it was investigating the organs of the female pelvis. But this poor woman was in such a condition that I was obliged to find out what was the matter with her" (231). Finding that her uterus was "retroverted," Sims began puzzling how to relieve the condition. Recalling a procedure he had only half paid attention to in medical school, Sims succeeds in restoring Mrs. Merrill's uterus to its proper position. Moreover, he discovers that the position (placing her on her hands and knees and inserting several fingers into her vagina) allowed atmospheric pressure to inflate the walls of the vagina, allowing him to examine her internally with greater ease. Purchasing a pewter spoon on his way back to his office, he rushes to try his new technique of examination on a slave woman, Betsey, who was suffering from vesico-vaginal fistula and was left by her owner, despite Sims's vehement protests of his inability to heal her and his unwillingness even to try. Sims, with the help of two student assistants, places Betsey into the position and is rewarded with the "puffing noise" of inrushing air. Then the moment of triumph: "Introducing the bent handle of the spoon I saw everything, as no man had ever seen before. The fistula was as plain as the nose on a man's face. . . . The walls of the vagina could be seen closing in every direction; the neck of the uterus was distinct and well-defined, and even the secretions from the neck could be seen as a tear glistening in the eye" (235). Sims sees the "truth" of the fistula, counterintuitively, as a nose on a *man's* face. It is as if what he is seeing were not so much the fistula in the woman's body, but the competitive success it will garner for him among male professionals. At the same time, the uterus reflects the experience of his vision, tearing like an eye. With the innovative technique he imagines he will soon perform, Sims plans to command the attention of fellow surgeons. Confidently, he spends the next three months expanding his hospital and scouring the countryside for slave women who suffer from fistulae, making deals with their owners and gathering eventually nine women in addition to the first three (whose masters had pressed Sims to attempt the surgery)[33] on whom to experiment. Even before he attempts the first surgery, he invites "about a dozen doctors there to witness the series of experiments I expected to perform" (237).

He did not succeed nearly as quickly as he hoped: it would take Sims three years to find adequate method and material for suturing vaginal walls. In this period, he subjected the slave women to surgery, without anesthesia, as frequently as once a month.[34] His eventual success at it led Sims to a better surgical market in New York, where after the founding of Woman's Hospital, he had a far larger field of patients, with a wider variety of disorders. While it is clear throughout Sims's career that his surgical techniques, like those of other gynecologists, were almost always developed before there was a clear, scientific rationale for it, this is nowhere clearer than in his operations to treat painful menstruation and infertility, where he would "split" or make incisions up the cervix, or amputate it entirely. As McGregor summarizes, "While Sims's experimentation with surgery on vesicovaginal fistula might be explained as an educated attempt to cure an otherwise miserable and untreatable female disorder, the cutting away of the cervical canal to restore normal and painless menstruation is not rationally defensible" (355). It was what Barker-Benfield describes as "his lifelong devotion to this knife to women's genitals," however, that earned Sims his international fame (108).

This is the literalization, then, of gynecological manhood where men become individually noted among men for their observation and aggressive "repair" of women's disordered reproductive organs. Conversely, women are passively individualized through men's diagnosis of their particular genital pathology. Like Morton, who reputedly could see a skull and know its racial individuality,[35] Sims saw female genitals and knew the woman: "I have seen the inside of an immense number of vaginas, and I never saw two that were in all particulars exactly alike. They are as different from each other as our faces and noses" (qtd. in Barker-Benfield 94).[36] This is the classic application of Meigs's high/low sexual geography, where the particularity of men resides in their thinking minds and speaking faces, and women's particularity lies in their passive, damaged genitals. In their ability to "know" the individual pathology of "others," men like Morton and Sims differentiated themselves in a field of professionals, not just from their research subjects, but more especially from other professional men.

In Sims's extensive use of woodcut illustrations in publishing the results of his three years' experiments on the women in Alabama, though, these "faces" were female—and they were also all white.[37] What was buried in Sims's representation of his work may also have been the logic that guided it: his cultured refusal to call attention to the "blackness" and enslavement of his first experimental subjects reduplicated the white cultural logic of segregation, proper flow, and social cleanliness that he had learned as a child.[38] In much the same way, we might note that Sims's response to the condition of

vaginal fistulae—which he repeatedly characterizes as "loathsome"—
was guided by accumulating cultural metaphorics of sexual uncontrollability and counterphobic calls for sexual "hygiene": self-control
among men and denial among women. If, as Gail Paster has noted,
"menstruation comes to resemble other varieties of female inconti-
nence—sexual, urinary, linguistic—that served as powerful signs of
woman's inability to control the workings of her own body" (83),
vesico-vaginal fistula would seemingly epitomize woman's reckless
flows. These sexual metaphorics were at least symbiotic with if not
dependent upon cultural structurations of race and its logic of con-
tainability. Ann Laura Stoler has recently analyzed the ways that
the growing availability in the nineteenth century of representations
of the genitals of "primitive" women, from the Hottentot Venus to
Women in Java (1897), allows us to see how "the sexual pleasures
of scientific knowledge combine with the pornographic aesthetics
of race" (184). Stoler shows how such representations "demand that
readers rivet their attention on genitalia in the making of race," insistently framing "dark" women as the object of a taxonomic, scientific
gaze while "white women were assiduously protected from it" (188).
My reading of Sims and the logics of early U.S. gynecology suggests,
however, that white women were not protected from that gaze but
were at least as obsessively the focus of it. If "other" women became the repository for white men's fantasies about sexuality, white
women's sexuality became the repository for "white" cultural anxieties about "purity." This fantasized and imperative "purity" provided
"white" women some protection—from Sims's earliest experimentation—but his gynecology, guided both by cultural logic and career
ambition, was all along aimed squarely at them—at the purity control
of "white" female sexuality.[39]

I do not mean, in my attention to Sims's efforts to master the clean
repair of fistulae, to diagnose his pathology as particular; after all, he
convinced a group of medical doctors and wealthy women patrons
to open an entire hospital, initially for the sole purpose of repair-
ing vaginal fistulae.[40] In Alabama as in New York, medical and lay
audiences enthusiastically received Sims's surgical innovations redirecting women's flows into their proper channels, for fistulae as for
fertility.[41] His work in New York opened up a pathway to his international reputation. And indeed, Sims's timely intervention and his aggressive presentation of its importance has governed his subsequent
historical treatment. Only recently has the severity and incidence of
fistulae among women come into question.

On Services to Fellowmen

We must ask what it means for fellow gynecologist Gaillard to describe Sims's gynecological innovations as a service "for [his] fellow
men" (see full quote above). The mainstay of Sims's work was practiced on *women*. For Sims to describe his vesico-vaginal repair as "one
of the most important discoveries of my age for the relief of suffering
humanity" is hyperbole, at least (*Story* 246), though that overstate-
ment has influenced even his severest critic, Barker-Benfield, who
does not question Sims's assessment of the widespread affliction of
women with fistulae and its severity, but only his reluctance to operate on it in the first place. McGregor's historical study clarifies that we
have no real numbers on the historical incidence of vaginal tearing.[42]
The evidence indicates that it traversed class lines and had long been
known to doctors as an incurable affliction. What seems most clear is
that it resulted from a prolonged labor, and that prolonged labors frequently burdened women who had been malnourished during their
childhood. Rickets, a disease of the skeletal system resulting from a
diet deficient in vitamin D, often caused deformities of the pelvis,
making it difficult for women to deliver normally. Here too, evidence
is scarce: because the disease was not fatal historians have been unable to measure its incidence demographically. But Sims's work, the
records of both the Woman's Hospital, and other doctors experiment-
ing with the procedure, document that a predominant number of
patients were from among the slave- and wage-laboring classes. As
McGregor summarizes: "Slavery was part of a different kind of political economy, but the experiences of blacks were in some ways parallel to those of wage labor—in meager diet and shelter. . . . Although
vesico-vaginal fistulas were not confined solely to black, Irish and
similar ethnic groups, rickets and disorders of childbirth frequently
struck among the more economically deprived" (178). Another scholar
has recently called into question Sims's claims regarding the debilita-
tion that fistulae presented to women, and particularly slave women,
such that they would be willing to endure repeated surgeries without
anesthesia.[43] Diana Axelsen comments: "While certainly a source of
chronic discomfort and possibly secondary irritation, and while obviously embarrassing in many contexts, vesico-vaginal fistula is not a
disorder involving chronic or severe pain. . . . In comparison to the
effects of excessive beatings, chronic malnutrition, and other forms
of physical and psychological aggression, [vaginal fistula] hardly con-

stitutes a probable motive for suicide [as Sims biographer Harris suggests]" (12). Sims did perform his fistula repair even on members of European royalty.[44] But more frequently among women of wealthier classes, Sims was called on to treat fertility problems, ovarian cancer, or cervical disorders. Without denying the physical boon that the procedure he developed offered to some women, what McGregor's study would seem to indicate is that the surgical procedure for fistula repair was less important as a medical "breakthrough" than it was for the symbolic authority it granted Sims in building his career and for the "founding" of gynecology. To put this another way, Sims's medical fame depended less on the specific basis of fistula repair than on the more abstract promise held out by his successful gynecological "treatment" of white women's sexual disorders.

And clearly, the abstract promise to supervise and repair white women's sexual disorders held a greater appeal for white men than women. This is not to deny that white women participated in beliefs about their need to manifest sexual purity during the era, but simply to observe that men had more professionally and symbolically at stake. To put this somewhat differently, there was no obvious logic propelling Sims, who had spent the first decade of his medical practice *avoiding* treating women's sexual disorders, into a career based entirely on them after he had pioneered his surgery for vesico-vaginal fistula. He might as easily have gone on, for instance, to treat a range of injuries and bodily disorders requiring delicate suturing. I am suggesting he does so because gynecological practice provided a symbolically satisfying avenue for establishing white male professional expertise—symbolically satisfying to the extent that it offered what I describe at the beginning of this chapter as a formal, institutional routing for the desires and anxieties generated within national manhood. Gynecological practice becomes another way for white men in the United States to extend the purview of professional male authority over culture (an issue I raised at the conclusion of chapter 3), and another arena in which they can "consolidate partnership with authoritative males" over the bodies of their "others"—here white and black women (Sedgwick, *Between Men* 38).

This partnership, though, was always only partially consolidated, as Barker-Benfield (perhaps too) neatly summarizes: "A man . . . looked to be confirmed in his self-making by democratic rivals. This was a paradoxical and therefore doubly self-defeating hope: such confirmation was doomed, of course, in its own terms—rivals would refuse to provide it" (98). Sims, defensive and contentious throughout his career among fellow professional men, worked a seemingly second-best sense of success through the admiration he got from women. Women patients followed him to New York City from Alabama, and back to the United States from his stays in Europe. One of Sims's eulogists, Dr. Joseph Tabor Johnson, reported, "It is said of him that no woman ever distrusted him, while his exceptional purity of speech and life, together with the personal magnetism of his smile, his words, his manners, attracted many to him and held them chained with the silken cords of love, gratitude, and esteem" (qtd. in Sims, *Story* 468). By evoking an image of enchained women (a common image for the bond of marriage), Johnson romantically subordinates women who are bestowing recognition *to* the man whose reputation is ostensibly confirmed by it (much in the tradition of *feme covert*).

Meigs chooses this very same image to clarify the relation between white women and medical men in his introductory lecture: "If we scan her position amidst the ornate circles of a Christian civilization, it is easy to perceive her intellectual force is different from that of her master and lord. I say her master and lord, and it is true to say so, since even in that society she is still in a manner in bonds, and the manacles of custom, of politics, or of bienseance not yet struck from her hands. She has nowhere been admitted to the political rights, franchises, and powers that man arrogates to men alone. The crown, when it rests on the brow of a woman is always a political accident, grievous and deprecable; and even then, where woman reigns, man governs" (*Lecture* 9). Compensation for men having to rely on women for the affection and admiration that they desire from other professional men will come in remembering, it would seem, that women are legally, socially, and even biologically subordinate to them. As for Byrnewood in the *Quaker City*, so too it seems that for Meigs, Johnson, and Sims, heterosexuality proved the safe haven but could not provide the emotional satisfaction promised in professional fraternity, the homosocial recognition of "equals."

Hearts of Nether Millstone

The images of chains and silken cords evoke not just white "wives" but also the African-descended enslaved women on whom Sims's practice got its start, and who he claimed "willingly consented" to repeated operations and in fact "clamor[ed] for his surgical attention"

(Sims, *Story* 234, 243). In this sense, the silken cords trace, as Young puts it, the way "forms of racism remain so intimately bound up with sexuality and desire" (*Colonial Desire* 182). As Young's analysis demonstrates, the "white" cultural imperative for sexual purity was intimately linked to the "imaginative phantasm of racial mixing" (142).

The erotically miscegenated phantasm of recognition from Other women (such as that which Sims claims from women like Anarcha, Lucy, and Betsey) seems widely to have triangulated desires for and imagined association with male authority, in the form of hypermasculine icons of colonialism and discovery. This desire, as I sketched it in my Introduction, was present for more than Melville's fictionalized Delano. Emphasizing for his students how "woman" can be depended upon to admire male prowess wherever she sees it, Meigs describes for his students how "Mungo Park in the Sahara, and Ledyard among the wildest Samoiedes, always received good, and not evil entreaty at the hands of women, whose husbands had hearts of the nether millstone" (*Lecture* 12–13).[45] In such moments we can trace these white men's compensatory, melancholic longings for human connectedness. These are longings that we could describe as being directed at other professional men with "hearts of nether millstone." Or, tracing back through the model of education Sims details, we might understand them also to evidence prior, unschooled, undifferentiating longings made "other" through the "mysteries" of civic and professional "pedagogism." We could consider how these naked nature moments encapsulate the organization of white manhood—its affective routings and hierarchizing, managerial aims—as they simultaneously register foreclosed desires for an expanded human community, foreclosed precisely through the structures—civic, pedagogical, institutional, professional—*of* national manhood.

5

The Melancholy of White Manhood, or,
Democracy's Privileged Spot

After Sims died, medical men across the nation remembered they liked him. To prove just how much, they passed resolutions formalizing their recognition:

> *Resolved,* That in the death of Dr. J. Marion Sims, we, his professional brethren, lament the loss of an affectionate colleague and a most able and ever-willing counselor.
>
> *Resolved,* That in recognition of his important disclosures in certain departments of our science, and in the impulse he has given to its electrical advancement, the people at large mourn the death of a most distinguished citizen.[1]

> *Resolved,* 1. That the sad intelligence of the sudden and unexpected death of Dr. J. Marion Sims, flashed throughout the civilized world with electric speed, has communicated to us a shock well calculated to overcome us with emotions of unaffected sorrow and abiding regret.
>
> *Resolved,* 2. That as Americans we feel justly proud of the brilliant and distinguished career of this eminent physician . . .
>
> *Resolved,* 3. That we shall ever recall the man as one who combined an unusual and attractive beauty of manly form, with a refinement and gentleness of manner, and a genial cordiality of deportment, betokening the "kind, true soul within," which seldom failed to win and fascinate all with whom he came into contact, calling forth the grateful love of woman and the admiring friendship of man.[2]

In death, the quarrelsome, defensive, contentious Sims became known by his fellows the way he had wanted in life. In death, these men resolved to remember the "gentleness" of the man few had been able to like; in death, they promised (and asked the nation to promise along with them) never to forget how they had always truly recognized the affectionate bonds between them.

This Sims, manly, attractive, *dead*, was a reconstruction. This reconstruction reworked his professional image and the vexed history of his relations with his colleagues. But even more importantly it reworked the corporate solidarity and professional identity of those colleagues whose resolutions and testimonials built a very particular kind of ritualized fraternal space. This is a space that links the practice of professional medicine explicitly to the fraternal title of civic management—not only do these medical "brethren" instruct all Americans to mourn this notable citizen and to reverence his important career, they elsewhere and at length compare Sims with "founding fathers" such as George Washington and Patrick Henry.[3] It is a space that certifies medical men's qualification for civic management precisely in their ability to recognize Sims's worth, in contrast to his severe misrecognition by the Ladies Board of Supervisors (who had demanded he limit his male surgical audience and accepted his resignation in lieu of his compliance; see chapter 4). As one of his memorialists prophesies: "When the names of these sickly sentimental governors shall long since have passed into oblivion, and their foolish rules and regulations, in connection with this hospital, shall have been wisely forgotten by the world, the name of Sims shall be known and read of all men as its great founder and patron, and emblazoned all over its walls . . . as its ensign-armorial and its shield to guard it against evil and unwise spirits."[4] This is a space where the memorializing of founding fathers deflects the "evil . . . spirits" of "foolish" and "unwise" women. It is a space that ritualizes manly remembrance not just to protect buildings or institutions but as importantly to armor professional brothers against haunting reminders of fraternity's irrational others. But finally, these memorial claims are so immoderate that it's hard not to wonder: what is really haunting these men? What is it they are warding off by putting such lavish energy into these eulogies? What does it mean that fraternity's best corporate energy goes into creating loving, "true" recognition for men who are *dead?*

This chapter traces the archaeology (or etiology) of middle-class and professional fraternal rituals to the political psychology of national

manhood. Throughout the nineteenth century, fraternal space prolif-
erated in the working and middle classes. From labor unions, political
parties, and fraternal lodges, to Christian and reform groups, to professional organizations and sports clubs, men extended the sphere of
male sociality well beyond their day at work.[5] These social spaces
offered themselves as a corrective to the abrasions of that workday,
a haven where a man could be truly recognized apart from his competitive working-role, could be rightly known in his individual particularity. This is what D. W. Bristol insists in his essay on the "Social
Influence of Odd Fellowship" (first published in 1848): "Here place
around him men in every circumstance of life, and of every creed
and profession, and before him a worthy object to enlist his feelings,
and then you will have evoked the true man. . . . Does he now enter
into the feelings and interests of those around him? Does he act here,
where all eyes except a few are shut out from him, with interest and
energy? Has he forgotten the caste which the world has arbitrarily
assigned to the men around him? Does he look at them with fellow feeling and honor them as men, not as rich or poor, but men
who are acting on the same broad bases as himself, and whose hearts
beat responsiveness to the same calls as his own?" (qtd. in Blumin
239). But as Stuart Blumin carefully details, these voluntary fraternal
associations were not socially heterogeneous; they were in the process of becoming more and more homogeneous by class and ethnicity
throughout the mid-century (see Blumin, ch. 6, "Coming to Order").
Furthermore, the social structures of these various brotherly shelters
were *not* disconnected from what Anthony Rotundo describes as the
"cut and thrust" culture of the marketplace (200–201).

Men's social spaces came increasingly to rely on rituals to constitute the affective exchange of brotherhood, informally through a
combination of what Rotundo describes as "verbal jousting" (201)
with jokes and complaints about women that were the key activities
at men's clubs and dinners, and formally through fraternal orders'
extraordinarily elaborate and explosively popular secret ceremonies
and rites. But men's obsessive decoration of fraternal space with rituals of brotherhood barely papers over the fundamental inability of
these havens to deliver what they promise. In a range of middle-
class fraternal imaginings and practices, we find a patterned strategy.
Men's rituals of friendship and brotherhood promise egalitarian emotional exchange. But they depend on elaborate and hierarchical structures that merely symbolize such exchange. These sterilized symbolic
spaces work, though, to help white men ward off having to confront

fraternity's psychic and political abortiveness. I will sketch this affective dynamic in an early instance before turning to the more formally instituted and professionally articulated practices that begin emerging mid-century. My analysis in this chapter, moving from Benjamin Rush's "dream" of a "Paradise of Negro Slaves" to discussions of fraternal order and structures of professional friendship, and returning finally to "Benito Cereno," shows fraternal practices as melancholic echo chambers, disrupted by the repeating claims of national manhood's others, crisscrossed by ungrievable losses.

I

Democracy's Others: A Dream

In 1798, Benjamin Rush, architect of the Republican Machine, offered to the public an account of a dream. This dream provides a concise instance of the affective routing I am interested in analyzing in this chapter, the way white men's recognition of (and even desire for) a heterogeneous, equalitarian, democratic community is trained into a reaffirmation of homogeneous, fraternally representative order. In his curious and abbreviated essay, "Paradise of Negro Slaves—A Dream," Rush sketches his adventure in a beautiful land occupied only by former slaves. This is a paradise the Christian God has allotted to people who, having suffered so fully during their earthly lives, have been exempted from purgatorial punishment.

This dream begins as an iconic (though one would presume seldom so explicitly enacted) challenge to the "natural" privilege of white manhood ordered by the 1790 naturalization law. As Rush encounters the negroes in a "beautiful grove, where a number of them were assembled for religious purposes," they "appeared cheerful and happy" (*Essays* 188). But when they see *him*, he notices, their appearance changes from happiness to one of "general perturbation." Finally, a representative comes forward to explain: "Excuse the panic which you have spread through this peaceful and happy company: we perceive you are a *white man.*—That colour which is the emblem of innocence in every other creature of God, is to us a sign of guilt in a man. The persons whom you see here were once dragged by the men of your colour from their native country, and consigned by them to labour—punishment—and death. . . . Our appearance of terror, therefore, was entirely the sudden effect of habits which have not yet been eradicated from our minds" (187). In the United States, as we have seen, the civic body was constituted inferentially in the Constitution, and explicitly by the first act of naturalization as iconically white and male.[6] That the Negroes identify Rush generically, as a white male, and read his category not as exemplary of virtue but *guilt* thus offers a presumptive challenge to the representative routing of democratic citizenship through national manhood. They remind Rush that *"the notion of the Good, the Good of the whole . . . was* never anything but the special (economic) interests of the propertied classes."[7]

What unbearably threatens to derail the virtuous claim of civic fraternity, its (homogenizing) promise to represent the (heterogeneous) Good of the Whole, is immediately redirected, and in a fascinating way. Rush reassures the man that he agrees with their assessment: "Your apprehensions of danger from the sight of a white man . . . are natural" (*Essays* 187). He attempts to explain that he, unlike his compatriots, is not a threat to the Good: "in me—you behold a friend. I have been your advocate" (187). He is interrupted in this apology by the Negro, who suddenly recognizes him in his individual particularity: "Is not your name [Benjamin Rush]?" and being answered in the affirmative, embraces him. This moment, Rush's ascension from (guilty) class to (innocent) particularity, provides a classic instance of white manhood's privilege, the liberal franchise of individual exceptionality. Named, particularized, and recognized by the all-but-unnamed blacks (we learn the name of only one: Scipio), Rush is exempted from the stained category.

The recognition bestowed by the Negroes in paradise rescues Rush from his guilty association, and incorporates him into a community of the Good. This moment might seem to gesture toward Rush's tentative construction of a broader, more inclusively imagined collective, where whites are incorporated into democratic community only on the basis of ethical behavior as it is recognized by its formerly oppressed black constituents. But this is where the dream begins decisively to tip in a different direction, for it seems that the rescue of white men's guilt *in toto* is the sole purpose of these (former?!) slaves. From this point in Rush's dream, a number of the blacks, individualized only by the atrocities committed upon them by their white masters, beg Rush for news of those men, imploring him to carry back their forgiveness and earnest wishes that the masters repent before they face eternal punishment. This dream—the "Paradise of Negro Slaves"—begins to betray the purpose indicated by its title: its investment is hardly the happy reprieve for the Negro slaves it apparently offers to sketch; instead, its pronounced desire is to rescue white manhood from guilty association, to repurify not just Rush's, but all white men's claim to represent the Good. It is a "paradise of Negro slaves" *for* white men, a world where slaves (like Rush's own?) forgive and want the best for their masters.

The accounts of these blacks and their appeals on behalf of their cruel masters—which seemingly could go on endlessly—are interrupted at last by the appearance of *another* white man: "All at once, the eyes of the whole assembly were turned from me, and directed towards a little white man who advanced towards them, on the opposite side of the grove, in which we were seated. His face was grave, placid, and full of benignity. In one hand he carried a subscription paper and a petition—in the other, he carried a small pamphlet, on the unlawfulness of the African slave-trade, and a letter directed to the King of Prussia, upon the unlawfulness of war. While I employed in contemplating this venerable figure—suddenly I beheld the who[l]e assembly running to meet him—the air resounded with the clapping of hands—and I awoke from my dream, by the noise of a general acclamation of—ANTHONY BENEZET!" (*Essays* 320). Their instant recognition of Benezet (d. 1784) ranks that abolitionist over Rush. But the character of that recognition places Rush in Benezet's company. It is the dead Benezet's dreamlike appearance that returns Rush to his own waking self. Rush claims this dream to have been inspired by his reading of an essay by another abolitionist, the British Thomas Clarkson (1760–1846),[8] and it is by recalling its occasion that we can most clearly see how the dream in fact creates for Rush not a heterogeneous community amongst the Negro slaves, but a privileged, fraternal, homogenous one, amongst white male abolitionists. Clarkson's good work is the impetus for a dream where first Rush's and then Benezet's ability to represent the Good is ratified by democracy's Others. These men represent a purer space for white manhood, indeed, its (original, destined) innocence, and thus the challenge offered by those dead slaves (in "Paradise") to whiteness is normalized, indeed incorporated in this fraternal fantasy of a guiltless white representivity.

II

Fraternal Order

Rush's dream concisely diagrams national manhood's operative structure, where white male exceptionality is experienced through the imagined reconstruction of white fraternity. It offers us a usefully simplified instance of the model linking representative citizenship to the abstract identity of white manhood, and of the psychic transfers entailed in national manhood's embrace of representative democracy. As I have outlined in chapters 1 and 2, anxieties about political division and social disorder, along with counterphobic imperatives for "wholeness" and "unity" were transferred onto democracy's "representative," the citizen *qua* individual. Correlatively, as I have been arguing in chapters 3 and 4 and will continue detailing here, the citizen's guilty knowledge of the actual *inequality* of the political order, his systematic inability to represent the Good of the Whole, was "handed off or loaded onto" democracy's Others through functional reconstructions of white fraternity.[9] This psychic re-ordering—or, in Young's term, recodification (*Colonial* 171)—of national anxieties delegated two important domains of responsibility to the civic manager. One was the management of the Other—a term and territory ever more broadly and diversely defined. The second, as important, was the management of the *self*, entailed by the emergence of such cultural ideals as self-making and male purity. Whereas the former worked to shore up and justify the uneven distribution of political rights and entitlements, the latter functioned to make the uneven economy a question of the "competitive edge," the "self-discipline," the "talent" of the individual.

The period from which I have drawn my texts and examples in the past two chapters, the 1830s through the 1850s, strikes me as an important transitional period in the articulation of national manhood, where the middle classes claim and rework its psychic energies and civic imperatives for the purposes of professional formation. The beginning of the great era of professionalization coincides with the severe, often devastating economic flux of the 1830s and 1840s and its resulting intensification of class stratification.[10] Notably, the class re-ordering that threatened to rend the illusion of national fraternity is ideologically counterbalanced by political and cultural developments such as the full "universalization" of white manhood suffrage,[11] the establishment of the first national voting day on November 7, 1848,[12] and the proliferation of organized male social spaces, including the beginnings of a reinvigorated fraternal movement.

I want to unpack the fraternal aspect here. This era of fraternal organization seems arguably an attempt to capture, locally and "in reality," the promised relief from managerial responsibilities for self and other held out by the civic imaginary: the reassuring grant of brotherly equality, the fraternal "sameness" of the white male citizen. Freemasonry had been active in America since the early 1700s. The late 1700s saw an important development, when a new group composed largely of mechanics and militia men established itself as "Ancient" Freemasons, breaking with the Freemasons they termed "Moderns," and inducting "tens of thousand of members" (see Carnes, *Secret Ritual* 23). Soon infamous for their drinking and carousing habits, and capturing a more serious notoriety in the Morgan affair of 1826, the Freemasons suffered a strong and organized backlash throughout the 1830s.[13] By the late thirties and early forties, though, old fraternal orders were revitalizing and new ones springing up. As Mark Carnes summarizes in his analysis of secret fraternal rituals in the nineteenth century, these new orders diverged significantly from the tavern brotherhood of the early Freemasons.[14] Groups such as the Odd Fellows placed a ban on alcohol at lodge activities, and began revising initiation rituals. Shortly the Freemasons would follow suit. Carnes notes that "from 1840 to 1860 American Masonry was entirely transformed," so much so that their British counterparts denounced the revised rituals as "too long, too complicated, and too theatrical" (*Secret Ritual* 28).

While it is hard to be sure now precisely what it was about these sober and obscure rituals that attracted millions of (mostly middle-class) white men,[15] it is clear that by mid-century, the success of various orders—groups with such diverse orientations as labor, profession, temperance, and religion—rose and fell over the appeal of their rituals. As Carnes observes, "Those who did publicly comment on the initiations often compared them to magnetism, an equally inexplicable and compelling force. This language suggested two important aspects of the phenomenon: There was something special about certain rituals that 'attracted,' 'charmed,' or 'lured' members, and many men were somehow predisposed to 'crave' or 'desire' them. All rituals were not successful, nor did all men crave them" (*Secret Ritual* 11). Though many of the rituals relied on religious imagery and rites, Carnes notes that they tended to downplay and even exclude focusing on Christ in favor of a universalist emphasis. Theoretically inclusive, the rituals thus implied the inadequacy of Christian worship to their broader purposes (60).[16] Structured to initiate the member into ever-higher levels of an all-male, universal family, the ceremonies "promised to reveal 'great mysteries,' 'impenetrable secrets' or equally arcane forms of religious knowledge" (Carnes, *Secret Ritual* 56). Typically featuring some kind of symbolic death, the initiate was commonly conducted through a series of intricate adventures—led through hell, or a forest, or a desert, forced to walk on nails, jump into dark pits, tied to stakes. Eventually, the candidate would be "rescued" by a wiser, older, mystic patriarch, and adopted into the next stage of brotherhood.

Beyond the raw silliness of men dressing up like Indians, Egyptian pharaohs, and knights on a regular basis,[17] there are other reasons to ask why this mystic form of fraternalism attracted so many men from the middle classes.[18] One important question is that of expense: in addition to dues, a member was constantly called on to contribute other moneys. Each new level entailed more costuming, more equipment, another initiation fee. Commenting on the work of Freemason historian Lynn Dumenil, Carnes highlights another paradox of this ritual-intense mid-century fraternalism. These productions worked imaginatively to separate "men from the outside world and plac[e] . . . them securely amongst the brothers of the lodge." Yet another question is raised by the time these practices consumed: the rituals became so long that they left little time for men to enjoy friendship or even casual association. For instance, like other increasingly successful orders, the revisionists in the Odd Fellows insisted on lengthy (as long as an hour) solemn, and elaborate rituals recited and enacted from memory—so much to the exclusion of fellowship that the Odd Fellows eventually would split with their British brothers over their differing sense of purpose (Carnes, *Secret Ritual* 27–28).

Though it is impossible to know exactly what made these mystic rituals so attractive for so many men by mid-century, it is arguable that intensifying cultural imperatives for male self-discipline led men to make sacrifices of time and money in order to gain purchase on a "pure" space of formal masculine affiliation that would allow them to leave outside all that threatened to contaminate them. There does seem to be a strong correlation between the rise of male-purity movements and fraternal men's desires for intensified ritualism; Carnes notes that the mid-century "infusion" of newly prosperous professionals and tradesmen into the orders "coincided with new demands for sobriety and self-restraint and with the rise of emotionally intense rituals" (*Secret Ritual* 24).[19] The more nineteenth-century culture emphasized the importance of men disciplining their bodily flows, insisting that men practice sexual abstention, dietary regimentation, and temperance in order to conserve their energy for proper (business) pursuits, the more necessary—repeatedly and formally necessary—

it became to consolidate an ideal form of properly channeled manhood. Or, to caption this point from a slightly different angle, if, as Mary Douglas has argued, rituals work to redress fears of social formlessness, we can see how strong imperatives for men's self-control, for bodily and identity boundary-maintenance ("individualism") responded to the massive social and economic changes accumulating at mid-century. Fraternal ritual offered to provide men a formally and emotionally focused time during which they could experience themselves as part of a controlled male body.

The various rituals—of Freemasons, Odd Fellows, Knights of Pythias, the Fraternal Order of Red Men, and others—would increasingly strive to create a structured space in which men could feel individually reconstituted within the abstract identity of (white) brotherhood. Like Charles Meigs's introductory lecture, these rituals strongly emphasized the degraded nature of the initiate's worldly self, and of the world outside the fraternity.[20] Elaborating on symbolic death and rebirth, initiations exterminated a specifically debased, sinful, unmanly, and dirtied self. Ceremonies described death in lurid details featuring dismemberment and putrification. Carnes summarizes the Odd Fellows' revised initiatory degree of 1845: "Like Adam, the candidate was 'naked' (his shirt had been removed) and he was repeatedly told 'Thou art dust' and placed on the floor to the exclamation, 'Low! level with the earth! This is the state of man!'" (Secret Ritual 50). In a Scottish Rite ceremony, the candidate began wearing a spotless uniform, only to have each item replaced with "more common clothing." Eventually, the ceremony's official would declare that "'these marks of indignity are not sufficiently humiliating'" and cover the initiate "with a black cloth sprinkled with ashes" (51). Indeed, abasement in the form of humiliation seems to have been central to the ceremonies. Carnes observes, "as if skeletons, skulls, bloody daggers, executioners' devices and funereal accouterments were not enough, ritualists frequently employed other mechanisms to unnerve the initiate" (54). With the candidate sufficiently soaked in his own shame and embarrassment, the ritual proceeded to rescue or rebirth the now-worthy candidate into a new family, his all-male secret brotherhood. As if drawing on Meigs's imagery (or vice versa) linking men's debasement to women's bodies, the rituals, as Carnes summarizes them, "affirmed that, though woman gave birth to man's body, initiation gave birth to his soul, surrounding him with brothers who would lavish on him the 'utmost affection and kindness'" (120).

Fraternal structures were not, however, egalitarian structures.[21] Like a concentrated form of J. Marion Sims's "early education," the adult man's symbolic humiliation in fraternal initiations reminded him to identify with male power. This power's appeal was in its hierarchical ordering, as lodge rituals affirmed: "All rituals established a hierarchy among members. . . . Initiates could not acquire manhood and gain entry into the masculine family of the lodge until they had won approval of the patriarchs." As Clawson summarizes, such hierarchy, expressed within the rituals and in the succession of degrees, "upheld a version of a social mobility available to all industrious men who would care to take advantage of it" (176). But more than a structural analogue, ritually instituted fraternal hierarchy worked affectively to install in "brothers" a desire for the "intimate inequality" that Julie Ellison has argued increasingly represented the emotional organization of male homosocial culture by mid-century.[22] Carnes concludes that the rituals contain symbols and metaphors that help men "effectively confront" the difficult conflicts of the "outside world" (*Secret Ritual* 144). Somewhat differently, I would suggest that fraternal rituals mirrored, distilled, and provided a kind of narcotic for conflicts men faced outside the lodges. In other words, ritualism seems to have provided men not so much the equipment to "confront" (if we can take that word in the sense of engaging critically) the disparities of the world outside so much as it offered them a standpoint that naturalized the emotional dissonances they experienced in the political and economic imbalances "outside" the lodge.[23]

Let me elaborate briefly. Fraternal rituals allowed groups of men to act in unison, as a single, coherent body. This was a body that exemplified the purpose and order they had been taught to long for—by national imperatives and by emergent capitalism with its twin deacons, the temperance campaign and the male-purity movement—and it was precisely their formalized, emotionally intense, affectively gratifying subordination to group leadership that allowed the fraternal order to function in a way that satisfied these needs.[24] Brotherhood was grounded—as Christopher Newfield even more precisely phrases it—in "rewarding subjection" (*Emerson* 125). The pleasures men experienced as part of a hierarchized, rigidly ordered fraternal "body" worked forcefully to naturalize the hierarchical entitlements white men enjoyed outside the lodge, as citizen-representatives of democracy. At the same time, it worked powerfully to rationalize the uneven distribution of wealth, the gains and losses, the pleasures and humiliations, that the men themselves experienced in economic competition.[25] Above all (for my analysis, at least), it provided a paradigm of internally ordered, *hierarchized "sameness."* It is in this symbolic space that we can begin to discern the cultural emergence of homophobia. As Newfield trenchantly observes, "[h]omophobia's sexual regime takes its modern structure by miming the shape of a national imperative" (*Emerson* 94)—representative democracy as it was symbolically expressed in vertically ordered relations among white men.[26] Increasingly, as scholars like Newfield, Ellison, and Michael Moon have argued, "homosexuality" was conceptualized as a kind of radical equality, a mob equivalent, a de-individualizing sameness, a dangerous construction of democracy that threatened to emerge from the ranks of the citizens.[27] The "rewarding subjection" of fraternal brotherhood, with its imperative for stratified sameness, mirrored and arguably intensified emerging middle-class (national) phobias about unmanaged sameness—the haunting specter of a mob united by its desire for social change.

Thus, I would argue, ritualized fraternity was framed by the specter of unmanaged sameness as well as by disordered difference; ritual space thereby depended structurally on these excluded others. In a chapter describing the way the highest level of the various orders tended to culminate—counterintuitively—in ceremonies that emphasized not combative manliness, but peaceful homecoming, a reconciliation of man's "masculine passions" with his *"feminine* identifications," Carnes questions the role of secrecy: "if all men could benefit from the truth of the rituals, why were they concealed at all?" He concludes that the secrecy of these orders points toward the men's deep concerns over "gender bifurcations of Victorian society"—their sense that they were forbidden to "express nurturing and paternal emotions" (*Secret Ritual* 149). I would insist, differently from Carnes, that lodge secrecy was symptomatic of members' simultaneous desires for and fear of the radical impulses represented by "Fraternity," its specifically "universal" Good. In their rituals, they would learn to love their Others, but only in the most symbolic, denatured, purified form—the symbolically pure mother, the symbolically noble Red Man, the symbolically mystic "primitive." In so doing, they exercised their sense that indeed, they stood, benevolently, for the Good. But these ritual enactments kept the men who participated in them away from their homes with real women and real children; they kept the men who joined in homogeneous racial and (mostly) homogeneous ethnic and religious company. These rituals *did* work to redress men's rightful sense that they were being deprived of something in the world outside the lodge. But I would say that rituals were like an opiate, allowing men to experience the "traumatic pleasure" of their social power (what MacCannell, following Rousseau, frames as the Good of the Whole haunted by its partiality) as their own "innocent" victimization.[28] Thus, as victims, men turned to fraternal mysticism to regain a sense of "wholeness"—a structure that reinforced existing power imbalances rather than encouraging social change in the form of democratic expansion.[29] They could not regain a sense of wholeness, however, without invoking their (many) others. As I will argue in the next section, democracy's excluded other becomes a melancholy revenant at the heart of the white fraternal imaginary, a haunting we can see also in less formalized spaces of fraternal ritual, in practices of professional affiliation and friendship.

III

Sanctum Sanctorum

Mary Ann Clawson has commented on the widespread influence of Masonic-style fraternalism in nineteenth-century culture: it "served as an organizational model for trade unions, agricultural societies, nativist organizations, and political movements of every conceivable ideological stripe, as well as for literally hundreds of social organizations" (5). Observing that the model extends even further, to "professional societies and business partnerships, combinations, and trusts" (230), Mark Kann notes that "efforts to strengthen male bonds were especially refined among middle-class professionals who participated in occupations and associations that claimed to reunite masculine virtues and commercial interests" (231). Most recently, Anthony Rotundo has noted that "[h]istorians who have studied the structure and habits of the middle-class workplace have always approached it as a product of economic rationality, class interest, or professional imperatives. We also need to understand it as the product of its own masculinity" (196). Locating professional boundaries both geographically and associationally, professional men moved work spaces away from the home, and sought to define themselves as a group in terms of narrowing, specialized criteria. In structures that evoke the "work" of fraternity ritual, professional domains developed courses of study and certification rituals that determined a candidate's eligibility for entry into his chosen career.[30] Indeed, the anxieties that Rotundo highlights as characterizing a young white man's choice of and entry into a career sound much like those that Carnes describes for fraternal initiates, writ large (see Rotundo, ch. 8 passim; Carnes, *Secret Ritual* 17–21 and passim).

Our culturally guided conception of men in the nineteenth-century workplace tends to envisage them through the lens of competitive individualism, as isolated actors—for instance, we might conceptualize Morton's professionalism as the lonely but dedicated work of the scientific lab. But Rotundo reminds us that "male work and sociability mixed promiscuously" (197)—for Morton as for other scientists in local university settings (Morton was Professor of Anatomy at the Pennsylvania Medical College), and in professional organizations that held regular meetings (like the Academy of Natural Sciences), as well as in formal and informal professional and socializing networks, like dinner gatherings and parties. Professional culture was a multilayered *male* culture, where men spent time not just during the day but in evenings, and on weekends, in the company of white men. Men distinguished themselves in all these subcultures, as Rotundo details, through professional expertise, personal discipline, and successful competitiveness (see 194–205). A man's ability to compete, though, was always conditioned by his ability to affiliate successfully in cooperative networks of fellow professionals.

Morton provides us with a particularly rich example of a figure who consolidated professional respect and cultural authority through a carefully built system of formal and informal relations with other men. First, he cultivated an enormous web of correspondents, who supplied him with crania (he obtained none on his own). As Morton's manuscript collection at the Historical Society of Pennsylvania indicates, he was a thoroughgoing networker. These are almost uniformly warm correspondences, mainly with men who seem to value their affiliation with the cordial, attentive, and generous Philadelphia scientist. His files are littered with letters from one- and two-time correspondents the world over, writing to thank Morton for his kind letter, copies of his most recent work and casts of crania, and to offer further information on the location and disposition of the crania they sent in response to his queries. These range from scientists of international repute, to casual scientists, from Ohio and Kentucky, Massachusetts and New York, Dublin and Lima, and virtually all stops between. As

William Stanton summarizes, casual scientists on the frontiers in particular, "recognized Morton's pre-eminence in the study of crania and were proud to contribute to his famous cabinet. In this manner, Morton was able to gather at the Academy of Natural Sciences the largest collection of crania in the world. . . . That army surgeons stationed at remote western outposts and explorers of the world's deserts took the trouble, often at great hazard to themselves (for some tribes had strong taboos against the desecration of the dead [!]), spoke eloquently of the wide reputation that Morton's collection had acquired" (28). Corresponding and supplying Morton with materials for his scientific researches thus offered these men an imagined affiliation with Morton and the science that he represented—lending them some of the growing cultural prestige of science. We might also imagine that for these men (as for Delano), association with Morton and his progressivist/rationalist/categorical scientific project conditioned their attitude toward local people whom they encountered.[31]

Morton seems also to have used this network to solicit further evidence for his scientific arguments, such as those on hybridity, as this letter from D. W. Dudley, of Lexington, Kentucky, suggests:

> I had the pleasure to receive your favor of the 27th a few days ago and I have read with great interest & satisfaction your memoir on animal hybridity. Notwithstanding a long life [that] has been actively devoted to the duties of our profession, yet I am unprepared to offer you any contributions upon which I could rely as worthy of consideration in reference to your interesting subject of inquiry. Like too many other objects of scientific investigation, hybridity seems to have elicited but little more than the productive curiosity of the intelligent public. A patient & persevering series of observations made under all the favorable circumstances arising out of a thorough knowledge of comparative anatomy and physiology, opens a new and interesting field of inquiry. As a pioneer, your countrymen will anticipate the development of new lights, & the establishment of new principles . . . resulting from your labors and investigations into the origin of the multiplication of circumstances under which it may exist. (Apr. 15, 1847; Morton Papers, Library Company of Philadelphia)

Morton constructed for himself a veritable army of researchers, who would write in with additional support for arguments he was working on—including offers of supporting quotes and logical analogies. In this way, Morton's craniological research and racial arguments became a corporate project, with a reach both national and international.

In Philadelphia, Morton made himself the center of another important social network for men of science and ideas. As William Stanton notes (summarizing from an 1851 Morton biography by the president of Philadelphia's Academy of Physicians, George B. Wood), Morton made a custom of holding "'weekly soirées' to which he invited friends and 'strangers distinguished in the various departments of learning and philosophy'" (27). The favorable regard of the local scientific community for Morton and his habitual gatherings was registered by Dr. Charles Meigs in his *Memoir* of Morton, read before the Academy of Natural Sciences: "I have . . . said that his love for his family was almost idolatrous, and many of us who are witnesses of the graceful and unaffected hospitality of his house, can testify as to the marks of his love and confidence as to them: and we must, with one accord, regret the dissolution of those pleasant reunions, in which we have participated there, with men of letters and science of our own country or from foreign nations, who, with us, observed the cordiality and simplicity of his manners, in which were joined, in just proportions, dignity and urbanity" (43). In a practice registered by other men as a professional service, Morton engineered a social space that offered a mannerly reprieve from the pressures of daily work, a private retreat where select company could build acquaintance, exchange information, and experience an emotionally charged professional confirmation in the audience of important friends and distinguished visitors.[32]

The most important of these professional and social networks for Morton was an "inner circle" of friends, Josiah Nott (1804–73), George Gliddon (1809–57), and Ephraim Squier (1821–88), his core group of compatriots in the battle over polygenesis. Morton had solicited a correspondence with Gliddon in 1837, two years before the publication of *Crania Americana*, hoping that the U.S. vice-consul to Cairo would be able to supply him with samples of Egyptian crania. As William Stanton notes, Morton's friendship with Gliddon "was of great value, for he was able now to verify his growing suspicion of the great antiquity of the races through his own researches" (50). Morton indicated his debt to Gliddon by dedicating *Crania AEgyptiaca* (1844) to him. Nott, whom Morton contacted first in 1844, served as point man. Aggressive and argumentative, he along with Gliddon enjoyed what he termed "parson-baiting"—making explicit attacks in the name of polygenesis on the authority of natural theology. Additionally, Nott's work on hybridity predated and paved the way, in inflammatory and colorful fashion, for Morton's more cautiously worded, carefully built, and scientifically accredited arguments. Squier, who introduced himself to Morton in a fund-raising tour for his mound-excavation project in Ohio, was like the younger brother in the group. Stanton observes that the crania he supplied to Morton were pivotal in cementing Morton's arguments that racial differences were "aboriginal" (82–88). When Squier found his first whole cranium, the sketches he sent immediately to Morton were answered by an enthusiastic letter from Morton declaring it the "perfect type" of its "race" (and thus steering Squier's own interpretation of it).[33] The group offered steady support (and Gliddon his usual advance promotion) as Squier dealt with the Smithsonian Board of Regents in the production of his book (written with his excavation partner, Edwin H. Davis), *Ancient Monuments of the Mississippi Valley* (1848).[34] In their correspondence, these men shared scientific materials and arguments and even a group vocabulary—compliments of Gliddon and Nott in particular—terms like "niggerology" for polygenesis, "moundology" for Squier's work excavating Indians mounds, and "parson-skinning" for successful shots against natural theologians.[35]

As a group made up by men with diverse talents and interests, they adeptly generated a widespread cultural and scientific interest in polygenesis. Their operation as a group is by no means exceptional to modern science. In his history of the beginnings of professional science in the United States, Robert V. Bruce observes that "the development of American scientific institutions in the nineteenth century cannot be fully understood without looking at a small group of men known . . . as the Florentine Academy, [or] the Lazzaroni" (217). This was a group of at most a half-dozen scientific men in Washington, Philadelphia, and Boston in the mid-1800s, who were instrumental in "organizing, raising support for, and guiding scientific institutions" (217). It is a group that has long been legendary as a scientific "cabal," though their actual influence has been widely contested.[36] Bruce identifies them as "a natural phenomenon in the development of organized science" (218): "So natural does such a pattern of association seem, in fact, that sociologists have generalized it for twentieth-century scientists. Small, close-knit, informal groups form, they say, quite consciously about an acknowledged leader, who usually serves as a model for at least the younger members. Such groups tend to generate 'tribal folklore,' with mock ceremonies. Held together best by the belief that they are advancing a radical new view in science, they may go beyond scientific objectivity in pushing it. And the impression they give of arrogance and exclusiveness often sets outsiders against them, thus making it harder for them to achieve their goals" (219).[37] While Morton and his colleagues, Nott, Gliddon, Squier, and eventually, the Swiss scientist Louis Agassiz,[38] were never to establish the financial clout of the Lazzaroni, in many other respects, their earlier group functioned similarly. The five men were all (variously) in correspondence by 1848, sharing sources, promoting each others' works, and collaborating on publications. Morton was pivotal to cementing the alliances between these four men and many others less centrally involved.

There are a host of productive interrelations between the public arena of professional science and this private discursive domain. This network, as their correspondence frequently affirms, is most prominently a space that ameliorates the competitive abrasions the men encountered in making their controversial, scientific arguments. It is a supportive space, where they can experience solidarity in their difficult, adversarial project. It is a compensatory space, where they can joke about the worries they experience as they are publicly attacked for their arguments and where they can exchange jokes about those who attack them. Along with documenting the professional support and promotions these men provide each other, their correspondence also privately reveals a great tenderness for one another, structured around their mutual admiration for Morton. In this aspect, the group is a haven where they can feel an almost familial support, where they can worry, for instance, over the illnesses of fathers and sons. It is a site where the professional, objective pursuits of the group interpenetrate with the emotional, subjective ones. Their correspondence thus provides them a "privileged spot" similar to the one Delano seeks with Benito Cereno, a "sociable" place where they can mutually reconfirm their sense of purpose, their superiority to what worries them, where they can experience validation for their project and their sense of self.

That Morton served as the "heart" of the group is clear in Nott's letter to Squier on the news of Morton's death in 1851: "I recd. a letter today from Gliddon giving me the melancholy news of Morton's death—I am really overwhelmed by this affliction and have not the spirit to write—He was our leader and I look around in vain for one to supply his place—all men of science knew his talent and learning and I need say nothing to you of his virtues—human nature can be no better than he was" (May 29, 1851; Squier Papers, Library of Congress). Nott and Gliddon memorialized his importance, professional and personal, in their 1854 compendium collection of arguments for polygenesis, *Types of Mankind,* which begins with Henry S. Patterson's "Memoir of the Life and Scientific Labors of Samuel George Morton." Patterson begins with a testimony to Morton's ability to inspire fraternal devotion:

> [A]lways there was this peculiarity to be noticed, that wherever a man had known Morton personally at all, he mourned not so much for the untimely extinction of an intellectual light, as for the loss of a beloved personal friend. Certainly the man who inspired others with this feeling, could himself have no cold or empty heart. . . . Quiet and unobtrusive in manners, and fond of the retirement of the study, it was only in the privacy of the domestic circle that he could be rightly known; and those that were privileged to approach nearest the *Sanctum Sanctorum* of his happy home, could best see the full beauty of his character. That sacred veil cannot be raised to the public eye but beneath its folds is preserved the pure memory of one who illustrated every relation of life with a new grace that was all his own, and who, in departing, has left behind him an impression on all hearts. (Patterson xix–xx; original emphasis)

In her recent analysis of Emerson's *Conduct of Life,* Julie Ellison argues that "sentimental or domestic configurations in men's texts are not necessarily, or not only moments in which men are 'feminized.' . . . They are also specific to masculine culture" (601). Her arguments offer a way to read Morton's charismatic role within his circle of devotees as an historically specific instance of the "constant process of rearranging masculine emotion in order to accommodate homophobic anxieties, homosocial desires and class differences" (601). Somewhat differently here, I want to borrow on the energy of Ellison's insight, about a sentimentality specific to nineteenth-century male culture, to consider the ways Morton's social networking structured reassuring and empowering experiences of affiliation for scientific professionals and casual scientists not just in Philadelphia but all over the nation. His genial habits provided circulatory paths for scientific theories, materials, and fellow-feeling that led, in treasured moments of professional intimacy, to his study, and to his *heart.* In this sentimental space, men could enjoy the "overflow" of "gentle affections." In this space they could presumably hope, like Morton, to be "rightly known."

A careful reading of this passage suggests that the individualizing fellowship men enjoyed within Morton's *Sanctum Sanctorum* depended structurally and symbolically on excluded others. The confluence of metaphors of difference, figured by race and gender, circulate in this passage in numerous ways. We can see how Morton's scientific reputation, which Patterson describes as a "white radiance," offers access to a scientific brotherhood both sexually purified and racially dominant. In addition, Patterson's description references a masculine point of view secure in its dominance over nature and the lesser bodies that inhabit the regions outside Morton's study. The womb-like metaphors of that "domestic" space relocate (female) procreative power from the kitchen (or parlor) to the study, the home/heart of the masculine scientific enterprise. The scientific identity-formation Patterson memorializes in Morton suggestively manages to evacuate actual femaleness while absorbing its domestic functions. Morton's study, seen from this vantage, functions as an emotionally charged, intellectually reproductive space that is pointedly, in David Noble's phrase, a "world without women." It culminates the professional arrogation of power and knowledge to science in the private regions of male affiliation.

Patterson eulogizes Morton in a language that appeals to interiority, to a private wholeness revealed in select companies of men. Refusing to detail this space, where Morton displayed the "full beauty of his character," for the curious masses, Patterson keeps Morton protected, in a symbolically domestic space held apart from the "public." His observance here provides suggestive confirmation for Gillian Brown's arguments about the domestic construction of nineteenth-century individualism. As Brown summarizes, "[i]n the midst of change the domestic sphere provided an always identifiable place and refuge for the individual: it signified the private domain of individuality apart from the marketplace" (3). Morton's domestic space was pointedly a social one, where he shared his private self amongst select company. Morton's *Sanctum Sanctorum* thus promises a privileged access to a pure world symbolically cordoned off from abrasive encounters with "otherness"—from, for instance, the black waiters that so upset Agassiz in his Philadelphia hotel,[39] from women who were challenging the rights, spaces, and habits of manhood, from the frictions, the woundings professional men experienced amongst other white men, in scholarly and marketplace competition.

But its value depends precisely on the space culturally associated with women—the domestic circle and its sentimental symbol, the heart—to demarcate the highest and most intimate form of professional men's association. Like fraternal orders' highest degrees, then, Morton's privileged space of friendship returned professional men to a symbolically feminine, sentimental domain. In this sense, Patterson's paean to Morton and his *Sanctum Sanctorum* evokes the "hermaphroditic figure of the father" that Eric Cheyfitz has outlined in his study, *The Trans-Parent*. There, Cheyfitz situates an analysis of Emerson's gendered language practices through a reading of Tocqueville's delineation of reconfigured familial politics (here specifically father-son relations) in the post-Revolutionary era: "Tocqueville characterizes this new, or natural, relation as more 'intimate' and 'sweeter,' or 'softer' . . . than its aristocratic counterpart. It is a relation marked by 'tenderness' and 'affection.' When contrasted to the relationship between a father and his sons in an aristocracy, the relationship between a father and his sons in a democracy, as Tocqueville describes it, appears as a maternal one. It would seem then, that the democratic father at whom we are looking, if we are to see him as natural, must appear before us clothed, at least partially, in one of the figures of nature, that of the mother, or Woman" (129). In this sense, Cheyfitz suggests, post-Revolutionary manhood comes to be, in Tocqueville's depiction and Emerson's handling, haunted by its relation to the "not me": "[a]t the moment she appears as a figure of repose, a figure of that natural place of repose, the home, woman also appears as an ironic figure, representing the contradictions within the word *freedom* that threaten to bring revolution" (138; original emphasis).

It is in just this way that I want to pressure Patterson's evocation of the "sacred veil" that "cannot be raised," the "folds" of which shield Morton from "the public eye." This veil holds out a suggestive range of metaphors for an explicitly feminized purity—Morton as a muse, or a vestal virgin, or a bride, threatened with the symbolic penetration of a male (public) gaze. But this is a bride (or a virgin or a muse) who is (this is the occasion of Patterson's "Memoir," after all) *dead*. In this figure, Patterson conveys the haunting of the "not me" that plagues and challenges the fraternal imaginary. It is a haunting that gives away the instability of white manhood's self-sameness, its declaration of independence, its constitutional authority to stand for the Good. This is a "haunting" that works spatially and symbolically. The culture of middle-class manhood, having claimed a sphere apart, compulsively returns to the domestic space, attempting to recreate it in the inner circle of lodge rituals, or in the physical occupation of domestic spaces emptied of actual women. In the evocation of women (and Indians, and primitives), these brotherly practices signal the extent to which the foreclosed domestic space of democratic human connectedness—foreclosed in men's identification with civic, representative, male power—haunts the fraternal imaginary of white manhood.

Above all, then, I would urge that we think about the way that Patterson's eulogy to Morton's *Sanctum Sanctorum* memorializes the white male melancholy that registers the multiple foreclosures of human exchange structuring white brotherhood in U.S. culture. This is a melancholy that simultaneously symptomatizes a longing for human interconnection *and* an identification with the very power that demands such renunciations. It is precisely this melancholy that returns me, finally, to Melville's "Benito Cereno."

IV

What Has Cast Such a Shadow?

I began this study wanting to unpack what Melville might have been referencing in the moment where Delano finds "confidence and ease" in his anthropologically triangulated ruminations on an African woman and her child. Specifically, I wanted to know how that imagined moment with Mungo Park compensated for the "privileged spot" Delano was near despair of ever sharing with Benito Cereno. Whereas in my first book, I was interested in "Benito Cereno" for what it had to say about the operations of racism, I became more interested here for what it has to say about the identity, or more specifically, what it seemed to be diagnosing as a particular standpoint of or logic within the practice of white manhood. In *The Word in Black and White*, I castigated Melville's "Benito Cereno" for its imaginative failure, for replicating "the same *structural* exclusivity of white male subjectivity in its own necessarily limited portrayal of Babo's motives and goals, and ultimate humanity" (130). At the conclusion of this study, *National Manhood*, I now want to argue something different. What I read as failure before is, as I now see it, the precise diagnosis of what I have been analyzing in this chapter as the melancholy of white (or representative) manhood. The point of the story *is* imaginative failure—or imaginative short-circuiting—of a very particular kind.

"Benito Cereno" carefully sets out Delano as the very type of optimistic, self-disciplined, fraternity-loving, economic, and rational

American manhood. He is an individual who is all but entirely sure that the world is good (a person of "singularly undistrustful good-nature, not liable, except on extraordinary and repeated incentives, and hardly then, to indulge in personal alarms, any way involving the imputation of malign evil in man" [47]), and entirely sure that he represents the Good (a person whose constitution unites, as he admits, "good nature, compassion and charity" [115]). On the *San Dominick*, as elsewhere, Delano takes life genially. He takes blacks genially too, deploring slavery and generously appreciating the slaves on the ship, like the woman and her babe ("pure tenderness and love" [73]), Atufal ("he has a royal spirit in him, this fellow" [62]), and Babo ("slave I cannot call him" [57])—all of whom remind him of free men of color he has watched with "rare satisfaction" from his porch in Massachusetts (84). His universalizing good will extends beyond national boundaries; indeed, he thinks of Benito Cereno, the Spaniard, as a "brother captain" (52).

The American captain represents what Eric Sundquist has characterized as the "carefully calibrated benevolence" of "the politics of Union" (154). Pridefully displaying his "republican impartiality" when he distributes the water on the ship, he watches with equal pleasure to see Don Benito reflect a similar "disinterestedness" in distributing the food (80). Careful readers (like Babo) will note, of course, that he betrays this republican impartiality even *as* he distributes the "republican element," reserving extra water for Benito Cereno, "whose condition, if not rank, demanded an extra allowance" (80). Without doubt, Delano reveals what we might more properly call his republican *partiality* by reserving the best of the pumpkins, all of the bread, all of the sugar, and all of the bottled cider for the whites on the ship. Don Benito countermands Delano on this point. But to forestall triggering Delano's "republican" suspicions, Babo wisely insists that at least a bottle of the cider be reserved for the Spanish captain.

In his republican way, then, Delano, like members of fraternal orders, is in search of the "fraternal unreserve," the equalizing "sociability" of brotherhood. He characterizes Don Benito's reserve as a Spanish habit (53), implicitly contrasting that hierarchizing, aristocratic restraint to his own more democratic, American "sociability." But the potential for community in Delano's world is radically fore-shortened by his identification of "brotherhood" with white male power (they are brother *captains* after all). Conditioned by the representative construction of democracy in Massachusetts, Delano's definition of brotherly community as a privileged spot excludes all but one of the humans on board the *San Dominick*, as I argue at length in *The Word in Black and White* (114–18). Delano's attitude toward the blacks on board the slave ship symptomatizes precisely the false promise of his practice of democracy. He notes with pleasure Babo's attention to Don Benito: "performing these and similar offices with that affectionate zeal which transmutes into something filial or fraternal acts themselves but menial; and which has gained for the negro the repute of making the most pleasing body-servant in the world; one, too, whom a master need be on no stiffly superior terms with, but may treat with familiar trust; less a servant than a devoted companion" (52). Such a "friend" provides the appearance of that relation to his master, while upholding his "superiority"—in other words, this is a person who handily can satisfy both aspects of liberal white male desire, to represent the Good, and to enjoy his own, particular good. This is why, of course, almost the instant Delano pronounces Babo a "friend," he offers to buy him from Don Benito. And such liberal, "genial" sympathies would be precisely the reason when, finally understanding that Babo is trying to kill not him, but Don Benito, Delano strikes him not just with his hand, but "harder" with his "heart" (99). In this moment of violent, specifically *emotional* foreclosure, Delano cements his identity as a republican, as a white man. Like J. Marion Sims, he realizes finally what "belong[s] always" elsewhere.

There is certainly melancholy in this story, as my arguments about the way fraternal enactments are haunted by the simultaneously challenging and barred other would predict. Don Benito is at the story's end its seeming embodiment. Haunted by Babo—so much so that to look on him is to faint (116)—Don Benito finds first command and then life utterly insupportable, entering a monastery and dying soon after. H. Bruce Franklin has observed that Melville changed the date of the actual event on which this story is based from 1805 to 1799, the year that marked the beginning of the civil war that would eventually lead to the declaration of Haitian independence by former black slaves. The slave uprising on the *San Dominick* in this sense gestures toward that most famous of slave uprisings in Santo Domingo, the second revolution for independence in the Western Hemisphere, a revolution that has haunted the racialized practice of U.S. democracy.[40] The uprising on the *San Dominick* is less injurious to Don Benito, though, than what Babo compels him to confront. Babo deprives Don Benito of his most treasured relationship with

Don Aranda. In the bleached bones of that friend, Babo forces him to confront the denuded promise of white fraternity, its violence, its attenuated humanity. Delano enters only to confirm this bitter lesson. Benito Cereno tries to explain this painful lesson to the captain (whose geniality, as the narrator notes, leaves him ever "wide of the mark"): "You were with me all day; stood with me, sat with me, talked with me, looked at me, ate with me, drank with me; and yet, your last act was to clutch for a monster, not only an innocent man, but the most pitiable of all men. To such degree may malign machinations and deceptions impose" (115). Benito Cereno's is the melancholy knowledge that the promise of white manhood actualizes a structural privilege but at the cost of satisfying human connections even *within* fraternity. Though Delano is in repeated and intimate contact with Don Benito, he does not "rightly" know him, nor, importantly, does he ever trust him. Delano is constantly on the watch for sabotage to the symbolic order of white male privilege, such that he is prepared to relieve Don Benito of the command of his own ship should he prove himself undeserving (69); such that Delano's chief mate, acting as his deputy, can shoot *white* officers on board the fleeing slaver, who seemed to have formed solidarity with the cause of the escaping blacks (101, 113). The captains' "brotherhood" is shadowed by revenant otherness such that relations within fraternity can never be any more than symbolic and conditional enactments of the "real" thing: fraternity is constantly haunted within (as Delano's recurring suspicions of Don Benito evidence) by its own violences toward its others. This is a violence that threatens always to return, in one form or another—as uprising, as revolution, as betrayal from within, when "white" men turncoat and league with those "others." Babo is at once an unbearable reminder of the presumptive challenge of humanity's other, and of the emotional hollowness of community structured within the privileged spot of white manhood.

If Don Benito embraces the melancholy of white manhood, Delano arguably embodies its manic repression. Yet he is as surely haunted by it. We see that haunting in two key instances. The more minor one comes when he begins "to feel a ghostly dread of Don Benito" (68). To manage the anxiety this evokes, Delano employs his rational skills, reassuring himself with arguments that no plot could be directed against him *personally*, but only his ship. But rehearsing the unlikelihood of "piratical" conspiracy only seems to fire his imagination, and he worries that his extension of kindness, his hospitable offers, will be repaid by violence. Delano fears deceptive appearances, fears the "spectacle of disorder" (70) that always lurks behind well-ordered relations like a "slumbering volcano" that can "suddenly let loose energies now hid" (68). Delano puts down these fears by promising himself that he will, "on some benevolent plea," withdraw command from Don Benito, invoking symbolic right order to assist him in repressing his worries. These thoughts, as the narrator comments, "were tranquilizing" (69).

Much more painfully, I would argue, though even less apparently, Delano is haunted by the ghost of his dead/lost friend. As he explains to Don Benito, lacking provisions for the proper storage of dead bodies, he once had to order the body of a dead brother/friend thrown into the ocean: "It was once my hard fortune, to lose, at sea, a dear friend, my own brother, then supercargo. Assured the welfare of his spirit, its departure I could have borne like a man: but that honest eye, that honest hand—both of which had so often met mine—and that warm heart; all, all—like scraps to the dogs—to throw all to the sharks! It was then I vowed never to have for the fellow-voyager a man I loved, unless, unbeknown to him, I had provided every requisite, in the case of a fatality, for embalming his mortal part for interment on shore" (61). In telling this painful story to Benito Cereno, Delano's incoherent logic gives lie to his "vow." It is not a religious concern over the dead man's spirit that drives him, but the grievous loss of human connection—the looks, the touches, the *love*—that Delano can brokenly acknowledge, but cannot allow himself fully to comprehend. Instead, he invokes a formula, a ritual to forestall his mourning: I will never have a friend/I will not lose the friend (his body). It is a hollow, substitutive logic. In Delano's repression, his refusal to confront what the loss of the brother-friend *means*, we can begin to sense how that figure is symbolically loaded up with *all* the losses of Delano's fraternal space: to mourn this larger loss would affect him unbearably.

We see the shadow of the unbearable in Delano's near-frantic pursuit of Benito Cereno's "withdrawments"—his obsessive need for Don Benito to meet with him in that privileged space, which is for Delano a ritualistically protected enactment of that lost friendship with his brother, the supercargo. He is always prepared for the interruption of this pleasant fraternal space (with secreted coffins and embalming fluid), but *not* for its entire (unbearable, ungrievable) refusal. Thus, out of the very same obsessiveness that drives his pursuit of Benito Cereno on board the *San Dominick*, Delano cannot—will not—comprehend Benito Cereno's melancholy. "Why moralize?" queries the man who represses his own grief much as he represses seasickness: by "ignoring the symptoms" (116, 76–77). Read this way, Delano's vaunted and shallow "geniality" thus becomes the sign of his repressed longing for and fear of (the loss of) human connection. And similarly, we can see how, in the moment that Delano betrays that geniality by ordering the vicious pursuit of the *San Dominick* for the sake of its human cargo, he is imaginatively or unconsciously recovering a privileged spot with this brother-friend by *taking his place* as "supercargo"—the man who has charge of the cargo.

Thus we might read Delano's melancholy, and the fraternal melancholy I have described in this chapter, through the psychoanalytic framework that Judith Butler so elegantly outlines in her essay, "Melancholy Gender/Refused Identification": "If melancholia in Freud's sense is the effect of an ungrieved loss, it may be that performance, understood as 'acting out,' is essentially related to the problem of unacknowledged loss. Where there is an ungrieved loss in drag performance, perhaps it is a loss that is refused and incorporated in the performed identification" (32). Butler's specific interest in the essay is to describe the sexualized formation of bodily ego, through the ungrievable loss that bars the "same" gender as an object of desire. I think, though, that Butler's frame might work to suggest as well how the bodily ego is not just gendered and sexualized, but raced and classed— indeed, made "representative"—through prohibited/recodified desires such as those I have been tracing in national manhood.[41] Here, we might consider how not just one categorical loss (a gender) is barred and enacted, but rather multiple categorical "losses" are rerouted into the fraternal space, onto the lost body of the (ungrievable) fellow.

This model provides a helpful framework for explaining fraternal ritual's obsessive recourse to communion with dead men—and not just in fraternal orders (where the most important ritual was always the member's actual funeral), but in professional associations (as we see in the entirely typical professional eulogy-rituals lavished on Sims and Morton) and more personal "fraternal" interactions among men (as we have seen with Rush and Delano). Over and over in this study it has become clear that "fraternity" works best—perhaps works only— with absent or dead men. Butler argues that: "[M]elancholia attracts the death instincts to the superego, where the death instincts are understood as regressive striving toward organic equilibrium, and the self-beratement of the superego is understood to make use of that regressive striving for its own purposes. Where melancholy is the refusal of grief, it is also always the incorporation of loss, the miming of a death it cannot mourn" ("Melancholy Gender" 30). What Butler is mapping for individual psychology finds a structural analogue in fraternal rituals. Her model can help us think about how the unevenness of a political identity formation such as "representative democracy" is recodified in individual psychology (or pathology), how corporate trauma becomes manifest in what we are in the habit of seeing as individual behavior. The bribe of national manhood worked (and works) to reroute democratic possibility into fraternal logic, where representivity—white men's individual ability to stand for the Good of the Whole—was (and is) the alibi. Accepting the bribe meant (and means) foreclosing a whole range of political practices and human connections. It is a loss national manhood must not and cannot acknowledge; its melancholy energies turn back onto the fraternal space itself where "democratic" relations and equalitarian emotional exchanges are ritually sought and rehearsed—and effectively renounced.

White manhood hides its many losses from itself: it is a nearly impossible (however nationally/institutionally productive) subject position to achieve and to maintain, and its human costs are high. This is precisely the lesson we learn from "Benito Cereno." Delano's enactment of white manhood—his hollow geniality, his pursuit of (human) cargo, his anxious seeking for that "privileged spot"—symptomatize the profound abbreviation of human identification that structures white brotherhood. That, I would now say, is the story's achievement: it diagnoses the imaginative and emotional short-circuiting of democracy entailed in the United States' rationally conceived, professionally instituted, fraternal construction of representative identity—the abstracting ideal of white manhood that does its work.

Afterword: The President in 2045, or, Managed Democracy

My analysis has described national manhood as (to rework Benedict Anderson's well-known phrase) an imagined fraternity, which works best—perhaps only—with absent or dead men. It functions, as my last chapter outlined, in a state of melancholy, a false and unhealthy nostalgia for a uniform, brotherly state of unity and wholeness that never in fact did or even could exist. In that sense we might identify the motivating spirit of national manhood as an *esprit de corpse.* My afterword carries forward this aspect of my argument in a more focused way, which allows me to draw out some issues that emerged though were not exactly central to my analysis of the subject of national manhood, and to extend some of the implications of that analysis to the present day.

Specifically, I want to outline how presidentialism works both symbolically and institutionally in the United States to route democratic energies into the affective containment structures—the melancholic *esprit de corpse*—of national manhood. Alternative possibilities and practices (and even our ability to imagine those possibilities) get blocked by the system we are in the habit of giving our consent to, and I will work to highlight some of those possibilities as I raise questions about and outline the consequences of the structures linking presidentialism to patterns of democratic foreclosure similar to those we have seen in national manhood. Our constitutionally conditioned habit of looking to the President has trained us to vest our desires in him for what we might otherwise see all around us. Or, to say this differently, people's ability to deal with messier, open-ended, democratic

heterogeneity is circuited through national manhood's presidentialism into constitutionally unhealthy longings for wholeness, unity, for
"democratic" homogeneity.

As my preceding analyses have detailed, more heterogeneous,
democratic longings are in (often tortured) evidence everywhere. Their
routing into national manhood dead-ends them. Presidentialism—
the national manhood it symbolizes and the democracy it manages
—keeps us all wishing for better, and keeps most of us locked in
the kinds of democratically abortive modes political (anti)theorist
C. Douglas Lummis outlines—sentimentalism, despair, cynicism, or
looking for satisfaction in the future, through science, "progress," or
religious faith. These postures keep us not in what Lummis calls the
state of democracy, but one I want to borrow on my own terms to describe as a state of democratic melancholy, reinforcing our desire to
experience "democratic" confirmation in the sight of a (future) president. It is, I insist, institutionally productive melancholy—productive
because its effects don't impede or interrupt but actually seem to
keep the system of national manhood running strong—even though
(or perhaps best when) it seems to be limping. (I will have more to say
on this image below.)

Once you've noticed it, it's not hard to find proliferating instances
of national manhood's melancholy (when I have given any version of
chapter 5 as a talk, people always come up with lists of texts I should
also discuss, a list that seems headed by "Bartelby the Scrivener"). I've
chosen to begin my arguments in this chapter with an analysis of a
story by Poe—"Some Words with a Mummy"—because there, white
manhood's melancholy seeks an antidote in one of its key placebos:
the idea of the (future) president. Poe's odd, seemingly antiprogressiv-
ist story neatly evokes the way presidentialism promises to manage
white male anxieties and democratic haunting. It suggestively confirms the symbolic space of the president as a *dead* space, a space of
and for disavowed mourning, simultaneously the locus of unacknowledged democratic denial *and* loss. My analysis of that story frames
the psychopolitical structuring of presidential identification, backgrounding my interest in presidentialism and democratic practice for
the next section. Then I turn to a couple of recent narratives about
"our" national desire(s) for the president, the movies *Air Force One*
and *Contact*, in order to update the implications of some of my arguments.

I

Some Words with a Mummy

In a striking though seldom noted story published in 1845, Edgar Allan Poe offers a nuanced commentary on psychopolitical imperatives fueling the United States' scientific interest in race and ancient civilization. In "Some Words with a Mummy," an unnamed narrator is summoned, just after retiring for the evening, to join his friend Dr. Ponnonner along with a select company to dissect an Egyptian mummy on loan from the City Museum. The men begin at 11 P.M., and by 2 A.M. have only finished unwrapping the mummy and examining his three coffins, where they discover his name, Count Allamistakeo. Deciding to reconvene the next night, the men are preparing to retire when someone half-jokingly suggests applying electric jolts to the body. To their surprise, they resuscitate the mummy, who excoriates them for their incivility and their primitive scientific abilities.

Stunned by the mummy's response, the group, which includes the famous Egyptologist George Gliddon and British travel-writer (James) Silk Buckingham, questions him at length. In sweeps narrow and broad, the mummy tears down the modern men's sense of political, scientific, and racial progress, suggesting that far from advancing, the civilization and civic order they represent has degenerated from earlier ages. They think otherwise only because of their inferior ability in historiography, which follows directly from their inferiority in science, technology, and political organization. "In imminent danger" as the narrator puts it, "of being discomfited," the men are left grasping at straws—clothing fashion and humbug patent medicines—to "prove" the superiority of their world to the one Allamistakeo is from (169). Happily, the mummy has not heard of "Ponnonner's lozenges or Brandreth's pills" and thus the modern men find cause for celebration: "Never was triumph more consummate; never was defeat borne with so ill a grace" (170). Indeed, the narrator avers, "I could not endure the spectacle of the poor Mummy's mortification. I reached my hat, bowed stiffly to him, and took leave." Once departed, though, the narrator reveals that contrary to the seeming triumph of his departure, he has been plunged into a kind of despair. He goes home and records his account of the evening, bitterly denouncing his wife and his family and indeed the entire age, in what reads as a suicide note. The narrator reveals at close his intention to be embalmed for two hundred years: "The truth is, I am heartily sick of this life and of the nineteenth-century in general. I am convinced that everything is going wrong. Besides, I am anxious to know who will be President in 2045" (170).

The story, which begins with the removal of a mummy from the sensationalist public space of the museum to the objective, private space of a scientific gathering, not only stages the spectacle of a revivified mummy discrediting modern science,[1] but it foregrounds the character of science's social investment through men who are entirely unprepared to countenance evidence that contradicts their presumptions about their privileged relation to knowledge, progress, human history, and indeed, humanity. The extent of their investment in the scientific fiction of progress (and their exclusive role in it both as discoverers of its order and representatives of its advancement) is signaled by their ludicrously desperate attempts to continue claiming it in the face of the mummy's rebuttals. Their panicky response not only raises questions about their scientific "objectivity," but more importantly, it allows us to glimpse what they work so hard to evade: a recognition of common humanity. In particular, the narrator's emotional ricochet from scientific faith in (white) progress, to despair, to a resurrectionist fantasy of presidential confirmation details in quick succession several of the exorcist strategies that ward off the democracy haunting white manhood.[2]

"Some Words with a Mummy" lampoons a particular, fraternal construction of national manhood as it diagrams the short-circuiting of its affective structure.[3] The story's concern is with the rupture in an emerging form of U.S. manhood that stakes its privileged relation to civic status not just through race, but gender, class, and political exclusions. U.S. democracy was abstracted as a fraternal, homogeneous space. Its reassuring grant of equality, however, was always unsettled in practice, not only by the vicissitudes of citizens' professional, political, and working interactions with other "white" men, but also and as insistently by citizens' daily encounters with democracy's "others": "white" women, African Americans, Native Americans, and a growing underclass fed by poor immigrant Europeans. In John Brenkman's words, "the synthesis of civic equality and [white] masculinity is disturbed" constantly by the repeating claims of these other groups to civic entitlement, to democratic access (241). These repeating, challenging encounters had become a symptom within the privileged spaces of U.S. fraternity by the mid-nineteenth century, a kind of haunting that Poe's story neatly delineates.

The Wonders of Egypt

This story has a great deal of fun spinning out what the Other of white civilization, scientific progress, and representative order might say if only given an opportunity to respond. Above all, it demonstrates Poe's attention to the converging popular and scientific appeals of Egyptology in the United States, which offered to document both "white" exceptionality and human "progress." Gliddon, a widely recognized public figure, was pivotal both in cultivating public, museum interest in the "wonders" of ancient Egypt and in promulgating its research value to racial science. As Thomas Gossett notes, Gliddon was "one-half serious student and one-half P. T. Barnum" (64). Born in England (1809), Gliddon spent his childhood in places like Malta and Alexandria, Egypt. After his schooling in England, Gliddon worked as his father's agent in Greece, Syria, and Cairo. In 1832, he was appointed U.S. vice-consul to Cairo, from whence he cultivated a large "expertise" in Egyptology. In the 1840s, Gliddon traveled to the United States with a collection of Egyptian materials and began a lecture tour with exhibits.

As William Stanton notes, his timing was perfect: "P. T. Barnum and Peale's Museum had popularized Egyptian relics, and during the thirties and forties the Egyptian influence became apparent in American architecture. . . . well-to-do Americans began to include Egypt as part of the Grand Tour" (47). Growing fascination with Egypt was intimately bound with discourses of national, class, and racial progress.[4] Drawing on Walter Benjamin's arguments about the ways nineteenth-century industrial capitalism drew on contrasting images of the "archaic" in order to consolidate the experiential "newness" of commodities, Anne McClintock delineates how the growing cultural fixation "with origins, with genesis narratives, with archaeology, skulls, skeletons and fossils—the imperial bric-a-brac of the archaic—was replete with the fetishistic compulsion to collect and exhibit that shaped the *musée imaginaire* of middle-class empiricism. The museum . . . became the exemplary institution for embodying the Victorian narratives of progress. In the museum of the archaic, the anatomy of the middle-class took visible shape" (40).[5] The ancient Egyptian revival launched in the 1820s with museum displays of mummies in New York, Boston, and Philadelphia was the counterpart of modern Egyptology, which, as John Irwin observes, began with Champollion's translation of the Rosetta stone (3). The museum displays and tours

of Egyptian artifacts, and scientific and academic debates on ancient
Egypt, offered a fascinated American public a way to conceptualize
U.S. culture in the contrastive terms of progress, a way to experience the U.S. social body as historically, nationally, and racially exceptional.[6] It offered the middle classes, in particular, confirmation
of their historic preeminence, their particular suitedness to bear the
mantle of civic management and representative national order.

Gliddon may have been the first publicly to lecture in the United
States on Egyptology.[7] His role in spectacularizing remnants of the ancient civilization was complemented by his work at turning the attention of scientists toward ancient Egypt's pivotal importance, not only
to achieving science's definitive break with biblical interpretation by
pushing human chronology back beyond theological consensus, but
also to emerging theories of separate racial origins. In 1843, when
Gliddon gave his Lowell Institute Lectures in Boston, he provided
timely publicity and indeed stood as the public focal point for a nexus
of arguments coming out of the scientific community that were tending toward claiming separate racial origins. Morton's *Crania Americana* (1839) had gestured toward though did not commit to a theory of
polygenesis. In 1843, the rebarbative Nott published his essay, "The
Mulatto, a Hybrid," which touched off waves of scientific speculation
and controversy through its arguments that mulattos, though more
intelligent than their black progenitors, were more sickly and less fertile, tending ultimately toward infertility and thereby documenting
the claim he would be making within the year (in his "Two Lectures"
[1844]), that blacks and whites were separate species.[8]

Gliddon seemingly nerved Morton to make that claim explicitly as
well. Providing the embalmed Egyptian heads Morton would use in
arguments before the American Philosophical Society in the spring
of 1843 to demonstrate that differences in internal crania capacity
between ancient Caucasian and ancient Negroid skulls corresponded
significantly with contemporary differences, Gliddon urged Morton
to press against theological arguments about chronology (see William
Stanton 50). Morton began, within the year, publicly arguing in
anatomy lectures for the doctrine of polygenesis, which argument he
obliquely forwarded in the 1844 publication of his *Crania AEgyptiaca.*
However unwilling he might have been at that point to argue explicitly in print for polygenesis, his conclusions—on the basis of cranial
measurements as well as on his examination of ancient paintings,
that "the valley of the Nile, both in Egypt and in Nubia, was origi-

nally peopled by a branch of the Caucasian race," and that "Negroes were numerous in Egypt, but their social position in ancient times was the same that it is now is, that of servants and slaves," and that "[t]he physical and organic characters which distinguish the several races of men, are as old as the oldest records of our species"—were ample fodder for Gliddon's more aggressive public proclamations (qtd. in Campbell 426–427).[9]

Because of widespread attention to archaeological remains in Egypt, the fact of that ancient civilization and evidences that ancient Egyptians were "black" had become a haunting challenge for those who were trying to argue that the black race was and always had been "inferior." As Robert J. C. Young summarizes, evidences that ancient Egypt was the product of a "black" or even a racially "mixed" culture had to be decisively refuted: "for the polygenesists, it had to have been a white civilization" (128). Recognizing this earlier than most, Gliddon—a bit like Ponnonner in the story—gathered a likely circle of friends, offering them layers of encouragement, in the form of a steady stream of "raw" materials, public support for their professional reputations, and his own steady (if somewhat manic) friendship and correspondence, in the form of sympathetic arguments and encouragement for their (similarly oriented) work.[10]

Eric Lott has commented on the "revealing continuity" between discourses of sciences (biology, geology, anthropology) and museum culture's fascination with racial difference and antiquities (77). But Young argues that Gliddon in fact participated with Nott and Morton in *engineering* that continuity: "The significance of their work was the way they brought the scientific and the cultural together in order to promulgate an indistinguishably scientific and cultural theory of race. Biology and Egyptology thus constituted *together* the basis of the new 'scientific' racial theory" (*Colonial* 124; original emphasis). This was a theory designed to put down the reminders of an equalitarian dispensation of humanity, of "white" nonexclusivity. It looked (obsessively) to the distant past both to avoid incriminating contact with the contemporary politics of racial formation and to justify the contemporary foreclosure of possibilities for a very different political practice, one grounded in a more democratically conceived interconnection, in a messier and more open-ended form of human recognition.

Allamistakeo

Poe's story exposes the cultural logic of Egyptology's science. It highlights the symbiotic connection between scientific and social desires, that science's social desire to fortify men's sensation of white male exceptionality through the reconstruction of white fraternity. We can see the gathering to examine the mummy in just this way. The late-night unwrapping is a fraternal ceremony of professional, white manhood: a brotherly rehearsal of sameness and coherence in the ritualistic unveiling of otherness. But the symbolically hollowed mummy turns literal revenant, whose return severely interrupts the privileged invocation of white manhood. In this fantastic plot device, the story reveals how absolutely fundamental it is for the ritualism of *esprit de corpse* that supplementary bodies (both those abjected and those idealized) stay absent and/or dead. At the same time it emphasizes how these absent/dead bodies never quite give what national manhood needs from them.

From the first moments that the mummy comes to life, it speaks as the haunt of civilized white manhood, chiding Gliddon and Silk Buckingham for their disrespectful consideration of his body and his feelings: "I really did anticipate more gentlemanly conduct from *you*. What am I to think of your standing quietly by and seeing me thus unhandsomely used? What am I to suppose by your permitting Tom, Dick and Harry to strip me of my coffins, and my clothes, in this wretchedly cold climate? In what light (to come to the point) am I to regard your aiding and abetting that miserable little villain, Doctor Ponnonner, in pulling me by the nose?" (159; original emphasis). As the mummy's first comments indicate, this science works only by keeping otherness on display, exempting the body and culture of the scientist from uncontrolled comparison. Once the mummy can speak, he can challenge the terms of the comparison: the result in Poe's story is at once humorous for the reader, and embarrassing— even devastating—for the middle-class narrator and his compatriots.

Gliddon responds to the mummy's charges in the depersonalizing language of modern science. As the narrator summarizes: "Mr. Gliddon's discourse turned chiefly upon the vast benefits accruing to science from the unrolling and disemboweling of mummies; apologizing, upon this score, for any disturbance that might have been occasioned *him*, in particular, the individual Mummy called Allamistakeo; and concluding with a mere hint, (for it could scarcely be considered more,) that, as these little matters were now explained, it might as well to proceed with the investigation intended" (161; original emphasis). The mummy refuses that devivifying hint, jumps down from the table, and, shaking hands with each member of the scientific party, installs himself as their speaking equal rather than their mute object. The men are thus forced into the precise dialogue their ritual unwrapping was designed to forestall.

This conversation forces them (almost) to recognize the inadequacy of the competitive orientation of their progressive, representative selfhood. Allamistakeo reveals in short order that these scientific "experts" have incorrect understandings of ancient Egyptian life spans (anywhere from 500 to 1000 years), chronology, embalming practices, and religion. The revivified mummy details the absolute unreliability of historical transmission, recounting how ancient Egyptian historians would have themselves embalmed alive, and then resuscitated a couple centuries later so that they could rectify the always-mistaken interpretations of their historical accounts. Indeed, the scientific moderns standing before him offer a case in point for Allamistakeo's method, since their understanding of ancient Egypt, by comparison to the mummy's account, is as "totally and radically wrong" as the ancient Egyptian historical lessons to which the mummy refers (165).

And Allamistakeo ridicules these men's attempt to date the Creation. Though Ponnonner presents this as a topic of "universal interest" the mummy ridicules it as a provincial, laughable speculation: "During my time I never knew any one to entertain so singular a fancy as that the universe (or this world, if you will have it so) ever had a beginning at all. I remember, once, and once only, hearing something remotely hinted, by a man of many speculations, concerning the origin of *the human race*; and by this individual the very word *Adam* (or Red Earth) which you make use of, was employed. He employed it, however, in a generical sense, with reference to the spontaneous germination from rank soil . . . of five vast hordes of men, simultaneously upspringing in five distinct and nearly equal divisions of the globe" (166; original emphasis). John Irwin observes that Allamistakeo's response here "subtly shifts the question of origin from a biblical to an epistemological ground; that is the question of recognizing an original human form is seen to be circumscribed by the more basic question of the origin of recognition itself, the origin of consciousness" (58). Another way to conceptualize Allamistakeo's challenge is to say that it ridicules the political project that underwrites their use both of religion and science, their desire one way or another to establish their own preeminence (sanctified origins, heroic progress) and to evade any recognition of alternate human possibilities.

He may expose those politics for the story's reader, but the men's defense mechanisms facilitate their avoidance of his epistemological and political challenges. Allamistakeo's glancing (and indeed, trivializing) reference to the theories of "a man of many speculations" works instead to trigger an association that gives life back to these scientific moderns. However he might have intended his point, the mummy has reminded them of Egyptology's pet theory, of the separate origins of the "five races." Buckingham quickly responds to the gestures of "one or two" of the men who "touched our foreheads with a very significant air," and goes on the offensive. Imputing the amazing knowledge demonstrated by the mummy simply to "the long duration of human life in your time," Buckingham trots out a favorite craniological "fact" as his *coup de grace:* "I presume therefore that we are to attribute the marked inferiority of the old Egyptians in all particulars of science, when compared with the moderns, and more especially, with the Yankees, altogether to the superior solidity of the Egyptian skull" (166).[11] The associative link that Buckingham makes, from the mention of five races to the craniological studies that "document" their separate origins, leads him to the suggestion that ancient Egyptian skulls evidence a "primitive" thickness. This chain of association highlights the contradictory demands Egyptology placed on the mute(d) body of the mummy. This science simultaneously seeks on the one hand a "white" body, where Egyptian civilization will serve as a classical exemplar of white/"Yankee" civilization, and, on the other, a primitive body, to serve as an anthropological other to modern science.

For his part, Allamistakeo refuses to be baited by an essentialist argument correlating physical bodily difference to intellectual and cultural ones; instead, professing not to understand Buckingham, he requests more information about the "particulars of science."[12] On that (relative, argumentative) ground, as it happens, the Yankee moderns cannot prevail, though they bring out all the ammunition, from phrenology, astronomy, and architecture to modern transportation, Transcendentalism, and democracy (regarding the last, Allamistakeo recalls experiments in constitutional democracy during his age, locating an Achilles heel in their competitive orientation: "For a while they succeeded remarkably well; only their habit of bragging was prodigious" [169]). Allamistakeo's refusal to engage as either classical exemplar or anthropological other reveals the limited conceptual basis of both impulses, their hierarchizing and teleological orientation. The mummy takes a direct swipe at the latter: "As for Progress," Allamistakeo opines, "it was at one time quite a nuisance, but it never progressed" (169).

The President in 2045

The extent to which these scientists were counting on the mummy's (mute) corporeality to accredit their fraternal incorporation, under such signs as modernity, whiteness, and above all, progressive rationality, is underscored in the narrator's emotional unraveling after leaving the gathering. We can best comprehend the narrator's troubled response by reading it as the story's index to the emotional short-circuiting of self-making, scientific white manhood. This is a practice of manhood haunted not just by an Egyptian mummy, but by multiple, ungrievable, contemporary losses within the democratic body, as we see in the narrator's final, hysterical repudiation not just of his wife but of his entire age in his search for a future president.

The tale of the mummy's interview is framed by the narrator's attempt to stabilize a coherently unified sense of self. His strategy for this offers a precise diagram for the psychic recodifications structured through national manhood, where his own (representative) failures at self-management are projected onto (democracy's) others. The narrator introduces the story by recounting his evening at home, before he is summoned by Ponnonner. He narrates his desire to eat a "light" supper and to retire early to bed, in order to recover from a demanding evening previously. In what looks suspiciously like a set of jabs at Ben Franklin, Poe's narrator inadvertently exposes himself as he praises his own self-discipline. Though he is "exceedingly fond of Welsh rabbit," he sagely pontificates that "[m]ore than a pound at once . . . may not at all times be advisable" (154). Having set this out as his ideal, the narrator's rationally defensive lack of self-discipline quickly emerges: "Still, there can be no material objection to two. And between two and three, there is merely a single unit of difference. I ventured, perhaps, upon four. My wife will have it five—but, clearly, she has confounded two very distinct affairs. The abstract number five, I am willing to admit; but, concretely, it has reference to bottles of Brown Stout, without which, by way of condiment, Welsh rabbit is to be eschewed" (154). Allocating any "miscalculation" about the meal to his wife, the narrator concludes his account of "a frugal meal" and retires to bed "with the aid of a capital conscience." Despite his "wretched headache" and firm conviction that the "wiser thing" is to sleep through "till noon the next day," the narrator is more than happy to answer Ponnonner's summons: "I leaped out of bed in an ecstacy, overthrowing all in my way; dressed myself with a rapidity truly marvellous; and set off, at the top of my speed, for the Doctor's" (154–55).

The narrator's eager retreat from the compromise and dissonance he projects onto his allegedly argumentative, miscalculating wife— whom he'll label a "shrew" at the close of the story—to the all-male enclave of his scientific friends prefaces his escape plan at the end. In both instances, he experiences the challenging heterogeneity of self and other as a threat that must not be engaged but disavowed. The particular appeal of Ponnonner's invitation to examine the mummy in the first instance is that it allows the narrator to escape the space where his other can talk back for one where it can't. This safer space is one of antiseptically ritualized sameness, where the scientific, brotherly rehearsal of the "corporeality and disincorporation" of the other promises to restabilize the narrator's interrupted sense of self (Albanese 5).

Unfortunately, the plan doesn't work, and when it doesn't—when science's carefully engineered space is interrupted by the uncooperatively revenant other—the narrator escalates his original strategy. Now, the abjected and rejected domestic space expands to include not just the shrewish wife and his family, but his entire milieu: "The truth is, I am heartily sick of this life and of the nineteenth-century in general. I am convinced that everything is going wrong" (170). Projecting his own self-division and sense of inadequacy onto his wife was not sufficient defense for the onslaught of the mummy; what disappoints him about his own self-control, about the limitations of what he stands for, is now so overwhelming he can only manage it by projecting onto his entire age. Failing his attempt to experience a redemptive sensation of pure self-identity in living fraternity, he frantically seeks a more virtualized form in the sight of an imagined president. His strategy literalizes the *esprit de corpse* of national manhood. He will transcend the haunting otherness that has spoiled "everything" by using the mummy's technique to escape to an idealized (symbolically dead) space with the "President in 2045" (170).

Thus we find in this elliptical story a useful diagnostic of the revenant heterogeneity perversely haunting scientific faith in white manhood's progress, and civic faith in presidentialism's preeminent, representative order. The mummy literalizes this haunting, but the narrator details the emotional pattern-response that is key to understanding the story's more serious cultural diagnosis. His desire for redemptive confirmation in the sighting of a future president is revealed as a literal dead-end; all the narrator has left as a final resort is to take the excavated, deadened place of his Other. "Some Words with a Mummy" unwraps that other to reveal at its ghostly center the melancholic, emotional hollowness of fraternally representative white manhood. And it suggestively exposes presidentialism as a strategy that allows that hollowed, haunted manhood to avoid the very democratic recognition that might revivify it—as something other than itself.

II

Presidentialism, Management, Democracy

Presidentialism offers a quadrennially redemptive paradigm of and guarantee for unified civic self-management. It provides a safely stratified order for the free (market) practice of democracy. In this section, I focus on the interfaces between the institutional structures of U.S. presidentialism and its symbolic import.[13] Along the way, I'll be pointing toward some of presidentialism's political consequences for democratic imagining—or what C. Douglas Lummis calls democratic sense (137–38)—in the United States. Poe's story suggests it is an emotional dead-end for progressive, scientific, white manhood; I'll be suggesting that it works to short-circuit the practice of democracy.

John Adams complained against the title of "president" because he found it too mundane and managerial—not sufficiently grand to inspire the respect he felt was necessary to such an office. Here he clearly misgauged the usefulness and versatility of that title for denoting the nation's executive officer. The *OED* tells us that "president" as a term designating the title of the person who "presides over the proceedings of a financial, commercial or industrial company" is an Americanism (the equivalent British usage is "governor"), and records its earliest usage in 1781, when the U.S. Congress granted a charter to and ordered the organizational structure for the Bank of North America. This idea, to make the national executive some-

how equivalent to the designated leader of an economic corporation
(one that in the 1780s still demanded public good and accountability
for private profit), precociously tapped the energy of corporatism's
late-century expansion and economic reordering. As Charles Sellers
reminds us, under British rule, corporations could only be chartered
as nonprofit agencies, and only by legislative act. Seven such char-
ters were organized in the colonial period. But after the Revolution,
"the number climbed to forty in the first decade . . . and passed three
hundred during the commercial boom of the 1790s" (44–45).[14] Titling
the nation's executive "president" displaced the more equalitarian
model of "confederation"[15] and made the nation analogous to a corporate body (treated by law as an individual); it drew on the emergent,
rationally entrepreneurial orientation of the corporation for conceptualizing democratic order.

Gary L. Gregg reminds us that under the Articles of Confederation, there was no single executive officer, and that "this lack of a
central figure within the government was more important than most
commentators and historians have noticed" (23). I'm arguing something a little different, that the transition *to* a governmental system
headed by a president, a national union embodied in the single person of the president, is more important than we are in the habit of
noticing. Presidentialism arguably anticipates the corporate model of
individualism Christopher Newfield has capably described (see *Emerson* 62–88). But more immediately, it reroutes the emergent radical
democratic energies I noted in chapter 1 into structures of practical,
political, and affective containment. The presidential reconstruction
of national unity, and of representivity, trains democratic energies
into what we might loosely call corporately managed sites[16] in at least
three ways: through constitutional rationalization, democratic institutionalization, and market routinization.

First, the president stands both as one aspect of, but even more
importantly, as the symbolic guarantor for, the Constitution's scientific system for national politics. The office of the president is designed, assure the Constitution's most famous defenders, to transcend
individual self-interest, specifically the local and contradictory self-
interest of the people. Under the federal plan, the president would
reflect a refined and rational version of "the sense of the people."
He will be able to do this because he will be chosen by men chosen
by the People, men whom the People trust to act as more organized
agents of sober discernment than the People ever could as a whole,

disordered body. These men would be elected as "most capable of analizing [sic] the qualities adapted to the station, and acting under circumstances favourable to deliberation and to a judicious combination of all the reasons and inducements which were proper to govern their choice" (Hamilton, Madison, and Jay 345). (This refining and distancing structure, apparently countermanded by the institution of direct presidential elections three generations later, is one "we" are still loathe to give up by amending the Constitution, though—or perhaps because—most citizens remain totally confused about the function of the electoral college.) This "mode of appointment" actualizes the striking image of one of Pennsylvania's delegates to the Constitutional Congress, James Wilson, who argued for direct elections with loose suffrage requirements in the case of the House of Representatives. As Madison records it, "He was for raising the federal pyramid to a considerable altitude and for that reason wished to give it as broad a base as possible" (qtd. in Ketcham 40).

The distance pyramidically installed between the people's general and "disorderly" interests and the president's judicious distillation of their (singular) interest delivers the president to the nation as a purified body, a man *in* but not *of* a body. Electoral distance, carefully commissioned electors, term limitations, and the "intermixture" of powers will all combine to provide a presidential entity who has risen above the personal passions and factional interest, who will preside democratically by transcending local investments and attending dispassionately to abstracted national interest. This is an argument that promises more representation for "the people" through what we might even think of as a tricameral legislature (see Riker 109). If a House and Senate aren't enough, now "the people" will find an even more concentrated and purified experience of representation in the executive body of the president—the concrete correlative for national manhood.

This argument notably resituates democratic negotiation, the face-to-face democracy emerging throughout the Confederation, as inadequate and even threatening to national order, except as it is defused through atomization and rationalization (*The Federalist* No. 10 stands as this argument's monument). This is an argument that even explicitly disqualifies the People from self-rule; precisely insofar as they *are* the people their own embodied, contradictory interests disqualify them from actual, unrefracted self-rule.[17] As Frederick M. Dolan points out, the Anti-Federalists were not simply objecting to the president/king parallel, they also—significantly—rejected the Federalist attempt rationally to "purify" politics of embodied interests. Dolan insists that we should give Anti-Federalists more intellectual credit for their oppositional project, which he analyzes as a "hermeneutics of suspicion": "Federalist political science emphasizes cool logic, clear and unambiguous assertions, solid argumentation, and above all political claims that appeal to a disembodied reasoner striving to objectify his world rather than to immediate passions and affections, which are necessarily narrowing and parochial. Disembodied reasoners are exactly what the anti-Federalists refused to be" (42). Anti-Federalists insist that politics can only proceed fairly by locally interested actors skeptically negotiating toward a consensual and conditional "general will"; presidential democracy suggests that only a disinterested, rationally disembodied, and "vigorous" president can adequately process and reflect the unified will of the People.

Dolan notes that constitutional government's appeal to Newtonian science, where government will henceforward be "grounded in nature's own laws of motion" has the paradoxical "effect of offering *mythical* reassurance, because the citizen can feel that his political system is modeled on heaven itself" (54). Perhaps as important, though, the Newtonian appeal of constitutional framing also implies the precision of machinery. A second way that presidentialism manages democratic energies is by channeling them into democratic machinery in the shape of institutions like balanced powers, independent judiciary oversight, and regular elections. These institutions promise to create a safer space for democratic freedom by regulating and regularizing its expression. This is a model of managed democracy that constrains and complements presidential powers. These institutions, like the president, both guarantee and stand for U.S. freedom.[18]

But they do so in the same way that the black Algerian "stands for" French Empire in Roland Barthes's analysis "Myth Today"—which is to say, mythologically. While such institutions as a bicameral legislature and national presidential elections might aid in the goal of achieving more spaces for democratic practice, they can never be tantamount to democracy, never equivalent to freedom. Elaborating on the distinction between "democracy as a principle in human affairs" and the "various institutions or actions through which people seek to realize this practice," Lummis helpfully frames this point: "All too often these become fused and confused, and we speak as if democracy were free elections or legal guarantees of human rights, or worker's control. Yet we do not say, for example, that peace is peace treaties, or that justice is trial by jury. That peace may be brought about by peace treaties or justice by jury trials, are hypotheses that, as we know from experience, prove true in some cases but not in all. We are able to judge the relative truth, or success, of these hypotheses because we have notions of justice and peace independent of our notions of trials and treaties" (12). The Constitutional defenders successfully tapped (as I argued in chapter 1) into tensions and anxieties that ordinarily emerge in democratic practice, tied them to a whole range of cultural and economic anxieties, and promised relief for those anxieties in institutional machinery for national unity and democratic order. This presidential institutionalization of democracy offered a reassuringly hierarchized substitute for the messiness of local interaction: a rationally stratified structure, the atomization of factional interests through electoral distance, and the ritual release of democratic energy in the form of elections.

Commenting on the way the expansion of suffrage works to augment (not challenge) national governmental authority, Benjamin Ginsberg details how expanded voting rights gesture toward a modern sphere of public opinion that is "in many respects an artificial phenomenon that national governments themselves helped to create and that their efforts continue to sustain" (*Captive* 32). One key component of the national rechanneling of public opinion comes, Ginsberg argues, when its social basis is redirected from class to market (36–40). In equating a unified political system with national economic health, harnessing the marketplace ideal for the expression of civic opinion, and providing a machinery for processing and refining that opinion, presidential federalism encourages civic actors to believe that they gain more liberty to compete "equally" in an impersonal free-market of political opinion through their participation in national elections than in local democracy. Reformulating the practice of nation through presidential incorporation worked to disconnect the "equality" of the voter from a recognition of actual inequalities in the market. This realm of virtual equality functioned to blunt class politics and vision while keeping everyone focused on the importance of the economy for national unity, what Publius/Hamilton calls the "brother moderation" that "concur[s] in erecting one great American system" (Hamilton, Madison, and Jay 55). Market routinization is thus a third way that corporate presidentialism manages democratic possibility.

The Presidential Imaginary of Democracy

One important structural effect of presidentially managed democracy is that it blocks our ability to imagine productive democratic processes built out of consensus *or* reciprocal dissensus (as Lani Guinier's fast ouster from the review process to confirm her appointment as assistant attorney general in charge of the civil rights division amply evidences). Instead, it hard-wires national order for majoritarianism, in multiple ways. First of all, as comparative democratic theorist Arend Lijphart observes, the one-person model for the executive office is perhaps the strongest majoritarian influence within presidential democracy. In an article revising his earlier comparative study of presidential and parliamentary democracies, Lijphart claims to have overlooked one important element in calculating how it is that presidential democracy tends so strongly toward majoritarianism: "I have come to the conclusion . . . that a third essential difference must be stated . . . that accounts for much of the majoritarian proclivity of presidential democracy. . . . Within parliamentary systems, the prime minister's position in the cabinet can vary from preeminence to virtual equality with the other ministers, but there is always a relatively high degree of collegiality in decision making. In contrast, the members of presidential cabinets are mere advisors and subordinates of the president" ("Presidentialism" 93). Presidentialism, which concentrates symbolic power "not just in one party but one person" (97) provides a model for strong individualism, of subordination within the (almost always) single-party cabinet, and competition with the (frequently) opposed majority Congress. This is the strong body promised by national manhood, and this symbolic presidential body has worked powerfully to limit if not foreclose such democratic ideals as reciprocity for the purposes of U.S. democratic practice.[19] Lijphart puts the point bluntly: "presidentialism is inimical to the kind of consociational compromises and pacts that may be necessary in the process of democratization and during periods of crisis" ("Presidentialism" 97).

Another of presidentialism's majoritarian proclivities comes in the president's claim to full democratic legitimacy as the only elected officer of the People. Because the president is not structurally accountable to other politicians (in the form of no-confidence motions), the ambiguity that rides between the charge of his partisan victory and his symbolic charge to represent the full electorate often results in a practice comparative political scientist Juan J. Linz summarizes as a presidential "propensity to identify the people with one's constituency and ignore those voting for one's opponents" (Linz and Valenzuela 25). The presidential claim to full legitimacy structurally orients democratic practice toward a homogenized (strongly unified), rather than a heterogeneous (functionally disunified) ideal. Thus presidentialism, like national manhood, conditions citizen inability to conceptualize productive dissensus; political dissensus can hardly be embodied by the president as anything but effeminate indecisiveness, a weakness unhealthy for nation.

And the stature of the office also works to precondition the nation's embrace of a politically narrowed two-party system. Particularly after the installation of the team ticket, where the "loser" really becomes a loser and not a vice president, the model of a dual-oppositional party system is structurally cemented. The fact that only large parties can hope to win the presidency mitigates against multiple-party viability, and thus again, democracy is structurally routed into a majoritarian, oppositional model where the "healthy" outcome is a unifying victory embodied in a single man, not a complex and conditional process of negotiation.[20] As the new president moves into office and claims his partisan agenda as the "People's mandate," and the runner-up fades from the public view and into the footnotes of historical accounts, U.S. "democratic" presidentialism teaches its citizens once again that democratic conversation, like cutthroat economic competition, is an oppositional, zero-sum debate, with clear winners and soon-to-be invisible losers.

And (as my arguments about national manhood would suggest), it effectively teaches even those who vote for the "loser" to subordinate themselves to and experience themselves as part of the "People's mandate." Voting, in other words, works powerfully to incorporate citizenry to the new presidential agenda, whether or not people agreed with it going into the voting booth. As Ginsberg explains, "political rights such as voting and representation serve to convince citizens that they actually control the state and thus stand to benefit from its power." Summarizing the results of two pre- and postelection polls that queried respondents on their trust in government and confidence in its responsiveness, Ginsberg notes a clear pattern of increased confidence after the presidential election among voters. Fifty-five percent of voters who felt they did not have satisfactory input into government felt they did after they voted for president—whether or not they voted for the candidate who won (*Captive* 42–46).[21]

Now: we can call such people idiots, unworthy of democracy. Or we can call them good citizens, team players in the democratic game. Or we can say that this is not an institution that is working for the practice of democracy in the first place. Given the hollowed-out quality of that word, it would be good for me to say something here about what I mean by democracy. I define democracy as a process of peoples' self-governing in the sense that Lummis outlines: democracy "describes an ideal, not a method for achieving it. It is not a kind of government but an end of government; not a historically existing institution but a historical project. That is, it is a historical project if people take it up as such and struggle for it" (22). People's exercise in voting for "losers" and willfully forgetting as they self-subordinate in the winner's circle exercise of presidential identification is at some level certainly a struggle. But by Lummis's definition, it would be hard to identify it as a struggle that results in democratic practice. Democracy happens when people have, and take responsibility for, self-governing power.

I differ with Lummis's extraordinarily helpful, clear, and passionate discussion of radical democracy in one important respect. He argues that democratic practice is motored by political virtue, which he defines as "the commitment to, knowledge of, and ability to stand for the whole" (37). As my arguments throughout this study, but especially in chapter 5 make clear, I think that ideal—the ability of the individual actor to stand for the whole—is exactly where democratic practice goes painfully wrong. No single citizen can stand for the "whole" unless "we" are all radically and repressively the same, unless some (even many) of "us" drop out (or into the margins) of the picture. I would say that democratic virtue is constituted precisely through the certainty that no one can stand for the whole, and through a willing engagement in the difficult, ongoing process of creating and recreating equalitarian grounds for reciprocally dissensual democratic processes.[22]

To return to the question of presidentialism, then. I'm not saying democracy must be practiced without institutions: in fact, I'm saying just the opposite: democratic energies can't be sustained for very long without institutions that complement and support them.[23] But we have to be able to know the difference between the institution that supports, and the practices of democracy. As far as I can see, presidentialism is bad for democratic practice. It's bad in the specific sense that it reroutes the radical practice of democracy—the hard work of achieving plus-sum democratic (dis)union—for a citizenry that learns from presidentialism to long for self-subordinating civic unity and national "wholeness." It channels democratic energies into nominally democratic, civically and economically stratifying institutions, where patriotic identification arrests questions about local social, political, and economic injustices. The presidential incarnation of national manhood's representative democracy blocks imagining democracy as the political and cultural processes of multiple and diverse bodies, engaging dissensually together in self-governance.[24] The president of national manhood leads us boldly into "our" future (2045 and beyond?), claiming "our" consent.

National Manhood's President

The Constitution enumerates congressional powers. There is no such list for the executive. Whatever presidential scholars might want to say about checks and balances (or their "adulteration"—as Roelofs calls it—in giving the executive legislative veto power; see *Poverty* 4), it's a fact that the office was left wide open for symbolic and actual expansion. Presidential scholars and analysts have an oft-repeated refrain about how the Constitutional allotment of power actually keeps the president comparatively "weak" and how the demands put on his office by public and international expectation combine with his structural dependency on other branches to create a lot of "frustration" for the president personally. Scholars call this the "paradox" or the "ambiguity" of presidential power. But the fact is, as Lijphart registers with a certain amount of annoyance, no one seems very committed to the idea of executive checks and cooperative government: *everyone* wants to believe the president has the power—the president, legislators, journalists, scholars, the citizenry.

Our longing for the power of the president keeps a myth alive, and it is one that, as Barbara Hinckley insists, has real consequences for our practice of democracy. She enumerates the key features of this myth: "Presidents are identical to nation, identical to government and powers of government, unique and alone [and] the moral leaders of nation" (135). One key aspect of her analysis has to do with the concentration of agency in the body of the president in a way that completely elides the cooperative efforts that produce every act of state: "Presidents, factually speaking, do not manage the economy, but it is part of the symbolism of the office that they are singularly responsible for the nation's well-being. We speak of the president's foreign policy or economic policy, collapsing a long and complex policy-making process into the work of a single individual. We use the singular—the president—in describing what all presidents do, thereby creating the impression of specialness and incomparability" (2). Our president is the culmination of the (middle-class) self-made man.[25] He serves as the apogee and guarantor of national manhood's particular mode of representivity: stratified order, market exchangeability, virtual presence, and virtualized democracy. And it literally doesn't matter whether individual men can live up to it. As Hinckley notes, "the more individuals are blamed for mistakes and scandals the less the office is touched . . . confidence is shaken in one president but not in the presidency" (136).

These are the symbolic demands of national manhood, or what Slavoj Žižek terms the "formal democratic subject." The hollow abstraction that structures the presidency finds its counterpart in this subject: "the subject of democracy . . . is none other than the Cartesian subject in all its abstraction, the empty punctuality we reach after subtracting its contents" (*Looking* 163). Žižek, who cynically generalizes this formal democratic subject to all democratic practice, still helpfully highlights the same dynamic of virtualized identification that Poe's story helps us see: "[i]t is because of this lack of identity [in the formal democratic subject] that the concept of *identification* plays such a crucial role. . . . the subject attempts to fill out its constitutive lack by means of identification, by identifying itself with some master-signifier guaranteeing its place in the symbolic network" (163; original emphasis)—with a hollowed out, abstracted president. While Žižek concludes that there is "no place" in democracy for "the fullness of concrete human content," I have been arguing somewhat differently and more specifically that national manhood's representative, presidential ordering of democracy leaves no room for the fullness of concrete human content, no place for the messy but rewarding work of democratic human interconnectedness. At the same time, it is haunted, fractured by desires and demands for such spaces.[26] It would be possible to find them, but we won't by looking to the president, now or in 2045. And still—as the summer movie fare of 1997 evidenced—we try.

III

The President's Two Bodies

The president embodies democracy as a paradigm of national manhood's unhealthy desires for unity, wholeness, and self-sameness. But the figure of the president is also loaded up with national manhood's ambivalent longings for a more heterogeneous democratic connectedness. These contradictory desires split the president in our "democratic" imaginary. The hard body of the president offers us a strong guarantee for national boundaries and self-identity. The soft body of the president holds out for us sensations of democratic recognition and equalitarian exchange. We can't seem to imagine having both at the same time and we can't figure out how to live without either one. And so neither provides us/U.S. a body we can live with for long. The hard body of the president keeps us hoping for more democratic connectedness than we are taught we can safely have; the soft body of the president delivers only a placebo version of that connectedness, and starts us worrying that he's not adequately protecting our boundaries, not quite keeping democracy clean and safe.

Michael Kimmel argues that a hard presidential body has been a key symbolic in presidential elections at least since 1840. In the race between Van Buren and Harrison over 80 percent of the eligible white male electorate turned out to vote a manly man into office—who promptly killed himself on the sharp edge of his machismo. Refusing to wear a coat for his oath of office, the Western military hero and Indian killer caught pneumonia on that bitterly cold day and died a month later (Kimmel 38–39).[27] But in a recent cycle that he dates as starting with Carter, Kimmel suggests that the nation has been flirting with the idea of a softer "new man" presidency. Choosing Carter and then panicking, we had an eight-year run of Reagan's cinematically flinty persona, followed by the drama of Bush's self-making from a rich-boy Yalie "lap-dog" veep into a macho strongman who could out-muscle Noriega and Hussein.[28] Then the electorate, ignoring Bush and Perot camp jibes about Clinton's "tassel-loafered lawyer crowd," put in office a man who promised he could "feel your pain" (Kimmel 270–98). And immediately, it would seem, began to worry over that choice.

Media treatment of Clinton reflects strong cultural ambivalence about the soft president.[29] Cultural theorist and feminist philosopher Susan Bordo notes that Clinton's "softness"—key attributes we alternately perceive as "virtues"—are nevertheless habitually cast as feminized defects: "The fact that he is a negotiator and consensus-seeker means that his is 'trying to please everyone' rather than taking a 'firm' stand. His genuine commitment to diversity gets translated as 'caving in' to interest groups. . . . Even Clinton's eating habits are feminized. Traditionally, hearty appetite is a mark of the masculine. 'Manwich,' 'Hungry Man Dinners,' 'Manhandlers' are products which boast their ability to satisfy men. . . . Clinton's love of food, on the other hand, continually gets represented as embarrassing, out-of-control, feminine 'binge' behavior" ("Reading" 723). Clinton was early viewed as pudgy, not stocky or hefty, in the anxious nation's eyes; his body became prima facie evidence for his various departures from the hard model of national manhood. The president who promises to feel the pain of the people elicits both longing and worry. Schooled by national manhood precisely to ignore personal pain (and not relieved much by that rhetoric anyway in the face of the intensifying national fallout of economic globalization), the NAFTA-generation electorate trains its ambivalence experimentally into fascinated anxieties about Clinton's loose bodily demeanor—and compensates by getting tough on national and internal borders with mean immigration and welfare "reforms."

As I was finishing revising this manuscript, two of the summer's biggest box-office draws were released, Air Force One and Contact. Given the clear presidential drama of one and the real-life presidential brouhaha over the other, I couldn't resist seeing them. I left convinced that both movies were a working-out of national desires for and anxieties about our current electoral engagement with a soft presidential body. They give us two different ways to convert those anxieties and sustain those desires. Air Force One locates the hard-soft drama between the family-man body of the person, and the "national" body of the president.[30] It gives us the reassuring display of the president morphing from the soft into the hard body and protects our (democratic) desires for the soft body by incorporating the nation as family: it's safe to love this president because he will protect his "family." Contact also constructs a (democratic) fatherly body; it solves the hard-soft dilemma by relocating the body in question. Contact promises us it will be safe and good to have a soft president—in the future, where it can finally be sustained either by heteronormative aliens or God. But both movies agree on one thing: the world we live in is neither safe nor ready for democratic trust, and it would be a mistake to be looking for it here and now.

Kick-Butt Action Hero

Beginning with a startling U.S. commando operation that kidnaps the Kazakhstan Republic's president, General Alexander Radek, *Air Force One* flaunts the nation's hard body in the form of military muscle. And in an extravagant diplomatic dinner in Moscow to honor the president (introduced as "the world's greatest leader") for backing the mission, we see a President Marshall outlining a strengthened moral backbone for that body. In what soon will be known as his "Be Afraid" speech, Marshall disarmingly begins in Russian with an admission of policy *weakness:* "remember our indifference; remember our silence." Switching back into English, he explains that he feels undeserving of honor, having "hid behind a rhetoric of diplomacy," failing to act before thousands of men, women, and children had been killed. Promising to make democracy safe globally and to prevent the threat of renewed cold war, Marshall warns the world that "atrocity and terror are not political weapons," and for those who use them, "your day is over . . . it's your turn to be afraid."

His confident presidential demeanor is not even jolted by the admonitions of his national security advisor ("Now it's public: get behind it!" he snaps). But back on Air Force One, we begin to see mounting evidence for the same "bodily" split that will soon be worrying his secretary of defense back in Washington: that the hard national body of the president can all too easily be compromised by the soft body of the particular man. As his staff follows him into his office, Marshall ineffectually tries getting them to leave him in peace to watch the Notre Dame–Michigan football game. He's so bad at this that he's soon begging them just to let him use the bathroom alone. By the time his wife and daughter arrive on the plane from the Russian ballet, he's fallen asleep on the job/couch. His wife (Hillary Rodham Clinton's devoted, tough but more properly subordinated brunet counterpart) Grace reassures her worried husband that even though his staff "hated" his "Be Afraid" speech, it was the right thing to do because he "spoke from [his] heart."

Soon the shooting starts. James Marshall looks bewildered, and it is Grace who sticks her head out into the hall to see what's going on. As Secret Service men whisk him to the escape pod, the president weakly protests, "Where's my family? I want my family." The drama of the movie here depends on us worrying that he's unable to uphold let alone stand as the nation's hard body, that at a time like this he's concerned about the wrong things, or, somewhat differently, that he's running away—as the terrorist Ivan Korshunov will shortly describe it—"like a weak dog." When he climbs back into the hold after the pod's ejection, he looks tentative, terrified, in strong contrast to the commanding Korshunov, who is coolly smoking a cigarette and ridiculing Vice President Kathryn Bennett as he conducts negotiations. This is a terrorist who's not just ruthless, he's ruthlessly smart. Keeping Grace and daughter Alice by his side, he knows exactly the hard/soft trap he's maneuvered for the U.S. president. When Grace insists that the United States does not negotiate with terrorists, that the president will not negotiate with him, he cocks an eyebrow, puts his gun to her head, and reminds us of the hard lesson Democratic presidential candidate Michael Dukakis learned: "It would be such bad politics," he sneers, if the president seemed not to care about the welfare of his wife.

Fortunately for us/U.S., the man whom Korshunov ridicules as "the most powerful man on earth" soon proves his mettle. Seemingly bumbling his way into a strategy, first benefiting and then sabotaged by blind luck, Marshall's initiation rite comes in the form of hand-to-hand combat. He proves his willingness to get blood on his, and from the point that he kills his first terrorist, he is clearly what *Variety*'s Todd McCarthy describes as a "kick-butt action hero" ("US Prexy" 37). As one of the joint chiefs of staff reminds us, *this* president did his time in Vietnam, flying "more helicopter missions than any other man on my command." When Washington discovers the empty pod and realizes he's still on the plane, the wifely VP Bennett storms: "That pod was designed for a reason! He has no right to take chances with his life!" In the theaters where I watched this, men laughed at her delivery. Why did they laugh? Probably because the movie's logic has already made it clear that it is time to take pleasure in the return of the hard Presidential body. This is a body that doesn't need protecting. What "silk-bloused" Kathryn fails to remember in this moment is that its strength is not just his right, it's *ours*.

Fortunately for us/U.S. too, Marshall doesn't just "kick butt," he also provides the sensation of caring for "our" pain. When he returns to the conference room where the hostages are being held, the relief of the symbolic return is immediately evident. "I never left" he reassures the incredulous roomful of terrified U.S. hostages, who know his presence will make all the difference. This moment converts any doubts about the president's "soft" family values into a family-arizing sensation of national pride; it is his love of family that will bring him back to protect *US*. The collapse of personal and national family (and the integration of soft/hard presidential values) becomes explicit as a technical aid declares to him: "It makes me so proud, Mr. President, that you stuck with us—whatever happens" (in the next moment he gives her a fatherly peck on the cheek). This is the sequence that repositions Defense Secretary Walter Dean's seemingly national concerns about the president's command as his own personal self-interest, indeed, as power-grabbing. Trying to convince Bennett to declare him incompetent and assume presidential powers herself, he urges: "Jim isn't making this decision as a president, he's making it as a husband and a father." But as the audience has learned, and Kathryn Bennett already knows, it is precisely as a husband and a father that he makes his best presidential decisions.[31] (And so we also cheer her heroism in the movie, which is constituted precisely through her resolute, wife-like subordination to his power, her steadfast refusal to relieve him of his power.)

The movie engineers its argument through a kind of legerdemain, where we get libidinal satisfaction in shows of deadly and uncompromising national strength (the commando mission kidnapping Radek, President Marshall's ever-more-climactic defeats of the terrorists, the Russian prison guards blowing away Radek on Marshall's order) all of which are aimed at making the world safe for a somewhat softer, more internationally cooperative national body. The movie offers us a counterintuitive nationalist thrill. We get a lesson in newer world-order U.S. globalism as we watch our Han Solo president cut the (other) ultranationalist bad guys off from the global community, personally ("get off of my plane!" he growls as he hangs Korshunov on his parachute lead).

Critics (and various viewers whom I've talked with about this movie) have marveled at the thrill it delivers despite its patently hollow plot. If my arguments about the melancholically hollowed symbolics of presidentialism have any value, it is then possible to see that this movie works exactly because of the emptiness of its plot, and even Ford's "monotone, physically unexciting" performance (McCarthy, "US Prexy" 38).[32] In a nationalist corollary to fraternal ritualism, the movie gives us a way to experience presidential democracy's affective foreclosures as our innocent victimization.[33] Cannily, *Air Force One* explicitly structures our redemption from the *threat* of emotional depletion, reassuring us it's not the presidential practice of democracy that is affectively "hollow." Just the opposite: we can see that it's Korshunov who is threatening explicitly to hollow our president. Holding Alice Marshall at gunpoint, he snarls to the president, "you lose a child, it hollows you out." Marshall, trembling with pain, clearly cannot bear the idea of becoming hollow. He confirms his presidential plenitude and innocent victimization by capitulating to the terrorists' bad-faith demands. In this moment, he stands for the love that we long to feel coursing through democracy, protecting us/U.S. In this moment, like one of the family, we know that any threat to our love for each other comes not from *US* but from "them."

And so we thrill to the self-administered democratic wounding suffered by the president next, as he cuts himself along with the tape binding his hands on the jagged shard of glass prominently featuring the presidential seal. This is a wound symbolically loaded with the pain of democratic foreclosure—a pain the movie lets us acknowledge only in order to project and disavow it. *Air Force One* offers placebo logic for our pain: that cut hurts, but it feels good because we know by that wound he/we will be "freed." Indeed. As Korshunov and his men embrace at the news of Radek's release, Marshall gets loose and goes on the offensive once again, teaching them that even they cannot afford a moment of softness. His purposeful self-laceration justifies and redeems our injured sense of democratic foreclosure. As he tells his daughter near the beginning when she complains indignantly about "cheating" in the Michigan–Notre Dame football game: "It's only cheating if they get caught. . . . it's the way of the world, kiddo." It's a cruel world. The president can't entirely change that, nor can we, as the rest of the movie proves. But he comes back to protect us, limping, with blood on his hands and tears in his eyes, assuring us our pain is not our fault.

Some Words with a D(e)addy

The summer's intellectual box-office hit *Contact* opened to a presidential controversy. Film consultant and former White House spokesperson Dee Dee Myers had early notified White House staffers that Zemeckis would be using clips from a few press conferences in the movie. What they hadn't realized, apparently, was that Clinton's press conference addressing the possible discovery of life forms on Mars and another on events in Iraq would be cut in as though Clinton was addressing the reception of a signal from the star Vega. When the movie was released, the White House immediately protested this distortion of presidential intention, complaining that these uses of Clinton's "image and words" were "fundamentally unfair" (see *Los Angeles Times*, July 15, 1997, A14). The event created a little media splash—but the producers of the movie did not feel that they were either in legal or ethical jeopardy, and the film continued showing with virtual Clinton prominently in view. Entertainment trade magazine *Variety* examined the stalemated question in July 1997, querying "if the Most Powerful Man in the Free World can't control the uses to which his image is put, who else possibly can?" (Voland 49).

The issue quickly died down, with Clinton apparently deciding it wasn't such a big deal after all. But Clinton could have been more offended. It's not just that he was misquoted. It's not just that he was digitally virtualized. What he didn't notice is that he's not even the playing the real president. He's just a visual/earthly body-double for the genuine democratic father in the movie. *Contact* solves the problem of the president's soft body by removing it from this world[34] and relocating it in a safer future from whence it can reassure us in our democratic loneliness: "none of us are alone."

Let me explain this a little more precisely. I am suggesting that "Clinton" is the mundane stand-in for the dead dad/alien whom we meet near the end of the movie. It is this "D(e)addy" who promises us we can have what President "Clinton" worries about in the movie —more human connectedness. This substitution is accomplished through a couple layers of logical and symbolic slippages. The logical substitution comes in a key axis for the movie's argument. In *Contact*, presidents are to fathers as science is to faith (note that I am not saying religious faith). Faith and Fathers win by absorbing the other. This corollary is established in a key scene at a White House reception. Four years after their first romantic tryst, and just hours after the meetings discussing Ellie Arroway's discovery of the plans for the enigmatic space machine, she and White House spiritual advisor Palmer Joss play out the romantic, champagne-laced argument that lies at the supposed heart of the movie. It's an argument that pits science against religious faith (soon we will see that in some cases even science comes down to a form of "faith"). Joss has been explaining with a great deal of charm and patience that he's not so much anti-technology as he is questioning whether science can deliver what it promises. People want "meaning" and that is the "one thing science hasn't been able to give them." Like a woman who has already won the argument and is enjoying it, Arroway patiently explains to *him* the principle of Ockham's razor ("all things being equal, the simplest explanation is usually the best")[35] and questions Joss about his belief in the Christian God. Maybe he didn't create us, she says. Maybe "we created him so we wouldn't have to feel so small and alone." She presses her point: "Are you sure you are not deluding yourself?" For her own part, she assures him, she would "need proof." Joss swiftly delivers that proof: "Do you love your father?" Well, he knows she does and we do too. It's hardly a fair question, but its presumed answer is one of the key locks for this aspect of the movie's collapse of "fathers" into a looser notion of faith (more on this below) and a key valence for the way the film resolves anxieties about a soft presidential body.

The symbolic slippages are worked out both through the character of Dr. Ellie Arroway and through the visual and affective correspondences between actor David Morse, his alien performance of Ellie's father at the movie's end, and Bill Clinton. The movie symbolically loads Ellie's loss—first of her mother who dies in delivery, and more especially of her father, who dies when she is nine—in national terms. It's not just that she spends her childhood on ham radio, connecting the nation with strings and pins mapping her random contacts and then using it, in a poignant moment, to try contacting her father after his funeral ("Dad, are you there? Come back"). It's also that her aloneness resonates with Palmer Joss's and President "Clinton's" concern for the spiritual direction of the nation, the way people are "more and more cut off from each other" despite advances in technology. And just so we don't miss seeing the way Ellie's "aloneness" exemplifies the loneliness of our nation's citizenry, Zemeckis gives us repeating shots of Arroway with the Washington Monument hovering behind her like the phallic, presidential ghost of her dead dad. Ted Arroway's, not Clinton's, is the soft body that literally can't be sustained in this world: he dies of a soft heart (myocardial infarction) as he brings popcorn to the star-gazing Ellie. If such a loving, soft body is impossible to sustain in our presidentially ordered democratic imaginary, the movie won't let us forget it is the one we (and not just Ellie) long for. Clinton works visually as a pale, ghostly/digital but somewhat more viable stand-in for David Morse's Ted Arroway. And "Clinton's" agenda serves as a paler version of the alien D(e)addy's promise, to remediate the way that, as his spiritual advisor Palmer Joss puts it, despite our ability to "surf the Web" we are "at the same time . . . emptier, lonelier, more cut off from each other than at any other time in human history."

After I saw this movie a second time, I met a fun and interesting couple in the parking lot, who had clearly understood the alien father's message as a national one. They were interested in the way the movie works subtly to highlight our growing civic disconnectedness, the way we are losing public space for community contacts, and losing ways even to conceptualize community identity in the United States. We spun out an energetic conversation for at least twenty-five minutes, agreeing on some things, arguing and interrupting each other over others, marveling sadly at the rareness of such random, friendly, and passionate discussions in a parking lot or anywhere. We said goodbye with just the same regret that the movie elicited. That chance conversation felt good to all of us, and Alice made the connection between our encounter and the movie's argument explicit. "How fun to have had this contact," she quipped as she climbed into her car. The movie activates desires for more and sustained interactions with other people. It made me wonder how much parking lot energy for "contact" it might be creating all over the nation. It works to remind us how much we want this, collapsing scientific faith and religious faith into what could be described as a kind of democratic faith: a faith in each other, the faith and courage to believe that however different we might all be, however "tiny and insignificant" we might all feel, we are also "rare and precious," and that only we, together, can undo this loneliness.

This is an energy, a desire for democratic action and connection that we can see not just as inchoate manifestations in parking lots, or as the nation's sudden worrying over closing bowling alleys. It is evident in forms that are more coherently and pointedly about democratic, face-to-face, self-governing community. We can see it in growing movements demanding direct and accountable representation through citizen pressure groups and calls for term limits. We can see it in movements for community controlled urban (re)development such as those in Boston, in neighborhood planning assemblies such as those in Burlington, Vermont, in local grassroots organizations for democratic self-education and social justice all over the nation. We can see it in Clinton's seizure of the democratic town meeting (and the eager public response) for his campaigning, or in the variation on that model more thoughtfully organized by the University of Texas's 1996 pre-election national deliberative poll. Though we have samples of this energy everywhere, it is certainly true that the American mainstream, guided by presidentialism, doesn't have much practice at growing (let alone naming) local democracy. To foster such energies in a more organized way, we might want to create structured support of release time in this era of the sixty hour corporate workweek and the four-job family. We would certainly need to create civic spaces for citizen deliberation and self-education something on the order of those created by the Zapatista Front in Mexico.[36] As the Chiapas Indians have shown mainstream Mexican citizens, we could cultivate the energy to start making radical democratic connections that would work for us now. But *Contact*'s father/president assures us we *can't* do it now. He tells us we have to wait.

The bad faith of the movie, to my mind, is that it reminds us of something we're missing without giving us a precise language for describing it, and it works very hard all the while to show us exactly why we can't have "it" now. It offers to hash out the differences between two key forces in our national culture, but does this in a way that just muddies the water. While the movie and its promotion promises us a "serious" debate between science and religion, the arguments between Arroway and Joss are always interrupted, either by sex or national affairs. We never get beyond an initial round of this debate. Instead, we get an ambiguous alien encounter combined with a normatively romantic resolution. First "parental" then heterosexual union replaces the messy hard work of actual community building (contact) across intellectual, cultural, ethical, and political differences. The movie actually despecifies both scientific and religious inquiry for the fuzzier terms of a more generalized "faith." This is a faith that offsets democratic hope for the here and now by relocating that hope, symbolized in the soft body of a father who looks and sounds like a president who feels our pain, to a more "progressed" or moral future.

This fuzzy resolution works to suspend viewers between two other modes that do the work of democratic evasion: sentimentalism and cynicism. Sentimentalism is the mode for what we might call clean contact, the one that happens somewhere in the virtual Pensacola of outer space, with its sweeping, depopulated, luminously white sands. In this never-never land, we have a spectacular, idealistic experience of contact, no difficult negotiations, no tests, just awe and a bath of love. It is wonderful to believe we could live in that world, where the alien/Other loves and admires us always and as gently as that D(e)addy loves Ellie.[37] Real contact with real people never works that way. To coin Lummis's phrase on this subject, "the particular advantage of wearing [sentimentalism's] rose colored glasses is that you can't see" the potential messiness of real human, political interaction, where it never goes that cleanly—not even with the most beloved of fathers (147).

Alternately, cynicism is the mode prepared by what we might think of as the movie's messy staging of contact in the present. In this "real" world, possibilities for human interconnection are threatened in mobs full of weird and dangerous characters. We learn not to want this in a key episode, where Arroway has a close encounter with dissensual, heterogeneous America. As she returns from the nation's capital to the New Mexico radio telescope site, we hear a radio announcer describing how, thanks to the "message from Vega," people from all over the nation "have come to participate in the best show in town." Arroway surveys the sprawling, carnival crowd—groups of partiers, Elvis imitators, Harley Davidson bikers, a cappella choirs, white supremacy groups, dancing girls, car buffs, and tent revivalists—registering this democratic assemblage of American diversity with a nervous, distanced ambivalence that turns finally to mild alarm. As one of the tent revivalists recognizes her as a project scientist, continuing in his denunciations of scientific rationalism while looking at her, she rolls up her window and faces away. And it turns out she was right to impose this barrier between herself and the messiness of the people, because that man shows up again to create an even bigger and more dangerous mess, blowing up the first transport mechanism. Thanks to her caution, she herself will be able to identify him as a "breach of security." This crazy ultra-white apocalyptic terrorist exposes the dangers not so much of religious extremism but of contemporary, "real" democracy, of letting real people get too close to us: there's bound to be an explosion, or at least a loud disagreement.

After her "contact" she again responds to the people in a way that reinforces the movie's message about the dangers of democratic human interconnectedness in this world. In this moment, Arroway betrays her sensible response to David Drumlin's cynical apology at the test launching: "I wish the world was a place where fair was the bottom line . . . unfortunately we don't live in that world." "Funny," she returns, "I always believed the world was what we made of it." Just moments after her moving admission to the congressional inquiry, that though she can "prove" nothing, she is sure she was given "something wonderful, a vision," that she wishes she could share so "that everyone could feel it if only for one moment," she encounters a second democratic mess/mass on the Capitol steps. They are reaching out to contact *her*, to have that feeling she just said in sworn testimony that she wanted to share with them. It is clear that this is either frightening or somewhat distasteful, and we are supposed to know she's as right to be wary now as she was last time. She pulls away.[38]

Funny. I always believed democracy was what we make of it. But D(e)addy and his earthly presidential stand-ins know better, and good for us that they do. Presidentialism promises the safe management of democracy; it promises to take care of democracy for us. It teaches us (over and over) that the world is not safe for democratic faith; that people are not prepared for democratic trust. U.S. presidentialism's symbolic resilience is extraordinary. Despite the slow but radical expansion of suffrage over the last century, the referential routing of national manhood remains virtually undisturbed. Trained by national manhood, we, like Poe's narrator and Ellie Arroway, put our faith in the (hard or soft) president of the future, whom, we believe, will never let *US* down. President D(e)addy marks the stalled space of democratic melancholy, a space where we are united in desiring, mourning the loss of, and disavowing our own agency within democracy. That president is an exceptionally effective switchboard for national manhood. As we look to him to provide for us a cleaned up, unifying, safely virtualized sensation of democratic contact, we miss what we might otherwise be working out, in a far richer disorderly way, all around us.

Notes

Introduction: Naked Nature

1   San Dominick is, as the editors of the Northwestern edition observe, an "archaic, anglicized spelling" of the Spanish Santo Domingo (presently Dominican Republic; see 583 n. 49.16). But it also alludes to the French side of Hispaniola, Saint Domingue, thus elliptically evoking the Haitian slave revolution for independence, which began formally in civil war in 1799. The flexibility of historical allusiveness that Melville achieves through this archaic usage is fascinating. As Thomas Ott details, after defeating the leader of the *gens de couleur*, Rigaud, Toussaint-Louverture turned his attention to invading the Spanish-controlled part of the island. In January 1801, Toussaint entered the capital of Santo Domingo. Observers were shocked at the ease with which Toussaint conquered the Spanish colony, having assumed that the "white" Spaniards' opposition to black rule would have prevented such an event (see Ott 116–18).

2   In a later edition, the U.S. explorer John Ledyard is substituted for Park. Both men were popular icons of colonialist manhood for their expeditions in exploration and ethnology in the nineteenth century. The Northwestern edition of "Benito Cereno" notes that the 1856 *Piazza Tales* edition revises the earlier Putnam's version from Park to Ledyard, but "neither name quite fits the sentence, since the famous African traveler Park (1771–1806) did not write the 'noble account' while John Ledyard (1751–89) did write it but about women of Asia, not of Africa. The explanation of this crux seems to be that when Melville first wrote the sentence he had in mind the passage in Park's *Travels in the Interior Districts of Africa* (1799) that quotes Ledyard's parallel 'noble account'—an account which Melville mistook or misremembered as Park's own" (584–85). Ledyard's account

from his Siberian journal appeared in the 1790 *Proceedings* of the African Association (264–65). His "eulogy" contrasts the behavior of the men and women he has encountered in his travels: "I have often observed among all nations, that the women . . . wherever they are found . . . are the same kind, civil, obliging, humane, tender beings; that they are ever inclined to be gay, cheerful, timorous, and modest. They do not hesitate, like men, to perform a hospitable or generous action. . . . With man it was often otherwise." Melville may perhaps have been confusing the two, though Park details several episodes where he received the attentions and particular kindnesses of African women in his account. Melville was not the only one to associate Ledyard and Park, as we'll see in chapter 4.

3   I am drawing here and throughout this book on Sedgwick's analysis of the triangulated structuring of male homosocial desire in her germinal study, *Between Men*.

4   And so these events must retroactively inform that moment when Delano looks on the African woman, whom we later know to be part of the rebellion and probably performing to lull his suspicions here. Retroactively, we can see how his invocation of an anthropologizing standpoint summons up the violently hierarchizing privileges of colonial force, cast as neutrally scientific observations about primitive, black, female "nature." His own personal investment in the economic privileges of white manhood in this scene may be occulted by his scientific/managerial standpoint, but is sharply revealed in his eventual recapture, testimony against and sale of this woman and her child.

5   In his second volume on the "invention of the white race," Allen painstakingly and convincingly argues that for the specific case of Virginia, the strategic cultural articulation and legal codification of a "supraclass" white race did not emerge until the beginnings of the eighteenth century. His study does not pursue the rearticulation of whiteness with national identity except in speculative and general ways; see vol. 2, ch. 13 passim, and especially 253–56, which reworks his critique of Morgan's paradox theory in the context of the emergence of a practice of "democracy" based on white supremacy. As he summarizes, "if racism was a flaw, then the 'rise of liberty' would have been better off without it—a line of reasoning that negates the paradox. On the other hand, if racism made the 'rise of liberty' possible, as the paradox would have it, then racism was not a flaw of American bourgeois democracy, but its very special essence" (2:256).

6   See Allen's critique of Morgan in 1:16–19; this section is part of a larger critique of the two prominent historical schools on the origin of white racism that forms the body of his introduction to the two volumes, 1:1–24.

7   "White" had already been used in the Articles of Confederation to modify "inhabitants," for the purposes of identifying population numbers for state tax assessments.

8 Thomas discusses manliness as a Constitutional ideal in a recent article; see 223–24; I will take up this discussion in more detail in chapter 1.

9 As Cheryl Harris observes, throughout this process whiteness was coming to function "as self-identity in the domain of the intrinsic, personal, and psychological; as reputation in the interstices between internal and external identity; and as property in the extrinsic, public and legal realms" (1725).

10 Rush continues here, obliquely clarifying the racializing aim of national education: "I do not wish to see our youth educated with a single prejudice against any nation or country; but we impose a task upon human nature, repugnant alike to reason, revelation and the ordinary dimensions of the human heart, when we require him to embrace, with equal affection, the whole family of mankind" ("Of the Mode" 90). I will address the racializing drives of national consolidation in chapter 1.

11 One such abstracted form is electoral politics. Historians like Stuart Blumin, Alan Dawley, and Paul Faler have commented on the curious way that political equality worked to direct laboring classes' focus away from growing economic inequality in the early nation. As Blumin summarizes: "[o]ne of the most distinctive features of American political history is the early date at which white workingmen were made part of the electorate. . . . strategies for the creation of mass parties left little room for the expression of class solidarities, which appeared with diminishing frequency, and in an increasingly localized fashion, as the parties developed within the peculiarly American context of a multiclass electorate" (255; see also Dawley and Faler 474–75).

12 Similarly, in his study of the "discovery of the asylum," Rothman finds the key expression of nineteenth-century "values" articulated in emerging penal practices: "a conscious effort to instill discipline through an institutional routine [that] led to a set of work patterns, a rationalization of movement, a precise organization of time, a general uniformity" (108).

13 However ironic the class stratification entailed by the professional demarcation of managerial manhood—in the management of democracy's and white manhood's (many) others—the fragmentation of even such a conditional community as national manhood is predicted in what Balibar has described as the "de-structuring" relation of capitalism to collectivity (Balibar and Wallerstein, Race 7–8).

14 See for example, Norton; Kerber; and Stansell.

15 I am not postulating national manhood as the only operative ideology or practice of manhood, but one that organizes and enlists various practices of manhood (such as those described by historian Roediger and literary critic Leverenz—working class, artisan, entrepreneurial, patrician, and many others) for the purposes of national formation, unity, and coherence. I would say that it aims to subordinate the claims of those local/class

manhoods to a national ideal, as we see when manhoods compete with each other not just through the language of manliness, but also through the language of nationalism—which men are more "American," which are less patriotic.

16 This certainly evokes Gilmore's model of "pressured manhood," but I wouldn't want the (transcultural/transhistorical) anthropological weight of his analysis to overtake the links I'm pointing up between U.S. national formation and white manhood per se.

17 Leverenz's arguments about the "self-doubling and male rivalry" that "loom under the rhetoric of self-fashioning" in the American renaissance were central to helping me conceptualize this argument (see 38).

18 This is not to say that colonial and Revolutionary literature never functioned in effectively "elitist" ways (through access to literacy, through rhetorical training, through access to print media, through gender and race bans on publication), but to draw attention to the more extensive systematization of high "Literature" around which the U.S. academy still structures the literary curriculum. This reorganization, and our professional promulgation of it, orders our student's relation to the literary in the same way that representivity orders their relation to democracy— something they can claim knowledge of only as they admire it from a distance. As Warner observes, "it was of no small importance that the years in which literary culture was established in this country were also the years of protracted constitutional crisis." He argues that the new "official hermeneutics . . . helped to determine a newly representative relation between literary textuality and the nature of subjectivity in the bureaucratic nation" (114–15). I will be examining the constitutional "crisis" as a key era for instantiating representative (or virtual) democracy through the formulation of national manhood in chapter 1.

19 The term "scientist" did not enter English usage until the 1830s (first *OED* entry is 1834); Yeo attributes the coinage of "scientist" as a generic term to Whewell in that year (cf. 110–11).

I

Purity Control: Consolidating National Manhood in the Early Republic

1 As Gunderson notes, Adams was the "only delegate to Congress to discuss women's rights in his letters during the years 1775–89" (64 n. 13). And he was ahead of most, as Davidson notes, in his fretting over the "spreading mood of populism" (156).

2 Wood characterizes these forces in terms Klaus Theweleit would love to tear into: "The Revolution resembled the breaking of a dam, releasing thousands upon thousands of pent-up pressures. . . . suddenly it was as if

the whole traditional structure, enfeebled and brittle to begin with, broke apart, and people and their energies were set loose in an unprecedented outburst" (*Radicalism* 232).

3 As Wood observes, "[n]o event in the eighteenth-century accelerated the capitalistic development of America more than did the Revolutionary War. It brought new producers and consumers into the market economy, it aroused latent and acquisitive instincts everywhere, and it stimulated inland trade as never before." Then end of the eight-year wartime "boom" led to a "bust": "Too many people had too many heightened expectations and were too deeply involved in the market and the consumption of luxuries to make any easy adjustments to peace. The collapse of internal markets and the drying up of paper money meant diminished incomes, overextended businesses, swollen inventories of recently imported manufactures, and debt-laden farmers and traders" (*Radicalism* 248–49).

4 Dumm provides a history connecting the emergence of the modern penitentiary in the United States to liberal democracy in his *Democracy and Punishment*. See especially chapter 4, "Republican Machines."

5 Consider, for instance, William Findley, who noted in his arguments against rechartering the Bank of North America, that Pennsylvanians were "too unequal in wealth to render a perfect democracy suitable to our circumstances," and Jeremy Belknap, who argued in a letter to Ebenezer Hazard that the foundations of republicanism entailed that "individuals" should "be poor and the State rich" and complained that "if 'Equality is the soul of a republic,' then we have no soul" (both qtd. in Wood, *Creation* 402, 425). See also Main 10–11.

6 It's worth noting here, though, the inadequacy of economic generalizations for the particular experiences of the poorer classes. In the midst of economic growth, we might consider Boydston's alternative summary of the period: "Peace brought little immediate relief: Great Britain did not re-open its empire to American trade; under the excuse of searching for renegade seamen, British ships preyed upon American carriers; and British traders dumped goods on the American market at prices that undercut local production. As states levied new taxes to pay war debts and creditors pressed for compensation, paper money depreciated wildly. Some Americans did well, but, as Jean Lee has observed, for many Americans the founding years of the republic w[ere] comparable to the Great Depression of the 1930s. In this milieu, households struggled merely to stay afloat and maintain some semblance of control over their own economic lives" (26). Wood's own argument foregrounds the widespread register of "crisis," when he accuses other historians of neglecting to forward politicized arguments against the Federalists. See Wood, *Creation* 413–14; 394 n. 2.

7 See also Main 177–80.

8 I want to note here that I'm fully persuaded by Wood's argument that

244 Notes to Pages 32–33

people across the states and across socioeconomic levels were registering the presence of some kind of crisis; I'm also fully persuaded by his move to locate the energy of the "crisis" in emerging political dissensus. Our difference lies in the relative values we attach to the notion of "dissensus," the ideal of "unity," and the Constitutional attempt to guarantee national unity. I'm interested here to pressure "fragmentation" as a culturally dystopic framing of what might actually be regarded in the terms of *health:* of human and cultural diversity, of local political variety, of what Newfield has described as the "disunited state of America": "Our national 'disuniting' began with our inception and it's not too soon to get over our regret about this. Our 'pluralistic,' 'consensual' union, however one feels about it, has always rested on a divided, antagonistic multiplicity of cultures whose overlap has been sporadic, conflictual, or incomplete. The burden of providing a unified government has for too long interfered with our ability to understand cultural actuality. . . . Disunity is not a problem — in fact, it is usually preferable to more efficient resolutions. *Disunity* is another word for *democracy*" ("Political Correctness" 336).

9 These were laws, for instance, that suspended usual methods for debt collection and confiscated property. See Wood, *Creation* 404.

10 Wood notes that "more such groups sprang up in the dozen years after Independence than in the entire colonial period" (*Creation* 325). Gilje argues that "[t]hroughout most of the eighteenth century, mobs theoretically represented a united community acting to protect agreed-upon morals and customs" and were granted — even by the wealthy elite — a kind of "quasi-legitimacy" (*Road to Mobocracy* 118, 5). Such toleration began to break down beginning in the 1780s, and though Federalists and Republicans continued to support their own out-of-doors actions, Gilje observes that they more and more harshly condemned the actions of their opponents as a national danger (see esp. ch. 4, "Political Popular Disturbances").

11 Ferguson points out that conservatives and propertied men reacted with growing alarm: "Tutored in the history of proletarian uprisings in the ancient world and believing themselves to have been the chief sufferers during the late war, they were convinced that from the beginning of the Revolution the propertied classes had been exposed to mob despotism. Three years after the end of the war they were not certain that the Revolution had truly ended" (243).

12 This is a state that is precisely *not* the product of institutions, but rather emerges out of a dynamic of trust and collective action. The state of democracy, explains Lummis, "is not the name of any particular arrangement of political or economic institution" — it is pre-institutional, "the state of affairs in which the people have the power" (22, 35; see also 111–13).

13 I want to underscore that I am not trying to present a romanticized tragedy

of democratic declension here. I am trying to pay attention to democratic alternatives and to the specific ideological and discursive conditions through which those possibilities were narrowed in the United States.

14   I am using the term "virtualization" to get at a fairly precise point (and one whose implications extend forward from this historical moment) about democracy, which is directed at the way the Constitution promised to "manage" democracy in order to make it "safe" for the people. To my mind, this constitutes a fundamental restraint on democratic energy and possibility (more on this in the afterword). Constitutional order promises to eradicate the stresses of heterogeneity by distancing people from its "dangerous" expression. As it develops in practice, federal democratic order cleans up the messiness of radical democratic practice by virtualizing it, abstracting its face-to-face negotiations through the managed competition of private voting booths and the symbolically distancing and organizing mechanisms of party politics. Through the developing systematization of Constitutional presidentialism and the universalization of white male suffrage, "the people" would come to surrender the idea of locally negotiated, face-to-face democracy for the routine expression of their opinion on ballots, and the embodiment of that "opinion" in the person of various elected officials, especially the president (see Lummis 19, for a pithy summary of the relation of "allowing the people to have their say" to democracy). My term, "virtualization," riffs both on the logic of virtual representation as described by Edmund Burke (see Pitkin 169–70) and rejected by the American colonists (see Wood, *Creation* 173–81), and on Baudrillard's evocative discussion of the operational simulation of the political economy. As Baudrillard notes, the electoral sphere is "the first large-scale institution where social exchange is reduced to getting a response" (65). Locating the emergence of mass media in the nineteenth-century "universalization" of suffrage (see 65), he argues that "'Classical' universal suffrage already implies a certain neutralisation of the political field, in the name of a consensus over the rules of the game. But we can still distinguish the representatives and the represented in this game, on the basis of a real social antagonism in opinions. The neutralisation of this contradictory referential, under the sign of a public opinion which from now on is equal to itself, mediatised and homogenised by means of anticipation (polls), will make possible an alternation, not of parties, but of their 'heads,' creating a simulated opposition between the two parties, absorbing their respective objectives, and a reversibility of every discourse into any other" (68). While it's interesting to see the way Baudrillard traces this logic into twentieth-century political economy, my claims for the purposes of this chapter are more limited and specific: that Constitutional order takes away power (removes the impetus and redirects the structures for direct democracy) from the people in order to guarantee national order,

all the while promising them recognition (the sovereignty of "the People")
as (a substitute for) power.

15   Two states (North Carolina and Rhode Island) refused to ratify until after
the reconstitution of national governance; votes were close in New Hampshire, New York, Massachusetts, and Virginia; the remainder all showed
fairly to very strong Federalist majorities. But the question of the popular
vote presents an entirely different picture: Charles Beard calculates that
in all likelihood, "not more than one-fourth or one-fifth of the adult white
males took part in the election of delegates to the state conventions," and
that "not more than 100,000 men favored the adoption of the Constitution at the time it was put into effect—about one in six of the adult [white]
males" (250). By state, Main figures: "It seems likely that the Antifederalists outnumbered the Federalists by as much as four to one in Rhode
Island and South Carolina and by perhaps three to one in New York and
North Carolina, and that they were slightly more than a majority in Massachusetts and Virginia. Probably the two sides were nearly equal in New
Hampshire in June 1788, although there had been an Antifederal majority
earlier. On the other hand, almost all of the citizens in Georgia, New Jersey and Delaware were Federalists. The situation in the remaining states
is uncertain; probably the Federalists had a clear majority in them, though
perhaps not as large as the margin of victory in the ratifying conventions
suggests" (249).

16   As Sharp has extensively detailed, the nation saw a continuation of local
actions and political dissensions through the 1790s. He insists, though,
that that whatever support the Anti-Federalists had culminated in 1788,
and dissipated with ratification. Though political dissension continued,
Sharp argues that their very ferocity was generated out of a common commitment to the Constitution, but one they *"failed to recognize* that they
shared" (8; original emphases). As he also notes, there was an "abortive
plan to call a new national convention to revive the whole question of
governance" spearheaded by Virginia and New York (29). Gilje notes some
Anti-Federalist actions such as effigy parades, jail rescues, street battles,
and demonstrations (*Road to Mobocracy* 97). Davidson offers a more helpful explanation: "Interpreting in radical terms the inherent indeterminacy
of the Constitution, many citizens invoked that document as the justification for their political zeal" (157).

17   There was little actual Anti-Federalist opposition to the office of the president. As Main notes, significant opposition focused on the issues of re-
eligibility and scope of powers, but not on the fact of the office: "Various
critics objected to every power that he had been given—his right to make
appointments and treaties, his influence over the army, his right to pardon, and most of all his veto. Yet there were many Antifederalists who did
not raise any serious criticism whatever, and the amendments that were
suggested in the state conventions did not call for radical change" (141).

18 The breadth and precision of Fliegelman's arguments are occasionally blunted by his unresponsiveness to feminist insights about gender in a way that can cut in both directions, where he is seemingly uninterested in the significance of misogyny rhetorically directed at women for his analysis, or generalizes "woman" out of rhetoric that is *not* gender-specific—as, for instance, when he quotes from child advice literature aimed at "fathers and mothers" and aims his own summary at "these too sensible mothers" (*Prodigals* 207).

19 See, for example, samples quoted in Burrows and Wallace, 193, 197, 215, 286. Kerber suggests that Burrows and Wallace's treatment is "restrict-t[ive]" in its failure to consider mother-daughter political analogies. The example she offers of such usage—one that "made more extensive use of this imagery than most"—does not even employ the word "daughter": "In this golden Age mutual Love subsisted between the Mother State and her Colonies, the Mother extended her Powerfull Arm to skreen [*sic*] and to Protect her Children. . . . In return, the Children have ever been Obedient to the requisitions of the Mother" (qtd. in Kerber 28 n. 31). Having located no specific mother-daughter or father-daughter analogies myself, I remain less sure that *daughter* (as opposed to "sons" and "children") worked as a significant category in Revolutionary rhetoric.

20 By this I mean specifically that the Articles' form of national governance specified that regardless of size, each state stood as equal within the Confederation, with one vote apiece.

21 See Boydston's assessment of historical attention to women's economic role. Wood offers the early-nineteenth-century example of Horace Mann's childhood, when, within a few short years, the children and mother of the family were making more money from the sale of straw braids than was the father from his farm (*Radicalism* 315). Rogin argues that the "family"—which had "provided revolutionaries with a model of virtue"—absorbed the brunt of these economic and political shifts: "household order could not sustain itself, in bourgeois society, against internecine conflict and market expansion" (*Fathers* 15). More specifically, Boydston observes that because "the market transition threatened the customary bases of manhood, women (and children) may disproportionately have borne the new pressures on household economies" (28).

22 In his study of "competency" in the early Republic, Vickers details, from the diary of Caleb Jackson, Jr., how at least one farming father, struggling to maintain a sense of "independence" within the context of growing market labor dependence, took in shoemaking but delegated the work to his sons: "There is no evidence that Caleb, Sr., ever stitched, lasted, or bottomed a single shoe. He passed the awl onto his sons in exactly the same way that early American farmwives delegated spinning or hatmaking to their daughters—as an occupation proper to dependence" (10).

23 This is one historical instance, then, of a process that Jeffords has de-

scribed more generally as "remasculinization," the "overarching characteristics of which enable individual men to reassert their participation in
masculinity" (xiii). This remasculinization, I will be arguing, is a more
durable "assemblage of culture in response to specific" and more public
occasions than Lockridge is willing to see in his analysis of the "patriarchal rage" of Thomas Jefferson and William Byrd (84). My arguments here
and throughout imply two critiques of Lockridge's conclusions. Though I
don't disagree with his assertion that there is likely no such thing as a unitary and specifically identifiable "male *ideology*" (84; original emphasis), I
do want to foreground the flexibility and durability of the "assemblage" of
ideas about manhood as they are harnessed for the sake of consolidating
a unifying national practice. And, I am insisting on the value of looking
carefully at the way these "rages" and anxieties are located onto women
(or blacks or Indians) in ways that rhetorically screen other causes (like
market competition and homosocial frictions) from scrutiny.

24   The moment of white male suffrage "universalization" completes national
manhood's cultural generalization as it grants adult men of European descent a civic-possessive investment in whiteness.

25   This is not to say that a trans- or supraclass notion of "white" identity
was invented in the early nation, but rather that it was adapted from
earlier or regional expressions and generalized for the purposes of articulating a unified national identity. In his painstaking rereading of colonial
Virginia's "racial" policies, Allen argues that the "invention of the white
race" does not occur in any formal way there until the early eighteenth
century, and that inculcating it among people who might prefer other
identifications was a long and ongoing social process of class disidentification (see vol. 2, esp. part 4). This was not, in other words, a social
identification conclusively achieved in Virginia simply by the passage of
laws and institution of practices privileging "whites." The national project
of correlating white identity with civic identity was similarly ongoing,
not conclusively achieved by the passage of the 1790 law of naturalization. We see the social incompletion of this legal declaration in a simple
set of statistics summarized by Sellers. It was not until the 1810s through
the 1830s that most states, in the South *and* North, disenfranchised free
blacks (New Jersey beat the pack in 1807): Maryland in 1810, Connecticut
in 1811, New York in 1821, Rhode Island in 1822, North Carolina in 1835,
Pennsylvania holding on until 1837 (see 127).

26   Scholars such as Roediger and Ignatiev have identified various ideological intensifications in racism and in the importance of "whiteness" to
the identity construction of various groups and individuals in the post-
Revolutionary period. Michael Goldfield has challenged Jordan's long-
accepted argument about racial liberalization in the United States prior to
the industrial revolution in his essay "The Color of Politics in the United

States." Goldfield argues that slavery was a "pivotal issue in the formation of the Union. . . . The centrality and dominance of racial slavery and
the hegemony of white supremacy throughout the land is perhaps nowhere more clearly seen than in the complete capitulation of Northern
delegates over the 1787 Fugitive Slave Law" (118–19). Where Jordan saw
a benign political spirit halted by the demands of machine technology,
these more recent historians of "race" find instead a (trans-party) impulse
to guarantee political hegemony via whiteness from the earliest moments
of nationhood.

Similarly, feminist contributions to historiography over the last two
decades have revised significantly a prior reading, that the industrial
revolution was the agent that revoked women's post-Revolutionary co-
partnership as economic producers in the home unit, replacing it with
the political disenfranchisement entailed by domesticity. By contrast,
Gunderson notes that the Revolutionary era's emphasis on romantic love,
which gave women an increasing opportunity to choose their own marital partners, did "not carry over necessarily into other areas of life"
(72). The change that the Revolution effected on women's sense of their
intellectual role in the early nation led to what Kerber characterizes as
an "ambivalent ideology" about women's political involvement (11). The
1780s was a period in which women like Judith Sargent Murray, Abigail
Adams, Susanna Rowson, and numerous anonymous "Female Advocates"
began experimentally to advocate for a larger political entitlement, and
numerous others responded with negative furor to the publication of
Mary Wollstonecraft's *A Vindication of the Rights of Woman* (1792). White
women made a few, temporary gains as some states, like Virginia, had
explicitly named women as citizens during the Revolution; New Jersey
actually gave them the vote. But generally, as Gunderson and Stansell
have demonstrated, "the ideological climate of the post-Revolutionary
decades seems to have reinvigorated, rather than undercut, an already
established, popularly based misogyny" (Stansell 20).

27   Dolan helpfully outlines how the "anti-Federalists took issue not only
with the national state designed by the Founders but with the latter's
vision of a rational political science as well" (38). Dolan provides a different interpretation of the personal attacks that have often been read as evidence of the Anti-Federalist's lack of political sophistication. He argues
that these kinds of arguments evidence their political belief in embodied
politics, thus their attempt to expose the particular, personal investments
behind apparently disinterested political arguments: "Viewed from that
angle, the anti-Federalist suspicions indeed issue in an 'unmasking' of the
Law of the Constitution, namely, that Law which insists on appearing as
pure, neutral, impersonal, and dispassionate" (47; see also ch. 2).

28   See for instance Bordo, *Flight*; Keller.

29   Here he is responding not just to the Confederate model, which worked on a one-vote, one-state, no-president model, but also to suggestions that the executive should be *multiple*, that is, three people should occupy the executive office *together*. For instance, Edmund Randolf of Virginia insisted at the Convention that he opposed a "unity of the Executive" on the grounds that it would too easily turn into a more monarchical form. George Mason, also of Virginia, liked the idea of a multiple executive because it could be used to ensure that no single state cornered the presidency, but that people of different regions could feel sure they had an advocate in the executive branch.

30   As scholars such as Jordanova and Stafford have demonstrated, the eighteenth-century scientific conceptions of "woman" were extensively linked to disorder, death, and decay; though the examples I am examining here are not explicitly gendered, they are evocative in their associations with such increasingly commonplace assumptions about "the feminine."

31   This section title is an allusion to Patemen's insightful arguments about the fraternal contract undergirding the construction of the modern, liberal subject. See especially ch. 2 in Pateman's *Disorders of Women*; see also Wendy Brown.

32   Let's just say it: everyone should read Boydston's excellent article, "The Woman Who Wasn't There." As she notes: "representations of the protected household and the private female became conventionalized after the Revolution in part as a response to the exceptional volitility and permeability of households during the revolutionary era and to the changing practices of gender within households and throughout society more generally" (39).

33   Thus, I would differ slightly with Erkkila's otherwise helpful and insightful analysis about women's power in the early United States. She argues that "[a]s a part of the process of constituting America both politically and culturally, the literature of the early national period seems almost obsessively concerned with the construction of sexual difference, the definition of male and female spheres and the reconstitution of female nature and desire under the sign of the father" (217). In the example she cites, Royall Tyler's *The Contrast*, Maria is recuperated not so much under the power of her father, who is revealed as a well-meaning fool, but under her *husband*, Colonel Manly.

34   Publius identifies these women as Mme. de Maintenon, the Duchess of Marlborough, and Mme. de Pompadoure. The first of these was secretly married to Louis XIV in 1684; she may have persuaded him to persecute the Huguenots. The second was confidant and advisor to Queen Anne from 1702 to 1710; she was extremely influential in that capacity until she fell out of favor. The third was the mistress of Louis XV, also reputed to be influential.

35 Warner has recently delineated the enduringly canny strategy of the Constitution, which depended for its juridical authority upon the consent of
the people, whose consent and indeed, very identity is created as they are
hailed in the preamble: "WE THE PEOPLE." Quite differently from the Declaration of Independence, which was signed by the individual members
of the Assembly, the Constitution is published unsigned, to be ratified by
the states whose members will then constitute that PEOPLE. Warner summarizes the strategic coup accomplished therein: "There is no legitimate
representational space outside of the constitutive we. When someone calls
out to the people, you will answer. You inhabit the people, but this is not
true of any group to which you belong, the people being the site where all
lesser collectivities are evacuated. . . . By means of print discourse we have
come to imagine a community simultaneous with but not proximate to
ourselves: separate persons having the same relation to a corporate body
realized only metonymically. The national community of the constitutional we is an aspect of the people's abstractness and may be contrasted
with the intense localism of the popular assemblies which were its main
rivals for the role of the people" (112). It is exactly the evacuation of lesser
collectivities in the name of consolidating a corporate body that I want to
consider in my reading of Publius's arguments for ratification. (Warner relies, as do I, on Louis Althusser's discussion of interpellation in his essay,
"Ideology and Ideological State Apparatuses.")

36 Cheyfitz locates this ideological shift from the figure of the father to
that of the husband in the next generation of national culture. Reading
Emerson's sexual politics through Tocqueville, Cheyfitz observes: "looking around the hearth of Tocqueville's American home . . . we must
maintain a double vision of the relationship between man and woman, at
once aristocratic (our view of husband and wife) and democratic (our view
of father and mother). What this double vision may suggest . . . [is] that
as the figure of the father loses power and authority in American culture
this figure may be trying to regain its force in the figure of the husband"
(Trans-Parent 181).

37 Eisenstein characterizes this as the originary move of liberal ideology,
which "would demystify the nature of government by specifying the importance of the individual in relation to the political contract. It would
do this while mystifying the place of the family in terms of politics and,
hence, the patriarchal bias of liberalism" (49).

38 In her study, Fierce Communion, Wall comments on a new, distinctive
emphasis on the mother in childrearing literature: "colonial writers had
often blurred the distinction between father and mother in delineating
childrearing responsibilities. . . . But in the late [eighteenth century], the
mother moves to the foreground. The responsibilities and special purposes of motherhood receive careful elaboration; before this period, only

one advice book published in the colonies addressed itself specifically to mothers" (139).

39 With stunning insight, Smith-Rosenberg has recently described this "highly problematic liberal economic subject": "If the eighteenth-century businessman was only as good as his credit, that is, if his autonomy was always compromised by his dependence on others to admit his credibility and hence create his credit-ability, and if the contracting nation was like the contracting businessman, then the nation's political independence and powers must be similarly compromised. Like men of commerce, the new nation would become subject to the judgment of its 'public,' that is, its private economic creditors, who were subject in their turn to the judgment of *their* creditors in an endless chain of dependency and interdependency. In these ways, Federalist rhetoric made subjectivity, like money, interchangeable (that is, exchangeable)" ("Dis-Covering" 852; original emphasis).

40 Wood suggests that this new conception of the nation as marketplace was a central factor in what he terms the "reform" of the Articles of Confederation: "All the massive movements of people westward, all the growing productive activity, all the endless trading, were creating a continental marketplace and a natural harmony of economic interests. Farmers could sell their produce to Americans and could buy their manufactured goods from Americans; and if the artificial political obstacles of the states could be eliminated, the whole country could be linked in trade and prosperity. . . . Sentiments like these . . . prepared the way for reform of the national government in 1787. . . . in time they contributed to a radically new conception of America's economy" (*Radicalism* 313). These reconceptualizations were, I would emphasize, dependent upon a radical abstraction of male particularity, which glued the (de-individualizing) market ethic of human exchangeability to the Revolutionary ideal of equality. National manhood suited out for the marketplace is an identity category where human particularity drops away in favor of interchangeability, as Cherniavsky notes: "the rational totalization of the political field depends on a system of representation conceptually autonomous from the particular subjects whose political representation it supposedly assures. The particularized, or embodied, subject remains as such unrepresentable; the subject's specificity is precisely what is voided in his accession to the status of citizen" (9).

41 This is not to overlook the ways women's activism and agitation on behalf of extending women's rights was a factor in such portrayals—for instance, Erkkila has called our attention to such activism as women's mobs and the "first national organization for women" during the Revolutionary period (see 189, 213). Rather, it is to call attention back away from the explicit figure for difference, femaleness, to the other kinds of differences that the symbolic female counterphobically contains.

42 I am not ignoring the possibility as Lockridge has recently argued, that outbursts of misogyny can occasionally be traced to men's tormented relations with women; I just want to insist on the critical importance of not confusing one with the other, especially when rhetoric encourages us to do so.

43 Though South Carolina's motion to include the qualifier "white" in the Constitution was defeated, it was deployed a year later to describe qualifications for naturalization. Appointed by President Washington, a three-member committee presented a bill that stipulated: "that all free white persons, who have, or shall migrate into the United States, and shall give satisfactory proof . . . that they intend to reside therein, and shall take an oath of allegiance . . . shall be entitled to all the rights of citizenship" (*U.S. Congress* 103–4). As Ringer and Lawless observe, "in the ensuing two-day debate no argument arose over the racial stipulation; the only topic debated was length of residence" (110). The revised bill, signed into law on March 26, 1790, was, if anything, more exclusive than previously, containing now a *gender* exclusion as well as a racial one (see *U.S. Congress* 103). As Ringer and Lawless note, this law remained on the books, surviving an attempt to strike it down during Reconstruction, until the McCarran Act of 1952, operating after slavery to exclude Asian immigration. See Ringer and Lawless 110.

44 Thank you to David Mazel for this observation.

45 The opportunity willingly to subordinate to a "new race" is not here available to all, as we see in contrast to the "mongrel breed" produced by the intermarriage of Indians with "whites" on the frontier (Crèvecoeur 77). There, degeneration, not regeneration, is the rule for the "white" settlers, the slothful condition manifested by the bodies created by intercourse both social and sexual offering proof—in Farmer James's eyes—of the impossibility of Indian incorporation into the (British) American body politic by conversion (78).

46 Jardine has offered the neologism of "gynesis" to describe the "transformation of woman and the feminine into verbs at the interior of [master] narratives" about modernity (25). In Schweitzer's useful summary, gynesis is "the effect produced when 'woman' is employed as a figure in discourse, used as the vehicle of man's contemplation, as the Other who makes possible his apprehension of interiority and subjectivity," and I would add for the purpose of my argument, civic fraternity (Schweitzer 32).

47 In her essay, "Why Mammals Are Called Mammals," Schiebinger details the politics of eighteenth-century obsessions with female breasts. As she notes, in Linnaeus's 1758 compendium, *Systema naturae*, he introduces two terms for categorization: mammals—"of the breast"—for warm-blooded vertebrates, and Homo sapiens—"man of wisdom"—to distinguish humans from other primates. Thus, Schiebinger summarizes, "within Linnaean terminology, a female characteristic (the lactating

mamma) ties humans to brutes, while a traditionally male characteristic (reason) marks our separateness" (40, 53–55).

48 Kerber observes that during the Revolutionary period, "if Americans lived in a world of the political imagination in which virtue was ever threatened by corruption, it must be added that the overtones of virtue were male, and those of corruption, female" (31). But even during the Revolution, the cultural definition of "virtue" had begun to shift from a public one, practiced by men and associated with political commitment to the Republican cause, to a private one, practiced by women and associated with sexual chastity. Importantly, as Bloch notes, "the movement toward a more personal, domestic, and feminized definition of morality in the 1780s and 1790s was linked to a greater acceptance of institutionalized public order" (40–41, 47, 55).

49 Gunderson locates the causality somewhat differently: "Political independence for American men thus heightened and reinforced the view of women as marginal on the American political frontier" (77).

50 See Kerber passim; Bloch 46–47; Boydston 34, 39.

51 Rotundo notes that boys in colonial New England were typically put to some kind of work by the age of six. By the early nineteenth century, however, a very different practice was developing: "Middle class boys were needed less to do the work of the family. They were increasingly isolated from males of the older generation. A growing proportion of them lived in large towns and cities, which brought them into contact with a denser mass of peers. And, in a world where autonomy had become a male virtue, there were positive reasons to give boys time and space of their own. In sum, the conditions were ripe in the nineteenth century for a coherent, independent boys' world" (32).

52 This figure is arguably evidence of what Eva Feder Kittay has described at length as "womb envy," an envy which Keller has convincingly argued has governed much of scientific inquiry in the modern age (see Keller, *Secrets*, chs. 2 and 3).

53 The Constitution neither eliminated the spirit of local democracy, nor did it resolve sectional political conflicts. Indeed, the years following its passage were some of the most politically turbulent in U.S. history, as citizens divided in sentiment over the French Revolution, the Federalist move toward declaring war against France, the Federalist effort to quash political opposition to the Alien and Sedition Acts, and the results of the election of 1800. These years saw a continuation of local political action, for instance the Whiskey Rebellion of 1794, for which George Washington called out more troops than he had commanded during the Revolution. See Sharp for a detailed account of these years; indeed, he notes that the "near-fatal flaw" of the Constitution was precisely that it "provided few mechanisms for resolving conflict" (2).

54 Feminist historians of science such as Keller have convincingly argued that Enlightenment scientific paradigms were underwritten by an active misogyny; others, such as Schiebinger, have pointed out that Enlightenment science actively contributed to the masculinization of both science and power. For the question of science and race, see Schiebinger; and Harding's useful collection, *The 'Racial' Economy of Science*. For a provocative analysis of scientific objectivity, see Halpin.

55 See Schiebinger and especially Laqueur for excellent discussions of the importance of gender for the consolidation of Enlightenment scientific paradigms and of the ways political shifts in the seventeenth and eighteenth centuries drove certain reconceptualizations of male and female sexual construction.

56 I think it is worth noting the overarching complexity of the cultural consolidation of national manhood that I am tracing, a movement never reducible to a single actor. Jefferson's pronouncements on "race" and black-white difference carried enormous weight and enduring authority in the process of national racialization. On the other hand, Jefferson remained throughout his career far more comfortable with the kinds of conditional political disunities that emerge in democratic practice—through the generational revolutions he early advocated, and the ward councils he later urged. For a discussion of Jefferson's ideas about "elementary republics" see Arendt 252–59.

57 Albanese has recently, more generally outlined the implications of this scientific strategy in her book, *New Science, New World*.

58 In the chapter, "Productions," Jefferson offers the reported rhetorical eloquence of the Mingo chief Logan to refute Buffon's assertion that all humans in the New World were degenerating because of the more primitive environment. Arguing that by factoring in the differences of circumstance, "we shall probably find that they are formed in mind as well as in body, on the same module with the 'Homo Sapiens Europaeus,'" Jefferson backs his argument with a report of the speech (see *Notes* 62–63).

59 Jefferson's text participates in a genre that would culminate shortly in guides like Julian R. Jackson's *Military Geography* (1850), and in particular, his treatise on *How To Observe* (1861), which advises travelers on how to collect cultural, geographical, and physical information useful to empire building and defense. We have only to consider here how in answer to the previous query on "Rivers," Jefferson is careful to point out the amenability of each he describes to gun-boat navigation, a reading that must direct us to see how the catalogue of "warriors" in the section on "Aborigines" serves similar interests.

60 Cherniavsky also reads Jefferson's observations on black albino women, and in terms very similar to my reading, though her interest is less in scientific discourse and national manhood than in the (national) production

of the sentimental (white) mother. She notes that: "These [albino black] women make their appearance in the *Notes* as mute figures, a designated 'anomoly of nature,' wedged in between an entry on native birds and remarks on the importation of the honey bee. They are as such less the agents of resistance than an emblem of Jefferson's dis-ease. But despite their status in the *Notes* as silenced and objectified figures, I would argue that they display an irreducible material remainder of the rationalized black body" (17).

61   I want to be clear: I am not saying that racism and misogyny in the early nation are reducible to the "same" thing but rather am pointing toward their imbrication in the production of national manhood.

62   Gilman's work has been fundamental to my own understanding here. But I want to stress that differently from Gilman, who sees this "fantasy of wholeness" as the product of "that primal moment in everyone's experience when we first became aware that we were different . . . unable to control our world" (*Disease* 5), I would argue that such fantasies are produced and maintained in far greater measure through social structures. Here I find Silverman's rereading of the "fantasy of the body in bits and pieces" more compelling: "Lacan suggests that it is 'organic disturbance and discord' which prompts the child to seek out the form of the 'whole body image.' However, it seems to me that the reverse is actually true: it is the cultural premium placed on the notion of a coherent bodily ego which results in such dystopic apprehension of corporeal multiplicity" (*Threshold* 21).

2

"That's Not My Wife, That's an Indian Squaw":
Inindianation and National Manhood

1   See Fitzgerald 2; original source in *Pennsylvania Packet*, 17 Jan. 1782.

2   Only one of these family murders was committed by a woman—who killed three children but not her husband (see Fitzgerald 8–9, 10).

3   Biddle's edition is a redaction of the explorers' journals (see below). Elliott Coues's 1898 edition is an interpolated reprint of Biddle. Reuben Gold Thwaites was the first to provide a full edition of the journals; Gary Moulton's edition is now considered to be the most authoritative in providing additional materials unavailable to Thwaites.

4   See Rotundo, ch. 1. He observes that manhood prior to the Revolution was understood in New England through the category "head of household." This ideology of manhood, far from isolating individual men, made them the leader of a "social trust," an assemblage of duties that did not distinguish individual men but upheld a communal ideal. This practice broke down, Rotundo argues, as the nation shrugged off the logic of self-submission in the Revolution, and became more comfortable with newer

ideological emphases in manhood, such as self-assertion. One way to begin reexamining the Yates episode and others like it is to consider the stresses arising out of this shift in definitions of manliness, from traditions that emphasize a man's place, as head of household in a community, to ones that isolate individual men, judging them in the "competition" by their ability to manage their household.

5   In the only extended analysis of these murders, Fitzgerald, whose emphasis is on religious doubt rather than economic and political/ideological stresses, does note that a composite of the murders includes always a "real or imagined downturn" in finances as the founding stage of the parricidal crisis (11). Without discounting the value of his arguments that this outbreak of familial murders locates a cultural reaction against natural religion or deism, I am more interested in considering other cultural factors; in this respect, I find Mathews's reading of the Second Great Awakening a more useful model. He focuses on postwar social stresses, and reads through revivalism evidence for ways that large segments of U.S. culture negotiated those stresses. Whatever our difference in explanatory apparatus, I share with Fitzgerald an interest in this episode as evidence of a reaction against the a-communal implications of new models of individualism.

6   This is the term for induction into the Fraternal Order of Red Men. See the final note in this chapter.

7   This address was an additional strategy in a long attempt to carry off such an expedition. As minister to France in 1786, Jefferson enlisted the aid of John Ledyard for discovering a Northwest passage. Ledyard, who had accompanied Captain Cook on his Pacific voyages and who had most recently attempted to establish mercantile enterprise in fur trade on the west coast of America, eagerly agreed to cross the Nootka Sound and then the continent, tracing the route of the Missouri. He was prevented in this journey, however, when his Russian passport was revoked. Jefferson renewed his attempts in 1792, appealing to the American Philosophical Society when news reached the United States that Captain Robert Gray had discovered the mouth of the Columbia River. This attempt failed when the French minister to the United States, Edmond Charles Genet, recalled botanist André Michaux, whom Jefferson had chosen for the task. Apparently, he did so to save face when Jefferson discovered or began to suspect that Michaux was working as a secret agent for France. See Jefferson's "Memoir" xx, ixx; Coues 1: xx n. 3; Dillon 5.

8   Jefferson adds: "The nation claiming the territory, regarding this as a literary pursuit, which it is in the habit of permitting within its own dominions, would not be disposed to view it with jealousy, even if the expiring state of its interests there did not render it a matter of indifference" ("Confidential Message" xxvii).

9   Jefferson explained to Lewis in a letter dated March 27, 1803, that while

Caspar Wister, Benjamin Smith Barton, and Benjamin Rush were all in on the secret, elsewhere, "the idea that you are going to explore the Mississippi has been generally given out. It satisfies public curiosity and masks sufficiently the real destination" (qtd. in Dillon 39). As Dillon summarizes, Jefferson "was less eager to apprise his political enemies in the United States of his grandiose scheme than he was to inform the Spanish, French and British governments" (34).

10   Jefferson outlines the territorial gains potential to displacing individual traders in the northwest of *any* national affiliation:

> In leading them [i.e., "Indians"] thus to agriculture, to manufactures, and civilization; in bringing together their and our settlements, and in preparing them ultimately to participate in the benefits of our government, I trust and believe we are acting for their greatest good. At these trading-houses we have pursued the principles of the act of Congress, which directs that the commerce shall be carried on liberally, and requires only that the capital stock shall not be diminished. We consequently undersell private traders, foreign and domestic; drive them from the competition; and thus with the good will of the Indians, rid ourselves of a description of men who are constantly endeavoring to excite in the Indian mind suspicions, fears and irritations toward us. ("Confidential Message" xxv)

11   This presidential prerogative, of locating democratic opposition in self-interested and unpatriotic individuals, is evidenced most recently by Bill Clinton. As Gregg notes: "In his television address to the nation on February 15, 1993, President Clinton disparaged opponents of his economic proposals as 'special interests' and 'defenders of a decline,' 'who've profited from the status quo.' He went on, 'When I was a boy we had a name for the belief that we should all pull together to build a better, stronger nation. We called it patriotism—and we still do'" (217 n. 18).

12   This is not to say that Jefferson's use of Logan's speech didn't have an instrumentalist dimension. As Fliegelman notes in his *Declaring Independence*, "Logan's speech, with its mixture of conciliation and anger, offered a displaced articulation of colonial grievance" (97).

13   As Goldberg summarizes, "Even the literature, art, languages, and general cultural expression are appropriated as proper objects of 'scientific' evaluation. They are judged not as works among works of art in general, but the works, or languages, or expressions of the Other, representative of the cultural condition and mentality, of the state of Otherness—artifacts not art, primitive formulations not rationally ordered linguistic systems, savage or barbaric or uncivilized expressions not high culture" (*Racist* 151).

14   Sellers comments on the "historic political coalition" that gathered around Indian removal "to champion the equality and independence of white male farmers, workers and small enterprisers" (312). Like Rogin,

Sellers reads Indian removal in the context of Jacksonian democracy. I don't think there is anything wrong with tracing some of this to Jackson and the emerging political imperatives that swept him into his presidency; like Rogin, I am looking for earlier roots to explain the intense and complex needs that seemed to drive white male support for Indian removal; differently from Rogin, I am less interested to locate these needs in human psychology and more interested to concentrate on the national structures that so effectively enlisted and bent certain psychologies in these directions, in the name of "democracy."

15 Lewis records on June 3: "what astonishes us a little is that the Indians who appeared to be so well acquainted with the geography of this country should not have mentioned this river on wright [sic] hand if it be not the Missouri; *the river that scolds at all others,* as they call it if there is in reallity [sic] such an one, ought agreeably to their account, to have fallen in a considerable distance below, and on the other hand if this right hand or N. fork be the Missouri I am equally astonished at their not mentioning the S. fork which they must have passed in order to get to those large falls which they mention on the Missouri. Thus have our cogitating faculties been busily employed all day" (Thwaites 2:115; original emphasis).

16 Curiously, before the end of the journey, Cruzatte would shoot Captain Lewis in the leg, after they had separated to hunt elk. Lewis suspected immediately that the shot was delivered by Cruzatte: "I called out to him damn you, you have shot me," believing that the shot had come from within forty yards. When Cruzatte didn't answer, Lewis's suspicions immediately turned to Indians, but finding no evidence of that, he returned to the pirogue. Cruzatte claimed, upon his arrival, to have shot at an elk, and Lewis concluded in his journal that "I do not believe that the fellow did it intentionally, but after finding that he had shot me was anxious to conceal his knowledge of having done so" (Coues 3:1115, text and n. 25).

17 The description of his decision is worth noting: "I determined to give it a name and in honor of Miss Maria W——d. called it Maria's River. it is true that the hue of the waters of this turbulent and troubled stream but illy comport with the pure celestial virtues and amiable qualifications of that lovely fair one; but on the other hand it is a noble river; one destined to become an object of contention between the two great powers of America and Great Britain" (Thwaites 2:131). If the river itself seemed to sully the dignity of its namesake, its value, as an object of competition, would do her justice! On Maria Wood as a possible romantic prospect, see Coues 2:354 n. 1; Dillon 182.

18 This is noted by Dillon 183.

19 Ambrose notes that Lewis medicates himself using "exactly what his mother would have done and had taught him to do" (235).

20 Jehlen reads this passage as being "pervaded by a Romantic conscious-

ness," insisting that the seeming despair at failure is a "commonplace of Romantic art." Jehlen reads the passage as ending "not in despair but in pride in the place" which is "also pride in oneself being of the place, a place in itself worthy of the greatest art" (159, 158). I agree with Jehlen's point that a Romantic consciousness is arguably developing in Lewis's descriptions of nature; I don't agree though that these moments ever definitively stabilize Lewis's sense of adequacy or command.

21 Lewis would record a passage the following month that seemingly explains his rather impersonal view of her here in terms of *her* passionlessness:

Sacajawea, our Indian woman, informs us that we are camped on the precise spot where her countrymen, the Snake Indians, had their huts five years ago, when the Minnetarees of Knife river first came in sight of them, and from which they hastily retreated three miles up the Jefferson, and concealed themselves in the woods. The Minnetarees, however, pursued and attacked them, killed four men, as many women, and a number of boys, and made prisoners of four other boys and all the females, of whom Sacajawea was one: she does not, however, show any distress at these recollections, or any joy at the prospect of being restored to her country; for she seems to possess the folly or philosophy of not suffering her feelings to extend beyond the anxiety of having plenty to eat and a few trinkets to wear. (Biddle 1:330; Coues 2:448)

22 Historians' eagerness to follow Lewis's diagnosis, based on his scanty and vague records of her symptoms, is actually startling. Note, for instance, this progression. In his 1959 study of "The Medical and Surgical Practice of the Lewis and Clark Expedition," Will has this to say:

Sacagawea recovered rapidly, undoubtedly in spite of somewhat rigorous measures adopted by the captains. Lewis' rather liberal use of opiates helped ease the pain of her acute illness, the total duration of which was six days. Pelvic pain, fever, rapid thready pulse and menstrual irregularity in a young woman under such circumstances seems most strongly to suggest acute pelvic inflammatory disease, either recently acquired or an exacerbation of a chronic infection. Sacagawea may also, though less likely, have been suffering with an acute exacerbation of latent post-partum infection or from appendicitis. It is regrettable that the account of her illness is so sketchy, but any diagnostic conjectures should be tempered by the fact that this was the only recorded serious ailment Sacagawea suffered during the entire journey. (290)

Dr. Will's essay won the 1957 John Farquhar Fulton Medal of the Society for the History of Medical Science, Los Angeles. He is more cautious than those who follow him (my principal quibble with him is that "lower region of the abdomen" by no means clearly designates "pelvic pain" and he evidently misses what even Coues understood, that nursing was a likely candidate for explaining Sacagawea's menstrual "irregularity"). In a 1979 study of the "medical aspects" of the expedition, *Only One Man Died*, Chuinard offers his diagnosis: "Will suspects that Sacajawea's illness was due to chronic pelvic inflammatory disease. . . . Her history as a captive-slave among the diseased and licentious Mandans lends probability to this diagnosis; if so, it was probably gonorrheal in nature" (289 n. 7). Here, the sloppiness of bland racism and sexism combine with a strong will to believe in the absolute virtue of Lewis's diagnosis: Sacagawea was *not* a "captive-slave" to the *Mandans;* she had been taken captive by Hidatsas. Chuinard's assessment of the Mandans as "diseased and licentious" is beneath comment. There seems little if any solid evidence for concluding that Sacagawea had gonorrhea, then, though this is the conclusion Ambrose condenses and forwards in his recent, popular, and influential study of Lewis, *Undaunted Courage:* "Chuinard conjectures that Sacagawea may have suffered from chronic pelvic inflammatory disease, because of gonorrheal infection" (241 n.). Ambrose himself concludes that, because Sacagawea recovered quickly, Lewis "wasn't far off in his diagnosis" of Sacagawea's "obstruction of the mensis" (241).

23   Lewis studied *very* briefly, as Will notes: Lewis was "delayed" in his arrival in Philadelphia "by miscalculations and misfortunes." When he finally reached the city, over a month behind his projected schedule, "the immediate necessity was the gathering of equipment and supplies" (274). The main of Rush's advice was supplied in written form to Lewis and Jefferson, a questionnaire about the physical history, morals, and religions of Native Americans, and a "Commonplace Book" of simple advice for medicinal treatment on the journey. See Will 275–79.

24   William Shippen began teaching midwifery to medical men in Philadelphia in the 1760s. But this was a category of medical interest and organized expertise that would not begin taking hold in medical culture before the late 1820s and early 1830s. What we are looking at in this episode is arguably an anticipatory moment to an organized field of medical expertise still a generation away. I want to highlight that one of that profession's organizing logics is incipient in this episode—the gynecological supplementation of managerial manhood. Chapter 4 details this argument.

25   I set off this term to highlight not just Lewis's practice of bleeding, but an entire range of medicine understood by both leaders of the party to be more "rational," "economical"—in short, more manly by the terms of my analysis above—than those practices of the Native Americans with which it is contrasted.

26   We don't have journals by Lewis for this last portion of the trip.

27   For my guess, I think it is entirely possible that she had the same intesti-

nal problems Lewis did—none of the historians who speculate wildly on "her region" seems to want to make anything of the fact that a few days after her recovery, she becomes ill again with the same symptoms after eating apples and dried fish (see June 19), and that Lewis at this point credits the food consumed as occasioning the return of her fever, chiding her husband for "indulging" her with such food.

28   Lewis's interest in Sacagawea's reproductive health was coextensive with his interest in the parturition of Native women more generally; his interest, in other words, was in identifying absolute sexual *and* racial difference, as we see in his subsequent observations: "It appears to me the facility and ease with which the women of the aborigines of North America bring fourth [*sic*] their children is reather [*sic*] a gift of nature than depending as some have supposed on the habitude of carrying heavy burthens on their backs while in a state of pregnancy" (Thwaites 3:41). He explains that all Native women he has encountered, whether required to carry such burdens or no, experience less pain and inconvenience in childbirth than white women; though Indian women who have conceived with white men "experience more difficulty in childbirth than when pregnant by an Indian"—this conclusion despite his own observation that Sacagawea's labor (February 11, 1805) "was tedious and the pain violent" (Thwaites 1:257).

29   Lewis's diagnosis highlights the humoral logic at work in his medical practice, where bloodletting and menstruation both provide necessary relief for a fluid imbalance or superfluity. For an excellent discussion of the relation of cultural and medical understandings of humoral theory and menstrual flow, see Paster's excellent study, *The Body Embarrassed*, especially ch. 2, "Laudable Blood." As Paster notes, while aspects of humoral medicine would seem to valorize women's ability to purge blood plethora monthly, in fact, menstrual flow became evidence for women's relative inferiority via the uncontrolled nature of the bleeding: "[the] physiological homology between the involuntary bleeding of the menstruating woman and the opened vein of the phlebotomist's patient, whether male or female, serves not to deny but to establish the difference between the two processes as an issue of self-control" (83).

30   Jefferson would diagnose Lewis's subsequent and mysterious death as suicide resulting from an insanity inherited from his father: "hypochondria." Some historians have puzzled over Jefferson's conclusion for two, linked reasons: first, because Jefferson had virtually adopted Lewis in the years prior to the expedition, and second, because there seems to be no recorded family history that would support such a conclusion. Dillon argues that Jefferson resorts to this explanation out of a sense that "his adopted son had . . . *failed* him by taking the coward's way out of difficulties" (342; original emphasis). But Jefferson's diagnosis—his attempt to project back

onto Lewis and Lewis's father his own burdened sense that he was failed by Lewis—is fascinating for its symbolic resonance, whether or not it is any more accurate than Lewis's conclusions about Sacagawea's illness.

31   I am quoting here from Sally Shuttleworth's essay, "Female Circulation: Medical Discourse and Popular Advertising in the Mid-Victorian Era" (57).

32   Walt Herbert brought this important point to my attention: as late as 1872, the *OED* reports that the word "fork" was used to designate "in the human body, the part at which the lower limbs proceed from the trunk."

33   There is a durable debate over whether Lewis was murdered or committed suicide on the Natchez Trace. There seem to be no reliable accounts from the original event, and thus there is a welter of countervailing specula-tion. From Coues's edition until the 1960s, the practical consensus was for murder, though theories tended not to converge. The guiding strand of this argument was that suicide is both irrational and unmanly, and that Lewis was neither (his reported last words: "I am no coward, but I am so strong. It is so hard to die" are no help here). Recent historians lean strongly toward the suicide theory, noting that neither Jefferson nor Clark doubted it. For a representative cross section, see Fisher; Dillon 335–50; Barth 515; Moulton 2:36; and David Chandler—the last of which (rather remarkably) argues that Jefferson was actually aware of the murderer, but so implicated in a set of conspiracies that he could not afford to expose the murderer, since that would entail exposing his own embroilment.

Most recently, Ambrose concludes in favor of suicide, forwarding an argument that coincides with mine. He observes that Lewis actually felt the entire mission was a failure—he did not find a cross-continent water passage and he felt sure that many of the tribal peoples his party encoun-tered would work against U.S. territorial and trading claims. Ambrose further emphasizes a "dark side" to Lewis's life, "barely hinted at in the available contemporary documents"—manifested near the end of his life in his heavy drinking and opium habit, his crumbling finances and lying (450; 471).

It is worth referring readers to Seller's suggestive analysis of drink-ing patterns in the United States between 1790 and 1830—there was an explosion of hard alcohol consumption in this period, with serious alco-holism becoming a visible problem. He summarizes, "the great Ameri-can whiskey binge was fed primarily by the anxiety of self-making men," noting that "the psychodynamics are the most evident in sons of success-ful fathers. When the national temperance crusade opened in the jubilee year, the country's two highest executive officials were suffering remark-ably similar anguish over their two oldest sons"—both Adams and Clay were dealing with sons who were alcoholic and even suicidal (260).

34   As Ambrose describes it, Lewis's life as President Jefferson's personal sec-retary was intimate, even by Jefferson's account: "They ate together, spent

evenings together — usually with guests — and worked closely together. . . . Jefferson wrote his daughter Martha, 'Capt. Lewis and myself are like two mice in a church' " (63).

35 In a somewhat different, fascinating argument about the "Western socio-spatialities structured by the Oedipal triad Father-Mother-Son," Nast and Kobayashi insist that:

> two taken-for-granted binaries in contemporary western scholarship (inside-outside and Man-Nature) do *not* in fact map directly onto each other. Rather, through critically interrogating the *bodies, visual regimes* and *spatialities* involved in their geo-political construction, the binaries map out a pyramidic socio-spatial terrain, within which are situated two very different sorts of masculinities — Father and Son. . . . The masculinity of the third term (Father) is rarely interrogated because it is characteristically *displaced;* it is hidden within the dis-embodied rubric of transcendental 'rationalities' and logics, an obscurantism involving strenuous cultural work. Consequently Man (as labour, maleness, citizen or human object of the scientific gaze) is confused with *Maleness-as God,* maker and bearer of logic (or worse, Logos itself). Nonetheless, *we* locate and name the third term (as Dorothy and Toto did the invisible Wizard), in the process of revealing merely another tier of the masculine. . . . [this model] challenges us to interrogate in spatial ways the differences between masculinities of Father and Son and . . . begin to describe the socio-spatiality of Western male-male relations in terms other than simply contradictory, variable or complicated. (87–88; original emphases)

36 Jefferson details later in his "Memoir" how then Governor (of Louisiana territory) Lewis found that territory "distracted by feuds and contentions among the officers of the government, and the people themselves divided by these into factions and parties. He determined at once to take no side with either, but to use every endeavor to conciliate and harmonize them. The even-handed justice he administered to all soon established a respect for his person and authority, and perseverance and time wore down animosities and *reunited the citizens again into one family"* (xxxviii; emphasis added).

37 Despite Lewis's assurances that the offer had Jefferson's support, no captaincy was forthcoming for Clark, who served most of the expedition as second lieutenant, the last few months at the rank of first lieutenant. Lewis, however, addressed him throughout as captain. See Coues 1:lxx-lxxi; Dillon 96–97. For Clark's relation, see Coues 1:lxxi–ii. Clark, never a great speller, cast his expectations suggestively, reporting that he had in fact been led to expect a commision as "Capt. of Indioneers" — which Coues emends to "Engineer." In a letter to Nicholas Biddle, Clark reports confidentially that though Lewis had treated him as an equal in every

respect, "I did not think myself very well treated as I did not get the appointment which was promised me." Perhaps his disappointment in this regard was redressed with his commission, after the expedition, as Indian Agent for Louisiana. Regarding historians' habit of subordinating Clark's role, see Steffen 43–52.

38 See especially Fliegelman, *Prodigals* 212–26.

39 Shortly, as Wiebe notes, this ideological strategy would be institutionalized in fraternal lodge practice: "The first rule of this [home club] lodge democracy was loyalty—inturning, unqualified—and to clear the way for this fraternal bonding, white Americans [read men] constructed a narrative of benign family dissolution" (72).

40 These materials are difficult to work with because they are so voluminous, and so widely available in (misleading) extracts. Most literary critics have relied on Biddle's two-volume account or versions extracted from it, and many do not realize that Biddle's account is not the journals as written by the two explorers. Indeed, few critics have realized that the Dover three-volume edition, reprinted from the Coues 1893 four-volume edition, is a (loosely) interpolated version of Biddle. Understanding the literary quality of Biddle's work thus necessitates a comparative analysis, using the journals from the expedition as they are reprinted in either Thwaites's eight-volume set, or Moulton's eleven-volume set.

41 Barth also argues that the expedition itself was actually structured around democratic practices, citing as evidence two "elections" held among the party—to elect a replacement for the deceased Sergeant Floyd, and to choose the location of the Clatsop winter encampment (this latter election included Sacagawea and Clark's slave, York; see Barth 518). I think that might be overidealizing some practices at the expense of noticing others. Lewis's concern that he and Clark be regarded as equals obviously did not extend to the construction of his party, which was a military one. The party was *symbolically* consolidated through a fraternal model: Lewis sought out like-minded and -bodied party members, unmarried men with navigational and hunting skills (see Dillon 47). If the party functioned as an *emblem* of national fraternity in its construction and in its subsequent representations, it is also important to read that "fraternity" as symbolic rather than experiential equality—that is, to heed the way in which military order guaranteed social hierarchy in the expedition. The group may have represented a masculine collectivity to the U.S. public (although, as I suggest above, I think part of its imagined appeal was fraternity combined with fantasies about Lewis and Clark's command over not just "Indians" but other white men), but it functioned for the male subordinates as a carefully ordered regiment, where every lapse in discipline was tried and corporally punished. Interestingly, (and here is where my emphasis diverges from Barth's) this discipline could be used to *enforce* political fra-

ternity—to the extent that early in the journey, after a harrowing series of court-martials for insubordination, sleeping on the watch, and desertion (all of which resulted in severe sentences of lashing, some running a gauntlet), Lewis held a "democratic" election. The men were ordered to vote amongst themselves for a sergeant to replace Charles Floyd, who died of an undetermined ailment in August 1804. Given such "freedom," we might analyze the cheerful and unanimous willingness of the men to carry forward, referenced variously by the two captains throughout the journey, as the result of a particular regime of discipline: the discipline of fraternity.

And in this regard, it is tempting to read symbolically the escape of the Frenchman, Liberté, from the party early in August. At first they assume he is lost, and spend several days searching for him: "We dispatched four men back to the Ottoes village in quest of our man Liberte" (Biddle 1:41; Coues 1:69). They eventually confirm his desertion, when a contingent of the party reports "they had also caught Liberté, but by a trick he had made his escape" (Biddle 1:46; Coues 1:77; cf. Thwaites 1:111).

42 Biddle's nationalist agenda extended eventually to the economic: this is the same Biddle who served as president of the second Bank of the United States from 1823 to 1836.

43 Jefferson had done a great deal to foster and maintain the nation's expectation of a narrative. He notes in his "Memoir" that "the humblest" of the nation's "citizens had taken a lively interest in the journey and looked forward with impatience for the information it would furnish" (xxxvi). Jefferson had encouraged the two captains to think of their record-keeping as publishable from the start. Before Lewis left for St. Louis, according to Moulton, he had made arrangements with Joseph Conrad to publish a three-volume set by subscription (2:36). Delayed for various reasons after returning to St. Louis and Washington, Lewis worked hard to get possession of all the records kept during the journey. He was frustrated in this when David McKeehan, a Pittsburgh book dealer, bought Patrick Gass's journal, turned it into a narrative, and published it in 1807. The book did surprisingly well, with six additional editions appearing between 1808 and 1814 (see Barth 504–5).

After Lewis's death in 1809, Clark took up the project of finding an editor and publisher. After a careful search, Biddle's qualifications seemed ideal.

44 Ziff, in his recent *Writing in the New Nation*, offers a rare reflection on the critical import of Biddle's work. See 159–73, where Ziff argues that Biddle's literary achievement was to add "cultural to political imperialism" (169).

45 Ironically, since Biddle declined to have his name appear in the edition, having been unable to see it though press due to his election to the state

senate, bibliographers assigned authorship to *Lewis*, repeating again the habit I have described above, of looking for a central authority to order the representation *of* fraternity.

46 I take all Biddle citations from the Biddle 1814 edition, because Coues is not always reliable, but I am providing readers corresponding citations to the more accessible Coues edition published by Dover.

47 I can find no corollary passage in the journals, which probably means Biddle solicited this memory from Clark in the process of working with him on the journals.

48 See Thwaites 4:37–39; Lewis/Clark entries for Feb. 2, 1806.

49 I have been unsuccessful in locating even a remotely corresponding passage in the *Journals*. The closest I can find comes in two passages, both by Clark: "The[y] Call themselves Chinnoks, I told those people that they had attempted to steal 2 guns &c. that if any one of their nation stole any thing that the Senten. whome they Saw near our baggage with his gun would most certainly Shute them, they all promised not to tuch a thing, and if any of their womin or bad boys took any thing to return it imediately and chastise them for it. I treated those people with great distance" (Thwaites 3:326); and "we find the Indians easy ruled and kept in order by a stricter indifference towards them" (Thwaites 3:243).

50 Jefferson himself would come very close to this direct an assertion, in his "Appendix No. 4, Relative to the Murder of Logan's Family" (published in 1800 and included in the Peden edition of *Notes*), where he at one point argues about the controversy over the speech's origins: "Whether Logan's or mine, it would still have been American" (230).

51 In an important analysis of the politics of the U.S. gothic form, which appeared just as I was finishing this book, Goddu observes that "the gothicized Indian provided the nation with a distinctive literary asset as well as a politically useful cultural image" (55). In a careful, chapter-length analysis of Neal's use of the gothic for the production of "American" literature and identity in *Logan*, Goddu concludes that the novel's "excesses expose too much about the contested and contradictory nature of this identity and make it an unsuitable model for the project of nation building" (70). See her chapter "Literary Nationalism and the Gothic: John Neal's *Logan*" 52–72.

52 See especially Neal, *American Writers* 120–40, 70–71.

53 See Lease 10–11. The Portland economy was, during this period of Neal's career (1805–12) seriously affected by Jefferson's non-intercourse policy and trade embargo (1807); but the pattern of short-lived mercantile businesses was common to the rapidly expanding economy of the early republic. As Kimmel summarizes: "[I]independent artisans, craftsmen, and small shopkeepers were on the defensive throughout the first half of the century. . . . In Philadelphia in 1819 three of four workers were idle, and

nearly two thousand were jailed for unpaid debts" (30–31). That Neal's mercantile partner, Pierpont, would end up in pauper's prison for a period in 1816 (Sears 22), was an experience entirely characteristic of the era.

54 The club was active from 1816 to 1818; its membership included, according to *Benét's Reader's Encyclopedia of American Literature*, John Pierpont, H. M. Brackenridge, Francis Scott Key, William Wirt, John Howard Paine, Rembrandt Peale, Samuel Woodworth and John P. Kennedy (251). Notes Neal biographer Lease: "The Delphian Club made a significant contribution to American letters from its founding to its dissolution in 1825. It did so rather casually. Each Saturday the members gathered for the advancement of literature and a jolly night out" (17). The evening consisted of performances of "epigrams and epitaphs, elaborate puns," with cheese, beer, and cigars. The group assigned each other "clubicular" names—hence Jehu O'Cataract. See Lease 17–23.

55 Neal was notorious not only for his outrageous plots, but his aggressive (and often aggressively negative) characterization of competing writers. Most notable was his three-year series of articles for the British *Blackwood's Magazine*, wherein he provided a summary review of U.S. authors. He took this on explicitly to counter Sydney Smith's 1821 dismissal of American literature; it is also clear that professional jockeying is at least as much his motive as in defending American literary production.

56 Briefly and very skeletally, the plot of *Logan:* The story begins in a British colony, with threats of violence coming from the aggressive chief Logan. The British governor, with the aid of a young, adopted Indian man, Harold, stave off the threat and enact a treaty. Harold, coming upon the wounded Logan, remembers him as his father and submits to his demand that Harold take up his war against the "whites." He returns to the settlement to get help with the body, but when he returns, it is missing. He goes back to the Indian village, and after a trial of misunderstanding with his beloved, Loena, the two proceed to Quebec, where the governor there decides to send Harold to Europe for an education so that he can return as a leader for his people. There are a series of mishaps en route; Harold meets his brother Oscar without recognizing him, and winds up in England, where he claims his inheritance (through Logan, his British father). There, he learns about Oscar, and Oscar's romance with the British governor's wife, Elvira, with whom Harold has had a secret affair, and a son, Leopold, who is commonly assumed to be the son of the now-dead governor. Leopold dies (see note below). Elvira and Harold live together for a time; Harold and Elvira go to America, then Harold returns to England to plead for Indian sovereignty to Parliament. Now reunited with Loena, he persuades Oscar who "knew" Loena in France but is now with Elrira, to return to America. They visit the rock where Logan supposedly died; he reappears and shoots Harold, who dies of the injury. Loena dies of

grief, then Logan. Oscar dies when Elvira tells him her "secret" (perhaps that her now-dead son Leopold was Harold's child—the narrative is not clear about this). Lease and Sears both provide more extended summaries, though they are both mistaken about the narrative's geneology of Logan. See Lease 89–96; Sears 39–45.

57   This is a strategic confusion that provides the logic that allows him in his theory of American literature to castigate writers for "aping" the English without recognizing his own recommendations for "manly" American literature as being also premised on imitation.

58   Throughout the first volume of the novel, Harold self-identifies unambiguously as Indian. However, after he travels to England and discovers his inheritance as son of George of Salisbury, he begins to distance himself from full identification with Native Americans. In his speech before Parliament, he will use both third person to refer to Indians, and first person, and first-person plural in referring variously to "red men," "my own people," and to Americans, his "countrymen." See 2:276–89.

59   He stakes his claim as well on the basis of parallel experiences: Harold's mother is revealed to have been slaughtered along with the rest of the family excepting Harold and Logan (neither of whom is apparently aware of the other's survival), exactly as the Mingo Logan's family was slaughtered.

60   Their capitulation in offering Loena to Logan is explicitly portrayed as one of high stakes, since the Logans apparently have been given to know by the British colonial government that their decision to make such an alliance would be prohibitive to treaty negotiations (1:89).

61   Note, for instance, in one of his confrontations with the British governor, Logan refers to "thy countrymen—*our* countrymen!" (1:92; original emphasis).

62   For a concise and evocative discussion of the capacity of "whiteness to be everything and nothing" see Dyer.

63   It might be worth noting here that the Iroquois Confederation, which had endured over two centuries and which some argue was the foundation for many of the Framers' ideas for democratic practice and confederational governance, broke apart during the American Revolution.

64   It is even better than that, actually: Leopold gets a fatal infection of croup seemingly *because he is forbidden* by his mother from calling Harold "pa," her injunction apparently aimed at maintaining the secrecy of their former adulterous connection.

65   It is easy to see in retrospect—and aside from the fact that its plot is easier to follow—why *Last of the Mohicans* became the culturally iconic text: there the son (the only one, and one who happens to be an Indian) gets killed so that only symbolic "fathers"—men unburdened by social obligations—are left; Cooper thus sidesteps the neurotic vantage of the son and

assumes the more symbolically stable (if sterile) position of the father. One could argue that his decision to do so complements the novel's misogynist obsession with racial purity. The British father Munro is a good father but has no sons; with the death of Uncas sons are literally removed from the text so that all relations take place in a desexualized contact zone of Indians and whites who pointedly will *not* mix. Thus for *Last of the Mohicans*, Indian identity is spiritually/symbolically excavated and expropriated solely through masculine relations, without any contamination from the (hetero)sexual realm. Cooper's novel is probably also successful because it so masterfully takes up *for the reader* the ideological/scientific vantage of Lewis and Clark, anthropologists and diplomats, par excellence.

66   Harold and Logan vie for the attention of Loena who also has a relation with Harold's brother Oscar; Harold and the British governor, as well as Logan's British son Oscar *all* have a romantic and sexual relationship with Elvira. We should also recall here the way (the white) Logan certifies his identity with (the Mingo) Logan through sexually reproductive relations with the daughters of Logan.

67   Newfield's *The Emerson Effect* is devoted to an elucidation of "corporate individualism." For key discussions, see 5, 38–39, and ch. 3, "Democratic Prophecy and Corporate Individualism."

68   See Carnes, *Secret Ritual* 177 n. 4. Schmidt notes that the IORM "claims to be the oldest secret order founded in America," basing their claim "on being the continuation of certain secret societies that were in existence" prior to the Revolution, and in particular, the "Sons of Liberty whose members 'worked underground to help establish freedom and liberty in the Early Colonies'" (287). As we know it today, the International Order of Red Men (IORM) was organized in 1834, and went national in 1847. Politically conservative by official policy (they are even formally anticommunist), it was not until they eliminated their all-white rule in 1974 that either African or Native Americans were admitted (see Schmidt 288–89).

3
"Our Castle Still Remains Unshaken":
Professional Manhood, Science, Whiteness

1   Gould has laboriously documented Morton's errors of procedure and interpretation: "Morton's summaries are a patchwork of fudging and finagling in the clear interest of controlling a priori convictions" (*Mismeasure* 54).

2   In his study of the emergence of the middle class, Blumin locates the 1830s and 1840s as the beginning period of a "revolution of work in the nonmanual sector . . . associated with changes in economic well-being and perceived social worth in ways that suggest the emergence of a new

middle class" (67). He argues that "the most significant elements of the change lay not in the structure or technology of specific tasks, but in a number of somewhat broader relations: first, in the increasing alignment of nonmanual work with entrepreneurship and salaried (as opposed to wage-earning) employment, and . . . second, in the increasing specialization of firms in the nonmanual sector; and third, in the increasing physical separation of manual from nonmanual work" (68). Alfred Chandler identifies the 1840s as the early years of a managerial revolution; similarly, Bledstein traces the rise of modern professionalism to the 1830s and 1840s. My arguments in this chapter and the next, about the formation of a professionalized middle class through managerial claims, are an attempt both to theorize emerging trends in their very early moments, and to pin this theorization to specific and, to my mind, key historical instances of those emerging practices.

3   Bledstein notes that "the intellectual pretensions of [professionals] . . . were specific in aim and definite in purpose . . . they attempted to define a total coherent system of necessary knowledge within a precise territory, to control the intrinsic relationships of their subject by making it a scholarly as well as an applied science" (88). Arguing that the culture of professionalism worked to provide an ordering system for democracy, he emphasizes "just how closely opportunity for the middle-class person seeking a career was to be tied to exercising social control over 'undisciplined' lower class persons" (179; see also 90–92). Bledstein's analysis has been extremely useful to my own thinking in these next several chapters; I am obviously extending the scope of his argument about professionalism's aims in my specific focus on the way professionalism is powered not just by the emergence of the modern middle classes but by the political psychology of national manhood.

4   In referencing *emerging* white middle-class cultural hegemony, I draw particularly on the insights of historians like Blumin, Faler, and Ryan, who point our attention toward the (not entirely exclusive, and indeed at times symbiotic) ways not just working-class identities but also middle-class identities were crucially in flux in the early- to mid-century. Two related aspects of these newer, emerging formulations of middle-class identity and power background my interest in this chapter as well as in chapters 4 and 5: first, the political psychology through which professional/managerial identities (where "scientists" are a subset of this larger grouping) were developing and becoming defined as *the* work identity—and the defining ethic—for the middle-class from mid-century forward; and second, that particular middle-class achievement, where the white middle-class way, successfully occulting its own particular self-interest, comes to stand as a universal good, a natural standard for (supra-class) cultural and self-realization. The theory of polygenesis—both

through its self-occulting standpoint and its multi-valenced certification of white "purity"—contributed in key ways to both these components of nineteenth-century middle-class development.

5   Child's apology for her "Americanism" is directed to the use of the word "sectionalism"; my borrowing of it for this section's subtitle directs its reference more ironically to the particularities of scientific racism—and its deep implications in gender politics—in the United States.

6   Drawing on the work of Edward Pessen, Jeffrey G. Williamson, and Peter H. Lindert, Voss notes that "recent historical research suggests that the period between 1820 and the Civil War was probably the most unequal period in American history" (28 n. 17). The trick, as Dawley and Faler suggest, is understanding how it could be known, then and since, as the "era of the Common Man," a notion fueled by the promise/ideology of self-making.

7   This collection was jokingly known as the "American Golgotha." Its representation of various "races" was at best uneven, as Gossett summarizes: "In the category of the English 'race' there were five skulls, in the American seven, and in the German eighteen. On the other hand, there were 338 Indian and 85 Negro skulls" (74).

8   Morton, while classifying the skulls as "ancient caucasian," describes their racial character as comprising a blend of "several distinct branches of the human family" including, with Caucasian, the Semitic and Austral Egyptian (*Crania AEgyptiaca* 1).

9   Morton separated the ancient crania by no other criteria than sight-judgment. He, along with his supporters, frequently insisted on his incredible abilities to distinguish "races" of bare skulls. As Gould summarizes: "Morton's subjective division of Caucasian skulls is clearly unwarranted, for he simply assigned the most bulbous crania to his favored Pelasgic group, and the most flattened to the Egyptians; he mentions no other criteria of subdivision" (*Mismeasure* 61). In other words, he chose the biggest skulls as "caucasian." See Gould's chapter on "American Polygeny and Craniometry" for a fuller discussion of Morton's scientific procedure and results. This debate over the "racial" classification of the ancient Egyptians still rages, most recently with classics scholar Mary Lefkowitz valiantly attempting to hold the Greek/white line against Martin Bernal's provocative reading of the race politics of pro-Greek/white Egyptology from the Enlightenment to present day, and his arguments about the African intellectual and cultural legacies of ancient Egypt.

10 Morton achieved this differential by sorting out the "Teutonic family" from the five other "families" included within the "Caucasian race" (Pelasgic, Celtic, Indostanic, Semitic, and Nilotic). Morton provides this justification for his procedure: "No mean has been taken of the Caucasian race collectively, because of the very great preponderance of Hindu, Egyptian

and Fellah skulls over those of Germanic, Pelasgic and Celtic families. Nor could any just *collective* comparison be instituted between the Caucasian and Negro group in such a table unless the small-brained people of the latter division (Hottentots, Bushmen and Australians) were proportionate in number to the Hindoos, Egyptians and Fellahs of the other group. Such a computation, were it practicable, would probably reduce the Caucasian average to about 87 cubic inches, and the Negro to 78 at most, perhaps even to 85, and thus confirmatively establish the difference of at least nine cubic inches between the mean of the two races" ("Observations on the Size" cf. 221–224). While he is concerned here to demonstrate some sort of equal basis for comparison, he noted elsewhere that "I have not hitherto exerted myself to obtain crania of the Anglo-Saxon race, except in the instance of individuals who have been signalized by their crimes, and this number is too small to be of much importance in a generalization like the present. Yet, since these skulls have been procured without any reference to their size, it is remarkable that five give an average of 96 cubic inches for the bulk of the brain; the smallest head measuring 91, and the largest 105 cubic inches. It is necessary, however, to observe, that these are all male crania; but, on the other hand, they pertained to the lowest class of society, and three of them died on the gallows for the crime of murder" (unedited ms., rpt. in Nott and Gliddon 308).

11   Though most of the scientific community agrees that race is an insufficient scientific/biological category (see for instance Guillaumin, "The Idea of Race" [in *Racism, Sexism, Power and Ideology*] and essays in section 2 of Harding, *'Racial'*), members of the scientific community yet endeavor to find valid classificatory measures. I am skeptical that "science" can achieve a neutral relation to this debate whether they are "pro-race" or "anti-race"—as this chapter will indicate.

12   See William Stanton's chapter "The Parson-Skinning Goes on Bravely."

13   Here William Stanton summarizes Nott, the only participant whom Stanton casts as having a pro-slavery agenda to further through scientific means: "A founder of the American School of anthropology, he had helped to execute a revolution in natural science, and, in company with his friends Morton and Gliddon, had overthrown the ancient and honorable doctrine of the unity of man. When their revolution was rendered irrelevant by the Darwinian invasion, he possessed the intellectual courage to relinquish a theory built upon a lifetime of labor and the good grace to accept the new. . . . Proud to agitate against the pious defenders of the old order, he followed the light of science to the end. One can ask no more" (188). See Fredrickson 78–82 (esp. 81), for his corrective response to Stanton's arguments about Nott. See Horsman, *Josiah Nott* 249–50, 302, and 320, for a different assessment of Nott's response to Darwinian theory.

14   Gould is far more willing than either of his colleagues to pursue the logi-

cal implications of this episode *for* science, and uses it and other such episodes to "criticize the myth that science itself is an objective enterprise" (*Mismeasure* 21; see also 55–56).

15 See for instance Horsman, who, citing Morton's *Crania Americana* as the "seminal [*sic*] publication of the new American ethnology," insists that "Morton was no southerner defending slavery, but a Philadelphia physician engaged in basic research" (*Race* 125).

16 And so it is important to underscore that Northern scientists and intellectuals found the theory widely persuasive. Indeed, as Gossett points out, polygenesis actually carried less clout in the South as a theory to support slavery: "The South would have noting to do with the argument of the polygenesists. In 1854, the fire-eating *Richmond Enquirer* declared that some might accept the 'infidel' doctrine of diversity because it seemed to be an excellent defense of slavery, but they would be wrong. Southerners could afford no such defenders as Nott and Gliddon if the Bible was to be the 'price it must pay for them'" (66). Historians of science have also noted polygenesis's lower currency in the South. William Stanton comments: "The Bible did lend considerable support to slavery, but so did science. Opting for the Bible was a mark of the South's already profound commitment to religion. Heretofore this had not necessarily been an anti-intellectual position. But when the issue was clearly drawn, the South turned its back on the only intellectually respectable [*sic*] defense of slavery it could have taken up" (194). Horsman details the quality of Southern reception of polygenesis, specifically to the radical polygenesis espoused by Josiah Nott in his publication of *Types of Mankind*: "As in the case of the *Southern Quarterly Review*, an initially favorable review produced an adverse reaction, and early in 1855, *Putnam's* published an article defending 'the moral, religious, and physical unity of the human race.' Most reviewers of *Types* accepted a high degree of contemporary racial inequality but could not accept the denial of biblical truth" (*Josiah Nott* 199). Given this, we have to wonder why historians focus so insistently on Southern players in their discussions of polygenesis: it seems arguable that the theory actually worked better to reconcile Northerners to slavery and racist institutional praxis.

17 Robert J. C. Young provides a more thorough discussion of this aspect of the polygenesis debate—the fact that "the more racial theory proposed permanent racial difference, the more obsessed its upholders became with the question of hybridity and the prospect of interracial sex" (133).

18 Stepan, for instance, details the British professor of surgery, Richard Owen, who used Morton's figures to argue against Cuvier's allegations that Negro crania were closer to those of apes than to those of Caucasians (*Idea* 16–17).

19 The term *scientist* came into wide usage during the early 1840s; as Noble notes, the word itself "first appeared in a review of a scientific book writ-

ten by a woman" in 1834. The reviewer was the British William Whewell; the book was Mary Somerville's *On the Connection of the Physical Sciences* (279).

20 By invoking a practice with an admittedly long history, but ineluctably one that is associated with racial persecution in the United States in a debate over the "intelligence" of U.S. racial groups, the editors belie their own confidence and vaunted objectivity. In the next column, the editors insist that this debate engages "burning matters," yet again invoking the racial violence of cross-burning and lynching in their own—it would seem somewhat neurotically "white"—defense.

21 Bachman published a number of articles between 1834 and 1842 in descriptive zoology and ornithology. He collaborated with John Audubon to publish a three-volume work on *Viviparous Quadruped of North America* (Daniels, *American Science* 203).

22 For example, Horsman argues that though "Bachman was an excellent naturalist, . . . [he] abandoned science for religious beliefs when he entered the unity controversy and defended the account of human origins given in Genesis" (*Josiah Nott* 200). William Stanton's treatment of Bachman is among the best, detailing how his work came close to reaching the insights achieved by Darwin in his evolutionary theory, though, Stanton argues, Bachman's biblically grounded "concept of a benevolent Nature prevented his seeing the struggle for survival as a factor in preserving favorable variations" (133). See also Gossett 60–63, who recognizes Bachman's scientific qualifications and credibility in the debate, though insisting that finally, Bachman "was seriously compromised both by his religious ideas and by his commitment to slavery" (63).

23 Agassiz had not been particularly interested in the debates over racial origins until he came to the United States in 1846, where, after encountering a black waiter in his Philadelphia hotel, he became an enthusiastic proponent of polygenesis. As Gould notes, "his conversion followed an immediate visceral judgment and some persistent persuasion by friends. His later support rested on nothing deeper in the realm of biological knowledge" (*Mismeasure* 44). For details on that encounter, see the note on Agassiz in chapter 5.

24 See, for instance, Montagu; Harding, *'Racial' Economy of Science* (esp. contributions by Lewontin, Rose, and Kamin); and Guillaumin for surveys of scientific opinion on the usefulness of race to science.

25 This methodology was one that Morton had earlier dismissively labeled "closet" naturalism (see *Crania Americana* 71).

26 Goldberg usefully describes this archive: "Production of social knowledge about the racialized Other, then, establishes a library or archive of information, a set of guiding ideas and principles about Otherness" (*Racist Culture* 150).

27 As Daniels details, discursive shifts in chemistry, natural history, botany, zoology, and geology in the early nineteenth century had, by the 1840s, accumulated in "a body of esoteric knowledge called 'science' . . . the term 'scientist' was also coined at this time to refer to those who had previously been designated 'natural philosophers' " ("Process of Professionalization" 66).

28 See also his essay, "The Process of Professionalization of American Science," where he discusses four stages of scientific professionalization. The first stage, "preemption," neatly describes Morton's part in the professionalization of science, "that stage in which a task which has customarily been performed by one group or by everybody in general comes into the exclusive possession of another particular group" (64). This debate, one of many in the nineteenth-century, worked to relocate the authority to describe and categorize humans and human groupings away from religion, granting science more and more exclusively the responsibility.

29 Morton asserts that he is being hounded as an infidel for his scientifically deduced beliefs; he also asserts, curiously, that the local religious community has raised no objection to his pronouncements on the topic (see "Additional Observations" 50).

30 Another way of framing this argument would be to turn the focus toward academic discourse, which is Young's strategy. Commenting on Bernal's observations, in *Black Athena*, that the emergence of professional scholarship was intimately linked to projects of racial rank-ordering, Young concludes that "the blunt fact that has not even now been faced is that modern racism was an academic creation" (*Colonial* 64). His argument here is important for all us academics who work on "race" (and those who don't): "This racialization of knowledge demonstrates that the university's claim to project knowledge in itself outside political control or judgement cannot be trusted and, in the past at least, has not been as objective as it has claimed; the university's amnesia about its own relation to race is a sign of its fear of the loss of legitimation" (64).

31 One of the better historical explications of this cultural development is Barker-Benfield; see part 1, "The Sexes in Tocqueville's America," 3–57, and esp. 98.

32 Evelyn Fox Keller provides a thorough discussion of "scientific autonomy," in which she compares modern, Western conceptions of masculine development/masculinity to the rhetorical posture of Western science: "the same interpretation of [masculine] autonomy also correlates with a conception of power as power over others, that is with power defined as domination. . . . Domination guarantees the indissolubility of difference by construing all difference as inequality—an inequality exacerbated by enforced vertical difference" (*Reflections* 97, 106; see 75–114 passim). The strategy of domination, as we see for Morton, applies differently but as usefully both to Bachman and the "inferior races."

33　According to Donald C. Peattie, in *Dictionary of American Biography*, Bachman traced his interest in natural history to his childhood; his family disapproved and throughout his youth he was forced to "pursue his studies surreptitiously." Stanton notes that Bachman turned down the offered presidency of South Carolina College in 1841 because accepting it would "put an end to my amusements in Nat. History" (qtd. in William Stanton 124).

34　Having acknowledged Bachman's standing "by common consent, in the front rank of American zoology," Morton proceeds to emphasize his theological title, "Rev. Dr.," carefully dissociating the "Dr." from science (the origin of Morton's own medical doctorate) by attaching it to Reverend (see "Letter" 1; "Additional Observations" 7). Bachman uses neither "Reverend" nor "Dr." in his own author signatures in the debate.

35　Sherwood comments that the ostensible source for the debate—chronological geology—was more an imaginary friction, "imaginary in that the two men were closer to one another than each cared publicly to admit" (314).

36　The Declaration of Independence utilized what Serres describes as the argumentative strategy of minimalization, his term for a strategy by which one claims absolute weakness with reference to the opponent, appealing for mercy or exemption on the grounds of moral fairness. Such is Jefferson's construction of the thirteen colonies in relation to Britain in his draft of the Declaration. See Serres 19–21.

37　For instance, here is Nott in typically colorful fashion:

> I received a letter today from Mr. Whitaker, Editor of the Southern Review (Charleston), informing me that a Rev. Mr. Curtis of Hillsboro North Carolina was about to make an onslaught on my *infidel* pamphlet, in the April No. of the Review—The editor says the article is written with ability & gives me this timely warning in order that I may reply if I think proper—he says his pages will be open to me— I presume I shall be skinned alive for not believing as the Presbyterians believe, the facts of science to the contrary notwithstanding.
>
> If the parson will keep his temper and write like a gentleman, I shall be glad to hear what he has to say & hope he may aid me in finding out the truth of the matter—but I presume he will prove scientific points as parsons generally do, by proving one end of the Bible out of the other—
>
> I shall probably amuse myself by giving him a thrust in some soft spot & should like to have the proper materials for doing so. (Mobile, Alabama; July 20, 1845, Library Company of Philadelphia)

38　Science, as Bledstein recognized, became central to U.S. culture as a managerial discourse of power. In providing a voice for professional manhood, in at least this instance *through* racism, it continued—and continues—to provide a hierarchizing vantage for "white" men (as well as to others seeking the vantage of white male authority) to participate in at a popular level long after it has been "officially" discredited by science. This is not an effect that has dissipated over time; rather, scientific racism/manhood has gained cultural power for its very diffuseness. For instance, on August 9, 1993, *Sports Illustrated* denounced then Florida State President Dale Lick for his comments about black athletes. In response, readers in the September 13 issue drew on a variety of popular science discourses, ranging from common sense ("To chastise him for saying what is obviously true is hypocritical"), to cross-"racial" universalism ("It's interesting to note that . . . [when] Barry Bonds was asked, 'What do you think made you such a fine ballplayer?' Bonds responded, 'Some of it is genetics . . .' "), to evolutionary competition ("Somewhere along the evolutionary trail, they [i.e., "blacks"] were naturally selected for a higher degree of athleticism. Nature isn't concerned with equality"). Scientific racism in popular discourse continues to demonstrate its flexibility and weight among the U.S. public; that one of the writers is female, and that another writer can quote a "black" athlete referencing "science" underscores the sensation of authority provided by scientific discourse all the more (all quotations taken from *Sports Illustrated*, Sept. 13, 1993: 8).

39   This is not to imply that Bachman was a gender radical. Indeed, it is more likely that we might conclude that he too had a strong investment in protecting paternalist/patriarchal authority. McClintock's arguments about Freud could quite possibly be a helpful wedge for examining the gender logic underwriting Bachman's claiming of a universal family of man: "The Oedipal theory reinvented paternal, familial authority as a natural, universal and inevitable fait accompli, at the precise moment . . . when the emergence of imperial bureaucracy was depriving the image of the father of symbolic power as the designated symbol for all political power" (93). To say, in other words, that Morton's arguments against monogenesis were also a strike against the incipiently feminist politics of sentimental reform is not to say that Bachman's championing of monogenesis and sentimental reform constitutes his feminist position.

40   My argument here would generalize and anticipate, then, the specific process Rotundo outlines, where the medical profession organized itself through and around the exclusion of women from its field of expertise: "The opposition to women practitioners did not stop the slow, steady trickle of women into the medical profession; but there were changes in the world of medicine after 1880 that created new problems for female physicians. One was the emergence of scientific medicine as a system of practice and belief that vanquished many of the alternative models to which female doctors adhered. At the same time that medical thinking coalesced around one set of ideas, the structure of the profession crystallized into a network of closely linked institutions—hospitals, dis-

pensaries, medical schools and professional societies. In this new world, opposition to women doctors could organize and take institutional root more easily than before" (215).

<h2 style="text-align:center">4
Gynecological Manhood: The Worries of Whiteness
and the Disorders of Women</h2>

1   Horsman explains that after the Civil War, Nott began to expand his interest in practicing gynecology, "when in the course of his normal, extensive medical reading he took up the writings of the famous Dr. J. Marion Sims, late of South Carolina and Alabama and now of New York" (*Josiah Nott* 314). He moved to New York in 1868 and with Sims's and Thomas Emmet's assistance, obtained an appointment at the Women's Hospital.

2   Bledstein summarizes the boundedness that the notion of "career" promised to lend individual actors: "This new notion of career was striking for its totality and self-sufficiency. The new individual professional life had gained both an inward coherence and self-regulating standards that separated and defined it independently of the general community" (172). What he captions as the "inner intensity of this new life" is precisely an energy I am interested to examine also in its corporate manifestations—the larger cultural promise of career logic to consolidate the purview and the community of white manhood.

3   I am of course borrowing here Sedgwick's important formulation: she describes one form of "male heterosexual desire" as a longing "to consolidate partnership with authoritative males in and through the bodies of females" (*Between Men* 38).

4   Laqueur characterizes such arguments in gynecological science as a "radical naturalization, the reduction of women to the organ that now, for the first time, marked an incommensurable difference between the sexes and allegedly produced behavior of a kind not found in men" (*Making Sex* 216).

5   Meigs can't settle on a category for these women: "It is true that we meet in the pages of History and Biography, the relations of strange phenomena in the lives and actions of certain women. There are Julia and Messalina, that are monsters. There is even somewhat questionable in the nature of such ladies as Elizabeth, or Mary of Medici.—We have the male powers of a Dacier and a Stael. We find the gentle and feminine Hemans sometimes bursting forth with a wild, impetuous and marital enthusiasm. Yet these are exceptions, are not rules, that fill us with surprise, as of things out of, or beyond the common course of nature" (*Lecture* 10).

6   In this chapter, I focus on how these counterdiscursive moments ("the heaven of sentimental relationship between males") were often structured through abjecting displacements, how manhood as a male accomplish-

ment could be—symbolically for many and actually for some—gynecologically routed. In the next chapter, I analyze counterdiscursive gestures
toward male community in practices of professional and social affiliation.

7   Reynolds identifies the novel as "the most popular novel before the appearance of *Uncle Tom's Cabin* (1852)" in his introduction to *Quaker City*
(Lippard vii).

8   Lippard's response to the city's elite as well as his gothicization of the
urban environment were not necessarily grossly exaggerated: as Barker-
Benfield notes, "the population of the United States increased by 226
percent between 1820 and 1860, but the urban population rose by 797 percent. Cities were swept by plagues and epidemics until late in the century
and were associated with a general rise in the death rate" (52).

9   While Lippard is at pains to stress the dignity of "mechanics" against the
deprecations of the wealthy elite throughout the novel, he draws both his
heroes from outside that class of manual laborers. Byrnewood Arlington is
from a wealthier family—corroborating Lorrimer's description of the Arlingtons as one of the "first families of the city," his parents have servants
and a parlor with lavish furnishings. Lippard's emphasis on the physical
space of the home emphasizes what Blumin describes as the mid-century
city's sorting of "its classes of people into increasingly distinct institutions and spaces" (146; see ch. 5 passim): though the house itself cannot
verify the Arlingtons as "one of the first families of the city," it certainly
does confirm their secure middle-class status. The class origins of Luke
Harvey, another favored character, are a little more difficult to pin down.
Though the female villain, Dora Livingstone, breaks off her engagement
to the "*poor* clerk" Harvey to marry the "*rich* merchant" Albert Livingstone (254), it is clear, as Blumin also documents, that the class alignment
of clerks and mechanics were diverging during the period from 1820 to 60.
Harvey's speech contains none of the class markers that Lippard bestows
on the mechanics of the Quaker City, except when he is masquerading as
the gang-boy "Brick-Top"—his predilection for disguise perhaps reflecting
widespread cultural anxieties about the middling sort as all being potential confidence-men making their way from one class status to another
(see Halttunen). This characterization may be truest of Gus Lorrimer,
whose class *origins* are never revealed in the novel, leaving readers to suspect that his wealth is the result, like his "marriage" to Mary Arlington,
of a con.

10 Reynolds argues that the novel satirizes temperance—doubtless it satirizes the hypocrisies of temperance reformers in the character of Reverend Pyne. It is not at all clear to me that satirizing the excesses and/or
hypocrisies of temperance, however, overbalance what seems to me to be
a strong temperance theme in the novel, or that the two are even contradictory projects.

11 This is not to indicate a contradiction in Lippard's politics, which seem highly consistent with the "mechanic ideology" outlined by Faler: "If there was a definite and clear hierarchy in the ranking of human needs, with material necessity first and other needs in various descending orders, human society should, in the view of the mechanics, reflect that hierarchy." Mechanic ideology did subscribe to social ranking; it simply argued that non-laborers, non-"producers"—those least valuable to the production of necessary goods—were unacceptably ranked above and allowed to exploit producing groups (31; see ch. 3 passim). My intention here is to highlight how apparently competing political ideologies become stressed along similar fault-lines. Thus, pro-labor Lippard can sound warnings strikingly similar in their images of racial incursion and social/ political breakdown to those raised by Jefferson and of Rush.

12 "The Jew" is, along with the three black characters in the novel (Dim, Mosquito, and Glow-worm), apparently constitutionally unable to disguise his "origins." Russ Castronovo briefly discusses another Lippard work, *The Legends of the American Revolution* (1847), where Lippard would again use the figure of racial otherness to "guard against a racial fracturing" of America's white body. Castronovo provides a larger context for his argument about the racial politics of U.S. monumentalist history in his chapter "Monuments, Fathers, Slaves." His treatment of an assemblage of texts, from Brown's *Clotel* (1853), to Melville's "The Bell Tower" and Lincoln's political speeches of the 1860s, is nuanced and instructive (see esp. 171–73; ch. 4 passim).

13 Newfield further notes that sodomy was "associated with a refusal to work and compete signaled by 'laziness,' 'sloth' and the neglect of business, and a willingness to congregate for no practical purpose" (*Emerson* 96). Devil-Bug's dream, then, suggestively corroborates my argument that *Quaker City* draws on fears of behaviors that threaten capitalist market practices at least as much as it challenges the class stratification that the economic system allowed.

14 It is tempting to argue that Lorrimer's biggest offense against Byrnewood is not the defilement of his sister so much as his withering dismissal of Byrnewood's class status: "you're not of our 'set'" he explains to the Arlingtons when they demand he marry the defiled Mary (547). Thus his murder becomes Byrnewood's necessary (competitive) response to the economic insult.

15 Reverend Pyne is another social climber, whose "daddy was a scavenger" and whose "mammy sold rags" (271).

16 Mabel's drugged condition evokes a key issue in contemporary gynecology. In *Uneven Developments*, Poovey traces British medical debates over the introduction of chloroform, which focused on similarities between the drug stupor and the appearances of women's sexual arousal. Poovey

argues that "the disagreement among medical men was fiercely argued because important issues were at stake: these included the authority of individual medical men within the profession and the social status of all medical men" (34; see ch. 2 passim).

17　John Campbell's 1851 *Negro-Mania* would soon provide the public a sampling of European medical accounts of women's racially unstable sexuality and reproductivity. See Campbell 140–41.

18　For a fascinating history of medical practices for obtaining corpses, changing public attitudes toward corpses, science, and medical experimentation on poor bodies in Britain during this period, see Richardson.

19　Streeby makes a similar point of the struggles between male characters in Lippard's *The Empire City* and *New York:* "these sadomasochistic, hypercharged, homosocial relationships expose social crises and different, even conflicting masculinities instead of reinforcing an overarching, homogenous model of manhood; they suggest that 'masculinity' is a plural, conflict-ridden, historically variable construct" (197).

20　Barker-Benfield summarizes: "Thomas Addis Emmet, Sims's disciple, rival, and colleague, and his successor as chief surgeon at the Woman's Hospital in New York City, called Sims the 'father' of American gynecology. . . . T. Gaillard Thomas, like Emmet a world-renowned gynecological surgeon, said at Sims's death: 'If all that Sims has done for gynecology were suppressed we should find that we had retrograded at least a quarter of a century. . . . If I were called upon to name the three men who in the history of all times had done most for their fellow men, I would say George Washington, William Jenner, and Marion Sims'" (91).

21　The fistulae did not necessarily occur *during* parturition, but frequently developed afterward. McGregor notes that "most women who suffered from the tears and tissue-sloughing involved endured extremely prolonged labors. The appearance of the fistulas often took several days, or even two or three weeks following parturition" (164). Prolonged labor seemed to be the root cause of fistulae, which resulted from a variety of factors—from childhood malnutrition and rickets, to impeded circulation in labor's second stage, where the head of the fetus could cut off circulation to the vaginal tissues, to misapplied forceps, to doctors' discouraging of and women's embarrassment to empty their bladders during labor. See McGregor 71–2, 165–75.

22　See D'Emilio and Freedman 148. See also Pivar 88–99. Sims also served as president of the American Gynecological Society (1880).

23　See also Barker-Benfield 105.

24　Sims invented the tool that became known as the Sims speculum among other gynecological instruments. See Haller 240–41.

25　As Kapsalis argues, the very origins of gynecology as well as many aspects of its ongoing practice are open to feminist interrogation and cultural critique. She notes: "Gynecology is not simply the study of women's bodies—

gynecology makes female bodies. It defines and constitutes female bodies" (6). She argues in her study, as I will argue below, that the inception of U.S. gynecology is rooted in its uneven application to raced female bodies. Commenting on contemporary gynecological practices, Kapsalis notes that "In most contemporary circumstances in the US, [the] ideal patient is insured, white, educated, mentally and physically able, thin and heterosexual. In experimental situations, the model is often poor and a woman of color" (6).

26   I was fortunate to be able to read Kapsalis's remarkable book as it was in production at Duke University Press, and just after I had completed drafting this chapter. Kapsalis and I have a similar commitment to taking into account the raced dynamics of Sims's experimentation. While my critical interest is in unpacking issues in the consolidation of white manhood, Kapsalis is concerned with the gendered and raced production of professional gynecology. Thus, unsurprisingly, our arguments parallel each other in many ways though our critical focus often diverges. I recommend readers to the entirety of her book, which should not be missed in simply consulting her excellent chapter on Sims (and his legacy's modern echo in the use of Norplant).

27   Kett notes that though public shaming had long been a basic method for social control, by 1830, "public shaming was no longer a primary method for maintaining social order among adults, but it continued to flourish in the schools" (Rites 47); Sims's schooling would not have been particularly unusual in this respect.

28   Sims's mother visited him at these schools regularly; his father however, visited less often. At one point Sims complains that though his mother came once a month to his boarding school, "my father came to see me but once during the six months" (Story 59).

29   The spectacle is not created by the cross-dressing, for he remains undiscovered even by a classmate who joins Dick until Dick reveals Sims as disguised. Rather, it seems to be a matter of fashion: "nor shall I ever forget how the beautiful women of Charleston stared at the strange bird sitting in the balcony with the countryman, Dick Barker" (Story 124).

30   Other grounds for building his professional manhood were his experiences during the Seminole War, where he achieves a sense of manhood through the charge of white male camaraderie combined with a sense of career possibility. As he summarizes: "This five weeks for me was a great thing. I went into that command perfectly unknown, and a boy in appearance, but a man in spirit; and I came out of it with one hundred and twenty friends. All of the command were devoted friends of mine and to me. It laid the foundation of my popularity so deeply that I was soon sent for as the doctor of the fellows that had been with me in that little excursion into the Creek nation" (169–70).

31   Barker-Benfield treats Sims's surgical theatricality, noting Sims's acquain-

tance with P. T. Barnum and concluding that "[t]he operating room was an arena for an exchange between men" (100–101). Kapsalis's remarkable analysis of gynecology and performance treats this aspect of Sims's career in more detail: see her ch. 2, "Mastering the Female Pelvis."

32   See McGregor 327–31; Barker-Benfield 100–101; Mackey's introduction to Sims's autobiography, 16–17. Sims claimed he was outraged by the limitations such restrictions would put on the medical education he provided in surgery. His colleague, Thomas Emmet, though, characterized his behavior in surgery quite differently: "[D]uring my entire association with Dr. Sims, I never received from him the slightest explanation or reason for anything he did. He was not a teacher and operated naturally with such rapidity that very few, unless they were familiar with his methods were able to receive much benefit from witnessing his operations" (qtd. in McGregor 155). Sims did attempt to withdraw his resignation, but was unsuccessful. Undaunted, as Kapsalis notes, in 1879, "Sims threw a gala event, something between a trade show and a circus. For four days he performed a series of varied operations on various women, ending in a dinner at Sims's house for some fifty or sixty physicians. As if in response to the Board of Lady Managers' reprimand . . . Sims's gala event openly defied the Board of Lady Managers' ideas about proper surgical performance protocol" (47–48).

33   It is grotesque to realize the sexual politics of a master's urgent desire that his slave's fistulae be repaired: given that fistulae did not prevent women from working, it becomes entirely possible (if not likely) that these men wanted the women "cleaned up" for the sake of their own sexual pleasure. What makes this even worse is that a repeat pregnancy would likely reopen the fistulae.

34   It is important that we know what many historians who treat Sims's work have tried to gloss: while it was widely acceptable to perform medical research on slave corpses, experimentation on *live* slaves was not a wide or accepted practice in Sims's era. As Sims's biographer Seale Harris notes, after three years of experimentation, "socially the whole business was becoming a marked liability, for all kinds of whispers were beginning to circulate around town—dark rumors that it was a terrible thing for Sims to be allowed to keep on using human beings as experimental animals for his unproven surgical theories" (99). For a summary of ongoing controversy over and professional defenses of Sims and his experimental procedures, see Kapsalis (48–49). For historical analysis of medical experimentation on slaves in Virginia, see Savitt ch. 9, who notes that seldom was Southern medical experimentation with black subjects "as blatant or dramatic as J. Marion Sims's use of Alabama slave women" (293).

35   Patterson records that, "[w]here a case admitted of doubt, I have known him to keep the skull in his office for weeks, and, taking it down at

every leisure moment, sit before it, and contemplate it fixedly in every position, noting every prominence and depression, estimating the extent and depth of every muscular or ligamentous attachment until he could, as it were, build up the soft parts upon their bony substratum, and see the individual as in life" (xxxviii). According to his papers at the Library Company of Philadelphia, Morton's ability correctly to identify crania by sight was disputed at least once: Peter Browne, a Philadelphia scientist who studied the hair of the various races, notified Morton by letter that one of the crania in his collection identified as a "negro of Philadelphia" is "not negro." He provides Morton his analysis of the hair and ends with this query: "I would be pleased to hear why the scull [sic] was esteemed to be of a negro" (Aug. 4, 1849; Morton Papers, Library Company of Philadelphia). For more on Browne, see William Stanton 149–54.

36   In their discussion of "faciality," Deleuze and Guattari note that " 'Primitives' may have the most human of heads, the most beautiful and the most spiritual, but they have no face and need none. The reason is simple. The face is not a universal. It is not even that of the white man; it is White Man himself. . . . Thus the face is by nature an entirely specific idea, which did not preclude its acquiring and exercising the most general functions: the function of bivocalization, or binarization" (*Thousand Plateaus* 176). Sims's use of facial metaphor for women's genitalia demonstrates the *intra*racial operations of "faciality's" binarization, along with its *inter*racial ones.

37   McGregor speculates that Sims's "loyalty to the system of slavery led him to mute the role of slavery in his early surgical experiments"—though that gives this shrewd gynecological entrepreneur less credit for strategy than he may deserve. His speculating that a Northern public, where he was seeking a new professional audience and a career advance in 1852, would question his use of slave women as experimental subjects for three years would make more sense as an explanation. McGregor goes on to note that "many medical practitioners reading this article undoubtedly inferred that the patients were enslaved, given the fact that the operations were experimental and performed in Montgomery" (63–64).

38   Sims and other doctors of the nineteenth century were ironically situated between burgeoning scientific arguments about racial incommensurability and their own limited access to cadavers for anatomy lessons; Southern and Northern practitioners alike were likely to rely on the corpses of blacks as the bodies of dead slaves were shipped north for medical purposes. As McGregor notes, "in order to accept the use of slaves for demonstration and experimental surgery, of black cadavers for anatomy lessons, medical men had to accept physiological parallels" (58).

39   See McGregor for a thorough discussion of the way Sims worked through class issues. Women's Hospital was in its original inception a charity hos-

pital; in New York, Sims would continue his experimentation with the same intensity, now on the bodies of poor white women. He kept his own practice on the side, often refusing to paying (middle- and upper-class women) patients procedures he could perform, but which he deemed too "dangerous" or "painful" for them. See esp. McGregor 269–70.

40   In Young's lucid conclusion to *Colonial Desire* he argues, quoting Deleuze and Guattari in *Anti-Oedipus*, that racism "is perhaps the best example through which we can immediately grasp the form of desire, and its antithesis, repulsion, as a social production: 'thus fantasy is never individual: it is *group fantasy*'" (168–69; original emphasis).

41   Neither Sims's operations for fistulae nor fertility were unproblematic. Doctors in this country and Europe complained that they could not duplicate Sims's successes, and as McGregor points out, since Sims seldom bothered with follow-up checks on his women patients, it is not altogether clear that they did not simply choose to avoid further surgical intervention by not returning with complaints (see, e.g., McGregor 180–81). Regarding his fertility treatments, both of Sims's treatments, surgical alteration of the cervix or injections of semen, could severely jeopardize women's fertility and their health: "Ironically, the procedure he advocated would not only cause an abortion if pregnancy was under way [*sic*], but cervical incision would at the very least complicate a subsequent labor and delivery. He denied such problems, instead calling upon examples of women who enjoyed repeated pregnancies following surgery" (241; see also 243).

42   Vaginal fistulae were uncommon by 1930 and rarely occur today, resulting more frequently from accidents in gynecological surgery than from women's actual labor and delivery.

43   McGregor explains that though Sims refused to bother anesthetizing the slave women on whom he experimented during surgery (believing blacks had a specific tolerance for physical pain), he did give them opium for up to two weeks after the surgery. (It is horrific to realize that after three years of harrowing pain, these women were sent back to their plantations, brutalized by monthly surgeries, possibly dealing with the effects of opium withdrawal, *and* the likelihood of repeat fistulae in subsequent childbirths.)

44   Among women of more moderate and wealthy incomes, fistulae were less likely to occur as the result of rickets, and more likely were attributable either to the failure to intervene in a prolonged labor, women's inability to urinate for hours or even days during a long labor, and/or the misuse of instruments designed to intervene in labor. Ironically, male doctors' takeover of childbirthing and their use of instruments like forceps may well have increased the incidence and/or damage of vaginal fistulae, which subsequently gynecological surgery was designed to repair.

45   Barker-Benfield discusses male-purity reformer John Todd's identification with Mungo Park, who seemingly related to his image of manly isolation

among savages more so than with his intimacies with African women (see 157). "Ledyard among the wildest Samoides" refers to his travels across Siberia.

5
The Melancholy of White Manhood, or,
Democracy's Privileged Spot

1 P. Goudin de Saussure, Secretary for the Medical Society of South Carolina, in Sims, *Story of My Life*, Appendix 2, 424.

2 Drs. Alexander Y. P. Garnett, J. M. Toner, Samuel C. Bussey, William G. Palmer, and W. W. Johnson for the Medical Society of the District of Columbia, in Sims, *Story of My Life*, Appendix 2, 450.

3 See Sims, *Story of My Life*, Appendix, remarks of Dr. Joseph Taber Johnson:

> When John Hancock, President of the Continental Congress, signed his name to the Declaration of Independence in 1776, it is said that he wrote his signature in characters so large and so loud that the cry for liberty, which they represented, was heard around the world. . . .
>
> Hancock, by his eloquence, wisdom and example, stimulated not only his associates but posterity to patriotism, learning, and noble deeds. Sims, by his brilliant genius, patient industry, wonderful skill, and dexterity, saved the lives of many. . . . Who shall say the former is more deserving of fame than the latter? (465–66)

4 Dr. W. O. Baldwin, in Sims, *Story of My Life*, Appendix 3, 438.

5 See Rotundo on "Male Sociability and Men's Work" at Rotundo 196–205; Wiebe, ch. 3 passim; Carnes, *Secret Ritual* 6–9; and Blumin's analysis of "Churches, lodges and the classless ideal" at 218–29.

6 See Ringer and Lawless's discussion of the Constitution's indirect "reaffirmation and relegitimization" of white entitlement, 108–9.

7 This is MacCannell, summarizing Rousseau, in "Postcolonial Unconscious" 31; original emphasis.

8 Rush probably refers to one of Clarkson's earliest essays: "An Essay on the Slavery and Commerce of the Human Species, Especially the African . . ." (1786, taken from his 1785 dissertation, which was also the first prize-winning dissertation at the University of Cambridge); "A Summary View of the Slave-Trade, and the Probable Consequences of its Abolition" (1787); "An Essay on the Impolicy of the African Slave-Trade" (1788). My thanks to Leigh Baldwin for ferreting out this information for me.

9 I am quoting here from MacCannell, "Postcolonial Unconscious" 32. In her suggestive Lacanian reading of modern democracy, MacCannell argues that European political orders failed to act on Rousseau's key insight, that the Good of the Whole was never anything but an alibi for the inter-

ests of the propertied classes. Instead, they have installed political systems based on the *"unconscious* internalization of the *law of the good"*
(31; original emphasis). Within these systems, she suggests, the democratic
subject will always be disturbed in his "traumatic enjoyment," the dual
imperative to follow his democratic desire, and his guilty knowledge that
what he pursues in the name of a common good, is always "at bottom . . .
a particular, private good": "the new democratic subject encounters, on
the one side, unbearable Superego pressures to enjoy, and, on the other,
manifold political, class and economic pressures against enjoyment by
all. This unresolved complex is handed off or loaded on to the colonial
subject, inflicting damage at many levels" (32). MacCannell's focus is on
colonial subjectivity, but I have found her theoretical framework useful
for my work at historicizing the political psychology of representative or
national manhood in the United States.

10   See Pessen, *Riches*. Obviously there are numerous other corollary developments in the 1830s through the 1850s that we might include in the
list that frames the professionalizing of the middle classes, like Indian
removal, the markedly brutal intensification of slave-management, the
emergence of temperance, pauper reform, etc. For an unusually deft and
thoughtful analysis of the middle classes in relation to such cultural shifts
in the period, see Sellers, chs. 8 and 12.

11   Rotundo correlates the growing political use of a rhetoric about unmanli-
ness to "universal" suffrage: "Charges of effeminacy became most extreme
—and most effective—after the vote was extended to all white males, regardless of property" in the 1820s and 1830s (270).

12   Both these developments—"universal" white manhood suffrage and a
nationally coordinated voting day—institutionalized a more virtualized
practice of democracy. Though he would not agree with my evaluation,
Wiebe usefully draws attention to the way representative, Constitutional
democracy atomized the citizen's concept of democratic community and
democratic action: "[w]here a tradition of town meetings existed, the new
democracy needed to break down the customary concept of voting as
the family-based community's coming together and replace it with one
of voting as an individual's act" (72–73). Virtual democracy brings the
nation together as "one body" in the sterilized privacy of the voting both,
substituting this spectacular homogenizing "event" for messier, face-to-
face, heterogeneous, participatory practices. The universalization of white
male suffrage seems to extend democracy at the very point that class
and party formation, combined with the vexed and abstracting logic of
"representation" and national centralization, take people's access to participatory equality one step further away. Indeed, Ginsberg has argued in
great detail that the extension of suffrage has often worked precisely as an
institution that redirects citizens away from more direct political action

(such as demonstrations and rioting). He observes that electoral policies in the United States have functioned to condition voter acquiescence to governmental powers by limiting their access to input on specific issues and policies, by redirecting their attention from class to market, and by replacing traditional opposition to government with a sense of proprietorship. See Ginsberg, *Consequences*, and *Captive*, esp. 32–58.

13 Falling on hard times, William Morgan, a stonemason, threatened to, and then actually did publish a book that advertised itself as an insider's exposé of secret Mason rituals. Local Masons tried to buy him off; failing there, they threatened him and his publishers. On the night of September 12, 1826, Morgan was abducted and was never again seen. For historical treatments of the Morgan affair and the anti-Masonic movement more generally, see Vaughn; Dumenil 5–7; and Formisano and Kutolowski.

14 I have relied heavily on Carnes's important study for my analysis in this section to characterize predominant features of mid- to late-century fraternalism. His book is the only major study to concentrate on fraternity rituals. His major conclusion describes how fraternal ritualism worked to ease boys from a female-role-identified childhood environment into a male-role-identified world in fraternal orders that would help them deal better with the world outside: "By emphasizing a surrogate father's benevolence and love, the ritual made it easier to identify with the male role; and by accepting the initiate into the family of patriarchs, the ritual made it possible to approach manhood with greater significance" (*Secret Ritual* 123). These stresses came about because of the pressures of separate spheres combined with the forces of moral reform:

> The implicit meanings of the symbols suggest that many men were deeply troubled by the gender bifurcations of Victorian society, which deprived them of a religious experience with which they could identify and of a family environment in which they could freely express nurturing and paternal emotions. . . . By affirming that men possessed traits socially defined as female, the symbols conveyed a message expressed nowhere else in Victorian America.
>
> These ideas and emotions could not be stated publicly. If men had acknowledged that the orders were an alternative form of religion, of family, and of social organization, the forces that had crushed Masonry in the 1820s might have again besieged the fraternal movement. (149)

While there is much to admire about Carnes's analysis, I find that his conclusions sympathize a little too uncritically with these middle-class men. It is hard to imagine, if even one in eight men were members of fraternal orders by the end of the 1800s, and that lodges were overwhelmingly composed from the middle classes, that these same men weren't also in powerful social and even political positions. It is also difficult to understand why, if men needed simply to be able to acknowledge that they were "like" women—emotional, vulnerable—their rituals featured the symbolic repudiation *of* women. Carnes's conclusions simplify his analysis, allowing an important aspect of fraternal orders' social function to drop from sight: how fraternities upheld the very uneven social, affective, and economic structures that their lodge rituals "mystically" redressed.

15 Carnes asserts that from mid-century on, membership was overwhelmingly middle class. Clawson argues otherwise, insisting that "large numbers of American working-class men did participate in fraternal orders in the late-nineteenth and early twentieth centuries. But this did not lead to the consolidation of working class solidarity" (89). In Clawson's view, Masonic-style fraternalism "exerted a special appeal to anyone seeking to establish or reaffirm a symbolic relationship to the figure of the producer-proprietor" (14). Given that "class" has never been a term noted for particular clarity, Carnes's and Clawson's difference may be at least in part one of definition: another student of fraternity, MacLean, uses the category petit-bourgeoise, or lower-middle class to limn the gray zone between working and middle class. See her chapter, "Men in the Middle: The Class Composition of the Klan," at MacLean 52–74. What is at least clear is that increasingly after mid-century, the initiation fees and the multiplication of "levels" of membership entailed heavy costs that fewer and fewer working-class men could afford (see Dumenil 13–17).

16 Other commentators than Carnes take the racial homogeneity of fraternalism more seriously into account. Of the Masons, Dumenil notes that "Masons insisted that their order was committed to the principle of *universality*, which they defined as the association of good men without regard to religion, nationality, or class . . . [but] the fraternity was in fact, predominantly a white, native, Protestant, middle-class organization" (9; original emphasis). She observes that "despite its insistence on the equality of men . . . in practice the order excluded non-whites" (9–10). For a study of the African American Masons, see Williams. Clawson observes that fraternal egalitarianism was "made possible by the exclusion of women, blacks, and ethnic minorities from the relevant social universe, a universe whose boundaries fraternal institutions helped to demarcate and guard. American fraternalism thus heightened the already great social and cultural distinctiveness of those white male workers who were also the most highly skilled and privileged segment of the wage-earning work force. The fraternal order was not, in other words, a neutral social arena in which some people happened, in random fashion, to unite as brothers. Rather, it was a form of association with a particular history and content, based on deeply grounded social and cultural assumptions" (110).

17 In his discussion of "fraternal fantasy" Schmidt notes that: "When a member attended his society's local meetings, he did not got to a hall but

to a 'court,' 'nest,' 'tent,' 'homestead,' 'grange,' 'circle,' 'lodge,' 'encampment,' 'pond,' 'forest,' 'caravan,' 'conclave.' . . . The principal officer was not called president, but 'Worshipful Grand Master,' 'Supreme Potentate,' 'Grand Illuminator,' 'Exalted Grand Master,' 'Sachem,' 'Supreme Chancellor' . . ." (9).

18   By the end of the century, estimates of membership ranged from one in eight to one in *five* men in the United States (Carnes, *Secret Ritual* 1).

19   Strikingly, Clawson notes that "the mobilization against drinking was paralleled by a new and narrower definition of the limits of fraternal obligation." Her observations seem to fit with my argument that as the fraternal man constricted and channeled his own bodily flows, he was less inclined to "open up" on behalf of others. Indeed, as Clawson continues: "The Independent Order of Odd Fellows continued to maintain, throughout the century, that the obligation of reciprocal relief was one of the order's defining characteristics, but its mode of practice tended to transform fraternal aid from a right (and a rite) to a kind of charity that would be afforded only to the deserving" (121): charity became a disciplinary practice, responding only to those who evidenced proper forms of self-discipline.

20   Dumenil describes how "Masonry ritual forms . . . accented the sacred-profane demarcation between Masonry and the rest of the world" (39).

21   Schmidt comments on the way "most fraternal groups pride themselves on their representative or democratic form of government" (15), and then notes the results of his own earlier study which "found that fraternal organizations were oligarchic in spite of their claims to be democratic" (16).

22   In her study of Emerson's *Conduct of Life* and other male conduct manuals, Ellison describes how Emerson increasingly delineates male friendship as "engagements that are simultaneously tender and hierarchical, affectionate and interested." She notes that "Emerson's success on the lecture circuit and his reception as an avatar of gentility depended partly on the existence of a male audience for his theory of masculinity, especially in the Midwest, where his sponsors included a number of young men's associations. The enthusiasm of this sector of Emerson's audiences suggests that his view of masculine encounters was part of a more widespread —though certainly not universal—way of configuring relations between men. The resemblance between Emerson's treatment of masculinity and the presentation of character in the contemporary conduct-of-life books is such that we can move toward some generalizations about homosocial affection in mid-nineteenth-century class settings" (584–85).

23   These dissonances were produced, say, by ideologies of individualism and market competition. Schein makes the striking observation in his study of old-line fraternal orders, that there is a "high visual correlation" between Elazar's mapping of individualist political culture and the geographic pat-

tern of old-line fraternal distribution (69). Elazar maps three political sub-cultures in the United States, "individualistic," "moral," and "traditional," arguing that individualistic political culture, differently from the other two, "emphasizes the conception of the democratic order as a market-place" (115; see his discussion 115–17, and maps 125–26, 135). Schein argues that there is "a definite correspondence between the individualistic culture region [as mapped by Elazar] and those areas of the United States that exhibited a strong fraternal acceptance. . . . The benevolent 'take care of your own' attitude of the old line fraternal order may have stemmed from the same attitude that supported egocentrism in the individualistic political" cultures (76–77; see figs. 5.1 and 5.3, on 70 and 72).

24 In *Threshold of the Visible World*, Silverman provides a suggestive critique of Lacan's assumption that "unity" or "wholeness" become psychic ideals from out of childhood sensations of "organic disturbance and discord." Comments Silverman: "It seems to me the reverse is actually true: it is the cultural premium placed on the notion of a coherent bodily ego which results in such a dystopic apprehension of corporeal multiplicity" (21). Drawing on the work of Henri Wallon and Paul Schilder, Silverman points out that subjects are constantly experiencing bodily "disintegration" in nonthreatening ways (e.g., hair, fingernails)—in ways that are actually experienced as "beneficent"—as the "precondition for change" (21). She underlines Schilder's suggestive point that "wholeness" does not in fact signify "psychic health" (22; see 20–22).

25 Clawson observes, similarly, that definitions of "the lodge as a cross-class institution that bound men together, regardless of who they were, enabled the fraternal order to legitimate the operation of the market by denying its consequences for social life" (176). With the expenses it imposed on members, along with its various unspoken exclusions by race and frequently, ethnicity, it allowed men tacitly to legitimate the exclusive operations of social life as they purchased into the fraternity's equalitarian ethos.

26 Some orders made the connection between lodge fraternity and national representivity most explicit. For instance, the U.S. Odd Fellows modeled their governance structures and symbolic apparatus on U.S. Constitutional order. As Schein summarizes of the 1824 Odd Fellow constitution: "Through a series of bureaucratic maneuvers that would come to characterize American Odd Fellowship, a system of government was instituted that was loosely modelled after the government of the United States. Individual lodges were organized into state bodies, or Grand Lodges, which in turn were organized and sent representatives to a national body, the Supreme Grand Lodge of the United States, headquartered in Baltimore. In this way, Odd Fellowship espoused democratic belief in the equality of membership . . . while providing a hierarchical structure which could govern the order as it wished to be governed" (32). He notes that in 1847,

the Sovereign Grand Lodge appropriated monies for the purchase of desks and chairs replicating those in the U.S. Senate (33).

27 Kann summarizes: "In time, the medical profession established a new litmus test for masculinity in studies . . . [that suggested] effeminate males were infected by sexual inversion and political subversion" (203).

28 This calls to mind Robert Bly and the Men's Movement today, where, as Boose observes, "as 'Iron John' and Bly's newly masculinized 'wild man' are celebrated in a reaffirmed hierarchy, the meaning of patriarchy for women goes totally ignored" (587). Of the contemporary manifestation of the "white male as victim" plot in current cinema, Kennedy observes that this crisis in white manhood "is not a terminal one, or even . . . historically new—traumas of male crisis/resolution have a significant dialectical presence in narratives of American identity. More to the point, I believe this crisis has in many ways been recognized and successfully managed by white males; the very rhetoric of crisis is one that has been franchised and mobilised by those incarnating it. Only one of the most obvious examples of this crisis management is the white male appropriation of 'victim status'" (90).

29 In his encyclopedic study of fraternal organizations, Schmidt comments on the strong conservative social and political orientation of the secret orders in particular, despite their own claims to be nonpolitical. The secret societies have been (and continue to be) far more resistant than benevolent/insurance orders to racial integration (see 13). As he summarizes, the secret orders' "long-standing opposition to racial integration, refusal to admit women, and other attempts to preserve the status quo indicate that most fraternal secret societies are quite conservative politically. In short, fraternal secret societies are no harbingers of social change" (14).

30 Bledstein, in his study of "the culture of professionalization," comments on the way the jurisdictional authority of the professionals in general drew on the combined mystique of esoteric ritual and the cultural authority of science: "The jurisdictional claim of [professional] authority derived from a special power over worldly experience, a command over the profundities of a discipline. . . . Hence, the culture of professionalism required amateurs to 'trust' in the integrity of trained persons, to respect the moral authority of those whose claim to power lay in the sphere of the sacred and the charismatic. Professionals controlled the magic circle of scientific knowledge which only the few, specialized by training and indoctrination, were privileged to enter, but which all in the name of nature's universality, were obligated to appreciate" (90).

31 For instance, consider this excerpt from a letter in Morton's file from S. J. Oakford, of Paita, Peru (June 14, 1847; Library Company of Philadelphia):
On my passage from Valparaiso to Lima I stopped for a few days at Arica, and while there was able, after some trouble with the local au-

thorities, to obtain permission to dig in the cemetery near that town. After opening some ten or twelve graves in which the mummies were in a broken and decayed state, we came to one which appeared to have been the grave of a chief together with his family, there were seven bodies in it, of various ages, the only one however that was perfect was that of a child. This I send you together with the sculls [*sic*] of the others and the various articles that were buried with them, consisting of some earthen jars, a wooden mug, and some pieces of wood painted with read stripes. The graves in the cemetery of Arica differ from those of the interior and of the northern coast of Peru, in containing but few warlike or domestic utensils, and these are of the rudest construction evidently the work of a poor and uncivilized race of people who in all probability subsisted by fishing, the clothes in which the bodies are wrapped are of the same material as those found in the interior but of much ruder manufacture.

You will notice upon the mummy some scarlet feathers, these I was assured by Mr. Kenderine (an English naturalist who resides in Arica) are from a species of parrot that is now only found in one of the interior provinces of Peru some 60 leagues distant from the burial place—That these people have been buried for long time is evident from the fact that the soil under which they lay has become as hard almost as stone, and can only be broken with the greatest difficulty by means of the crowbar and pick axe—These remains have been packed in sand from the surface of the hills under which they were buried, and shipped on board the Barque St. Joseph for Baltimore. . . . I am sorry that I was not allowed to send you better specimens but the Government of Peru in their wisdom have seen fit to prohibit under sever penalties the shipping of all native curiosities and it was only by special permission from the officers of customs in Arica that I was able to obtain these few.

Letters such as these make it clear that men were willing to go to great lengths in order to provide assistance to Morton. This excerpt is suggestive also in the way it raises questions about how the modern project of science worked to caption any group—national or local governments ("tribes")—who resisted it as "difficult"—as being primitive in their superstitiousness.

32 Rotundo notes that dinner and evening parties were increasingly an important form of business entertainment in the nineteenth century: "In this convivial atmosphere, men made new business contacts and entered discussions that might lead to significant transactions" (199; cf. 197).

33 See Morton's letter to Squier April 10, 1847:

Your favour of the 6th inst. was rcd. this morning, and I rejoice with you over your discovery of a truly *aboriginal skull.* Nothing of the kind was ever found more certainly characteristic than this relic, and you may distribute casts of it as a *perfect type* of the race to which it belongs; that race which is indigenous to the American continent, have been planted here by the hand of Omnipotence, and which in all its numberless localities, conforms with more or less precision, and for the most part with amazing exactness in its cranial proportions to the skull you have now discovered.

. . . Look into the Crania Americana, and observe the Peruvian head there figured and how admirably they correspond with yours, which has, however a less receding forehead than usual. Every new observation on this subject goes to confirm my previous conclusions, that our Indian population, of all epochs have belonged to a single homogenous race. . . . This type, I grant, has its varieties, but these may be in a great measure referred to to [*sic*] a plurality of centers or origins, all of which, however, point to that primitive organization which you now have so fine an example. (Squier Papers, Library of Congress)

34 The Smithsonian was unwilling for Squier to take into print his speculations on polygenesis.

35 Morton, as far as I can tell, never participates in using this language, though it is a constant feature of the letters Nott and Gliddon send to him. Beach notes a similar phenomenon in another mid-century scientific group, known as the American Lazzaroni: "Many of their letters to one another speak as much of tender oysters and foolproof home brew as they do of science. Most of them delighted in calling one another by pet names. Everyone was serious in calling [Alexander Dallas] Bache 'the Chief,' but quite jovial in dubbing Henry, Pierce and Agassiz, 'Smithson,' 'Functionary' and 'Fossilary,' respectively" (119).

36 For instance, Beach contests the idea that members of the U.S. Scientific Lazzaroni ever concertedly or even consciously forwarded a scientific agenda: "they were nine men who were conscious of having some special relationship to one another for social purposes only" (131–32).

37 In their study of twentieth-century "Networks of Informal Communication Among Scientifically Productive Scientists," Griffith and Miller distinguish between "low and background levels of communication networking" (an example of this would be Morton's wide correspondence), "loose communication networks among active scientists" (for instance, men who might count running into each other at Morton's soirees), and "highly coherent groups within science" (Morton's circle, the Lazzaroni). They characterize the latter thusly:

[E]ach of these several groups [in their study] seemed convinced that it was achieving the overthrow of some major position within its discipline. . . . By way of opposition, they all offered a distinctively different theory or approach and new or modified research methodology;

and each maintained its beliefs over a period of time, ultimately demonstrating some substantial scientific achievements. In this process, none of the groups continuously observed the attitude of disinterested objectivity that is commonly regarded as a norm of science; two groups even ventured actively into professional politics to obtain or protect appointments and research support.

Another major characteristic shared by coherent groups studied is an identifiable leader who may be a major source of conceptual and methodological innovation, and who generally serves as a scientific model for at least younger members of the group. (139)

38 Agassiz, originally a proponent of monogenesis, changed his mind after a visit to Philadelphia spent largely in the company of Morton, at the Academy of Natural Sciences. Between examining Morton's crania collection under his tutelage, and then encountering "real" blacks at the dining room of his hotel, Agassiz soon changed his mind and became a prominent supporter of the theory of polygenesis. See William Stanton 100–103.

39 Agassiz would record the encounter in what Gould characterizes as a "remarkably candid" 1846 letter to his mother:

It was in Philadelphia that I first found myself in prolonged contact with negroes; all the domestics of my hotel were men of color. I can scarcely express to you the painful impression that I received, especially since the feeling they inspired in me is contrary to all our ideas about the confraternity of the human type and the unique origin of our species. But truth before all. Nevertheless, I experienced pity at the sight of this degraded and degenerate race, and their lot inspired compassion in me in thinking they really are men. Nonetheless, it is impossible for me to repress the feeling that they are not of the same blood as us. In seeing their black faces with their thick lips and grimacing teeth, the wool on their head, their bent knees, their elongated hands, their large curved nails, and especially the livid color of the palm of their hands, I could not take my eyes off their face in order to tell them to stay far away. (qtd. in Gould, *Mismeasure* 44–45)

The passage continues in (abjecting) detail. It is a passage so rich in contradiction that it begs analysis. This experience would be the basis on which Agassiz would lend his support to Morton and Nott's arguments about "natural repugnance."

40 Dayan, in her evocative essay "A Receptacle for that Race of Men," traces how "independent Haiti, the first black republic, became a focus of [U.S.] racial obsession" (805). See also Sundquist's discussion of "Benito Cereno" and Haitian-U.S. politics, 146–49.

41 Butler might find my suggestion incompatible with her own model, where she locates the foreclosure of homosexual desire as a "preemptive loss, a mourning for unlived possibilities" ("Melancholy" 27). As my specific

analysis of Sims and my arguments throughout indicate, the loss of a range of democratic human connections are not entirely "unlived"—the living memories of such interactions making the work of their refusal so obsessive and culturally pervasive in the practices of male fraternalism. I am not sure "unlived" is a necessary category for the explanatory model: here I find Brenkman's cultural critique of psychoanalysis more helpful. Brenkman's critique of the Oedipal takes into much fuller account the process of lived social relations for "individual" histories of psychic formation. He incorporates the concept of "retrodetermination" to explain how the "splitting" of women into the mother/whore dichotomy emerges, at a later period in a boy's life, when he is acculturated into his sexist, patriarchal culture through his learned identification with his father: "[T]he formation of the Oedipus complex requires that the interaction of mother, father, and son acquire, for the son, specific meanings. Those meanings turn out to be social meanings and cultural valuations. They are not parts of an intrinsic psychological response but have to be acquired through a long, multi-layered process. . . . The Oedipus complex is intregal to a process of socialization-individuation whose goal is for young men to adapt to the symbolic-institutional configuration made up of male-dominated monogamy, the restricted family, capitalist social relations, and patriarchal culture" (26, 29; on Brenkman's use of the term "retrodetermination," see 21). His model for discussing psychic foreclosure—a bar on or routing of affections that emerges out of cultural structures and retrodetermines earlier experiences and evaluations—seems a little more specifically useful to the kinds of arguments I am making in this book about national manhood and representivity.

Afterword: The President in 2045, or, Managed Democracy

1   As Scott Trafton recalled to my attention, this spectacular surprise in Poe's story strikingly foreshadows the sensational scandal of George Gliddon's 1850 Boston lectures, which he advertised on the promise of unwrapping one of two female mummies, the daughters of Egyptian priests. William Stanton summarizes the climax: "Night after night the "enlightened assemblage" sat in awed silence as Gliddon removed the shroud. At last he withdrew the final remnants and the ancient relic was revealed to the audience. It was the body of a man . . . A sharp burst of uproarious laughter broke strangely from some two thousand well-bred Boston throats and echoed resoundingly in the local press. Attempting to explain the fiasco, Gliddon sent a serialized five-and-one-half column letter to the editor of the Boston *Transcript* to show it was all due to the illegibility of the inscription on the mummy case" (146–47). Trafton, completing a manuscript entitled "Egyptland: The Cultural Politics of Egyptomania,

1800–1900" provides a more careful analysis of this event in his important and much-needed reexamination of the sociopolitical contexts of Egyptology in the United States.

2   Lummis discusses a series of "moves" that reorient people in directions other than "democratic faith"—including despair (the flip side of sentimentalism), and faith in progress. I am positing a variation on the category of "progress," faith in the (future) president, a seemingly "democratic" faith that routes us away from the hard work of achieving actual democracy now. Following Lummis, I would argue that this works in much the same way as a faith in progress, except that it replaces scientific agency with a comfortingly hierarchized, fraternally representative, civic agency: "We put our faith in the human beings of the future, and the 'human beings of the future' will never let us down because they are, like God, the products of our imagination" (150).

3   This is by no means to say that the story gives evidence of lampooning white manhood in general, but rather, that it takes aim at a particular construction of white male identity, participating thereby in a broader ideological construction of white manhood in the early nation, under the rubric of competition.

4   For an engaging reading of the cultural politics underwriting the United States' most recent Egyptian fascination, see McAlister.

5   For other useful analyses of middle-class formation in relation to the modern museum, see Hooper-Greenhill 185–90; Stewart 154–66.

6   Describing the converging interests of "popular and orthodox" science in American antiquities, Zochert notes that: "The central question of American antiquities, and certainly the most confusing, involved the origins of the American Indian. The difference between contemporary Indian culture and pre-Columbian Indian culture was itself indistinct. Nevertheless, there was a consensus that Western earthworks and the associated artifacts represented a culture higher than that manifested by contemporary Indians. . . . So confused was the issue, and so imprecise the arguments—even among orthodox scientists—that when contemporary Indians contended that 'they had seen the common Indian mound built,' the implications of this observation for American antiquities [i.e., collected by popular and orthodox scientists from the mounds] went unnoticed" (14–15).

7   See William Stanton 207 n. 2, for sources offering evidence on this possibility.

8   On Nott, his essay, and his arguments on behalf of polygenesis, see William Stanton 66–68 and passim; Horsman, *Josiah Nott* 81–103; and Robert J. C. Young 126–33.

9   Morton's logical calisthenics in the project are really amazing. Separating out skulls with large cranial capacity from those with smaller, grouping the larger as Caucasian and the smaller as Negroid, Morton then acknowl-

edges there are significant variations within each group, breaking the Caucasian skulls into three "types" (Egyptian, Pelasgic, Semitic), while arguing that variation within the skull category "Negroid" does not compromise the category but rather offers evidence of racial "mixing" with the higher, Caucasian types. Quite similarly of the drawings he observed, Morton was forced into a little logical legerdemain. Wriggling around historical evidences, such as Herodotus's explicit characterization of the Egyptians as "black," Morton notes that "On the monuments the Egyptians represent the men of their nation red, the women yellow. . . . It is not, however, to be supposed that the Egyptians were really red men, as they are represented on the monuments. This color, with a symbolic signification, was conventionally adopted for the whole nation" (qtd. in Campbell 399–400). Offering a welter of circumnavigatory "evidence" (such as accounts referring to Egyptians "blushing") Morton insists that "from the preceding facts, and many others which might be adduced, I think we may safely conclude, that the complexion of the Egyptians did not differ from that of the other Caucasian nations in the same latitude" (qtd. in Campbell 401).

10 For example, Gliddon would write to Morton from Savannah, Georgia, on January 9, 1848: "since we first talked, 10 years ago, of getting "two or three *Mummy* skulls," what a revolution in ethnological opinions have you not created! Perhaps, owing to my vagabond life, I see the evidences more than you do; perhaps, as your pupil in most things, and colleague in a few, I take deeper interest than others in the subjects of your studies—but certain it is, that as your faithful friends, no one is happier than when I hear the praises of *Morton*" (Morton Papers, Library Company of Philadelphia; original emphasis). Recognizing Gliddon's indefatigable promotion of their work, Nott notes in a letter to Ephraim Squier that "He *will* make us great men in Europe whether we want it or not—it is strange that 'large streams from little fountains flow'" (Sept. 30, 1848; Squier Papers, Library of Congress; original emphasis).

11 Just a year previous, in his 1844 *Crania AEgyptiaca*, Morton had also —more scientifically—attacked this theory, tracing it to Herodotus and noting that "some modern authors have also attributed to mummy skulls a density which is not characteristic, but is adventitiously acquired by the inflation of bitumen into the diploic structure during the process of embalming" (qtd. in Campbell 390).

12 Neither this story nor my reading of it should be taken to represent Poe's attitudes toward science. As Limon's far more detailed treatment summarizes, Poe's attitude toward science throughout his career is "duplicitous always (where Poe seems to be antiscience, he is less antiscience than where he seems to be proscience" (96; see ch. 3, "Poe's Methodology").

13 I intend to use that term—*presidentialism*—with a bit of historical looseness in this section. I am using the term both to refer to the Constitutional

restructuring of government headed by an executive office, and to the symbolic dimensions that office has accrued, both by merit of its (vaguely defined) place in this scheme of government, and through its practice over time. It may well be true that it is not until the twentieth century that, in Livingston's phrasing, "the sovereignty of the presidential state—not the people—[became] a manifest necessity" (52), when the symbolic importance of local and national legislatures was subordinated to the economic, corporatist role of the president. I don't think arguments over the exact timing of the growth of presidential power negate or diminish any of the arguments I am making here about the affective routing that presidentialism entails—has entailed from 1789 to our own time—for democratic practice.

14 Sellers details how these early corporations soon forged a link between the idea of public good and private profit, effectively convincing courts at least that because corporate entrepreneurship was socially beneficial, large debtors like corporate officers should not be impeded from continuing their entrepreneurial work on behalf of such social good by, say, being imprisoned for debts and bankruptcy (47–90).

15 This word is culturally retrodetermined by its association with the southern Confederacy, and with the South's prior proslavery states-rights agitation. I'm asking my readers to set aside those reactions, and think about the model laid out by the Articles: confederated republics, consensual unanimity required to amend, one state, one vote. I'm not saying this institutional model guaranteed more democracy than the Constitution, but I am suggesting that it provides, at the level of national government, a model that insists on structural equalitarianism instead of structural subordination.

16 I'm aware that I'm using the ideas of corporatism and management anachronistically here. Nevertheless, I want to insist that presidentialism drew on the same incipient logic as emerging corporatism—and that both were crucially influenced by the psychopolitical imperatives of national manhood. I'm locating that political synergy at a much earlier moment than most (presidential scholars and historians locate the presidency's symbolic and practical adoption of corporate logic in the late nineteenth century), though certainly some scholars have also drawn the connection I'm making here. See for instance Wolfe's arguments about the presidential office as a "locus of modernization," where he notes that the "American presidency has been the major instrument by means of which modernizing elites have sought to overcome or remove obstacles to the expansion and revitalization of capitalism" (22; see 22–24).

17 Indeed, as Livingston summarizes, "the role of the president as the embodiment of a sovereign state is to make of the diverse and factious people a lifeless, apolitical abstraction. . . . the president does not, then, so much represent the occupationally aggregated people as negate them" (52).

18 Of course, many have observed that the Framers were aiming for "federal" or "republican" and not necessarily "democratic" institutions. But it was through these institutions that "democracy" was claimed in the Jacksonian era, and it is precisely these institutions to which we point when evidencing U.S. "democracy" today.

19 Lummis would call this ideal of dissensual reciprocity "democratic trust": "The appropriate object of trust is not a thing, fact, theory, or event, but a person. Trust means expecting that a person will do something or refrain from doing something. But it is trust only when the person has the freedom to do otherwise. Trust presupposes the freedom of the other. It is not trust if I expect you to digest your dinner. . . . It is not trust if I brainwash you and expect you to act accordingly. It is trust if I expect you will not betray me when you could" (143–44).

20 Numerous studies correlated strong presidentialism with limited party options. In their study of party systems and consolidated democracies, for example, political scientists Stepan and Skach measured for "effective" political parties in forty-one political systems: "Of the thirty-four parliamentary democracies, eleven had between three and seven effective political parties. Both of the semipresidential democracies . . . had between three and four effective political parties. However, no pure presidential democracy had more than 2.6 effective political parties. These data indicate that . . . consolidated presidential democracies are not associated with the type of multi-party coalitional behavior that facilitates democratic rule in contexts of numerous socioeconomic, ideological, and ethnic cleavages and of numerous parties in the legislature" (121). Lijphart elaborates on the consequences of two-party politics for democratic representation: In two-party systems, only one issue dimension—usually the socioeconomic or the left-right dimension—tends to dominate. In multi-party systems, one or more additional dimensions—religious, cultural-ethnic, urban-rural, foreign policy and so on—is probably present. Consequently, the pressures toward a two-party system exerted by presidentialism are also likely to squeeze out all other issue dimensions—which may be quite important to political and other minorities" ("Presidentialism" 98).

21 See also Ginsberg's *Consequences of Consent,* the entirety of which is devoted to an analysis of "elections, citizen control and popular acquiescence." There Ginsberg notes that the "introduction of the election had a number of vitally important consequences. The most obvious of these was a diminution of the likelihood of disruption and disorder . . . elections limit the frequency of citizen participation . . . [they] limit the scope of mass political participation . . . [and they] limit the intensity of political activity by converting it from a means of asserting demands to a collective statement of permission" (30–31).

22 I have been informed here not just by Lummis, but by, among others, Laclau and Mouffe; Corlett; Newfield's essay on the political correctness

debates and managerial democracy; Silverman's valuable rethinking of Lacan's discussion of "the body in bits and pieces"; and long-ago conversations about civil dissensus with Wahneema Lubiano. All of these critics have useful insights on the value of disunity to the practice of democracy. For instance, Laclau and Mouffe: "Only if it is accepted that the subject positions cannot be led back to a positive and unitary founding principle—only then can pluralism be considered radical. Plurality is *radical* only to the extent that each term of this plurality of identities finds within itself the principle of its own validity without this having to be sought in a transcendent or underlying positive ground of meaning of them all and the source and guarantee of their legitimacy. And this radical pluralism is *democratic* to the extent that the autoconstituitivity of each one of its terms is the result of displacements of the egalitarian imaginary" (167; original emphasis). In his Derridean analysis of political community, Corlett insists that "the culprit is the underlying distinction between unity and diversity" (22), which he seeks not to mediate but supplement with his project for "community without unity." Corlett critiques liberal and communitarian theories that "continue fighting the flux, maintaining patterns of subjectivity across time," a fight that "involves protecting citizens from the worst of life even as it denies them its joys." He (provocatively, if abstrusely) argues instead for the life-affirming, "insane" embrace of the radical discontinuity of history, sovereignty, nation, and subjectivity (181).

   Newfield is more helpfully forthright, in a passage from which I quoted earlier (in the notes of chapter 1): "Our 'pluralistic,' 'consensual' union, however one feels about it, has always rested on a divided, antagonistic multiplicity of cultures whose overlap has been sporadic, conflictual, or incomplete. The burden of providing a unifying cultural government has for too long interfered with our ability to understand cultural actuality. Even our defensiveness about this has blocked a more creative contribution to public life. Disunity is not a problem—in fact, it is usually preferable to more efficient resolutions. *Disunity* is another word for *Democracy*" ("Political Correctness" 336; original emphasis). Disunity, as Silverman insists, drawing on the earlier work of Schilder, can also be another word for psychic health, allowing us to reconceptualize the supposed organic/psychic basis for rigid ideals of national unity. For Schilder, she notes, both routine bodily and psychic "disintegration is beneficent rather than tragic; it is the precondition for change, what must transpire if the ego is to form anew. . . . [He] thus gestures toward the possibility of living the heterogeneity of the corporeal ego outside the logic of the psychic paradigm upon which Lacan places so much emphasis in 'The Mirror Stage' and 'Some Reflections on the Ego'" (*Threshold* 21).

23 As Chantal Mouffe observes, "[t]here is no threshold of democracy that once reached will guarantee its continued existence" (6).

24 For a more concrete map of the way a version of such a process might work, see Fishkin. He argues for a system he calls "a democracy of civic engagement," which would protect four basic democratic conditions, political equality, deliberation, participation, and non-tyranny (63, 34). He notes that this system is grounded in a productive conflict: "instead of a unified and coherent ideal in which these valued parts fit together in a single clear vision of what we should be striving for, we have conflicting values." His appeal is to "ideals without an ideal," a recognition that there "is not a single ideal vision progressively to be realized. Rather there are conflicting portions of the ideal picture and emphasis on each would take us in a different direction" (63).

25 The "self-made man" is, in just that way, an ideology that disguises co-operative family efforts that support and advantage the man in his business and professional "making," as Ryan details in *Cradle of the Middle Class*, and as Leverenz pithily summarizes: "the emerging ideology of individualism . . . erected an ideal of free, forceful and resourceful white men on the presumption of depersonalized servitude from several subordinated groups" (44).

26 I have been framing this argument, about the affective foreclosure of democratic desire entailed by national manhood's will to unity and power, throughout *National Manhood*. Lummis describes it with an emphasis a little different from mine. In detailing the split that occurs within the human subject of democratic empire, he argues that it is "possible to cut ourselves off from the fates of our fellow human beings, but we know now that the cutting, as it were, must go on within our own nervous systems. What we cut off is not other people, but one of our own sense organs. . . . Aside from the general inadvisability of this kind of self-mutilation, it directly contradicts the essence of radical democracy. That is, it is a lobotomy of the very sense that radical democracy must seek to develop, the sense that makes political virtue possible—what might be called *democratic sense*" (137–38; original emphasis). He locates this charge in the "now" because, he argues, we can no longer believe in the "natural inferiority of certain races or of women," which once were arguments "considered beyond doubt." I have shown in *National Manhood* precisely how that self-mutilation emerges not "now," but in the founding moments of national manhood. This affective foreclosure, this civic self-mutilation was entailed in the consolidation of white manhood as a national ideal; its articulation was fueled by national manhood's imperatives for self-identity, territorial expansion, and racial purity.

27 Harrison fought in battles against Native peoples in the Northwest Territory before being appointed ex-officio superintendent of Indian affairs for Indiana Territory in the early 1800s. As Peterson summarizes, he "was often upset by disregard for Indian rights, yet he negotiated treaties that

gained millions of acres for the government" (18). In 1811, he led a force against the organized forces of the Shawnee near Tippecanoe Creek. This engagement soon earned him, notes Peterson, "a commission as brigadier general in the Regular Army and, eventually, full command of the Army of the Northwest" (18).

28   As Ehrenreich notes in her essay "Warrior Culture": "After the U.S. invasion of Panama, President Bush exulted that no one could call him 'timid,' that he was at last a 'macho man.' The press, in even more primal language, hailed him for succeeding in an 'initiation rite' by demonstrating his 'willingness to shed blood'" (100).

29   Clinton is clearly working to take control of that public ambivalence, for instance, in his recent actions against tobacco industry giants, and his staging of first the bipartisan compromise budget bill ceremony, and then his first executive Lone Ranger exercise of the line-item veto two days later, all this to the tune of the highest presidential approval ratings since Reagan.

30   These are the "two bodies" of the president that (more directly than my punning allusion to it in my arguments about the hard and soft bodies) evokes the older doctrine of the "king's two bodies"—the natural body and the sovereign body, the body politic. For a compelling analysis of U.S. presidential absorption of this doctrine, see Rogin, "The King's Two Bodies: Lincoln, Wilson, Nixon and Presidential Self-Sacrifice" in *Ronald Reagan, The Movie.*

31   In what has to be the movie's weirdest exchange, Marshall reminds his Veep of their no-negotiation policy. "Kathryn, we've got a job to do," he says sternly from the cellular phone in the luggage hold. And then, in precisely the voice he must have stopped using with his twelve-year-old daughter at least eight years before, he queries: "If you give a mouse a cookie . . . ?" Kathryn's shoulders relax and she obediently chimes in, "He'll want a glass of milk." Whatever.

32   See also for instance Morgenstern's assessment of Ford's performance: "Mr. Ford wants his character to be seen as a classically tight-jawed comic-strip hero" (A12).

33   Oldman actually gets some amazing lines about capitalism-as-freedom: "You talk as though you had nothing to do with this infection you call freedom. . . . You have given my country to gangsters and prostitutes. You have taken everything from us: there is nothing left." His communist nostalgia combined with his ultranationalism makes him expendable, though.

34   It is worth pointing out that all the shots of Clinton are from the shoulders up—he is cropped either by camera or podium; the only place where we see a full-body president (as he leaves the key press conference), it would seem clearly to be a body double.

35   In philosopher William of Ockham's phrasing, "plurality is not to be posited without necessity," or "what can be explained by the assumption of fewer things is vainly explained by the assumption of more things" (xxi).

36   For a helpful account of the Zapatista uprising's radical democratic practices and vision, see Nash.

37   And what a white fantasy that is! The alien/Other turns out to be "white" like us; he isn't mad about anything, he just loves us and wants us to know how precious and rare we are. No fuss, no mess, no confrontation, just unconditional acceptance. There is a great deal to be said about the ways this movie navigates anxieties about whiteness that emerge as the disavowed aftershocks of the Oklahoma City bombing.

38   She pulls away to lean into the shelter of a heterosexual union, with "Father" Palmer Joss. This is worth backgrounding and thinking about a little. Arroway graduated from high school in 1979, and entered college on the tidal wave of feminism's strong entry into academia. It is absolutely painful to watch her surprise and confusion as men walk on her professionally and take credit for her accomplishments. She never knows what to do about this; she doesn't even know how to articulate it. It's as though feminism never existed (except that she gets to be a research scientist and is the second person chosen for the space mission). She forgives Palmer Joss for the biggest professional screw job of her career because, he later tells her, he couldn't stand to lose her romantically. She succeeds professionally despite this, and it is just as painful to watch how happy he is at the corner she gets backed into at the congressional hearing. It's clear he likes it when she no longer has all the answers. It is not just that he feels her pain; it starts to look as though he wants her *in* pain. Arroway leans on Joss as they walk out of the hearing; she climbs into the car, silent (with the Washington Monument still hovering behind her), and waits for him to give the last word to the media. The next time we see her, eighteen months later, she is surrounded by small children at the New Mexico radio telescope site, redeeming both her "hard" research orientation and her rigidly a-normative aloneness in a new, maternal demeanor. In this way, *Contact*, like *Air Force One*, proffers an invidious message about white women's symbolic admission to national manhood: on the condition of their willing and even infantilizing heterosexual subordination.

Bibliography

Adams, Alice E. *Reproducing the Womb: Images of Childbirth in Science, Feminist Theory, and Literature.* Ithaca: Cornell UP, 1994.

Adams, John. *The Works of John Adams, Second President of the United States.* Boston: Little, Brown and Co., 1854.

Albanese, Denise. *New Science, New World.* Durham: Duke UP, 1996.

Allen, Theodore W. *The Invention of the White Race: The Origin of Racial Oppression in Anglo-America.* Vol. 2. New York: Verso, 1997.

———. *The Invention of the White Race: Racial Oppression and Social Control.* Vol. 1. New York: Verso, 1993.

Ambrose, Stephen. *Undaunted Courage: Meriwether Lewis, Thomas Jefferson and the Opening of the American West.* New York: Simon and Schuster, 1996.

Appleby, Joyce. *Capitalism and a New Social Order: The Republican Vision of the 1790s.* New York: New York UP, 1984.

Arendt, Hannah. *On Revolution.* New York: Viking, 1963.

Armstrong, Nancy, and Leonard Tennenhouse. *The Imaginary Puritan: Literature, Intellectual Labor and the Origins of Personal Life.* Berkeley: U of California P, 1992.

Aspiz, Harold. "Sexuality and the Pseudo-Sciences." *Pseudo-Science and Society in Nineteenth-Century America.* Ed. and introduction by Arthur Wrobel. Lexington: UP of Kentucky, 1987. 144–65.

Axelsen, Diana E. "Women as Victims of Medical Experimentation: J. Marion Sims' Surgery on Slave Women, 1845–1850." *Sage* 2.2 (1985): 10–12.

Bachman, John. *The Doctrine of the Unity of the Human Race Examined on the Principles of Science.* Charleston: C. Canning, 1850.

———. "An Investigation of the Cases of Hybridity in Animals, Considered in Reference to the Unity of the Human Species." *Charleston Medical Journal* 5 (1850): 168–97.

———. "Reply to the Letter of Samuel George Morton, M.D., on the Question of Hybridity in Animals." *Charleston Medical Journal* 5 (1850): 466–508.

———. "Second Letter to Samuel George Morton, M.D." *Charleston Medical Journal* 5 (1850): 621–60.

Badinter, Elisabeth. *XY: On Masculine Identity.* Trans. Lydia Davis. New York: Columbia UP, 1995.

Bailyn, Bernard. *The Ideological Origins of the American Revolution.* Cambridge: Belknap, 1971.

Balibar, Etienne. "The Nation Form: History and Ideology." Ferdinand Braudel Center. *Review* 13.3 (1990): 329–61.

Balibar, Etienne, and Immanuel Wallerstein. *Race, Nation, Class: Ambiguous Identities.* Trans. Chris Turner. London: Verso, 1991.

Barkan, Elazar. *The Retreat of Scientific Racism: Changing Concepts of Race in Britain and the United States Between the World Wars.* New York: Cambridge UP, 1992.

Barker, Martin. "Biology and the New Racism" in Goldberg, *Anatomy,* 18–37.

Barker-Benfield, G. J. *The Horrors of the Half-Known Life: Male Attitudes Toward Women and Sexuality in Nineteenth-Century America.* New York: Harper and Row, 1976.

Barth, Gunther. "Timeless Journals: Reading Lewis and Clark with Nicholas Biddle's Help." *Pacific Historical Review* 63.4 (1994): 499–519.

Baudrillard, Jean. *Symbolic Exchange and Death.* Trans. Iain Hamilton Grant. London: Sage Publications, 1993.

Beach, Mark. "Was There a Scientific Lazzaroni?" *Nineteenth Century American Science: A Reappraisal.* Ed. George Daniels. Evanston: Northwestern UP, 1972. 115–32.

Beard, Charles. *An Economic Interpretation of the Constitution of the United States.* 1913. New York: Free, 1986.

Bederman, Gail. *Manliness and Civilization: A Cultural History of Gender and Race in the United States, 1880–1917.* Chicago: U of Chicago P, 1995.

Ben-David, Joseph. *The Scientist's Role in Society: A Comparative Study.* Chicago: U of Chicago P, 1971.

Benjamin, Maria. "Elbow Room: Women Writers on Science, 1790–1840." *Science and Sensibility: Gender and Scientific Inquiry, 1780–1945.* Ed. Maria Benjamin. London: Basel Blackwell, 1991. 27–59.

Berger, Maurice, Brian Wells, and Simon Watson, eds. *Constructing Masculinities.* New York: Routledge, 1995.

Berlant, Lauren. *The Anatomy of National Fantasy: Hawthorne, Utopia and Everyday Life.* Chicago: U of Chicago P, 1991.

Berlin, Ira. "From Creole to African: Atlantic Creoles and the Origins of African-American Society in Mainland North America." *William and Mary Quarterly* 53.2 (1996): 251–88.

Bernal, Martin. *Black Athena: The Afroasiatic Roots of Classical Civilization.* 2 vols. New Brunswick: Rutgers UP, 1987.

Bhabha, Homi. *The Location of Culture.* New York: Routledge, 1994.

Biddis, Michael D. *Images of Race.* New York: Holmes and Meier, 1979.

Biddle, Nicholas, ed. *The History of the Lewis and Clark Expedition.* 2 vols. Philadelphia: Bradford and Inskeep, 1814.

Bledstein, Burton J. *The Culture of Professionalism: The Middle Class and the Development of Higher Education in America.* New York: Norton, 1976.

Bloch, Ruth H. "The Gendered Meanings of Virtue in Revolutionary America." *Signs: Journal of Women in Culture and Society* 13.1 (1987): 37–58.

Blumin, Stuart. *The Emergence of the Middle Class: Social Experience in the American City 1760-1900.* New York: Cambridge UP, 1989.

Boney, F. N. "Notes and Documents: Slaves as Guinea Pigs: Georgia and Alabama Episodes." *Alabama Review* 37.1 (1984): 45–51.

Boose, Lynda. "Techno-Muscularity and the 'Boy Eternal': From Quagmire to Gulf." *Cultures of United States Imperialism.* Ed. Amy Kaplan and Donald Pease. Durham: Duke UP, 1993. 581–616.

Bordo, Susan. *The Flight to Objectivity: Essays on Cartesianism and Culture.* Albany: State U of New York P, 1987.

———. "Reading the Male Body." *Michigan Quarterly Review* 32.4 (1993): 696–737.

Boulton, Alexander O. "The American Paradox: Jeffersonian Equality and Racial Science." *American Quarterly* 47.3 (1995): 467–90.

Bowler, Peter J. *The Non-Darwinian Revolution: Reinterpreting a Historical Myth.* Baltimore: Johns Hopkins UP, 1988.

Boydston, Jeanne. "The Woman Who Wasn't There: Women's Market Labor and the Transition to Capitalism in the United States." *Wages of Independence: Capitalism in the Early Republic.* Ed. Paule Gilje. Madison: Madison House, 1997.

Bozeman, Theodore Dwight. *Protestants in an Age of Science: The Baconian Ideal and Antebellum Religious Thought.* Chapel Hill: U of North Carolina P, 1971.

Brenkman, John. *Straight, Male, Modern: A Cultural Critique of Psychoanalysis.* New York: Routledge, 1993.

Brown, Gillian. *Domestic Individualism: Imagining the Self in Nineteenth-Century America.* Berkeley: U of California P, 1990.

Brown, Laura. *Ends of Empire: Women and Ideology in Early Eighteenth-Century English Literature.* Ithaca: Cornell UP, 1993.

Brown, Norman O. *Life Against Death: The Psychoanalytic Meaning of History.* Middletown: Wesleyan UP, 1959.

Brown, Wendy. *Manhood and Politics: A Feminist Reading in Political Theory.* Totowa: Rowman and Littlefield, 1988.

Bruce, Robert V. *The Launching of Modern American Science, 1846-1876.* New York: Knopf, 1987.

Bullough, Vern, and Martha Voght. "Women, Menstruation, and Nineteenth-Century Medicine." *Bulletin of the History of Medicine* 47 (1973): 66–82.

Burke, John G. "Mineral Classification in the Early Nineteenth Century." *Toward a History of Geology.* Ed. Cecil J. Schneer. Cambridge: MIT P, 1969. 62–77.

Burrows, Edwin G., and Michael Wallace. "The American Revolution: The Ideology and Psychology of National Liberation." *Perspectives in American History* 6 (1972): 167–306.

Butler, Judith. *Bodies That Matter: On the Discursive Limits of "Sex".* NY: Routledge, 1993.

———. "Endangered/Endangering: Schematic Racism and White Paranoia." *Reading Rodney King, Reading Urban Uprising.* Ed. and introduction by Robert Gooding-Williams. New York: Routledge, 1993.

———. "Melancholy Gender/Refused Identification." *Constructing Masculinity.* Ed. Maurice Berger, Brian Wallis, and Simon Watson. New York: Routledge, 1995. 21–36.

Butterfield, Herbert. *The Origins of Modern Science.* Rev. ed. New York: Free, 1965.

Campbell, John. *Negro-Mania: Being an Examination of the Falsely Accused Equality of the Various Races of Men . . .* 1851. Miami: Mnemosyne, 1969.

Canquilheim, George. *Ideology and Rationality in the History of Life Science.* Trans. Arthur Goldhammer. Cambridge: MIT P, 1988.

Carnes, Mark C. "Middle-Class Men and the Solace of Fraternal Ritual." *Meanings for Manhood: Constructions of Masculinity in Victorian America.* Ed. Mark C. Carnes and Clyde Griffen. Chicago: U of Chicago P, 1990. 37–52.

———. *Secret Ritual and Manhood in Victorian America.* New Haven: Yale UP, 1989.

Carstensen, Vernon, ed. *The Public Lands: Studies in the History of the Public Domain.* Madison: U of Wisconsin P, 1963.

Castoriadis, Cornelius. *Political and Social Writings.* Vol. 3. *Recommencing Revolution: From Socialism to Autonomous Society.* Trans. David Ames Curtis. Minneapolis: U of Minnesota P, 1988.

———. *The Imaginary Institution of Society.* Trans. Kathleen Blamey. Cambridge: MIT P, 1987.

Castronovo, Russ. *Fathering the Nation: American Genealogies of Slavery and Freedom.* Berkeley: U of California P, 1995.

Cawelti, John G. *Apostles of the Self-Made Man.* Chicago: U of Chicago P, 1965.

Chamberlain, J. Edward, and Sander L. Gilman, eds. *Degeneration: The Dark Side of Progress.* New York: Columbia UP, 1985.

Chandler, Alfred D., Jr. *The Visible Hand: The Managerial Revolution in American Business.* Cambridge: Belknap, 1977.

Chandler, David Leon. *The Jefferson Conspiracies: A President's Role in the Assassination of Meriwether Lewis.* New York: William Morrow, 1994.

Cherniavsky, Eva. *That Pale Mother Rising: Sentimental Discourses and the Imitation of Mothering in Nineteenth-Century America.* Bloomington: Indiana UP, 1995.

Cheyfitz, Eric. *The Poetics of Imperialism: Translation and Colonization from The Tempest to Tarzan.* New York: Oxford UP, 1991.

——. *The Trans-Parent: Sexual Politics in the Language of Emerson.* Baltimore: Johns Hopkins UP, 1981.

Child, Lydia Maria. *An Appeal in Favor of that Class of Americans Called Africans.* 1834. Introduction by Carolyn L. Karcher. Amherst: U of Massachusetts P, 1996.

Chodorow, Nancy J. *Femininities, Masculinities, Sexualities: Freud and Beyond.* Lexington: UP of Kentucky, 1994.

Chuinard, Eldon G., M.D. *Only One Man Died: The Medical Aspects of the Lewis and Clark Expedition.* Glendale: Arthur H. Clark, 1979.

Clark, Christopher. "Rural America and the Transition to Capitalism." *Wages of Independence: Capitalism in the Early Republic.* Ed. Paule Gilje. Madison: Madison House, 1997.

Clark, Ella E., and Margot Edmunds. *Sacagawea of the Lewis and Clark Expedition.* Berkeley: U of California P, 1979.

Clawson, Mary Ann. *Constructing Brotherhood: Class, Gender and Fraternalism.* Princeton: Princeton UP, 1989.

Cohen, Patricia Cline. "The Helen Jewett Murder: Violence, Gender, and Sexual Licentiousness in Antebellum America." *NWSA Journal* 2.3 (1990): 374–89.

——. "Unregulated Youth: Masculinity and Murder in the 1830s City." *Radical History Review* 52 (winter 1992): 33–53.

Cohen, Phillip. "Tarzan and the Jungle Bunnies: Class, Race and Sex in Popular Culture." *New Formations* 5 (summer 1988): 25–30.

Comaroff, Jean, and John Comaroff. *Ethnography and the Historical Imagination.* Boulder: Westview, 1992.

——. *Of Revelation and Revolution: Christianity, Colonialism, and Consciousness in South Africa.* Vol. 1. Chicago: U of Chicago P, 1991.

Corfield, Penelope J. *Power and the Professions in Britain, 1700–1850.* New York: Routledge, 1995.

Corlett, William. *Community Without Unity: A Politics of Derridean Extravagance.* Durham: Duke UP, 1989.

Cott, Nancy F. "Eighteenth-Century Family and Social Life Revealed in Massachusetts Divorce Records." Cott and Pleck 107–35.

——. "Passionlessness." Cott and Pleck 162–81.

Cott, Nancy F., and Elizabeth H. Pleck, eds. *A Heritage of Her Own: Toward a New Social History of American Women.* New York: Simon and Schuster, 1979.

Coues, Elliott. *History of the Expedition under the Command of Lewis and Clark.* 1893. 4 vols. in 3. New York: Dover Publications, 1964.

Crenson, Matthew A. *The Federal Machine: Beginnings of Bureaucracy in Jacksonian America.* Baltimore: Johns Hopkins UP, 1975.

Crèvecoeur, J. Hector St. John de. *Letters from an American Farmer*. Ed. Albert Stone. New York: Penguin, 1981.

Daniels, George H. *American Science in the Age of Jackson*. New York: Columbia UP, 1968.

———, ed. *Nineteenth-Century American Science: A Reappraisal*. Evanston: Northwestern UP, 1972.

———. "The Process of Professionalization in American Science: The Emergent Period, 1820–1860." *Isis* (summer 1967): 63–78. Rpt. in *Science in America Since 1820*. Ed. Nathaniel Reingold. New York: Science History Publications, 1976.

Davidson, Cathy N. *Revolution and the Word: The Rise of the Novel in America*. New York: Oxford UP, 1986.

Dawley, Alan, and Paul Faler. "Working-Class Culture and Politics in the Industrial Revolution: Sources of Loyalism and Rebellion." *Journal of Social History* 9 (summer 1976): 466–80.

Dayan, Joan. "Amorous Bondage: Poe, Ladies and Slaves." *American Literature* 66.2 (1994): 239–73.

———. " 'A Receptacle for that Race of Men': Blood Boundaries and Mutations of Theory." *American Literature* 67.4 (1995): 801–13.

———. "Romance and Race." *Columbia History of the American Novel: New Views*. Ed. Emory Elliott. New York: Columbia UP, 1991: 89–109.

De Grazia, Alfred. *Public and Republic: Political Representation in America*. New York: Knopf, 1951.

Deleuze, Gilles, and Félix Guattari. *Anti-Oedipus: Capitalism and Schizophrenia*. Trans. Robert Hurley, Mark Seem, and Helen R. Lane. Minneapolis: U of Minneapolis P, 1983.

———. *A Thousand Plateaus: Capitalism and Schizophrenia*. Trans. Brian Massumi. Minneapolis: U of Minneapolis P, 1987.

D'Emilio, John, and Esther Freedman. *Intimate Matters: A History of Sexuality in America*. New York: Harper and Row, 1988.

Denton, Michael. *Evolution: A Theory in Crisis*. Bethesda: Adler and Adler, 1986.

Dillon, Richard. *Meriwether Lewis: A Biography*. New York: Coward-McCann, 1965.

Dimock, Wai Chee. "Class, Gender, and a History of Metonymy." Dimock and Gilmore 57–104.

Dimock, Wai Chee, and Michael T. Gilmore, eds. *Rethinking Class: Literary Studies and Social Formations*. New York: Columbia UP, 1994.

Ditz, Toby L. "Shipwrecked; or, Masculinity Imperiled: Mercantile Representations of Failure and the Gendered Self in Eighteenth-Century Philadelphia." *Journal of American History* 81.1 (1994): 51–80.

Dolan, Frederick M. *Allegories of America: Narratives, Metaphysics, Politics*. Ithaca: Cornell UP, 1994.

Dominguez, Virginia R. *White By Definition: Social Classification in Creole Louisiana.* New Brunswick: Rutgers UP, 1986.

Donzelot, Jacques. *The Policing of Families.* Foreword by Gilles Deleuze. Trans. Robert Hurley. New York: Pantheon, 1979.

Douglas, Ann. *The Feminization of American Culture.* New York: Anchor/ Doubleday, 1988.

Douglas, Mary. *Purity and Danger: An Analysis of the Concepts of Pollution and Taboo.* 1966. New York: Routledge, 1991.

Duffy, Timothy P. "The Gender of Letters: Charles Eliot Norton and the Decline of the Amateur Intellectual Tradition." *The New England Quarterly* 69.1 (1996): 91–109.

Dumenil, Lynn. *Freemasonry and American Culture, 1880–1930.* Princeton: Princeton UP, 1984.

Dumm, Thomas L. *Democracy and Punishment: Disciplinary Origins of the United States.* Madison: U of Wisconsin P, 1987.

———. *United States.* Ithaca: Cornell UP, 1994.

Durey, Michael. *Transatlantic Radicals and the Early American Republic.* Lawrence: U of Kansas P, 1997.

Dye, Nancy Schrom, and Daniel Blake Smith. "Mother Love and Infant Death, 1750–1920." *Journal of American History* 73.2 (1986): 329–53.

Dyer, Richard. "White." *Screen* 29.4 (1988): 45–64.

Easlea, Brian. *Fathering the Unthinkable: Masculinity, Science and the Nuclear Arms Race.* London: Pluto, 1983.

———. *Science and Sexual Oppression: Patriarchy's Confrontation with Women and Nature.* London: Weidenfeld and Nicolson, 1981.

Easthope, Anthony. "The Masculine Myth." *What a Man's Gotta Do: The Masculine Myth in Popular Culture.* Boston: Unwin Hyman, 1990. 166–73.

Edelman, Lee. *Homographesis: Essays in Gay Literary and Cultural Theory.* New York: Routledge, 1994.

Ehrenreich, Barbara. *The Hearts of Men: American Dreams and the Flight from Commitment.* New York: Anchor/Doubleday, 1984.

———. "The Warrior Culture." *Time* 15 Oct. 1990: 100.

Ehrenreich, Barbara, and John Ehrenreich. "The Professional-Managerial Class." *Between Labor and Capital.* Ed. Pat Walker. Boston: South End, 1979.

Ehreneich, Barbara, and Deidre English. *Complaints and Disorders: The Sexual Politics of Sickness.* Glass Mountain Pamphlet No. 2. New York: Feminist, 1973.

Eiseley, Loren. *Darwin's Century: Evolution and the Men Who Discovered It.* New York: Anchor, 1958.

Eisenstein, Zillah R. *The Radical Future of Liberal Feminism.* Boston: Northeastern UP, 1981.

Elazar, Daniel J. *American Federalism: A View from the States.* 3rd ed. New York: Harper, 1984.

Ellison, Julie. "The Gender of Transparency: Masculinity and *The Conduct of Life.*" *American Literary History* 4.4 (1992): 584–606.

Erkkila, Betsy. "Revolutionary Women." *Tulsa Studies in Women's Literature* 6.2 (1987): 189–223.

Faler, Paul G. *Mechanics and Manufacturers in the Early Industrial Revolution, Lynn, Massachusetts 1780-1860.* Albany: State U of New York P, 1981.

Faucounier, Gilles. *Mental Spaces: Aspects of Meaning and Construction in Natural Language.* Cambridge: MIT P, 1985.

Fausto-Sterling, Anne. *Myths of Gender: Biological Theories about Women and Men.* New York: Basic, 1985.

Ferguson, E. James. *Power of the Purse: A History of American Public Finance, 1776-1790.* Chapel Hill: U of North Carolina P, 1961.

Feyerabend, Paul. "Consolation for the Specialist." *Criticism and the Growth of Knowledge.* Ed. Irme Lakatos and Alan Musgrave. Cambridge: Cambridge UP, 1965. 197–230.

Fisher, Vardis. *Suicide or Murder? The Strange Death of Meriwether Lewis.* Chicago: Swallow, 1962.

Fishkin, James S. *The Voice of the People: Public Opinion and Democracy.* New Haven: Yale UP, 1995.

Fitzgerald, Neil King. "Towards an American Abraham: Multiple Parricide and the Rejection of Revelation in the Early National Period." Diss. Brown U, 1971.

Fliegelman, Jay. *Declaring Independence: Jefferson, Natural Language and the Culture of Performance.* Stanford: Stanford UP, 1993.

——. *Prodigals and Pilgrims: The American Revolution Against Patriarchal Authority 1750-1800.* Cambridge: Cambridge UP, 1982.

Formisano, Ronald, and Kathleen Smith Kutolowski. "Anti-Masonry and Masonry: The Genesis of a Protest, 1826-1827." *American Quarterly* 29.2 (1977): 139–65.

Foucault, Michel. *The Birth of the Clinic: An Archaeology of Medical Perception.* Trans. A. M. Sheridan Smith. New York: Vintage, 1973.

——. *Discipline and Punish: The Birth of the Prison.* Trans. Alan Sheridan. New York: Vintage, 1979.

——. *The Order of Things: An Archaeology of the Human Sciences.* New York: Vintage, 1973.

——. *Power/Knowledge: Selected Interviews and Other Writings. 1972-1977.* Ed. Colin Gordon. NY: Pantheon, 1980.

Franklin, H. Bruce. *The Wake of the Gods: Melville's Mythology.* Stanford: Stanford UP, 1963.

Fredrickson, George M. *The Black Image in the White Mind: The Debate on Afro-American Character and Destiny, 1817-1914.* New York: Harper and Row, 1971.

Freeman, Joanne B. "Dueling as Politics: Reinterpreting the Burr-Hamilton Duel." *The William and Mary Quarterly* 3rd ser. 53.2 (1996): 289–318.

Fuchs, Cynthia J. "The Buddy Politic." *Screening the Male: Exploring Masculinities in Hollywood Cinema.* Ed. Steven Cohan and Ina Rae Hark. New York: Routledge, 1993. 194–210.

Fuller, Steve. *Social Epistemology.* Bloomington: Indiana UP, 1988.

Gallagher, Catherine, and Thomas Laqueur, eds. *The Making of the Modern Body: Sexuality and Society in the Nineteenth Century.* Berkeley: U of California P, 1987.

Garber, Marjorie. *Vested Interests: Cross-Dressing and Cultural Anxiety.* New York: Routledge, 1992.

Gilje, Paul. "The Rise of Capitalism in the Early Republic." *Wages of Independence: Capitalism in the Early Republic.* Ed. Paule Gilje. Madison: Madison House, 1997.

———. *The Road to Mobocracy: Popular Disorder in New York City, 1763–1834.* Chapel Hill: U of North Carolina P, 1987.

Gilman, Sander L. *Difference and Pathology: Stereotypes of Sexuality, Race, and Madness.* Ithaca: Cornell UP, 1985.

———. *Disease and Representation: Images of Illness from Madness to AIDS.* Ithaca: Cornell UP, 1988.

Gilmore, David. *Manhood in the Making: Cultural Concepts of Masculinity.* New Haven: Yale UP, 1990.

Ginsberg, Benjamin. *The Captive Public: How Mass Opinion Promotes State Power.* New York: Basic, 1986.

———. *The Consequences of Consent: Elections, Citizen Control and Popular Acquiescence.* Reading: Addison-Wesley, 1982.

Gliddon, George. *Ancient Egypt: A Series of Chapters on Early Egyptian History, Archaeology, and Other Subjects . . .* Philadelphia: Peterson, 1848.

———. *Otia Aegyptiaca: Discourses on Egyptian Archaeology and Hieroglyphical Discoveries.* London, 1849.

Goddu, Teresa A. *Gothic America: Narrative, History, and Nation.* New York: Columbia UP, 1997.

Goldberg, David Theo, ed. *Anatomy of Racism.* Minneapolis: U of Minneapolis P, 1990.

———. *Racist Culture: Philosophy and the Politics of Meaning.* Oxford: Blackwell, 1993.

Goldfield, Michael. "The Color of Politics in the United States: White Supremacy as the Main Explanation for the Peculiarities of American Politics from the Colonial Times to the Present." *The Bounds of Race: Perspectives on Hegemony and Resistance.* Ed. Dominick LaCapra. Ithaca: Cornell UP, 1991.

Gorz, Andre. "On the Class-Character of Science and Scientists." *The Political Economy of Science.* Eds. Hilary Rose and Steven Rose. London: Macmillan, 1976. 59–71.

Goshgarian, G. M. *To Kiss the Chastening Rod: Domestic Fiction and Sexual Ideology in the American Revolution.* Ithaca: Cornell UP, 1992.

Gossett, Thomas F. *Race: The History of an Idea in America.* New York: Schoken, 1963.

Gould, Stephen Jay. *The Mismeasure of Man.* New York: Norton, 1981.

———. *Outogeny and Phylogeny.* Cambridge: Belknap, 1977.

Gregg, Gary L. *The Presidential Republic: Executive Representation and Deliberative Democracy.* New York: Rowman and Littlefield, 1997.

Greenblatt, Stephen. "Filthy Rites." *Daedalus* (summer 1982): 1–16.

Greene, John C. *American Science in the Age of Jefferson.* Ames: Iowa State UP, 1984.

Greene, John. *Science, Ideology, and World View: Essays in the History of Evolutionary Ideas.* Berkeley: U of California P, 1981.

Greenfield, Bruce. *Narrating Discovery: The Romantic Explorer in American Literature 1790–1850.* New York: Columbia UP, 1992.

Griffith, Belver C., and James Miller. "Networks of Internal Communication Among Scientifically Productive Scientists." *Communication Among Scientists and Engineers.* Ed. Carnot E. Nelson and Donald K. Pollock. Lexington: Heath Lexington, 1970. 125–40.

Grosz, Elizabeth. *Volatile Bodies: Toward a Corporeal Feminism.* Bloomington and Indianapolis: Indiana UP, 1994.

Guillaumin, Collette. *Racism, Sexism, Power and Ideology.* New York: Routledge, 1995.

Guillory, John. "Literary Critics as Intellectuals: Class Analysis and the Crisis of the Humanities." *Rethinking Class: Literary Studies and Social Formations.* Ed. Wai Chee Dimock and Michael T. Gilmore. New York: Columbia UP, 1994. 107–49.

Guinier, Lani. *The Tyranny of the Majority: Fundamental Fairness in Representative Democracy.* New York: Free, 1994.

Gunderson, Joan R. "Independence, Citizenship, and the American Revolution." *Signs: Journal of Women in Culture and Society* 13.1 (1987): 59–77.

Guralnick, Stanley. "Geology and Religion Before Darwin: The Case of Edward Hitchcock, Theologian and Geologist, 1793–1864." *Isis* 63 (1972): 529–43. reprinted in *Science in America Since 1820.* Ed. Nathaniel Reingold. New York: Science History, 1976. 116–130.

Hall, Catherine. *White, Male and Middle Class: Explorations in Feminism and History.* New York: Routledge, 1992.

Haller, John S., Jr. *American Medicine in Transition 1840–1910.* Urbana: U of Illinois P, 1981.

Haller, John S., Jr., and Robin M. Haller. *The Physician and Sexuality in Victorian America.* Chicago: U of Illinois P, 1974.

Halpin, Zuleyma Tang. "Scientific Objectivity and the Concept of 'The Other'." *Women's Studies International Forum* 12.3 (1989): 285–94.

Halttunen, Karen. *Confidence Men and Painted Women: A Study of Middle-Class Culture in America, 1830-1870.* New Haven: Yale UP, 1982.

Hamilton, Alexander, James Madison, and John Jay. *The Federalist Papers.* Ed. Garry Wills. New York: Bantam, 1982.

Hamlin, Christopher. *A Science of Impurity: Water Analysis in Nineteenth Century Britain.* Berkeley: U of California P, 1990.

Harding, Sandra. *The Science Question in Feminism.* Ithaca: Cornell UP, 1986.

Harding, Sandra, and Jean F. O'Barr. *Sex and Scientific Inquiry.* Chicago: U of Chicago P, 1987.

Harding, Sandra, ed. *The 'Racial' Economy of Science: Toward a Democratic Future.* Bloomington: Indiana UP, 1993.

Haraway, Donna. *Primate Visions: Gender, Race and Nature in the World of Modern Science.* New York: Routledge, 1989.

Harris, Cheryl I. "Whiteness as Property." *Harvard Law Review* 106.8 (1993): 1709-71.

Harris, Seale, M.D. *Woman's Surgeon: The Life Story of J. Marion Sims.* New York: Macmillan, 1950.

Hartman, Geoffrey H. "The Reinvention of Hate." *The Yale Review* 84.3 (1996): 1-12.

Herbert, T. Walter. *Dearest Beloved: The Hawthornes and the Making of the Middle Class Family.* Berkeley: U of California P, 1993.

———. "Mozart, Hawthorne, and Mario Salvio: Aesthetic Power and Political Complicity." *College English* 57 (April 1995): 397-409.

Herndl, Diane Price. *Invalid Women: Figuring Feminine Illness in American Fiction and Culture 1840-1940.* Chapel Hill: U of North Carolina P, 1993.

Herrnstein Smith, Barbara. "Belief and Resistance: A Symmetrical Account." *Critical Inquiry* 18 (autumn 1991): 125-39.

Hibbard, Benjamin Horace. *A History of the Public Land Policies.* New York: Peter Smith, 1939.

Hinckley, Barbara. *The Symbolic Presidency: How Presidents Portray Themselves.* New York: Routledge, 1990.

Hindle, Brooke, ed. *Early American Science.* New York: Science History, 1976.

———. *The Pursuit of Science in Revolutionary America, 1735-1789.* Chapel Hill: U of North Carolina P, 1956.

Hinsley, Curtis M. *Savages and Scientists: The Smithsonian Institution and the Development of American Anthropology 1846-1910.* Washington D.C.: Smithsonian Institution, 1981.

Hoch, Paul. *White Hero, Black Beast: Racism, Sexism and the Mask of Masculinity.* London: Pluto, 1979.

Holton, G. *Thematic Origins of Scientific Thought.* Cambridge: Harvard UP, 1973.

Hooper-Greenhill, Eilean. *Museums and the Shaping of Knowledge.* New York: Routledge, 1992.

Horlich, Stanley Allan. *Country Boys and Merchant Princes: The Social Control of Young Men in New York*. Lewisburg: Bucknell UP, 1975.

Horsman, Reginald. *Josiah Nott of Mobile: Southerner, Physician, and Racial Theorist*. Baton Rouge: Louisiana State UP, 1987.

———. *Race and the Manifest Destiny: The Origins of American Racial Anglo-Saxonism*. Cambridge: Harvard UP, 1981.

Howe, Daniel W. "The Political Psychology of *The Federalists*." *William and Mary Quarterly* 44.3 (1987): 485–510.

Hubbard, Ruth, and Elijah Wald. *Exploring the Gene Myth: How Genetic Information is Produced and Manipulated by Scientists, Physicians, Employers, Insurance Companies, Educators and Law Enforcers*. Boston: Beacon, 1993.

Hudson, Liam. *The Cult of Fact*. London: Cape, 1972.

Hudson, Liam, and Bernadine Jacot. *The Way Men Think: Intellect, Intimacy, and the Erotic Imagination*. New Haven: Yale UP, 1991.

Ignatiev, Noel. *How the Irish Became White*. New York: Routledge, 1995.

Irwin, John T. *American Hieroglyphics: The Symbol of the Egyptian Hieroglyphics in the American Renaissance*. Baltimore: Johns Hopkins UP, 1983.

Itzhoff, Seymour W. *The Decline of Intelligence in America: A Strategy for National Renewal*. Westport: Praeger, 1994.

Jacobus, Mary. *Reading Woman: Essays in Feminist Criticism*. New York: Columbia UP, 1986.

Jacobus, Mary, Evelyn Fox Keller, and Sally Shuttleworth. *Body/Politics: Women and the Discourses of Science*. New York: Routledge, 1990.

JanMohamed, Abdul R. "The Economy of Manichean Allegory: The Function of Racial Difference in Colonial Literature." *Critical Inquiry* 12 (1985): 59–87.

———. "Sexuality on/of the Racial Border: Foucault, Wright, and the Articulation of "Racialized Sexuality." *Discourses of Sexuality: From Aristotle to AIDS*. Ed. Domna Stanton. Ann Arbor: U of Michigan P, 1992. 94–116.

Jardine, Alice. *Gynesis: Configurations of Woman and Modernity*. Ithaca: Cornell UP, 1985.

Jatinder, K. Bajaj. "Francis Bacon, the First Philosopher of Science." *Science, Hegemony and Violence: A Requiem for Modernity*. Ed. Ashish Nandy. Delhi: Oxford UP, 1991.

Jefferson, Thomas. "Jefferson's Confidential Message Recommending a Western Exploring Expedition." 18 Jan. 1803. *Statesman's Manual. Presidents' Messages, Inaugural, Annual and Special from 1789–1846*. Comp. Edwin Williams. Vol. 1. New York: Edward Walker, 1849. xxv–xxvii.

———. "Memoir of Meriwether Lewis." Rpt. in Coues 1:xv–xlii.

———. *Notes on the State of Virginia*. Ed. William Peden. New York: Norton, 1954.

Jeffords, Susan. *The Remasculinization of America: Gender and the Vietnam War*. Bloomington: Indiana UP, 1989.

Jehlen, Myra. "The Literature of Colonization: The Final Voyage." *The Cambridge History of American Literature*. Ed. Sacvan Bercovitch. Vol. 1. New York: Cambridge UP, 1994. 149–68.

Johns, Elizabeth. *American Genre Painting: The Politics of Everyday Life*. New Haven: Yale UP, 1991.

Jordan, Cynthia S. *Second Stories: The Politics of Language, Form and Gender in Early American Fictions*. Chapel Hill: U of North Carolina P, 1989.

Jordanova, Ludmilla, ed. *Languages of Nature: Critical Essays on Science and Literature*. London: Free Association, 1986.

———. *Sexual Visions: Images of Gender in Science and Medicine Between the Eighteenth and Twentieth Centuries*. New York: Harvester Wheatsheaf, 1989.

Juster, Susan. *Disorderly Women: Sexual Politics and Evangelism in Revolutionary New England*. Ithaca: Cornell UP, 1994.

Kann, Mark E. *On the Man Question: Gender and Civic Virtue in America*. Philadelphia: Temple UP, 1991.

Kaplan, Amy, and Donald Pease, eds. *Cultures of United States Imperialism*. Durham: Duke UP, 1993.

Kapsalis, Terri. *Public Privates: Performing Gynecology from Both Ends of the Speculum*. Durham: Duke UP, 1997.

Karcher, Carolyn. *First Woman in the Republic: A Cultural Biography of Lydia Maria Child*. Durham: Duke UP, 1994.

———. *Shadow Over the Promised Land: Slavery, Race and Violence in Melville's America*. Baton Rouge: Louisiana State UP, 1980.

Keller, Evelyn Fox. *Reflections on Gender and Science*. New Haven: Yale UP, 1985.

———. *Secrets of Life, Secrets of Death: Essays on Language, Gender and Science*. New York: Routledge, 1992.

Kennedy, Liam. "Alien Nation: White Male Paranoia and Imperial Culture in the United States." *Journal of American Studies* 30.1 (1996): 87–100.

Kerber, Linda K. *Women of the Republic: Intellect and Ideology in Revolutionary America*. New York: London, 1980.

Kern, Louis J. "Stamping Out the 'Brutality of the *He*': Sexual Ideology and the Masculine Ideal in the Language of Victorian Sex Radicals." *ATQ* 5.3 (1993): 225–39.

Ketcham, Ralph, ed. *The Anti-Federalist Papers and the Constitutional Convention Debates*. New York: Mentor, 1986.

Kett, Joseph. *The Formation of the American Medical Profession: The Role of Institutions, 1780–1860*. New Haven: Yale UP, 1968.

———. *Rites of Passage: Adolescence in America, 1790 to the Present*. New York: Basic, 1977.

Kimmel, Michael. *Manhood in America: A Cultural History*. New York: Free, 1996.

Kittay, Eva Feder. "Womb Envy: An Explanatory Concept." *Mothering: Essays* in *Feminist Theory*. Ed. Joyce Treblicot. Tottowa: Rowman and Allanheld, 1984. 94–128.

Kohut, Heinz. *The Restoration of the Self.* New York: International Universities, 1977.

———. *Self-Psychology and the Humanities: Reflections on the New Psychoanalytic Approach.* New York: Norton, 1985.

Kristeva, Julia. *Powers of Horror: An Essay on Abjection.* Trans. Leon S. Roudiez. New York: Columbia UP, 1982.

Kuhn, Thomas S. *The Structure of Scientific Revolutions.* 2nd ed. Chicago: U of Chicago P, 1970.

Laclau, Ernesto, and Chantal Mouffe. *Hegemony and Socialist Strategy: Towards a Radical Democratic Politics.* London: Verso, 1985.

Lakoff, George, and Mark Johnson. *Metaphors We Live By.* Chicago: U of Chicago P, 1980.

Laqueur, Thomas. *Making Sex: Body and Gender From the Greeks to Freud.* Cambridge: Harvard UP, 1990.

———. "Orgasm, Generation, and the Politics of Reproductive Biology." *Representations* 14 (1986): 1–41. Rpt. in Gallagher and Laqueur. 1–41.

———. "Sexual Desire and the Market Economy During the Industrial Revolution." *Discourses of Sexuality: From Aristotle to AIDS.* Ed. Domna Stanton. Ann Arbor: U of Michigan P, 1992.

Larson, Magali Sarfatti. *The Rise of Professionalism: A Sociological Analysis.* Berkeley: U of California P, 1977.

Laslett, Peter. *Philosophy, Politics, and Society.* Oxford: Basil Blackwell, 1956.

Lastrucci, Carlo L. *The Scientific Approach.* Cambridge, MA: Schenkman, 1963.

Latour, Bruno. *The Pasteurization of France.* Trans. Alan Sherridan and John Law. Cambridge: Harvard UP, 1988.

———. *Science in Action: How to Follow Scientists and Engineers through Society.* Cambridge: Harvard UP, 1987.

———. *We Have Never Been Modern.* Trans. Catherine Porter. Cambridge: Harvard UP, 1993.

Latour, Bruno, and Stephen Woolgar. *Laboratory Life: The Social Construction of Scientific Fact.* London: Sage, 1979.

Lease, Benjamin. *That Wild Fellow John Neal and the American Literary Revolution.* Chicago: U of Chicago P, 1972.

Ledyard, John. "Ledyard's Eulogy on Women." *Proceedings of the African Association* (1790): 264–65.

Lefkowitz, Mary, and Guy MacLean Rogers, eds. *Black Athena Revisited.* Chapel Hill: U of North Carolina P, 1996.

———. *Not Out of Africa: How Afrocentrism Became an Excuse to Teach Myth as History.* New York: Basic, 1996.

Leo, John R. "'. . . in other folks' time': 19th-Century Constructions of the Masculine: An Introduction." *ATQ* 5.3 (1991): 141–50.

Lerner, Richard. *Final Solutions: Biology, Prejudice and Genocide.* University Park: Pennsylvania State UP, 1992.

Leverenz, David. *Manhood and the American Renaissance.* Ithaca: Cornell UP, 1989.

Levine, Robert. *Conspiracy and Romance: Studies in Brockden Brown, Cooper, Hawthorne and Melville.* New York: Cambridge UP, 1989.

Levy, Anita. *Other Women: The Writing of Class, Race, and Gender, 1832–1898.* Princeton: Princeton UP, 1992.

Lewontin, R. C. "Facts and the Factitious in Natural Sciences." *Critical Inquiry* 18 (autumn 1991): 140–53.

Lewontin, R. C., Steve Rose, and Leon J. Kamin. *Not in Our Genes: Biology, Ideology and Human Nature.* New York: Pantheon, 1984.

Lijphart, Arend. *Democracies: Patterns of Majoritarian and Consensus Government in Twenty-one Countries.* New Haven: Yale UP, 1984.

———. "Presidentialism and Majoritarian Democracy: Theoretical Observations." *The Failure of Presidential Democracy.* Ed. Juan J. Linz and Arturo Valenzuela. Baltimore: Johns Hopkins UP, 1994. 91–105.

Limon, John. *The Place of Fiction in the Time of Science: A Disciplinary History of American Writing.* New York: Cambridge UP, 1990.

Linz, Juan J., and Arturo Valenzuela, eds. *The Failure of Presidential Democracy.* Baltimore: Johns Hopkins UP, 1994.

Lippard, George. *The Quaker City, Or, The Monk of Monk Hall.* Ed. and introduction by David S. Reynolds. Amherst: U of Massachusetts P, 1995.

Litvak, Joseph. "Back to the Future: A Review-Article on the New Historicism, Deconstruction, and Nineteenth-Century Fiction." *Texas Studies in Literature and Language* 30.1 (1988): 120–49.

Livingston, James. "The Presidency and the People." *Democracy* 3.3 (1983): 50–57.

Lloyd, Genevieve. *The Man of Reason: 'Male' and 'Female' in Western Philosophy.* Minneapolis: U of Minnesota P, 1984.

Lockridge, Kenneth A. *On the Sources of Patriarchal Rage: The Commonplace Books of William Byrd and Thomas Jefferson and the Gendering of Power in the Eighteenth Century.* New York: New York UP, 1992.

Lott, Eric. *Love and Theft: Blackface Minstrelsy and the American Working Class.* New York: Oxford UP, 1993.

Lubiano, Wahneema. "Like Being Mugged by a Metaphor: Multiculturalism and State Narratives." *Mapping Multi-Culturalism.* Ed. Avery Gordon and Christopher Newfield. Minneapolis: U of Minnesota P, 1996. 64–75.

Lummis, C. Douglas. *Radical Democracy.* Ithaca: Cornell UP, 1996.

MacCannell, Juliet Flower. "The Post-Colonial Unconscious, or the White Man's Thing." Journal for the Psychoanalysis of Culture 1.1 (1996): 27–41.

———. *The Regime of the Brother: After the Patriarchy.* New York: Routledge, 1991.

MacDonald, Sharon, and Gordon Fyfe, eds. *Theorizing Museums: Representing Identity and Diversity in a Changing World.* Oxford: Blackwell/Sociological Review, 1996.

MacKenzie, John M., ed. *Imperialism and the Natural World.* Manchester: Manchester UP, 1990.

MacLean, Nancy. *Behind the Mask of Chivalry: The Making of the Second Ku Klux Klan.* New York: Oxford UP, 1994.

Main, Jackson Turner. *The Antifederalists: Critics of the Constitution, 1781–1788.* Chapel Hill: U of North Carolina P, 1961.

Martin, Emily. *Flexible Bodies: Tracking Immunity in American Culture—From the Days of Polio to Age of AIDS.* Boston: Beacon, 1994.

Martin, Robert K. *Hero, Captain and Stranger: Male Friendship, Social Critique and Literary Form in the Sea Novels of Herman Melville.* Chapel Hill: U of North Carolina P, 1986.

Masson, Jeffrey Moussaieff. *A Dark Science: Women, Sexuality and Psychiatry in the Nineteenth Century.* Trans. Jeffrey Moussaieff Masson and Marianne Loring. New York: Farrar, 1986.

Mathews, Donald G. "The Second Great Awakening as an Organizing Process, 1780–1830: An Hypothesis." *American Quarterly* 21.1 (1969): 23–43.

Matthews, Glenna. *The Rise of Public Woman: Woman's Power and Woman's Place in the United States 1630–1970.* New York: Oxford UP, 1992.

McAlister, Melani. "The Common Heritage of Mankind: Race, Nation and Masculinity in the King Tut Exhibit." *Representations* 54 (spring 1996): 80–103.

McCarthy, Todd. "US Prexy as Last Action Hero." *Variety* 21–27 July 1997: 37–38.

———. "Zemeckis Connects with *Contact.*" *Variety* 14–21 July 1997: 43, 54.

McClintock, Anne. *Imperial Leather: Race, Gender and Sexuality in the Colonial Contest.* New York: Routledge, 1995.

McDade, Thomas M. *Annals of Murder: A Bibliography of Books and Pamphlets from Colonial Times to 1900.* Norman: U of Oklahoma P, 1961.

McGregor, Deborah. *Sexual Surgery and the Origins of Gynecology: J. Marion Sims, His Hospital and His Patients.* New York: Garland, 1989.

McWilliams, Wilson Carey. *The Idea of Fraternity in America.* Berkeley: U of California P, 1973.

Meigs, Charles D. *Females and their Diseases.* Philadelphia: Lea and Blanchard, 1848.

———. *Lecture on Some of the Distinctive Characteristics of the Female.* Philadelphia: T. K. and P. G. Collins, 1847.

———. *A Memoir of Samuel George Morton, M.D., Late President of the Academy of Natural Sciences of Philadelphia.* Philadelphia: T. K. and P. G. Collins, 1851.

Melville, Herman. *Piazza Tales and Other Prose Pieces, 1839–1860.* Ed. Harrison Hayford, Alma A. Macdougall, and G. Thomas Tanselle. Chicago: Northwestern UP and the Newberry Library, 1987.

Micale, Mark S. "Hysteria Male/Hysteria Female: Reflections on Comparative Gender Construction in Nineteenth-Century France and Britain." *Science and Sensibility: Gender and Scientific Inquiry 1780-1945*. Ed. Maria Benjamin. London: Basil Blackwell, 1991.

Midgley, Mary. *Evolution as a Religion*. London: Methuen, 1985.

Miles, Robert. *Racism After 'Race Relations'*. New York: Routledge, 1993.

Miller, John Chester. *The Wolf By the Ears: Thomas Jefferson and Slavery*. Charlottesville: U of Virginia P, 1991.

Miller, Toby. "A Short History of the Penis." *Social Text* 43 (fall 1995): 1–26.

Modleski, Tania. *Feminism Without Women: Culture and Criticism in a 'Postfeminist' Age*. New York: Routledge, 1991.

Montagu, Ashley, ed. *The Concept of Race*. London: Collier, 1964.

Moon, Michael. *Disseminating Whitman: Revision and Corporeality in* Leaves of Grass. Cambridge: Harvard UP, 1991.

———. " 'The Gentle Boy from the Dangerous Classes': Pederasty, Domesticity, and Capitalism in Horatio Alger." *Representations* 19 (summer 1987): 87–107.

Morgan, Edmund S. *Inventing the People: The Rise of Popular Sovereignty in England and America*. New York: Norton, 1988.

———. "Slavery and Freedom: The American Paradox." *Journal of American History* 59 (1972–73): 5–29.

Morgenstern, Joe. "Film: Macho President; Dweeb Engineer." *Wall Street Journal* 25 July 1997: A12.

Morton, Samuel George. "Additional Observations on HYBRIDITY IN ANIMALS, and on Some Collateral Subjects; Being a Reply to the Objections of the Rev. John Bachman M.D." Charleston: Steam Power P of Walker and James, 1850. Rpt. from *Charleston Medical Journal* 5 (1850).

———. "Appendix. Notes on Hybridity, designed as a Supplement to the memoir on that subject in the last number of this Journal." *Charleston Medical Journal* 6.1 (1850): 145–52.

———. *Brief Remarks on the Diversities of the Human Species, and On Some Kindred Subjects*. Philadelphia: Merrihew and Thompson, 1842.

———. *Catalogue of Skulls of Men*. 3rd ed. Philadelphia: Merrihew and Thompson, 1849.

———. *Crania AEgyptiaca; or Observations on Egyptian Ethnography, Derived from Anatomy, History and the Monuments*. Philadelphia: J. Pennington, 1844.

———. *Crania Americana; or, a Comparative View of the Skulls of Various Aboriginal Nations of North and South America*. Philadelphia: John Pennington, 1839.

———. *Ethnological Scrapbook, collected and arranged by Samuel George Morton, M.D.* Library Company of Philadelphia. N.p.: Philadelphia, n.d.

———. "Hybridity in Animals, Considered in Reference to the Question of the Unity of the Human Species." *AJS* 3 (1847): 39–50, 203–12.

———. "Letter to the Rev. John Bachman, D.D., on the Question of Hybridity in Animals, Considered in Reference to The Unity of the Human Species." Charleston: Steam Power P of Walker and James, 1850.

———. "Notes on Hybridity, designed as a further supplement to a Memoir on that subject in a former number of this Journal." *Charleston Medical Journal* 6.3 (1851): 301–8.

———. "Observations on Egyptian Ethnography, Derived from Anatomy, History and Monuments." *Transactions of the American Philosophical Society* ns 9 (1846): 93–159.

———. "Observations on the Size of the Brain in Various Races and Families of Men." *Academy of Natural Sciences Proceedings* 4 (1849): 221–24.

Moscucci, Ornella. "Hermaphroditism and Sex Difference: The Construction of Gender in Victorian England." *Science and Sensibility: Gender and Scientific Inquiry 1780–1945.* Ed. Maria Benjamin. London: Basil Blackwell, 1991.

Mosse, George L. *Toward the Final Solution: A History of European Racism.* Madison: U of Wisconsin P, 1985.

Mouffe, Chantal. *The Return of the Political.* London: Verso, 1993.

Moulton, Gary E. *Journals of the Expedition of Lewis and Clark.* 11 vols. Lincoln: U of Nebraska P, 1983.

Mueller, Dennis C. *Constitutional Democracy.* New York: Oxford UP, 1996.

Mulkay, Michael. *Science and the Sociology of Knowledge.* London: Allen and Hyman, 1979.

Nandy, Ashish, ed. *Science, Hegemony and Violence: A Requiem for Modernity.* Delhi: Oxford UP, 1991.

Nash, June. "The Fiesta of the Word: The Zapatista Uprising and Radical Democracy in Mexico." *American Anthropologist* 99.2: 261–274.

Nast, Heidi J., and Audrey Kobayashi. "Re-Corporealizing Vision." *Body Space: Destabilizing Geographies of Gender and Sexuality.* Ed. Nancy Duncan. New York: Routledge, 1996. 75–93.

Neal, John. *American Writers: A Series of Papers Contributed to Blackwood's Magazine (1824–25).* Ed. with introduction by Fred Lewis Pattee. Durham: Duke UP, 1937.

———. *Logan, A Family History.* 2 vols. Philadelphia: Carey and Lea, 1822.

Nelson, Carnot E., and Donald K. Pollock, eds. *Communication Among Scientists and Engineers.* Lexington: Heath Lexington, 1970.

Nelson, Dana D. *The Word in Black and White: Reading 'Race' in American Literature, 1638–1867.* New York: Oxford UP, 1992.

Newfield, Christopher. *The Emerson Effect: Individualism and Submission in America.* Chicago: U of Chicago P, 1996.

———. "The Politics of Male Suffering: Masochism and Hegemony in the

American Renaissance." *differences: A Journal of Feminist Cultural Studies* 1.3 (1989): 55–87.

———. "What Was Political Correctness? Race, the Right, and Managerial Democracy in the Humanities." *Critical Inquiry* 19.2 (1993): 308–36.

Nissenbaum, Stephen. *Sex, Diet, and Debility in Jacksonian America: Sylvester Graham and Health Reform.* Chicago: U of Chicago P, 1980.

Noble, David. *A World Without Women: The Christian Clerical Culture of Western Science.* New York: Knopf, 1992.

North, Douglass. *The Economic Growth of the United States 1790–1860.* Englewood Cliffs: Prentice Hall, 1961.

North, Douglass, and Robert Paul Thomas, eds. *The Growth of the American Economy to 1860.* Columbia: U of South Carolina P, 1968.

Norton, Anne. *Reflections on Political Identity.* Baltimore: Johns Hopkins UP, 1988.

Nott, Josiah. "Diversity of the Human Race." *De Bow's Review* 10 (1851): 113–32.

———. "Dr. Nott's reply to 'C'." *Southern Quarterly Review* 8 (1845): 148–90.

———. "Two Lectures on the Natural History of the Caucasian and Negro Races." *Southern Quarterly Review* 6 (1844).

Nott, Josiah C., M.D., and George Gliddon. *Types of Mankind, or Ethnological Researches Based Upon the Ancient Monuments, Paintings, Sculptures, and Crania of Races . . .* Philadelphia: Lippincott, Grambo, 1854. Miami: Mnemosyne, 1969.

Novak, Michael. *Choosing Our King: Powerful Symbols in Presidential Politics.* New York: Macmillan, 1974.

Nussbaum, Felicity A. " 'Savage' Mothers: Narratives of Maternity in the Mid-Eighteenth Century." *Cultural Critique* 20 (winter 1991–92): 123–57.

Ockham, William of. *Philosophical Writings.* Indianapolis: Hackett, 1990.

Okin, Susan Moller. "Women and the Making of the Sentimental Family." *Philosophy and Public Affairs* 1 (1982): 65–88.

Omi, Michael, and Howard Winant. "By the Rivers of Babylon: Race in the United States." *Socialist Review* 71 (1983): 31–65; 72 (1983): 35–68.

Ormiston, Gayle L. and Raphael Sassower. *Narrative Experiments: The Discursive Authority of Science and Technology.* Minneapolis: U Minnesota P, 1989.

Ott, Thomas O. *The Haitian Revolution, 1789–1804.* Knoxville: U of Tennessee P, 1973.

Pascoe, Peggy. "Miscegenation Law, Court Cases, and Ideologies of 'Race' in Twentieth-Century America." *Journal of American History* 83.1 (1996): 44–69.

Paster, Gail Kern. *The Body Embarrassed: Drama and the Disciplines of Shame in Early Modern England.* Ithaca: Cornell UP, 1993.

Pateman, Carole. *The Disorder of Women: Democracy, Feminism and Political Theory.* Stanford: Stanford UP, 1989.

——. *Participation and Democratic Theory.* New York: Cambridge UP, 1970.

Pattee, Fred Lewis, ed. *American Writers, a Series of Papers Contributed to Blackwood's Magazine (1824-25).* By John Neal. Durham: Duke UP, 1937.

Patterson, Henry S., M.D. "Memoir of the Life and Scientific Labors of Samuel George Morton." *Types of Mankind.* Ed. Josiah Nott and George Gliddon. Philadelphia: Lippincott, Grambo, 1854. Miami: Mnemosyne, 1969.

Paulding, James Kirke. *Slavery in the United States.* New York: Harper, 1836. New York: Negro Universities, 1968.

Penley, Constance, and Sharon Willis, eds. *Male Trouble.* Minneapolis: U of Minnesota P, 1993.

Pessen, Edward. *Jacksonian America: Society, Personality and Politics.* Homewood: Dorsey, 1969.

——. *Riches, Class, and Power Before the Civil War.* Lexington: Heath, 1973.

Peterson, Norma Lois. *The Presidencies of William Henry Harrison and John Tyler.* Manhattan: UP of Kansas, 1989.

Pfiel, Fred. *White Guys: Studies in Postmodern Domination and Difference.* New York: Verso, 1995.

Pfister, Joel. *The Production of Personal Life, Class, Gender and the Psychological in Hawthorne's Fiction.* Stanford: Stanford UP, 1992.

Pitkin, Hanna Fenichel, ed. *Representation.* New York: Atherton, 1969.

Pivar, David J. *Purity Crusade: Sexual Morality and Social Control 1868-1900.* Westport: Greenwood, 1973.

Pleck, Elizabeth H., and Joseph H. Pleck. *The American Man.* Englewood Cliffs: Prentice Hall, 1980.

Pleck, Joseph H. *Myth of Masculinity.* Cambridge: MIT P, 1981.

Poe, Edgar Allan. "Some Words with a Mummy." *The Science Fiction of Edgar Allan Poe.* Ed. Harold Beaver. New York: Penguin, 1976.

Polan, Dana. "Methods Against: Stanley Aronowitz and the Critique of Scientistic Reason." *boundary 2* 18.2 (1991): 227–37.

Poovey, Mary. "The Social Constitution of 'Class': Toward a History of Classificatory Thinking." *Rethinking Class: Literary Studies and Social Formations.* Ed. Wai Chee Dimock and Michael T. Gilmore. New York: Columbia UP, 1994. 15–56.

——. *Uneven Developments: The Ideological Work of Gender in Mid-Victorian England.* Chicago: U of Chicago P, 1988.

Prude, Jonathan. "Capitalism, Industrialization and the Factory in Post-Revolutionary America." *Wages of Independence: Capitalism in the Early Republic.* Ed. Paule Gilje. Madison: Madison House, 1997.

Pugh, David G. *Sons of Liberty: The Masculine Mind in Nineteenth-Century America.* Westport: Greenwood, 1983.

Reingold, Nathaniel, ed. *Science in America Since 1820.* New York: Science History, 1976.

Reynolds, David. *Beneath the American Renaissance: The Subversive Imagination in the Age of Emerson and Melville.* New York: Knopf, 1988.

Rhonda, James. "Jefferson and the Imperial West." *Journal of the West* 31.3 (1992): 13–19.

Richards, Thomas. *The Imperial Archive: Knowledge and the Fantasy of the Empire.* London: Verso, 1993.

Richardson, Ruth. *Death, Dissection and the Destitute.* London: Routledge and Kegan Paul, 1987.

Riker, William H. "Electoral Systems and Constitutional Restraints." *Choosing an Electoral System: Issues and Alternatives.* Ed. Arend Lijphart and Bernard Grofman. New York: Praeger, 1984. 103–10.

Ringer, Benjamin B., and Elinor Lawless. *Race—Ethnicity and Society.* New York: Routledge, 1989.

Ripley, William Z. *The Races of Europe: A Sociological Study.* New York: D. Appleton, 1910.

Robinson, Forrest. "A Combat with the Past: Robert Penn Warren on Race and Slavery." *American Literature* 67.3 (1995): 511–31.

Roediger, David. *Towards the Abolition of Whiteness.* New York: Verso, 1994.

———. *The Wages of Whiteness: Race and the Making of the American Working Class.* New York: Verso, 1991.

Roelofs, H. Mark. *The Poverty of American Politics: A Theoretical Interpretation.* Philadelphia: Temple UP, 1992.

———. "The Prophetic President: Charisma in the American Political Tradition." *Polity* 25.1 (1992): 1–20.

Rogin, Michael Paul. *Fathers and Children: Andrew Jackson and the Subjugation of the American Indian.* 1975. New Brunswick: Transaction, 1991.

———. "Liberal Society and the Indian Question." *Ronald Reagan, the Movie, and Other Episodes in Political Demonology.* Berkeley: U of California P, 1987.

———. *Subversive Genealogy: The Politics and Art of Herman Melville.* Berkeley: U of California P, 1979.

Ronda, James P. *Lewis and Clark Among the Indians.* Lincoln: U of Nebraska P, 1984.

Rose, Hilary, and Steven Rose, eds. *The Political Economy of Science.* London: Macmillian, 1976.

Rose, Steven. "Scientific Racism and Ideology: The IQ Racket from Galton to Jensen." *The Political Economy of Science.* Ed. Hilary Rose and Steven Rose. London: Macmillian, 1976. 112–41.

Rosen, David. *The Changing Fictions of Masculinity.* Urbana: U of Illinois P, 1993.

Rothman, David. *The Discovery of the Asylum: Social Order and Disorder in the New Republic.* Boston: Little, Brown, 1971.

Rotundo, E. Anthony. *American Manhood: Transformations in Masculinity from the Revolution to the Modern Era.* New York: Basic, 1993.

Rush, Benjamin. *Essays: Literary, Moral and Philosophical.* Ed. with introduction by Michael Meranze. Schenectady: Union College P, 1988.

———. "Observations Intended to Favor a Supposition That the Black Color (as it is called) is derived From Leprosy." *Transactions of the American Philosophical Society* 4 (1799): 289–97.

———. "Paradise of Negro Slaves—A Dream." *Essays, Literary, Moral, and Philosophical.* Philadelphia: Thomas and Samuel Bradford, 1798. 315–20.

———. *The Selected Writings of Benjamin Rush.* Ed. Dagobert D. Runes. New York: Philosophical Library, 1947.

Rushton, J. Phillipe. *Race, Evolution, and Behavior: A Literary History Perspective.* New Brunswick: Transactions, 1995.

Russett, Cynthis Eagle. *Sexual Science: The Victorian Construction of Womanhood.* Cambridge: Harvard UP, 1989.

———. "On Slave-Keeping." *Runes,* 1773: 3–18.

———. "On the Mode of Education Proper in a Republic." *Runes,* 1798: 87–96.

Ryan, Mary P. *Cradle of the Middle Class: The Family in Oneida County, NY 1790–1865.* New York: Cambridge UP, 1981.

———. *The Empire of the Mother: American Writing About Domesticity 1830–1860.* New York: Haworth, 1982.

Sahli, Nancy. *Women and Sexuality in America: A Bibliography.* Boston: G. K. Hall, 1984.

Samuels, Shirley. "The Family, the State, and the Novel in the Early Republic." *American Quarterly* 38.3 (1986): 381–95.

Savitt, Todd L. *Medicine and Slavery: The Diseases and Health Care of Blacks in Antebellum Virginia.* Urbana: U of Illinois P, 1978.

Saxton, Alexander. *Rise and Fall of the White Republic: Class Politics and Mass Culture in Nineteenth-Century America.* New York: Verso, 1990.

Schein, Richard Huot. "A Geographical and Historical Account of the American Benevolent Fraternal Order." M.S. thesis, Pennsylvania State U, 1983.

Schiebinger, Londa. *Nature's Body: Gender and the Making of Modern Science.* Boston: Beacon, 1993.

———. "The Private Lives of Plants: Sexual Politics in Carl Linnaeus and Erasmus Darwin." *Science and Sensibility: Gender and Scientific Inquiry 1780–1945.* Ed. Maria Benjamin. London: Basil Blackwell, 1991. 121–43.

———. "Skeletons in the Closet: The First Illustrations of the Female Skeleton in Eighteenth-Century Anatomy." *The Making of the Modern Body: Sexuality and Society in the Nineteenth-Century.* Ed. Catherine Gallagher and Thomas Laqueur. Berkeley: U of California P, 1987. 42–82.

———. "Why Mammals Are Called Mammals: Gender Politics in Eighteenth-Century Natural History." *American Historical Review* 98.2 (1993): 382–411.

Schmidt, Alvin J. *Fraternal Organizations.* Westport: Greenwood, 1980.

Schneer, Cecil J. *Toward a History of Geology.* Cambridge: MIT P, 1969.

Schwalbe, Michael. *Unlocking the Iron Cage: The Men's Movement, Gender Politics, and American Culture.* New York: Oxford UP, 1996.

Schweitzer, Ivy. *The Work of Self-Representation: Lyric Poetry in Colonial New England.* Chapel Hill: U of North Carolina P, 1991.

Scott, Jean W. "Gender: A Useful Category for Historical Analysis." *American Historical Review* 91 (1986): 1053–75.

Sears, Donald A. *John Neal.* Boston: Twayne, 1978.

Sedgwick, Eve Kosofsky. *Between Men: English Literature and Male Homosocial Desire.* New York: Columbia UP, 1985.

———. *Epistemology of the Closet.* Berkeley: U of California P, 1990.

Sellers, Charles. *The Market Revolution: Jacksonian America, 1815–1846.* New York: Oxford UP, 1991.

Sennett, Richard. *Authority.* New York: Knopf, 1980.

———. *The Fall of the Public Man: On the Social Psychology of Capitalism.* New York: Vintage, 1974.

Serres, Michel. *Hermes: Literature, Science, Philosophy.* Ed. Josue B. Harai and David F. Bel. Baltimore: Johns Hopkins UP, 1982.

Sharp, James Roger. *American Politics in the Early Republic: The New Nation in Crisis.* New Haven: Yale UP, 1993.

Sherwood, Morgan P. "Genesis, Evolution, and Geology in America Before Darwin: The Dana-Lewis Controversy, 1856–1857." *Of Geology.* Ed. Cecil J. Schneer. Cambridge: MIT P, 1969. 305–16.

Shreeve, James. "Terms of Estrangement." *Discovery* November 1994: 56–63.

Shuffleton, Frank, ed. *A Mixed Race: Ethnicity in Early America.* New York: Oxford UP, 1993.

Shuttleworth, Sally. "Female Circulation: Medical Discourse and Popular Advertising in the Mid-Victorian Era." *Body/Politics: Women and the Discourses of Science.* Ed. Mary Jacobus, Evelyn Fox Keller, and Sally Shuttleworth. New York: Routledge, 1990. 47–68.

Silverman, Kaja. "Masochism and Male Subjectivity." *Camera Obscura* 17 (1988): 31–66.

———. *The Threshold of the Visible World.* New York: Routledge, 1996.

Sims, J. Marion, M.D. *The Anniversary Discourse Before the New York Academy of Medicine.* New York: Samuel S. and William Wood, 1858.

———. *The Story of My Life.* NY: D. Appleton and Co., 1885.

Smith, Adam. *An Inquiry into the Nature and Causes of the Wealth of Nations.* Ed. Edwin Cannan. 1776. New York: Modern Library, 1937.

Smith, Daniel Scott. "Family Limitation, Sexual Control, and Domestic Feminism in Victorian America." *A Heritage of Her Own: Toward a New Social History of American Women.* Ed. Nancy F. Cott and Elizabeth H. Pleck. New York: Simon and Schuster, 1979. 222–45.

Smith, Samuel Stanhope. *Essay on the Causes of the Variety of Complexion and Figure in the Human Species.* Ed. Winthrop Jordan. 1787. Rpt. and rev. 1810. Cambridge: Harvard UP, 1965.

Smith, Stephanie. *Conceived by Liberty: Maternal Figures and Nineteenth-Century American Literature.* Ithaca: Cornell UP, 1994.

Smith-Rosenberg, Carroll. "Dis-Covering the Subject of the 'Great Constitutional Discussion,' 1786–1789." *Journal of American History* 79.3 (December 1992): 841–73.

———. *Disorderly Conduct: Visions of Gender in Victorian America.* New York: Knopf, 1985.

———. "Domesticating 'Virtue': Coquettes and Revolutionaries in Young America." *Literature and the Body: Essays on Populations and Persons.* Ed. Elaine Scarry. Baltimore: Johns Hopkins UP, 1988. 160–83.

———. "Sex as Symbol in Victorian Purity: An Ethnohistorical Analysis of Jacksonian America." *Turning Points: Historical and Sociological Essays on the Family.* Ed. John Demos and Sarane Spence Boocock. Chicago: U of Chicago P, 1978. S212–47.

———. "Subject Female: Authorizing American Identity." *American Literary History* 5.3 (1993): 481–511.

St. George, Robert, ed. *Possible Pasts.* Ithaca: Cornell UP, 1998.

Stafford, Barbara Maria. *Body Criticism: Imagining the Unseen in Enlightenment Art and Medicine.* Cambridge: MIT P, 1991.

Stallybrass, Peter, and Allon White. *Politics and Poetics of Transgression.* Ithaca: Cornell UP, 1986.

Stansell, Christine. *City of Women: Sex and Class in New York, 1789–1860.* New York: Knopf, 1986.

Stanton, Domna C., ed. *Discourses of Sexuality: From Aristotle to AIDS.* Ann Arbor: U of Michigan P, 1992.

Stanton, William. *The Leopard's Spots: Scientific Attitudes Toward Race in America 1815–1859.* Chicago: U of Chicago P, 1960.

Steffen, Jerome O. *William Clark: Jeffersonian Man on the Frontier.* Norman: U of Oklahoma P, 1977.

Steinberg, Stephen. *The Ethnic Myth: Race, Ethnicity and Class in America.* Boston: Beacon, 1989.

Stepan, Alfred, and Cindy Skach. "Presidentialism and Parliamentarianism in Comparative Perspective." *The Failure of Presidential Democracy.* Eds. Juan J. Linz and Arturo Valenzuela. Baltimore: Johns Hopkins UP, 1994. 119–136.

Stepan, Nancy Leys. *"The Hour of Eugenics": Race, Gender and Nation in Later America.* Ithaca: Cornell UP, 1991.

———. *The Idea of Race in Science: Great Britain: 1800–1960.* New York: Archon, 1982.

———. "Race and Gender: The Role of Analogy in Science." *Anatomy of Racism.* Ed. David Theo Goldberg. Minneapolis: U of Minnesota P, 1990. 38–57.

Stewart, Susan. *On Longing: Narratives of the Miniature, the Gigantic, the Souvenir, the Collection.* Baltimore: Johns Hopkins UP, 1984.

Stoler, Ann Laura. *Race and the Education of Desire: Foucault's History of Sexuality and the Colonial Order of Things.* Durham: Duke UP, 1995.

Streeby, Shelley. "Opening up the Story Paper: George Lippard and the Construction of Class." *boundary 2* 24.1 (1997): 177–203.

Sundquist, Eric. *To Wake the Nations: Race in the Making of American Literature.* Cambridge: Belknap, 1993.

Theweleit, Klaus. *Male Fantasies. Volume I: Women, Bodies, Floods, History.* Foreword by Barbara Ehrenreich. Trans. Stephen Conway. Minneapolis: U of Minneapolis P, 1987.

———. *Male Fantasies. Volume II: Male Bodies: Psychoanalyzing the White Terror.* Foreword by Anson Rabinbach and Jessica Benjamin. Trans. Erica Carter and Chris Turner. Minneapolis: U of Minnesota P, 1989.

Thomas, Kendall. " 'Masculinity,' 'The Rule of Law,' and Other Legal Fictions." *Constructing Masculinity.* Ed. Maurice Berger, Brian Wallis, and Simon Watson. New York: Routledge, 1995.

Thwaites, Reuben Gold. *The Original Journals of the Lewis and Clark Expedition.* 8 vols. New York: Dodd, Mead, 1904–5.

Tiger, Lionel. *Men in Groups.* New York: Random, 1969.

Todorov, Tzvetan. *On Human Diversity: Nationalism, Racism and Exoticism in French Thought.* Trans. Catherine Porter. Cambridge: Harvard UP, 1993.

Tompkins, Jane. *West of Everything: The Inner Life of Westerns.* New York: Oxford UP, 1992.

Toulmin, Stephen. "The Construal of Reality: Criticism in Modern and Postmodern Science." *Critical Inquiry* 9 (Sept. 1982): 93–111.

Tuana, Nancy. *The Less Noble Sex: Scientific, Religious and Philosophical Conceptions of Woman's Nature.* Bloomington: Indiana UP, 1993.

Tyler, Royall. *The Contrast.* Rpt. in *The Heath Anthology of American Literature.* 2nd ed. Vol. 1. Lexington: D. C. Heath, 1994.

U.S. Congress, "Naturalization Act" (26 March 1790) 103 Public Statutes at Large of the United States of America.

van Ginneken, Jaap. *Crowds, Psychology and Politics 1871–1899.* New York: Cambridge UP, 1992.

Vaughn, William Preston. *The Anti-Masonic Party in the United States, 1826–1843.* Lexington: UP of Kentucky, 1983.

Vickers, Daniel. "Competency and Competition: Economic Culture in Early America." *William and Mary Quarterly* 3rd ser. 47 (1990): 3–29.

Voland, John. "Prez Presses Tech Buttons." *Variety* July 21–27, 1997: 749.

Voss, Kim. *The Making of American Exceptionalism: The Knights of Labor and Class Formation in the Nineteenth-Century.* Ithaca: Cornell UP, 1993.

Wahlen, Matthew D., and Mary F. Tobin. "Periodicals and the Popularization of Science in America, 1860–1910." *Journal of American Culture* 3.1 (1980): 195–203.

Wahrman, Dror. *Imagining the Middle Class: The Political Representation of Britain, c. 1780–1840.* New York: Cambridge UP, 1995.

Wald, Priscilla. *Constituting Americans.* Durham: Duke UP, 1995.

Wall, Helena. *Fierce Communion: Family and Community in Early America.* Cambridge: Harvard UP, 1990.

Waller, Margaret. *The Male Malady: Fictions of Impotence in the French Romantic Novel.* New Brunswick: Rutgers UP, 1993.

Ward, David. *Poverty, Ethnicity, and the American City 1840–1925: Changing Conceptions of the Slum and the Ghetto.* Cambridge and New York: Cambridge UP, 1989.

Warner, Michael. *The Letters of the Republic: Publication and the Public Sphere in Eighteenth-Century America.* Cambridge: Harvard UP, 1990.

Wetherell, Margaret, and Jonathan Potter. *Mapping the Language of Racism: Discourse and the Legitimation of Exploitation.* New York: Columbia UP, 1992.

White, Hayden. *The Content of Form: Narrative Discourse and Historical Representation.* Baltimore: Johns Hopkins UP, 1987.

Wiebe, Robert H. *Self-Rule: A Cultural History of American Democracy.* Chicago: U of Chicago P, 1995.

Wiegman, Robyn. *American Anatomies: Theorizing Race and Gender.* Durham: Duke UP, 1995.

Wilentz, Sean. *Chants Democratic: New York City and the Rise of the American Working Class, 1788–1850.* New York: Oxford UP, 1984.

Will, Drake W. "The Medical and Surgical Practice of the Lewis and Clark Expedition." *Journal of the History of Medicine and Allied Sciences* 14.3 (1959): 273–97.

Williams, Loretta. *Black Freemasonry and Middle Class Realities.* Columbia: U of Missouri P, 1980.

Wills, Gary. *Inventing America: Jefferson's Declaration of Independence.* New York: Doubleday, 1978.

Wilson, Adrian. *The Making of Man-Midwifery: Childbirth in England, 1660–1770.* Cambridge: Harvard UP, 1995.

Wilson, Daniel J. *Science, Community, and the Transformation of American Philosophy 1860–1930.* Chicago: U of Chicago P, 1990.

Wolfe, Alan. "Presidential Power and the Crisis of Modernization." *Democracy* 4.2 (1981): 19–32.

Wood, Gordon S. *The Creation of the American Republic, 1776–1787.* New York: Norton, 1969.

———. *The Radicalism of the American Revolution.* New York: Vintage, 1991.

Wrobel, Arthur. "Phrenology as Political Science." *Pseudo-Science and Society in Nineteenth-Century America.* Lexington: UP of Kentucky, 1987.

———, ed. *Pseudo-Science and Society in Nineteenth-Century America.* Lexington: UP of Kentucky, 1987. 122–43.

Wyllie, Irvin. *The Self-Made Man in America: The Myth of Rags to Riches.* New Brunswick: Rutgers UP, 1954.

Yacovone, Donald. "Abolitionists and the 'Language of Fraternal Love'." *Mean-*

ings for Manhood: Constructions of Masculinity in Victorian America. Ed. Mark C. Carnes and Clyde Griffen. Chicago: U of Chicago P, 1990. 85–95.

Yeo, Richard R. *Defining Science: William Whewell, Natural Knowledge and Public Debate in Early Victorian America.* New York: Cambridge UP, 1993.

Young, Robert J. C. *Colonial Desire: Hybridity in Theory, Culture and Race.* New York: Routledge, 1995.

Young, Robert M. *Darwin's Metaphor: Nature's Place in Victorian Culture.* Cambridge: Cambridge UP, 1985.

Yoval-Davis, Nira, and Floya Anthias. *Woman-Nation-State.* New York: St. Martin's, 1989.

Yudice, George. "Civil Society, Consumption, and Governmentality in an Age of Global Restructuring: An Introduction." *Social Text* 45 (winter 1995): 1–44.

Ziff, Larzer. *Writing in the New Nation: Prose, Print, and Politics in the Early United States.* New Haven: Yale UP, 1991.

Žižek, Slavoj. "Eastern Europe's Republics of Gilead." *New Left Review* 183 (1990): 50–62.

———. *For They Know Not What They Do: Enjoyment as a Political Factor.* New York: Verso, 1991.

———. *Looking Awry: An Introduction to Jacques Lacan through Popular Culture.* Cambridge: MIT P, 1992.

———, ed. *Mapping Ideology.* New York: Verso, 1994.

Zochert, Donald. "Science and the Common Man in Antebellum America." *Science in America Since 1820.* Ed. Nathaniel Reingold. New York: Science History, 1976.

Zuckerman, Harriet, Jonathan Cole, and John T. Bruer, eds. *The Outer Circle: Women in the Scientific Community.* New York: Norton, 1991.

Index

Davidson, Cathy N., 242 n. 1, 246 n. 16

Dawley, Alan, 107, 241 n. 11, 272 n. 6

Dayan, Joan, 296 n. 40

Deleuze, Gilles, 73, 97, 125, 285 n. 36, 286 n. 40

D'Emilio, John, 282 n. 22

Democracy's Other(s), 11, 67, 100–1, 181–82, 188, 195, 200, 207, 214

Democratic community, 26, 197, 203, 204–5, 207, 210, 214, 225, 288 n. 12

Democratic dissensus, 32–34, 204–5, 215–16, 223–23, 225, 236–37, 243 n. 8, 288 n. 12, 301 n. 19, n. 20; as heterogeneous democracy, 60

Democratic faith (or trust), 227, 234, 298 n. 2

Democratic institutionalization, 219–20. *See also* Virtual democracy

Democratic melancholy, 175, 188, 196–97, 199–203, 204–5, 207, 231, 232–37

Democratic virtue, 223

Disciplinarity, 23–25, 128, 130, 132

Dillon, Richard, 75, 257 n. 9, 259 n. 17, n. 18, 262 n. 30, 263 n. 33, 264 n. 37, 265 n. 41

Disorderly women, 42–45, 46–47, 53, 56–57, 59–60, 61, 136, 146–47, 154–55, 168. *See also* Feminine flows; Gynecology; White Woman

Ditz, Toby, 36

Dolan, Frederick M., 218, 219, 249 n. 27

Donzelot, Jacques, 15

Douglas, Ann, 133

Douglas, Mary, 185

Dukakis, Michael, 229

Dumenil, Lynn, 184, 289 n. 13, 290 n. 15, n. 16, 291 n. 20

Dumm, Thomas, 13, 243 n. 4

Dyer, Richard, 124, 269 n. 62

Edelman, Lee, 75, 81

Egyptology, 118, 110, 206, 208–24

Ehrenreich, Barbara, 304 n. 28

Eisenstein, Zillah, 251 n. 37

Elazar, Daniel J., 291 n. 23

Ellison, Julie, 186, 187, 194, 291 n. 22

Emerson, Ralph Waldo, 165, 194, 196, 251 n. 36, 291 n. 22

Equality: as "benign" hierarchy, 20–21, 60, 75–77, 98, 186–88, 198, 265 n. 41, 292 n. 26; and/vs. exchangeability, 46, 63, 75–76, 98, 100, 252 n. 40; whiteness as, 60, 137

Erkkila, Betsy, 250 n. 33, 252 n. 41

Esprit de corps(e), 176–79, 188, 196–97, 199–203, 204, 211, 215

Excorporation, 37–38, 54, 57–60

Faler, Paul, 107, 145, 241 n. 11, 271 n. 4, 272 n. 6, 281 n. 11

Fantasy of wholeness, 38, 60, 256 n. 62, 301 n. 22

Father, the, 22, 34–35, 63, 73, 74–76, 92–100, 102, 107, 196, 269 n. 65; as democratic father, 232–37; and fatherhood, 90, 93; and fathering, 97, 160, 163, 264 n. 35; and transistorized patriarchy, 99–100

Federalist Papers, 26, 60, 75; and gender, 42–48, 51; and managed diversity, 41–44; and national fraternity, 38–39; and presidency, 65; and rational distance, 39–41

Feminine flows, 69–70, 72–73, 151, 154–55, 160, 171, 259 n. 17, 262 n. 29. *See also* Disorderly women; Gynecology

Ferguson, E. James, 244 n. 11

Findley, William, 243 n. 5

Fisher, Vardis, 263 n. 33

Fishkin, James, 303 n. 24

Fitzgerald, Neil, 62, 256 n. 1, n. 2, 257 n. 5

Fliegelman, Jay, 22, 34, 35, 49, 76, 99, 247 n. 18, 258 n. 12, 265 n. 38

Foreclosed democracy/community, 103, 131, 150–51, 165–66, 174–75, 187–88, 198–99, 204–5, 231, 303 n. 26

Formisano, Ronald, 289 n. 13

Foucault, Michel, 24, 123

Franklin, Benjamin, 55, 214

191, 193–94, 196–97; and debate
with Bachman, 112, 119–32, 133;
and inner circle of friends, 191–94;
and Lewis and Clark expedition,
102; on natural repugnance, 104,
114–16, 121; political investment
in whiteness, 113–14, 116; and professional networking, 189–97; professional status, 103, 111–13, 117;
his "Sanctum Sanctorum," 194–97.
See also Craniology; Male sentimentalism; Polygenesis; Scientific
standpoint; Sentiment/Sympathy
Moss, Henry, 57
Mouffe, Chantal, 301 n. 22, 302 n. 23
Moulton, Gary, 256 n. 3, 263 n. 33,
265 n. 40, 266 n. 43
Murray, Charles, 115, 117, 118
Murray, Judith Sargent, 248 n. 26
Myers, Dee Dee, 231

Naked nature, 2–4, 50, 135, 175, 197,
240 n. 4
Nash, June, 305 n. 36
Nast, Heidi, 264 n. 35
National domestication, 66–67,
72–73, 76–77, 108
National manhood: and abstracting whiteness, 14, 52, 203; and
affective foreclosure, 175, 202–
203, 204, 303 n. 26; as alibi for
class stratification (*see* Universal white manhood suffrage); as
anxiety-producing, 16–19, 22; as
civic mandate for self-control, 11–
14; as family romance, 63, 90; as
guarantee for national unity, 13,
27–28, 34, 81–82, 241 n. 15; and
homophobia, 97; and imagined
fraternity, 17–18, 19–22, 181–82,
202–203; and managerial aims,
14, 133, 175; as nostalgic fantasy
of powerful manhood, 37, 45, 49;
and professional manhood, 15, 133–
34, 135–37; referential power of,
28, 203, 237; and structural oedipalization, 22, 45, 63, 73–74, 97.

See also Representivity; Scientific
standpoint
Neal, John, 26, 61, 63, 67, 78, 88–
90, 94, 95, 99, 100, 107, 267 n. 51,
n. 52, n. 53, 268 n. 54, n. 55; *Logan:
A Family History:* 26, 63, 78, 269
n. 58–61, n. 64, 270 n. 66; fatherly
ideal, 93–98; and fraternity, 93–99;
"last of the Logans," 90–92; plot
sketch of, 268 n. 56
Newfield, Christopher J., 98, 99, 147,
186, 187, 217, 243 n. 8, 281 n. 13,
301 n. 22, 270 n. 67
Noble, David, 195, 274 n. 19
Norton, Ann, 241 n. 14
Nott, Josiah, 111–113, 115, 117, 132,
135, 136, 142, 191–94, 209, 210, 273
n. 13, 274 n. 16, 277 n. 37, 279 n. 1,
295 n. 35, 296 n. 39, 298 n. 8, 299
n. 10
Nussbaum, Felicity, 53

Ormiston, Gayle, 25, 51
Ott, Thomas, 239 n. 1

Park, Mungo, 2, 3, 175, 197, 239 n. 2,
286 n. 45
Paster, Gail, 171, 262 n. 29
Pateman, Carole, 250 n. 31
Pattee, Fred Lewis, 89
Patterson, Henry S., 126, 194–97, 284
n. 35
Patterson, Robert, 64
Paulding, James Kirke, 24, 106–9,
132, 134
Peattie, Donald C., 277 n. 33
Perot, H. Ross, 226
Pessen, Edward, 272 n. 6, 288 n. 10
Peterson, Norma Lois, 303 n. 27
Pitkin, Hanna Fenichel, 245 n. 14
Poe, Edgar Allan, 205–8, 211, 214,
216, 225, 237, 297 n. 1, 299 n. 12
Poovey, Mary, 281 n. 16
Potter, Jonathan, 124
Prichard, James, 117
Publius, 11, 33, 38, 39, 41, 42, 45–47,
51, 52, 250 n. 34, 251 n. 35

Dana D. Nelson is Associate Professor in the
Department of English at the University of Kentucky.
She is the author of *The Word in Black and White:
Reading "Race" in American Literature, 1638-1867*.

Library of Congress Cataloging-in-Publication Data
Nelson, Dana D.
National Manhood: Capitalist Citizenship and the
Imagined Fraternity of White Men
p.   cm. — (New Americanists)
Includes bibliographical references and index.
ISBN 0-8223-2130-0 (alk. paper).
ISBN 0-8223-2149-1 (pbk. : alk. paper)
1. White men—United States—Psychology.   2. White
men—United States—Attitudes.   3. Middle class
men—United States—Psychology.   4. Middle class
men—United States—Attitudes.   5. Men—United
States—Identity.   6. Masculinity—United States.
7. Racism—United States.   8. Sexism—United States.
I. Title.   II. Series.
HQ1090.3.N42   1998   305.31—dc21   98-14396 CIP